D1649905

THE
FAMILY
COURT
PRACTICE
2017

AUTUMN SUPPLEMENT
AND WELSH MATERIALS

THE FAMILY COURT PRACTICE 2017

AUTUMN SUPPLEMENT AND WELSH MATERIALS

Family Law
LexisNexis®

Published by LexisNexis
LexisNexis
Regus
Terrace Floor
Castlemead
Lower Castle Street
Bristol BS1 3AG

British Library Cataloguing-in-Publication Data
A catalogue record for this book is available from the British Library.

ISSN 1350 1860

ISBN 9781784733643

This volume is typeset by Letterpart Ltd, Caterham on the Hill, Surrey.

CASE EDITOR: Samantha Bangham LLB

SENIOR EDITOR: Jonathan Cailes

COMMISSIONING EDITOR: Gregory Woodgate LLB, LLM, Barrister

Printed in Great Britain by Hobbs the Printers Limited, Totton, Hampshire SO40 3WX

Introduction

Welcome to the Family Court Practice Autumn Supplement, which updates the 2017 edition of the Red Book. Included in this edition are all the latest legislative, case-law and guidance updates, plus revised commentary.

We are a year on from the Brexit decision and it seems we are none the wiser as to what it will mean for family law in England and Wales (or any other area for that matter). While the European Union (Withdrawal) Bill makes its way through Parliament and negotiations continue in Brussels, we can only surmise there will certainly be repercussions for the two European instruments: Brussels IIA, which deals with child and matrimonial matters, and the Maintenance Regulation 2009, dealing with cross-border maintenance matters. In addition, case-law emanating from the Court of Justice of the European Union will, presumably, no longer be binding on us. Currently, there are far more questions than answers, not least for the implications on international private law children disputes and international divorce and finance proceedings.

Perhaps by the time of the Autumn Supplement in 2018 the way forward will be clearer.

Legislation

One of the key legislative amendments is the Family Procedure (Amendment No 3) Rules 2017, which insert a new Part 3A dealing with the participation of vulnerable persons in proceedings and giving evidence. It places a duty upon the court to consider the vulnerability of a party or witness and to consider how they might participate in the court proceedings or give evidence. Rule 3A.7 lists a number of matters to which the court must have regard, including, inter alia, intimidation of the party or witness, whether actual or perceived, their particular mental or physical disorders and current medical treatment, and the background of the party or witness.

Guidance

The President of the Family Division has issued a new Practice Direction 12J – Child Arrangements and Contact Orders: Domestic Abuse and Harm. The Practice Direction supplements FPR Part 12, and incorporates and supersedes the President's Guidance in Relation to Split Hearings (May 2010) as it applies to proceedings for child arrangements orders. Specifically, the Practice Direction provides a far broader definition of 'domestic abuse' as opposed to 'domestic violence', the former including ill-treatment and coercive behaviour, for example. In addition, the Practice Direction makes mandatory requirements for a number of matters to be included in court orders.

No-fault divorce

The Court of Appeal judgment *Owens v Owens* [2017] EWCA Civ 182 has once again brought the issue of no-fault divorce to the fore. The decision meant that the husband and wife had to remain married in accordance with current law since the wife's allegations of unreasonable behaviour on the part of the husband were not made out. In the judgment, the court noted there was a strong argument that the law no longer reflected modern-day realities and that no-fault divorce was called for. The recent publication of the Nuffield Foundation's report *Finding Fault? Divorce Law and Practice in England and Wales* further supports the call to an end of fault-based divorce, stating that the law as it currently stands increases conflict and suffering for separating couples and their children, encourages dishonesty, and undermines the aims of the Family Justice System. However, despite strong professional and public support for a change in the law, the Government has informed the Law Commission that 'now is not the right time' for a full review of marriage law.

Local authority liability

In the case of *Armes v Nottinghamshire County Council* [2017] UKSC 60, the Supreme Court held the local authority vicariously liable for physical and sexual abuse suffered by the claimant while in two different foster placements during the 1980s. However, the court stopped short of finding that the local authority owed a non-delegable duty to ensure reasonable care is taken for the safety of children in care while they were in the care and control of foster parents. This landmark case will, no doubt, lead to local authorities reviewing their processes of overseeing such placements.

International children law – anticipatory wrongful retention

The Court of Appeal decision in *Re C* [2017] EWCA Civ 980 found that anticipatory retention of a child was recognised by the Hague Convention and that, as is so often the case, it was a question of fact as to whether anticipatory retention had occurred by reference to the evidence of the circumstances. The main issue of contention between the judges in this majority judgment was whether it was necessary for the retaining parent to communicate their intentions with the left-behind parent. The majority held that it was not, while Black LJ dissented. A hearing has now taken place in the Supreme Court and its final decision is awaited.

Judicial news

The representation of family lawyers in the Supreme Court has increased with the appointment of Baroness Hale of Richmond as President and the addition to the panel of Lady Black of Derwent, a founding author of The Family Court Practice who continues to serve as a consulting editor.

E-working in the family jurisdiction

The programme of digital reform continues to progress. The President of the Family Division, Sir James Munby, and the Deputy Chief Executive and Courts and Tribunals Development Director (HM Courts and Tribunals Service), Kevin Sadler, have communicated the changes that will be coming into effect in the next year to help achieve the aim of an entirely paperless court process (wherever possible). Following on from Divorce Online, the Public Law Project launched in October and will seek, like for divorce, to digitise proceedings from start to finish. A recent survey found that many family courts are already using e-working either to file documents, access court documents or submit bundles. A further roll-out of digital solutions has been put on pause to allow a risk assessment to take place regarding business continuity and data security. Further regular updates will continue to be provided and the sharing of experiences and views with HMCTS is greatly encouraged.

Delinking of financial proceedings from divorce

An upshot of the process of court reform has been the emergence of the possibility of separating divorce from financial proceedings. A pilot scheme in the South West Regional Divorce centre in Southampton has taken place, which envisages that the main divorce proceedings will remain in the specialist centre and staff and judiciary at the local hearing centres can work independently on the contested financial proceedings. A separate financial remedy file, using the same case number as the divorce proceedings, will be created at the local hearing centre and HMCTS staff will ensure that the dates of any decree nisi or absolute are highlighted on the file.

The next step will involve the legal delinking of the two proceedings that can be achieved by changes to the FPR, practice directions and forms without the need for primary legislation. In his 17th View from the President's Chambers, Sir James Munby concluded that 'the need for continuing reform is clear, not least to create systems and procedures that can easily be navigated by the litigants in person who increasingly dominate the worlds of both divorce and money. The way forward is clear. The programme ... is, no doubt, challenging but, I am sure, eminently "do-able" given appropriate commitment and energy. We – all of us – must seize the moment'.

Samantha Bangham, *Law Reporter, Family Law Reports*

Contents

PART II: Statutes

PART III: Procedure Rules

PART IV: Statutory Instruments

PART V: Practice Guidance

PART VI: European Material

PART VII: Welsh Materials

Table of Cases

References are to page numbers.

PART II

Statutes

Administration of Justice Act 1960

12 Publication of information relating to proceedings in private

Page 244.

Re W (Children) [2017] EWFC 61, [2017] All ER (D) 88 (Aug)

(Family Court, Sir James Munby P, 17 August 2017) Family proceedings – Orders in family proceedings. The Family Court allowed an application for disclosure in circumstances where the applicant had indicated her intention to bring claims in the Queen's Bench Division for damages for misfeasance in public office after, despite an order prohibiting it, the name of a trial judge in a matter in which SW had been a witness, was published. The requested disclosure was deemed necessary in the circumstances.

Background

The present case concerned an earlier judgment of the Court of Appeal (see [2016] All ER (D) 159 (Nov)) that, among other things, made findings in respect of the potential breach of private life rights of SW (for details of the finding in respect of SW, see [2] of the judgment).

It was ordered, among other matters, that: (i) the only judgment of the judge that was to be made public was an amended and redacted version of the full fact-finding judgment; and (ii) pursuant to s 4(2) of the Contempt of Court Act 1981, there should be no publication of any report of the proceedings, or any part of the proceedings, before that court. For the avoidance of doubt, that prohibition extended to the naming of the trial judge and the court in which he or she had been sitting (the November order).

In fact, and despite the November order, the name of the judge was published.

In May 2017, in a witness statement, SW indicated her intention to bring claims in the Queen's Bench Division for damages for misfeasance in public office, and for breaches of her rights under arts 6, 8 and 14 to the European Convention on Human Rights against the Lord Chancellor and/or the Ministry of Justice. In light of SW's intention, she applied for disclosure of papers to her solicitors instructed in the proposed civil action of the papers in the appeal.

Application granted

Issues and decisions

Whether the disclosure requested by SW would be authorised to enable her to commence the Queen's Bench proceedings.

Subject always to the imposition of any necessary safeguards and conditions, family courts should not stand in the way of, and should, on the contrary, take all appropriate steps to facilitate, the proper administration of justice elsewhere (see [7] of the judgment).

The November order would be varied by deleting the words which extended the prohibition to the naming of the trial judge and the court in which she or he had been sitting. Accordingly, SW might identify the judge in the court of disclosure to the proposed defendants and in any documents filed in the Queen's Bench Division proceedings. Disclosure would include permission for SW, or any solicitor and/or barrister instructed by her to disclose and/or communicate any information and/or documents relating to the appeal and the earlier care proceedings that had been the subject of the appeal (see [7] and annex of the judgment).

William Tyzack for SW.

Andrew Norton QC and Gemma Kelly for the local authority.

Adoption and Children Act 2002

Page 252.

Re B (Child) [2017] EWCA Civ 264, [2017] All ER (D) 107 (Apr)

(Court of Appeal, Civil Division, Black and Sir Ernest Ryder (P), 12 April 2017) Family proceedings – Orders in family proceedings. The Court of Appeal, Civil Division granted the mother leave to appeal out of time but dismissed her appeal against an adoption order. Although there might have been issues around the way in which the change of circumstances test under s 47 of the Children Act 1989 had been applied, the judge had not erred in the evaluative exercise involved at the second stage by refusing the mother leave to oppose adoption.

Digest

Care and placement orders were made in respect of B, a 4-year-old girl. In making the orders, the judge found that the key issues were the mother's mental health, and the impact that would have on her ability to care for B. B was placed with adopters who applied for an adoption order. The mother indicated that she opposed the adoption; that was treated as an application for leave to oppose the adoption. The mother had become pregnant again. With the support of her parents, she moved to the Republic of Ireland and gave birth to another child, C. She cared for C herself with the help and support of her parents. The mother's application for leave to oppose her adoption was dismissed. The judge, applying the two-stage test under s 47 of the Children Act 1989 (change in circumstance and welfare), found that although the birth of C and the move to Ireland were a change in circumstances, it did not amount to relevant change of circumstances. That was because the change comprising the existence of C and the fact of the mother's caring for her was not a change that went to the underlying reasons for which the care and placement orders had been made in respect of B. Those reasons were the finding that there was an enduring personality disorder that remained untreated and unrecognised by the mother and her family. He dealt briefly with the welfare stage of the mother's application (in case he was wrong about the change of circumstances) and concluded that the mother could not succeed at the second stage of the test any more than at the first. The mother appealed. The proposed appeal by the mother was commenced considerably out of time. She therefore required not only permission to appeal, but also an extension of the time for doing so.

The mother submitted that the manner in which certain letters from the Irish social services had been dealt with meant that she did not have time to discuss the letters with her barrister and that the judge should have allowed time for that to happen because the information was potentially of central importance in evaluating the change that the mother said had occurred.

The court ruled:

The question of whether time was to be extended was connected with the merits of the appeal. Considering the way in which the question of change of circumstances had been handled at the hearing, there was force in the mother's complaint about the way the information from Ireland had been dealt with, given that it was potentially of central importance in evaluating the change that the mother said had occurred. On balance, the judge should have adjourned the hearing to another date so as to enable the mother's challenges to the letters to be explored further. Nevertheless, that did not meant that the appeal should be allowed. The judge had taken the precaution of going on to consider the next stage of the process, in case he had been wrong about the question of change of circumstances, and he had not erred in the evaluative exercise involved at that stage by refusing the mother leave to oppose adoption. His careful consideration of the law had left no doubt that he had the proper principles in mind when he had come to address the second stage of the process under s 47(5) of the Act (see [32], [43], [46], [47], [52], [59] of the judgment).

The correct course was to extend time and give permission to appeal. However, given the appeal would be dismissed, an adverse conclusion at the second stage led inevitably to the refusal of leave to oppose adoption, so the judge's order was not affected by any defects in the way in which his conclusion as to the change of circumstances had been reached (see [58], [59] of the judgment).

P (a child) (adoption order: leave to oppose making of adoption order), Re [2007] All ER (D) 334 (Jun) applied.

Per curiam: 'When an oral hearing takes place in relation to an application for permission to appeal, … the judge will often give a judgment. Parties involved in the appeal need to ensure that they have sight of that judgment because it will almost certainly assist considerably in indicating the likely focus of any subsequent hearing in relation to the appeal. Judgments given in relation to questions of permission to appeal are routinely transcribed, so copies should be obtainable without difficulty (see [3] of the judgment).

The mother appeared in person.

Katherine Wood (instructed by Northumberland County Council Legal Services) for the Respondent.

PART 1
ADOPTION

Chapter 1
Introductory

1 Considerations applying to the exercise of powers

Page 255.

By virtue of Children and Social Work Act 2017, s 9, in Adoption and Children Act 2002, s 1(4)(f), after 'relatives,' in the first place it occurs, there is inserted 'with any person who is a prospective adopter with whom the child is placed,'. Section 1 is thereby amended to read:

1 Considerations applying to the exercise of powers

(1) Subsections (2) to (4) apply whenever a court or adoption agency is coming to a decision relating to the adoption of a child.

(2) The paramount consideration of the court or adoption agency must be the child's welfare, throughout his life.

(3) The court or adoption agency must at all times bear in mind that, in general, any delay in coming to the decision is likely to prejudice the child's welfare.

(4) The court or adoption agency must have regard to the following matters (among others) –

    (a) the child's ascertainable wishes and feelings regarding the decision (considered in the light of the child's age and understanding),

    (b) the child's particular needs,

    (c) the likely effect on the child (throughout his life) of having ceased to be a member of the original family and become an adopted person,

    (d) the child's age, sex, background and any of the child's characteristics which the court or agency considers relevant,

    (e) any harm (within the meaning of the Children Act 1989) which the child has suffered or is at risk of suffering,

    (f) the relationship which the child has with relatives, with any person who is a prospective adopter with whom the child is placed, and with any other person in relation to whom the court or agency considers the relationship to be relevant, including –

        (i) the likelihood of any such relationship continuing and the value to the child of its doing so,

        (ii) the ability and willingness of any of the child's relatives, or of any such person, to provide the child with a secure environment in which the child can develop, and otherwise to meet the child's needs,

        (iii) the wishes and feelings of any of the child's relatives, or of any such person, regarding the child.

(5) In placing a child for adoption, an adoption agency in Wales must give due consideration to the child's religious persuasion, racial origin and cultural and linguistic background.

(6) In coming to a decision relating to the adoption of a child, a court or adoption agency must always consider the whole range of powers available to it in the child's case (whether under this Act or the Children Act 1989); and the court must not make any order under this Act unless it considers that making the order would be better for the child than not doing so.

(7) In this section, 'coming to a decision relating to the adoption of a child', in relation to a court, includes –

(a) coming to a decision in any proceedings where the orders that might be made by the court include an adoption order (or the revocation of such an order), a placement order (or the revocation of such an order) or an order under section 26 or 51A (or the revocation or variation of such an order),

(b) coming to a decision about granting leave in respect of any action (other than the initiation of proceedings in any court) which may be taken by an adoption agency or individual under this Act,

but does not include coming to a decision about granting leave in any other circumstances.

(8) For the purposes of this section –

(a) references to relationships are not confined to legal relationships,

(b) references to a relative, in relation to a child, include the child's mother and father.

(9) In this section 'adoption agency in Wales' means an adoption agency that is –

(a) a local authority in Wales, or

(b) a registered adoption society whose principal office is in Wales.

Commencement date: 31 October 2017.

Chapter 3
Placement for Adoption and Adoption Orders

Placement of children by adoption agency for adoption

24 Revoking placement orders

Page 264.

R (on the application of EL) v Essex County Council [2017] EWHC 1041 (Admin), [2017] All ER (D) 113 (May)

(Queen's Bench Division, Administrative Court (London), Charles J, 8 May 2017) Family proceedings – Orders in family proceedings. The Administrative Court quashed the defendant local authority's decision to place the claimant's daughter for adoption in reliance on a placement order and declared that the child had not been lawfully placed for adoption. The authority had acted unfairly and so unlawfully in having made the decision to place the child, and so in having placed her for adoption in pursuance of that decision and the placement order.

Digest

Care and placement orders were made in respect of the claimant's daughter, aged 6, on the basis that the defendant local authority's plan for her adoption was approved. The claimant's application for permission to appeal against that order was dismissed. In reliance on the placement order, the child was placed for adoption. The claimant sought judicial review of that decision.

The issues for determination included whether, applying the guidance given in *Re F (a child) (placement order)* ([2008] All ER (D) 09 (May)) (*Re F*), the decision to place the child had been procedurally unfair. Consideration was given to s 24 of Adoption and Children Act 2002 (s 24).

The application would be allowed.

In the context of the important watershed between when a placement that could and could not be made by an authority without the leave of the court, the reasoning and conclusions reached in *Re F* showed that good practice or a fair process was: (i) not confined to a deliberate decision not to provide certain factual information; (ii) not confined to cases in which analogies could be made with the participation of the father in the care proceedings in *Re F*; (iii) not confined to the disclosure of facts, but extended to a consideration of whether it was fair that a parent was kept in the dark about something by the adoption agency/authority and was so prevented or hindered from making an application under s 24; and (iv) an approach based on the application of the principle of fairness. Accordingly, *Re F* was authority in the field for an approach that examined what information that had been provided and what information that should have been provided by an adoption agency/authority on both legal and factual matters to a parent was necessary to the determination of the question as to whether a parent had been unfairly kept in the dark and so prevented from or hindered in making an application to the court under s 24. *Re F* was not authority for the proposition that, before an application for leave to make an application to revoke a placement had been made, the authority could simply get on with its plan for adoption and, in effect, conduct a race between placement and issue of an application for leave to apply to revoke the placement order. Not only was a race between an underinformed parent and the adoption agency likely to be unfair, it was also likely to create significant risks to the achievement of a result that best promoted the welfare of the child and the timely completion of a plan for adoption (see [37], [44], [49] of the judgment).

The claimant had established that the authority had acted unfairly and so unlawfully in having made the decision to place the child, and so in having placed her for adoption in pursuance of that decision and the placement order. Before the authority had embarked on the implementation of a placement plan, fairness, common sense and straightforwardness had required the authority to inform the claimant that, unless she issued an application under s 24 for permission to revoke the placement order by a certain date, it would proceed with its placement plan by placing the child. That could have been done by the authority before or when the placement plan had been made. If before, the claimant should have been informed of the placement plan when it had been made and, in any event, the date chosen for the commencement of the placement plan should have allowed a reasonable time for the claimant to make her application. That course of action would have addressed the points on fairness and good practice in making and implementing a decision to place pursuant to a placement order made in *Re F*, having regard to the watershed for placement without leave provided for by the Act. That was because it would have made the claimant aware of what she could do and the urgency of the situation. Also, it had the advantage that it crystallised whether the threatened challenge at the placement stage would be made and so addressed the risks involved in proceeding with a placement plan knowing that a parent had indicated that they still wished to challenge the adoption process as and when they could. Other steps might have had the same effects and that was not the only way in which the authority could have acted fairly. However, its approach of not having communicated with the claimant about what it had been doing and she could do had been unfair (see [60]–[63], [83] of the judgment).

The decision to place the child would be quashed and it would be declared that the child had not been lawfully placed for adoption (see [79] of the judgment).

F (a child) (placement order), Re [2008] 2 FLR 550 applied; *R v Secretary of State for the Home Department, ex p Doody* [1993] 3 All ER 92 applied.

Per curiam: 'It seems to me that it would be sensible for those responsible for issuing guidance concerning the adoption process and for the Family Court (and its Rules Committee) to consider: i) what information should be given to parties to the care proceedings and others involved in the adoption process about the stages of the adoption process and the ways in which it can be challenged. The approach taken by the Upper Tribunal (see Rule 40 of the Tribunal Procedure (Upper Tribunal) Rules 2008) may be of interest and it is a confirmation of the point that the communication of relevant information on how individuals may challenge decisions is an ingredient of a fair process, and ii) more generally what guidance should be given on *Re F* and what fairness requires in the context of a decision to place for adoption.' (see [48] of the judgment).

Ashley Thain (instructed by Sparlings Benham & Brough) for the claimant.

Nicholas O'Brien (instructed by Essex County Council) for the authority.

The making of adoption orders

47 Conditions for making adoption orders

Page 280.

Re A and another (Children) [2017] EWHC 1293 (Fam), [2017] All ER (D) 17 (Jun)

(Family Division, Sir James Munby P, 26 May 2017) Adoption – Order. The Family Court determined that the English courts had jurisdiction to hear the applicants' application for an adoption order of two children born in Scotland. It was further determined that there should not be a stay of proceedings in the English court because of the principle of forum non conveniens, on the basis that Scotland, and not England, was the forum conveniens.

Digest

A and O were siblings, born in 2012 and 2013, respectively. They were born in Scotland to Scottish parents. In March 2014, the local authority's adoption and permanence panel held meetings in relation to the children, and unanimously recommended that both children were in need of permanent substitute care, achieved by adoption via an application for a permanence order with the authority to adopt. In June 2015, the authority recommended that the children should be match with the applicants. In July, the children moved into the full-time care of the applicants in England. In October 2016, the applicants issued applications for adoption orders in the family court in England.

It fell to be determined whether the English court had jurisdiction to hear the application for an adoption order. In the event that it did have jurisdiction, it then fell to be determined whether, despite having jurisdiction, the case should be stayed so that it could be heard in Scotland in accordance with the principle of forum non conveniens, on the basis that Scotland, and not England, was the forum conveniens. Consideration was given to the provisions of the Adoption and Children Act 2002.

The court ruled:

(1) The court had jurisdiction to hear the application for an adoption order pursuant to the Act irrespective of whether A and O were, or were not, habitually resident in England. Likewise, the court had jurisdiction to dispense with the parents' consent, notwithstanding that they are not habitually resident in England. The application was properly made. A and O's parents and the authority were properly joined: each of the parents as a parent who had parental responsibility and the authority as an adoption agency that had taken part in the arrangements for adoption of the children. The task for the court would be (i) to decide whether adoption was in the best interests of A and O, judged by the test of 'the child's welfare, throughout his life', having regard to the various provisions in the 'welfare checklist', and applying the principles explained in the authorities; and (ii) to decide whether the welfare of A and O 'requires' their parents' consent to be dispensed with (see [46] of the judgment).

P (children) (adoption: parental consent), Re [2008] All ER (D) 265 (May) applied; *B (a child) (care order: proportionality: criterion for review), Re* [2013] All ER (D) 103 (Jun) applied; *W (A Child), Re* [2016] All ER (D) 25 (Aug) applied.

(2) The applicants had been entitled to issue the proceedings in England. Two other factors pointed in favour of England and not Scotland being the more appropriate forum. One was that, if the present proceedings were stayed so that an application could be made in the Court of Session, there would, with one exception, be an unavoidable need to instruct new counsel and solicitors, and to appoint a new guardian – something productive only of delay and undesirable discontinuity. The other was that a minimum period of 18 weeks had to elapse after the petition had been lodged before there could be a final hearing. That further delay would be most undesirable, not least given the time that had already elapsed since the proceedings

commenced. However, the imperative demands of justice and fairness, and the equally pressing demands of humanity and common decency, required that the state, which, at the behest of one state agent – the authority – and through the actions of another – the court – was being invited to dispense with the parents' consent to the making of adoption orders, had to, if those proceedings were to remain in the court, meet the parents' costs, not merely of travel to and from the court for the final hearing but also of their overnight accommodation near the court starting on the night before the final hearing commenced and, thereafter, for the duration of the hearing. If and to the extent that those costs would not be met by the Legal Aid Agency then they had to be met by the authority. In fact, the authority had agreed to pay the parents' travel expenses for hearings dealing with welfare issues, including their accommodation costs. On that footing, but only on that footing, the clear conclusion would be that the stay should be refused (see [60], [61], [65], [66] of the judgment).

Jonathan Buchan for the applicants.

Lorraine Cavanagh for the parents.

Alan Inglis for the local authority.

Christopher Blackburn for the children's guardian.

Post-adoption contact

52 Parental etc consent

Page 288.

Re W (A child) (No 3) (Adoption order: appeal) [2017] EWHC 1032 (Fam), [2017] All ER (D) 38 (May)

(Family Division, Sir James Munby P, 5 May 2017) Adoption – Order. The Family Division held that, consistently with its order of 12 April 2017, dispensing with the parents' consent to the adoption of a child and making an adoption order in favour of adopters, the formal adoption order should be dated 12 April 2017. It would not be treated as not being made until after the determination of the father's renewed application for permission to appeal to the Court of Appeal, Civil Division.

Digest

On 12 April 2017, the court decided to dispense with the parents' consent to the adoption of a child and make an adoption order in favour of adopters (see [2017] All ER (D) 199 (Mar)). It subsequently refused the father's application for a certificate with a view to a leap-frog appeal to the Supreme Court or, alternatively, permission to appeal to the Court of Appeal, Civil Division. However, the court granted the father a stay for a period of 21 days. The father had renewed his application for permission to the Court of Appeal.

A question had arisen as to whether, consistently with the order of 12 April 2017, the formal adoption order should be dated 12 April 2017 or whether it should be treated as not being made until after the determination of the proceedings in the Court of Appeal.

The court ruled:

If the father's appeal was successful, the adoption order, if it had been made, would be set aside. If, on the other hand, the father's appeal was not successful, it was right that the adoption, with its concomitant change of status, should take effect from the date of the judgment, namely, 12 April 2017, and not from some date, sometime in the future, after the proceedings in the Court of Appeal had concluded. There could be no prejudice to anyone, for the stay prevented anything being done in pursuance of the adoption order until such time as the Court of Appeal determined that the stay should cease to operate (see [8], [9] of the judgment).

The adoption order would be sealed and dated 12 April 2017 (see [10] of the judgment).

W (a child) (adoption order: leave to oppose), Re; H (children) (adoption order: application for permission for leave to oppose), Re [2014] 1 FLR 1266 distinguished; *W (Children) (adoption proceedings: leave to oppose), Re* [2016] 1 FLR 454 distinguished; *B (adoption: jurisdiction to set aside), Re* [1995] 3 All ER 333 applied.

Chapter 6
Adoptions with a Foreign Element

Bringing children into and out of the United Kingdom

83 Restriction on bringing children in

Page 299.

Re V (A Child) (Recognition of Foreign Adoption) [2017] EWHC 1733 (Fam), [2017] All ER (D) 59 (Jul)

(Family Division, Pauffley J, 7 July 2017) Family proceedings – Adoption. The applicants, Nigerian nationals at the time resident in the UK in a temporary capacity, had applied for recognition of a Nigerian adoption order. The Family Court, following examination of all the relevant criteria for the recognition of foreign adoptions, acceded to the application.

Background

The applicants were husband and wife and Nigerian citizens. They were lawfully resident in the UK in a temporary capacity. It was the applicants' shared intention to return to Nigeria in 2019 when the husband was expected to have attained a significant medical qualification having completed his current placement. The applicants had adopted their 2-year-old son, V, in Nigeria. V lived abroad with maternal relatives and had almost daily contact using social media with the applicants.

The applicants could not apply for a declaration that V was their adopted child pursuant to s 57 of the Family Act 1986 because they could not satisfy the criteria that he had been domiciled in the UK at the time of the application or habitually resident for 1 year preceding the application. Nor were the applicants eligible to seek a domestic adoption because they could not satisfy the requirements of s 83 of the Adoption and Children Act 2002 and reg 4(2) of the Adoptions with a Foreign Element Regulations 2005, SI 2005/392.

The Regulations required prospective adopters to obtain a certificate from the Secretary of State for Education, which, among other things, certified that if an adoption order was made the child would be authorised to enter and reside permanently in the UK. That certificate could and would not be issued. Further, the applicants had been informed by the local adoption agency that they were ineligible to be assessed as prospective adopters for V because they did not have indefinite leave to remain.

Accordingly, the only route available to the applicants was to apply for recognition of the Nigerian adoption order at common law. The present proceedings, therefore, were an application under the inherent jurisdiction for recognition of the Nigerian adoption order.

Issue

Whether, given the circumstances of the case, the court would recognise the Nigerian adoption order. Although the intervening Secretary of State for the Home Department was neither supportive nor directly resistant to the application, the Secretary of State sought a rigorous examination of the various issues rather than inviting the court to accede or refuse the application.

Decision

The criteria for the recognition of foreign adoptions were: (i) the adoptive parents had to have been domiciled in the foreign country at the time of the foreign adoption; (ii) the child had to have been legally adopted in accordance with the requirements of the foreign law; (iii) the foreign adoption had to, in substance, have the same essential characteristics as an English adoption, namely, the concept of adoption in the foreign jurisdiction had to substantially conform with the English concept of adoption; and (iv) there had to be no reason in public policy for refusing recognition (see [14] of the judgment).

The evidence clearly demonstrated that the applicants had their permanent home in Nigeria and had not relinquished their shared domicile of origin. The husband had completed his medical training in Nigeria. His work and study placement in the UK was solely directed to enhancing his Nigerian practice. There were a number of other evidential matters that in combination satisfied the fact that the applicants had been at the time of the adoption order (and continued to be) domiciled in Nigeria (see [24], [26] of the judgment).

The evidence unequivocally supported a finding that the applicants had made all of the central decisions as to how and by whom V was looked after day by day. It had been of critical importance to the judge's assessment of his welfare needs that she had seen for herself how well-attached V had been to the wife at the time of the hearing. It was also relevant that the wife had undertaken his direct, albeit not consecutive care, for 2½ months prior to the adoption hearing and that the wife had strongly supported the adoption. V's adoption had not been anything other than legal and in accordance with Nigerian law (see [39], [41] of the judgment).

The terms of V's adoption order made clear that the applicants had assumed the full parental rights, duties and obligations of natural parents in respect of V and the birth rights of his unknown parents had been extinguished. The applicants had not sought to deceive or to mislead in any way and, in all her dealings with the relevant Nigerian probation officer, the wife had been transparent and entirely honest. The important factors for the probation officer and the judge had been the altogether pleasing bond that had developed between the wife and V and his future best interests. There was no public policy reason for refusing recognition of V's adoption order (see [48], [51], [52] of the judgment).

Valentine's Settlement, Re, Valentine v Valentine [1965] 2 All ER 226 followed; *GS v SS* [2016] All ER (D) 53 (Dec) followed.

Application allowed.

Kathryn Cronin for the applicants.

Claire van Overdijk for the Secretary of State.

Charging Orders Act 1979

2 Property which may be charged

Page 359.

New commentary has been provided to accompany Charging Orders Act 1979, s 2:

> **'made against that person as trustee of the trust'** (s 2(1)(b)(i))—Where a beneficiary claimed that the trustee had brought proceedings in relation to the trust property without her consent, it was held that that was purely a matter between her and the trustee and a charging order was made to secure an order for costs made against the trustee (*Kamran v Davenport* [2017] EWHC 1844 (QB)).

Child Abduction and Custody Act 1985

SCHEDULE 1

CONVENTION ON THE CIVIL ASPECTS OF INTERNATIONAL CHILD ABDUCTION

Article 3

Page 375.

Re C (Children) [2017] EWCA Civ 980, [2017] All ER (D) 94 (Jul)
(Court of Appeal, Civil Division, Black, Sharp and Thirlwall LJJ, 12 July 2017) Family proceedings – Orders in family proceedings. Under the Hague Convention 1980, wrongful retention could occur before the previously agreed date of return (anticipatory retention) and whether anticipatory retention had occurred was a question of fact to be resolved by reference to the evidence of the circumstances. In the light of that finding, the Court of Appeal, Civil

Division held that the judge had failed to consider or address that key issue when considering whether the 'circumstances surrounding the children's applications for British citizenship' amounted to 'anticipatory retention'. The case would be returned for a rehearing.

Digest

In proceedings under the Convention on the Civil Aspects of International Child Abduction 1980 (the Hague Convention), the father sought an order for the summary return of his two children from the UK to Australia. The mother had failed to return the children following an agreed period of living with them in the UK. The children had come to the UK on a 6-month visitor's visa. In order to legitimise a longer stay, the mother (without telling the father) on 4 November 2015 applied for British citizenship for them. The children were granted British citizenship on 3 February 2016. That operated in addition to their Australian citizenship. The mother conceded that she had retained the children in the UK against the father's wishes in breach of his rights of custody under the Hague Convention. Central to the debate were arts 3, 12 and 13 of the Hague Convention (see [10] of the judgment). There was no common ground between the mother and the father as to when the retention had occurred.

The date of retention was critical to the outcome of the case as the application of the Hague Convention was dependent on where the children were habitually resident immediately before the retention. Five possible dates were canvassed for the retention (see [12] of the judgment). On three of those dates, anticipatory retention might have occurred. Anticipatory retention was the issue of whether, as a matter of law, a child could ever be wrongfully retained on a date prior to the end of the agreed period of temporary absence from his or her 'home country'. The judge found that there was no legal binding principle in relation to anticipatory retention. He found that the children had been habitually resident in the UK at the time of the event, which he had identified as wrongful retention so that the Hague Convention had no role and the application was refused. The father appealed.

Appeal allowed.

Issues and decisions

(1) Whether there was such a principle as 'anticipatory retention' in English law and if so what the proper approach to it should be.

There was no obvious answer to the vexed question of what the proper approach should be to anticipatory retention. The English authorities had not determined it conclusively. A review of the English cases showed that cases often seemed to depend upon the particular facts, and there had been no extensive discussion of the pros and cons of possible approaches to what was a complex problem (see [97] of the judgment).

AZ (a minor) (abduction: acquiescence), Re [1993] 1 FLR 682 considered; *G (children) (abduction: habitual residence), Re* [2007] All ER (D) 505 (Nov) considered; *S (a child) (abduction: settlement), Re* [2009] All ER (D) 314 (Jul) considered; *H (Children) (Jurisdiction: Habitual residence), Re* [2014] All ER (D) 277 (Jul) considered; *A (children) (jurisdiction: return of child), Re* [2014] 1 All ER 827 considered; *H (Children) (Jurisdiction: Habitual residence), Re* [2015] 1 FLR 1132 considered; *BP v DP (Children: Habitual Residence)* [2016] All ER (D) 15 (Apr) considered.

(2) Whether there was unanimity of approach in other countries on the question of anticipatory retention.

Following a review of the decision of the courts of other countries, it could be seen that there were different views on the subject. What mattered was to appreciate the range of approaches and, if possible, the reasoning behind them (see [64]–[97] of the judgment).

CM Petitioner and Respondent against ER (AP) Respondent and Reclaimer 2017 Scot (D) 18/3 considered.

(3) Whether the Hague Convention recognised anticipatory retention and what the implications might be to the length and complexity of hearings.

Having regard to the nature and purpose of the Hague Convention, wrongful retention could occur before the previously agreed date of return. Whether that had or had not occurred was a question of fact. The court would not attempt to catalogue the attributes of an actionable anticipatory retention, even though there might be those who complained that it would be desirable for the court to give such guidance. There was clarity at the two ends of the spectrum, but much middle ground that was relatively uncharted. It was not necessary to a finding of anticipatory retention that the retaining parent should have communicated to the other parent either an intention to retain or any acts he or she had taken in furtherance of that intention. Very often that would be the case but it was not essential. Ultimately, however, whether anticipatory retention had occurred was a question of fact to be resolved by reference to the evidence of the circumstances.

It was difficult to forecast with any certainty what impact the clear recognition of anticipatory retention would have upon hearings in cases under the Hague Convention. Running a case of anticipatory retention might introduce complexity into the proceedings and extend the length of them. The extent of the problem might depend upon the nature of the events that could qualify as anticipatory retention. Case management was not a complete answer to the potential problem (see [99], [122], [123, [133], [176] of the judgment).

In order that the summary nature of proceedings under the Hague Convention was retained, the time had come for judges dealing with such cases to review their practices to ensure that they were adopting an appropriately robust approach to them (see [161]–[170] of the judgment).

B (minors) (abduction) (No 2), Re [1993] 1 FLR 993 considered; *C (B) (child abduction: risk of harm), Re* [1999] 2 FLR 478 considered; *D (a child) (abduction: custody rights), Re* [2007] 1 FCR 1 considered; *E (children) (international abduction), Re* [2011] All ER (D) 62 (Jun) considered; *AR v RN* [2015] 3 All ER 749 considered.

(4) Whether the judge had correctly rejected the three dates as a possible date for anticipatory retention. There had been a failure by the judge to address or grapple with the evidence when considering whether anticipatory retention had occurred on/by 4 November 2015, the date the mother had applied for British citizenship for the children. The critical issue, for the purposes of the judge's decision on that aspect of the case, was not whether the mother had been required to give certain information to the Home Office, but whether what had been said by her to the Home Office in her solicitor's letter was true. The judge had failed to consider or address that key issue when considering whether the 'circumstances surrounding the children's applications for British citizenship' amounted to 'anticipatory retention'. Having regard to the importance of the point, he should have done so (see [180] of the judgment).

(5) Whether there were points to note in cases of wrongful retention under the Hague Convention.

The fact that habitual residence might change even at the very early stages of an agreed period of absence from the home country might lead to injustice, as viewed from the perspective of the 'left behind' parent. The Hague Convention was effective in providing a swift remedy when children were wrongfully removed or retained after a short absence, it did not easily resolve cases where children were removed from their country of habitual residence for prolonged periods by agreement.

In the modern world, agreements between parents that one or other or both of them would move across the world with their children for a period of months, a year, or more were increasingly common. Parents (particularly estranged parents) who were considering such an arrangement had to understand that if one of them should change their mind, the children could remain permanently in the new country, against the wishes of the other parent either because the defence of settlement under art 12 of the Hague Convention would apply or because habitual residence might change during the currency of the agreement between the parties thereby ousting the Hague Convention altogether. Legal advisers would be bound to counsel against such agreements and arrangements (see [188] of the judgment).

A majority of the court held that the appeal would be allowed. The case should be sent back to the High Court for a rehearing before a different judge (see [44], [187] of the judgment).

Decision of Judge Bellamy [2016] EWHC 3535 (Fam) reversed.

David Williams QC and Jacqueline Renton (instructed by Ellis Jones Solicitors) for the father.

Henry Setright QC and Michael Gration (instructed by Crosse & Crosse Solicitors) for the mother.

Article 12

Page 382.

F v M and another [2017] EWHC 949 (Fam), [2017] All ER (D) 17 (May)

(Family Division, Hayden J, 26 April 2017) Child – Practice. The Family Division ruled that the grant of refugee status to the second respondent child, A, by the Secretary of State for the Home Department would be an absolute bar to any order by the Family Court seeking to effect an earlier order the applicant father had obtained seeking the return of A to Pakistan.

Digest

The father (F) and the mother (M) were both born in Pakistan and Pakistani nationals. In April 2006, their son, A, was born in Pakistan. Following a visit to the UK with A in August 2014, M remained in the jurisdiction and did not return to F, as planned, in Saudi Arabia. In October, F commenced divorce proceedings in Pakistan but they would subsequently lapse due to passage of time. In December, A commenced school in the UK. That same month, A and M's visitors' visa for the UK expired. In June 2015, A applied for asylum. In July, a final hearing took place in respect of F's application for what was said to be the 'summary return' of A to Pakistan. During that hearing, F and M entered into a consent order that provided for A's return to Pakistan by August. Both parties gave undertakings to the court, including M's undertaking to withdraw her asylum application and that of A. M did not withdraw either asylum application, and A did not travel to Pakistan. In October, M and A were granted, separately, 'refugee status' in the UK, by the Secretary of State for the Home Department. Subsequent to that determination, F made attempts to enforce the order of July 2015 (for details of the subsequent proceedings see [10]–[13] of the judgment). The present case had followed a successful appeal (for details of that case see *Re H (a child) (international abduction: asylum and welfare)* [2016] All ER (D) 79 (Oct)). Subsequently, the matter was remitted to the Family Court for consideration of the implications of the asylum determination to the family proceedings.

It fell to be determined whether A's refugee status was an absolute bar to the Family Court ordering his return to Pakistan.

The court ruled:

The determination of the refugee status of any adult or child fell within an area entrusted by Parliament to a particular public authority. A court could not exercise its powers, however wide they might be, so as to intervene on the merits in an area of concern entrusted by Parliament to another public authority. It mattered not that the chosen public authority was one that acted administratively whereas the court, if seized of the same matter, would act judicially (see [41], [42] of the judgment).

In the present case, the public authority entrusted with the determination of the refugee status of any adult or child was the Secretary of State. Accordingly, the grant of refugee status to a child by the Secretary of State was an absolute bar to any order by the Family Court seeking to effect the return of a child to an alternative jurisdiction (see [41], [44] of the judgment).

W (a minor), Re [1985] AC 791 applied.

D Fottrell QC, T Wilson and M Brewer for F.

H Setright QC and B Jubb for M.

D Williams QC and J Renton for A.

Norton QC and A Payne for the Secretary of State for the Home Department.

Kathryn Cronin and Julia Gasparro for the Joint Council for the Welfare of Immigrants, the interested party.

FE v YE (Secretary of State for the Home Department intervening) [2017] EWHC 2165 (Fam), [2017] All ER (D) 54 (Sep)

(Family Division, Mostyn J, 25 August 2017) Family proceedings – Orders in family proceedings. The Family Division provided guidance on where an asylum claim would halt an application under the Hague Convention on Civil Aspects of International Child Abduction 1980. The father had applied, pursuant to the Convention, for the return of his two children from the UK to Israel. Days prior to the present proceedings, the subject children had been refused asylum and were subsequently ordered to be returned to Israel. However, the order would not take effect until 15 days after the promulgation of the decision on the mother and children's appeal against the refusal of the grant of asylum.

Background

The father and mother were both Israeli and ethnically Arab. In June 1993, they were married. They had four children; a son aged 22, a daughter aged 20, and 7-year-old twins (a boy and a girl).

The two eldest children live in Israel with the father.

In June 2016, the mother travelled to Thailand with the twins. Instead of returning to Israel, she travelled to London with the twins. The mother subsequently applied for asylum for herself, listing the children as dependents. She made asylum claims for the children in their own right somewhat later. The mother said that she came from a very large family and that, from her birth, she had been grossly mistreated by her father and her brothers.

The father initially attempted to persuade the mother to return home but, on failing to do so, issued proceedings pursuant to the Hague Convention on Civil Aspects of International Child Abduction 1980. The Secretary of State for the Home Department, who had refused the asylum claim of the mother and the twins a few days before the present hearing, intervened.

Issues and decisions

Whether the children should be ordered to be returned to Israel.

Where a grant of asylum had been made by the Secretary of State it was impossible for the court later to order a return of the subject child under the Convention. Equally, it was impossible for a return order to be made while an asylum claim was pending. Such an order would place the country in direct breach of the principle of non-refoulement (see [17] of the judgment).

If an asylum claim had been refused, but an appeal had been mounted, then it was possible, indeed desirable, for the court to hear the return application but to provide that no return order should take effect until, at the earliest, 15 days after the promulgation of the decision by the tribunal (that was one day more than the time allowed for seeking a further appeal) (see [19] of the judgment).

Where there was an application under the Convention running in parallel with an application for asylum, it was vital that the Secretary of State was informed of that at the earliest opportunity, and was invited and encouraged to deal with the asylum claim with maximum speed. Similarly, where the asylum claim had been determined prior to the hearing under the Convention, but where an appeal was being mounted, it was highly important that the First-tier Tribunal (Immigration and Asylum Chamber) (the FTT) was invited and encouraged, indeed urged, to deal with the appeal as soon as possible (see [20] of the judgment).

A summary adjudication of the mother's case was that her fears had no objective foundation and she did not have a genuine subjective fear. Even if the mother's fears had objective justification, there was ample legislative protection afforded to women in danger in Israel. Not only would the mother be fully protected by Israeli domestic violence measures, but she would also have the facility to relocate to the other end of the country, if she so wished, without any hindrance. For those reasons the mother's defences were rejected (see [34]–[36] of the judgment).

It would be ordered that the twins be returned to Israel, but that order should not take effect until 15 days after the promulgation by the FTT of its decision on the appeal by the mother and the twins against the refusal of the grant of asylum by the Secretary of State. If the FTT were to allow the appeal, then the return order would be stayed. If the FTT were to dismiss the appeal, but the mother signified an intention seeking leave to appeal on a point of law, then the case would have to be returned to the present court to decide if the return order should be stayed further or if it should be implemented (see [36] of the judgment).

F v M and Another [2017] All ER (D) 17 (May) considered.

Jacqueline Renton for the father.

Henry Setright QC and Brian Jubb for the mother.

Alan Payne and Robert Cohen for the intervening Secretary of State, as intervener.

Article 13

Page 388.

H v K and others [2017] EWHC 1141 (Fam), [2017] All ER (D) 05 (Jun)

(Family Division, MacDonald J, 11 May 2017) Minor – Custody. The Family Court ordered the summary return of two children to their jurisdiction of habitual residence, the United States, in circumstances where the mother had abducted them from that jurisdiction. There were advantages to the children's welfare being determined in the jurisdiction of their habitual residence within court proceedings that had already been constituted and engaged in the issue of welfare. Further, it was only by returning the children that could ensure the continuation of each child's relationship with their father.

Digest

In May 2006, the parties married. Initially, they lived in Colorado, United States. In October 2006, their first child, B, was born. In 2008, their second child, M, was born. That same year, the father purchased a property in Hawaii and the family moved there the next year. They remained in Hawaii until October 2012. In October 2013, the mother and children returned to Hawaii, without the father's consent. Thereafter, the father went to Hawaii. In October 2014, the mother filed for divorce (for details of proceedings after the filing of divorce, see [9]–[13], [15]–[19] of the judgment). In April 2016, the court in Hawaii granted the mother permission to take the children to London to attend a memorial service for their maternal grandmother. The order prescribed the period to which the permission applied to be between 5 to 18 July 2016. The same order had granted the father permission to take the children to New York prior to London, which the father had complied with. Rather than return the children to the jurisdiction of the US on 18 July, the mother took the children first to France, then to the Spanish mainland and then to Tenerife, before returning to the UK. The father returned to the court in Hawaii, which ordered the return of the children to the jurisdiction of the US, granted full custody of the children to the father and suspended the mother's visitation rights. The mother failed to comply with the order to return the children. Following the location of the children at the home of a maternal aunt, the father applied, pursuant to the Child Abduction and Custody Act 1985 and the 1980 Hague Convention on Child Abduction, for an order for the summary return of the two children to the jurisdiction of the US.

Despite the mother's concessions, she resisted the return of the children on two grounds under the Convention. First, pursuant to Art 13(b) of the Convention, that the summary return of the children to the jurisdiction of their habitual residence would expose each of the children to physical or psychological harm, or otherwise place them in an intolerable situation. Secondly, pursuant to Art 13 of the Convention, that the children objected to their return to the jurisdiction of their habitual residence, and had each attained an age and degree of maturity at which it was appropriate for the court to take account of their views. It fell to be determined, in the circumstances, whether the court would order the return of the children to the US.

The court ruled:

The return of the children ought not to be deferred until stipulated orders had been obtained in the court in Hawaii. The protective measures offered by the father and available in the jurisdiction of the US were sufficient, taking the mother's case at its highest, to protect the children from a grave risk of physical or psychological harm or being otherwise placed in an intolerable situation. Article 13(b) had not provided, in the present case, a proper basis for refusing to return the children to the jurisdiction of their habitual residence. The views expressed by each of the children amounted to an objection to being returned to the US. Further, each of the children had attained an age and a degree of understanding at which it was appropriate for the court to take account of their views. Nevertheless, the law was clear that the children's objections were not determinative of the outcome of the instant proceedings, but gave rise to a discretion, the exercise of which required the court to decide whether to order the return of the children in the face of their objections. Exercising the discretion, the return of the children to the jurisdiction of their habitual residence would be ordered, despite their stated objections. The reasons for reaching that decision were that: (i) there was evidence before the present court, and before the court in Hawaii, that the children's expressed views had been influenced by their mother; (ii) there were manifest welfare advantages in the children's welfare being determined in the jurisdiction of their habitual residence within court proceedings that were already constituted and already heavily engaged in the issue of welfare;

(iii) only by returning the children to the jurisdiction of their habitual residence could the court ensure the continuation of each child's relationship with their father, which was manifestly in each child's best interests; and (iv) the aim of the Convention had to be carefully borne in mind (see [61]–[65] of the judgment).

There would be an order for the summary return of the children to the jurisdiction of habitual residence, the US (see [66], [67] of the judgment).

Jacqueline Renton for the father.

Edward Devereux QC for the mother.

Shabana Jaffar for the children.

Re GP (Wrongful removal) [2017] EWHC 1480 (Fam), [2017] All ER (D) 116 (Jun)

(Family Division, Hayden J, 20 June 2017) Minor – Removal outside jurisdiction. A mother removed her 11-year-old child from Italy to live in the UK, in breach of the father's custody rights. The Family Division ordered the return of the child to Italy, notwithstanding the child's objection and the risk of the mother's imprisonment if she returned to Italy. The court rejected the mother's submission, under Art 13(b) of the Hague Convention on the Civil Aspects of International Child Abduction 1980, that there was a grave risk of harm to the child if she was ordered to return to Italy. It held that the possibility of the mother's imprisonment in Italy did not amount to intolerability, within the meaning of Art 13(b) of the Convention, that the child's objections were not wholly authentic, and that the father's undertakings, concerning financial support, offered sufficient reassurance in respect of the child's return.

Digest

The proceedings concerned a child, GP, who was aged 11. The applicant, GP's father, was born in Italy and her mother was born in Latvia. In May 2001, the couple married in Italy. Some 4 years later, GP was born in Latvia. In September 2010, the parties returned to Italy on a permanent basis. In 2011, divorce proceedings commenced. In July 2014, an Italian court granted joint custody to the mother and the father, as well as contact and maintenance orders. Following their separation, the mother removed GP from the family home to another area in Italy. The father reported the unlawful removal to the police and court proceedings were commenced. In November, the mother was sentenced to 1 year's imprisonment for removing GP. An appeal against that decision was dismissed. The mother subsequently removed GP to the UK, where they presently lived, alternating between Shrewsbury during the week, and Derby at the weekends. The father sought GP's return to Italy. In January 2017, proceedings commenced in the UK. A location order was issue, which was eventually served on the mother in March.

There was no dispute that, at the time of her removal, GP had been habitually resident in Italy. The mother accepted that, by removing GP to the UK, she had acted in breach of the father's rights of custody. However, in her defence, she relied on Art 13(b) of the Hague Convention on the Civil Aspects of International Child Abduction 1980 (the Hague Convention) (Art 13(b)) and submitted that: (i) there was a grave risk that GP's return would expose her to physical or psychological harm or otherwise place her in an intolerable situation; and/or (ii) GP objected to being returned and had attained an age and degree of maturity at which it was appropriate to take account of her views. The mother submitted that GP's return would put her in an 'intolerable' situation because: (a) the father was only able to make limited financial provision (EUR 300 a month); (b) no accommodation had been provided for the mother or GP; (c) the mother was unlikely to find satisfactory employment; and (d) she faced a custodial sentence on her return to Italy. In relation to the latter, there was evidence that that custodial sentence could be converted to community service. In respect of GP's objection to being returned to Italy, the court considered the evidence of the CAFCASS officer, J, who assessed GP's maturity to be broadly commensurate with her chronological age. J stated that GP told her that she did not wish to return to Italy. J was concerned about the reliability of GP's allegations of domestic abuse when she was aged 2, and considered that they were unlikely to reflect GP's own memory. J indicated that GP asked to meet with the judge. The court considered the 'Guidelines for Judges Meeting Children who are subject to Family Proceedings April 2010' and the relevant authorities. The judge met with GP prior to giving his decision and considered her objections to returning to Italy. He also considered undertakings that the father gave, including an offer of some financial support, albeit limited, to assist with accommodation if the mother and GP returned to Italy. Reference was made to Art 11(4) of Council Regulation (EC) No 2201/2003 (Brussels IIA).

PART II

The court ruled:

(1) The principles to be applied in respect of Art 13 were as follows: (i) there had to be a grave risk of the harm alleged to the child; (ii) intolerable harm meant a situation that the particular child should not be expected to tolerate in the circumstances; harm included both physical and psychological harm and encompassed exposure to the physical and psychological harm done to a parent; (iii) the source of the risk of harm was irrelevant, such that it might stem from the subjective perception of a parent, which could have intolerable consequences for the child; (iv) if the risk was serious enough, the court was not only concerned with the child's immediate future as the need for protection might persist. It was settled law that the burden of proof lay with the person who opposed the child's return. The standard of proof was the balance of probabilities. Article 13(b) was not to be constructed narrowly; by its very terms, it was of restricted application. It was rarely appropriate to hear oral evidence of the allegations made under Art 13(b). The risk of the harm had to be 'grave'; it was not enough for the risk to be 'real'. It had to have reached such a level of seriousness as to be characterised as 'grave'. A relatively low risk of death or really serious injury might properly be qualified as grave, while a higher level of risk might be required for other less serious forms of harm. Intolerability denoted a situation that the particular child in the particular circumstances of the case should not be expected to tolerate. The source of the risk was irrelevant, for example where a mother's subjective perception of events led to a mental illness, which could have intolerable consequences for the child. When assessing the risk that a child faced on return, the court would have regard to protective measures. Critically, pursuant to Art 11(4) of Brussels IIA, a court could not refuse to order a child to return when Art 13(b) was raised when it was 'established that adequate arrangements can be made to secure the protection of the child after return'. Where there were disputed allegations, which could neither be tried nor objectively verified, the focus of the inquiry was bound to be on the sufficiency of any protective measures that could be put in place to reduce the risk. The clearer the need for protection, the more effective the measures would have to be. Inherent in the Hague Convention was the assumption that the best interests of children as a primary consideration were met by a return to the country of their habitual residence following a wrongful removal. That assumption was capable of being rebutted only in circumstances where an exception was made out. It was well established that there were two limbs to the child objections defence. It was necessary for the respondent to show that the child objected to being returned and the child had attained an age and degree of maturity at which it was appropriate to take account of his or her views. If each of those first two 'gateway' limbs was established, the court then had discretion about whether or not to order a summary return (see [13], [14], [22] of the judgment).

In the present case, the submission that there was a grave risk of harm to GP if an order to return her was made was rejected. While the court was satisfied that GP was sincere in her expression of her resistance to returning to Italy, it was clear that those views were coloured and influenced by the mother's own wishes. The objections were therefore not wholly authentic. The mother's risk of imprisonment, however that risk be calibrated, did not carry the weight it was asserted should be given to it. While the possibility that the mother might serve a period in custody was not discounted, and that that, if it happened, would be traumatic to GP, it did not seem, on a proper construction, to amount to intolerability even in a subjective sense, namely: 'a situation which this particular child in these particular circumstances should not be expected to tolerate'. Moreover, to conclude otherwise would be to undermine the central principle of comity, which underpinned the present proceedings. While the father's undertakings, constrained by his financial circumstances did not ensure that GP's 'landing' was as 'soft' as the mother would wish it to be, it offered sufficient reassurance. The court was encouraged that the mother agreed to accompany GP, and expressed the hope that she would, despite the history of her behaviour, use her best endeavours to minimise the upset to GP that the present decision would, undoubtedly, cause (see [19], [31], [34] of the judgment).

GP would be ordered to be returned to Italy at the end of the school year (see [35] of the judgment).

E (Children) (International abduction), Re [2011] All ER (D) 62 (Jun) applied; *KP (a child) (abduction: child's objections), Re* [2014] All ER (D) 24 (May) applied; *M (Children) (Republic of Ireland) (Child's Objections) (Joinder of Children as parties to appeal), Re* [2015] All ER (D) 03 (Feb) applied; *S (A child) (International abduction: subjective fear of risk), Re* [2012] 2 All ER 603 considered; *X v Latvia (Application 27853/09)* [2014] 1 FLR 1135 considered; *R v RH and another* [2016] All ER (D) 29 (Dec) considered.

Per curiam: 'For The Hague Convention to have both legitimacy and efficacy, the principle of international comity, whilst not unassailable, must always be central to these applications. For the Convention to work, children who have been abducted by a parent (it is important to use that term) from their country of habitual residence must expect to be returned. A parent's efforts to defeat that process require to be evaluated with healthy scepticism . . .' (see [33] of the judgment).

Mehvish Chaudhry for the father.

Paul Hepher for the mother.

F v M and another [2017] EWHC 949 (Fam), [2017] All ER (D) 17 (May)

See Child Abduction and Custody Act 1985, Sch 1, Art 12, above.

Children Act 1989

PART I
INTRODUCTORY

1 Welfare of the child

Page 422.

L v L and another [2017] EWHC 1212 (Fam), [2017] All ER (D) 144 (May)

(Family Division, MacDonald J, 19 May 2017) Family proceedings – Orders in family proceedings. The Family Division made a child arrangements order for a 14-year-old girl who suffered from anorexia nervosa and a severe depressive illness to live with her father and spend time with her mother, subject to the directions and/or conditions upon discharge from hospital, although there was no date set for her discharge. The child's wishes to live with her mother had to be viewed through the prism of the developmentally inappropriate weight of responsibility she felt for her mother's health and wellbeing.

Digest

The present proceedings concerned with N, aged 14, who suffered from anorexia nervosa and a severe depressive illness. N was held for treatment under s 3 of the Mental Health Act 1983. Her father applied for a series of orders under the Children Act 1989, including a child arrangements order, providing that N live with him and spend time with her mother following N's discharge from hospital. The father relied on the evidence of a consultant child and adolescent psychiatrist that an order was required to provide N with the certainty she needed to begin to overcome her illness and that the mother was not currently capable of fully meeting N's needs. The Children's Guardian also supported the making of a child arrangements order, although N had made clear that she wished to live with her mother.

The primary question for the court was whether it was better for N to make a child arrangements order at present than to make no order at all, in circumstances where there was no date set for her discharge and, in consequence, any order made would not come into effect for an as yet unspecified period.

The application would be allowed.

It was in N's best interests to make a child arrangements order that provided that, upon her discharge, she lived with her father and, subject to the satisfaction of certain conditions, spent time with her mother. Although careful regard had been paid to N's expressed wish to live with her mother upon discharge, that had to be balanced against the fact that N felt a great deal of responsibility for her mother's health and wellbeing. N's wishes and feelings had to be viewed through the prism of the developmentally inappropriate weight of responsibility she felt for her mother's health and wellbeing. In the short to medium term, an order that did not accord with N's wishes might have a detrimental impact on her emotional equilibrium, but the result of such an order would not be an enduring intent on N's part to remain ill. In circumstances where N felt so responsible for her mother's wellbeing, to leave the issue outstanding would result in N continuing to feel a responsibility to influence decisions that were the subject of dispute between her parents. N needed to have all responsibility for the decision of where she was to live upon her discharge removed from her. That meant taking that decision at the present stage, notwithstanding that it might be some months before any order made by the court came into effect. Having regard to the totality of the evidence before the court, the mother was not, at present, in a position to meet N's needs as a full-time carer. However, the father, with the support of his wife, had greater physical and emotional capacity to meet N's needs than the mother, given the mother's manifest and complex difficulties. The nature and extent of the time N should spend with her mother upon discharge was not capable of categorical definition. However, it was plain on the evidence as it stood that it would be in N's best interests to spend time with her mother on discharge. Accordingly, it was in N's best interests to make an order that provided that she would spend time with her mother upon discharge subject to directions and/or conditions to ensure that the nature and extent of such contact was the subject of consultation between the parents and the professionals working with N at the time, to ensure that the mother was mentally and physically well enough to meet N's needs, and to ensure that the mother had had the requisite psycho-education needs to address N's dietary needs (see [46], [47], [49], [51], [53], [56], [58] of the judgment).

A child arrangements order would be made that N live with her father upon discharge and spend time with her mother, subject to the directions and/or conditions set out in the child arrangements order (see [61] of the judgment).

The father appeared in person.

Hannah Markham QC for the mother.

Jane Rayson for N.

PART II
ORDERS WITH RESPECT TO CHILDREN IN FAMILY PROCEEDINGS

General

8 Child arrangements orders and other orders with respect to children

Page 438.

Re E-R (Child Arrangements) (No 2) [2017] EWHC 2382 (Fam), [2017] All ER (D) 07 (Oct)

(Family Division, Cobb J, 11 September 2017) Child – Care. The father had been principally, if not exclusively, responsible for the failure of the child arrangements in respect of his daughter, T. The Family Division, having considered the matters in the round, concluded that the child arrangements order ought to be varied. Arrangements for T to spend time with her father would be made, those arrangements would be expressed to be the minimum and should apply unless otherwise agreed between the parties in writing.

Background

The child, T, was 8 years old. She lived with Mr and Mrs H, who were family friends of her deceased mother, who had passed away in 2015.

In April 2016, following a contested hearing, arrangements were settled for T's future upbringing. Under that child arrangements order, T was to have her home with Mrs H and Mr H and was to see her father at pre-arranged times during weekends, summer holidays, Christmas holidays, half-terms and Easter (for further details of the child arrangements order of April 2016, see [7], [8] of the judgment).

The child arrangements order was largely ignored and very soon breached by the father and Miss B, the father's partner. By September, Mrs H felt compelled to issue a fresh application seeking the court's further directions, specifically seeking further definition of the time that T was to spend with her father and with Miss B. Over the following months, directions were given in the case generally, the April 2016 child arrangements order was suspended and reworked on a temporary basis.

At the present proceedings, the father made it known he sought for T to be placed in his full-time care. Alternatively, the father made an application for an order attaching a warning notice, under the Children Act 1989, s 11I to the original child arrangements order so that he could enforce contact as against Mrs H.

Issues and decisions

Whether, and to what extent, there would be changes to the child arrangements order of April 2016.

Future child arrangements for T had to be crafted by reference to the guiding principle that they meet T's best interests; it was the duty of the court, under the Children Act 1989, to make arrangements for her which promoted her welfare, having taken into account the range of factors adumbrated in s 1(3) of the Act and more generally (see [52] of the judgment).

The father had not, in all the circumstances, been able to establish any, or any substantive, case for a transfer of primary care for T in her best interests. His application for a warning notice to be attached to the child arrangements order of April 2016 would be rejected. First and foremost, there was already a warning notice on the order of April 2016; had the father looked at the order he would have seen that. The father had been principally, if not exclusively, responsible for the failure of the child arrangements, not Mrs H. The father had been unable to give a commitment to visit T even monthly going forward (see [64], [65] of the judgment).

Having considered the matters in the round, having regard to the findings and assessments of the parties, and with T's best interests as the prominent and guiding consideration, the child arrangements order made in April 2016 ought to be varied. The order should reflect, for the avoidance of doubt: (i) the undertakings given by the parties prohibiting each from making disparaging remarks about one another in front of T or in the presence and hearing of T until further order; (ii) the continuing obligation, pursuant to an existing order, for the father and Miss B to notify Mrs H or any change of address; (iii) the provision permitting Mrs H to remove T from the jurisdiction for up to 28 days; and (iv) there should be a recital on the face of the order that the court expected the parties to attend for mediation, conciliation or for family therapy (see [66], [67] of the judgment).

Arrangements for T to spend time with her father would be made, those arrangements would be expressed to be the minimum and should apply unless otherwise agreed between the parties in writing (see [68] of the judgment).

Clare Renton for Mrs H.

The father and Miss B appeared in person, assisted by a McKenzie friend.

Mary Hughes for T.

11J Enforcement orders

Page 465.

LL v Lord Chancellor [2017] EWCA Civ 237, [2017] All ER (D) 123 (Apr)

(Court of Appeal, Civil Division, Longmore, Jackson and King LJJ, 10 April 2017) Contempt of court – Committal. The Court of Appeal, Civil Division reversed the decision of the trial judge and held that the claimant father of a child, M, was entitled to compensation under Art 5 of the European Convention on Human Rights on the basis that the wrongful committal to prison by the judge for contempt of court had amounted to a gross and obvious irregularity.

Digest

In family proceedings, LL, the father of a child, M, was wrongly committed to prison for contempt of court. By an application under Pt 19 of the Family Procedure Rules 2010. LL claimed damages and a declaration against the defendant Lord Chancellor in respect of his unlawful imprisonment. He contended that the Lord Chancellor had acted contrary to Art 5 of the European Convention on Human Rights and accordingly, LL was entitled to damages pursuant to ss 6, 7(1) and 9(3) of the Human Rights Act 1998. The Lord Chancellor denied liability. He maintained that the errors made by the committing judge had not amounted to 'gross and obvious irregularity' and therefore LL was not entitled to any remedy other than a successful appeal against the judge's decision, which he had already achieved. At trial, LL's claim was dismissed on the basis that the judge's conduct had not amounted to a gross and obvious irregularity, which was noted to be a very high threshold. LL appealed against the rejection of his claim for a declaration and damages.

The central issue was whether the procedural errors made by the judge in the original proceedings were so serious as to constitute 'gross and obvious irregularity'. Six procedural errors were identified: (i) the inclusion of a recital that was a source of confusion; (ii) failure to recuse herself on the grounds of apparent predetermination; (iii) requiring LL to give evidence, instead of warning him that he need not give evidence, then plunging straight in to cross-examination without permitting any evidence-in-chief; (iv) conflating non-compliance with certain orders with deliberate non-compliance; (v) relying upon LL's failure to secure M's return to the UK by a certain date by means of proceedings in the Singapore courts, when that was not possible; and (vi) giving LL no opportunity to make submissions in mitigation before sentenced was passed.

The appeal would be allowed.

It was established law that a period of detention was lawful if, and only if, it complied with the applicable sub-paragraph of Art 5(1) of the Convention. Detention under Art 5(1)(a) or (b) of the Convention would not be lawful if the court acted without jurisdiction or there was a gross and obvious irregularity in the court's procedure. In considering whether the court's errors amounted to 'gross and obvious irregularity' or 'flagrant denial of justice', where appropriate, their cumulative effect could be considered. The word 'obvious' in that context meant obvious to anyone familiar with normal court procedure (see [88] of the judgment).

When one looked cumulatively at the errors that were linked, it could be seen that collectively they had amounted to 'gross and obvious irregularity'. For a judge to include a veiled instruction within a recital, which could not be complied with, and then to commit LL to prison for non-compliance was a 'gross irregularity'. All the more so, when one took into account the other linked errors. All five errors enumerated above were obvious. It followed that the Lord Chancellor could not justify LL's detention under Art 5(1)(a) or (b) of the Convention. The errors made had crossed the line (see [104], [108], [109], [111], [112], [116], [121] of the judgment).

Hammerton v Hammerton [2007] All ER (D) 393 (Mar) applied.

Decision of Foskett J [2015] All ER (D) 139 (Nov) reversed.

Jamie Burton and Angela Patrick (instructed by Hodge Jones & Allen LLP) for LL.

Oliver Sanders QC and Elliot Gold (instructed by Treasury Solicitor) for the Lord Chancellor.

13 Change of child's name or removal from jurisdiction

Page 470.

F v L [2017] EWHC 1377 (Fam), [2017] All ER (D) 63 (Jun)

(Family Division, Russell J, 9 June 2017) Minor – Removal outside jurisdiction. The Family Division allowed the mother's appeal against the judge's decision, refusing her application to relocate with the child, D, to Italy. The judge had made a fundamental procedural error in failing to resolve the issue of the future care of D prior to considering the application for relocation and had failed to consider or make any finding in respect of complaints of the father's controlling and coercive behaviour, as alleged by the mother.

Digest

The mother and father had met in their native Italy when they were both teenagers. In 2001, the father moved to the UK for work. In 2012, D was born in the UK. In 2013, the mother moved to the UK. After D was born, the father lost his job. During a trip to Italy in 2015, the relationship between the mother and father broke down. Since May 2016, the parties lived separately and had shared care of D between themselves. The mother applied to relocate to Italy with D. In January 2017, in addition to the mother's relocation application, cross-applications were considered in respect of who should be D's main carer and where his primary residence should be. During the hearing, the mother made numerous complaints about the father's controlling and emotionally abusive behaviour. The judge refused the mother's application to relocate. The mother appealed.

First, it was contended that the judge had made a fundamental procedural error in failing to resolve the issue of the future care of D prior to considering the application for relocation.

Secondly, it was contended that the judge had failed to consider or make any finding in respect of complaints of the father's controlling and coercive behaviour. Consideration was given to the welfare checklist as set out in s 1(3) of the Children Act 1989 (the welfare checklist).

The court ruled:

It was well established law that when the future care of a child was in dispute, that had to be resolved before an application for removal from the jurisdiction could be considered. The welfare of a child was best served by considering issues of care and who could best provide that care was an issue that was to be decided in advance of considering relocation (see [8] of the judgment).

It was abundantly clear from her judgment that the judge, who had correctly identified the case-law in respect of relocation cases and had set it out at the beginning of her judgment, had started off where she should ought to have concluded. It was not until the end of her judgment that the judge had considered what arrangements there should be for D, and her analysis and reasoning for that most fundamental part of her decision was dealt with barely any reference to, or analysis of, the welfare checklist or of the issues directly connected with D's care. The judge's belated, deferred analysis of D's future care was flawed, not only because it had been carried out after she had decided on the issue of relocation, but also because the judge's consideration of D's overall welfare needs had been considered within the context of relocation not as part of the necessary primary analysis of which parent had been best placed to meet those needs. Further, the judge had been wrong not to have considered and made findings in respect of the complaints of abusive and controlling behaviour on the part of the father as alleged by the mother. The judge had simply split D's time between two homes. That was an unsophisticated and over-simplistic approach. It was not clear from the judgment why the judge had considered it appropriate not to carry out any fact-finding as, if there had been any basis for them, the father's behaviour towards the mother was ultimately likely to have had an effect on D (see [9]–[11], [13] of the judgment).

The matter would be remitted to a different circuit judge for re-hearing in the first instance of the arrangements for D and, thereafter, of any renewed application by the mother to relocate to Italy (see [15] of the judgment).

Payne v Payne [2001] All ER (D) 142 (Feb) applied.

Michael Bailey for the mother.

The father was represented by a McKenzie friend.

PART II

PART III
SUPPORT FOR CHILDREN AND FAMILIES PROVIDED BY LOCAL AUTHORITIES IN ENGLAND

Provision of Services for Children and their Families

Page 484.

Armes v Nottinghamshire County Council [2017] UKSC 60, [2017] All ER (D) 87 (Oct)

(Supreme Court, Lady Hale DP, Lord Kerr, Lord Clarke, Lord Reed, Lord Hughes SCJJ, 18 October 2017) Negligence – Duty of care. The defendant local authority was vicariously liable to the claimant for the abuse she had suffered as a child while being placed with foster parents while in the care of the defendant. The Supreme Court found that the conditions in the case of *Cox v Ministry of Justice* had been met and reversed the decision of the Court of Appeal, Civil Division. However, the Supreme Court found that the authority was not under a non-delegable duty of care.

Background

As a child, the claimant was abused physically and sexually by foster parents with whom she had been placed while in the care of the defendant local authority. The authority was not negligent in the selection or supervision of the foster parents. The matter came before the court with the question of whether the authority was, nevertheless, liable to the claimant for the abuse she had suffered, either on the basis that the authority was in breach of a non-delegable duty of care, or on the basis that it was vicariously liable for the wrongdoing of the foster parents (see [4]–[8] of the judgment for the relevant statutory schemes). The trial judge found that the authority was not responsible in law for the tortious conduct of the foster parents, either on the basis of vicarious liability, or on the basis of a non-delegable duty of care. An appeal against the judge's decision was dismissed by the Court of Appeal, Civil Division. The claimant appealed.

Appeal allowed.

Issues and decisions

(1) Whether the authority was liable to the claimant on the basis of non-delegable duties of care.

To say that an authority was under a duty to ensure that reasonable care was taken for the safety of children in care, while they were in the care and control of foster parents, having regard to ss 10, 20 and 21 of the Child Care Act 1980, was too broad, and the responsibility with which it fixed authorities was too demanding (see [37], [39], [40], [47], [49] of the judgment).

Harris v Perry [2008] All ER (D) 415 (Jul) considered; *Barrett v Enfield London Borough Council* [1999] All ER (D) 632 considered.

(2) Whether the authority was liable to the claimant on the basis of vicarious liability.

Applying the approach adopted in *Cox v Ministry of Justice* [2016] All ER (D) 25 (Mar) (*Cox*) to the circumstances of the present case, considering the factors such as relationship between the activity of the foster parents and that of the local authority, risk creation, control and the ability to satisfy an award of damages, all pointed towards the imposition of vicarious liability. The Court of Appeal had rejected vicarious liability principally on the basis that the authority had not exercised sufficient control over the foster carers. That analysis had been influenced by the reasoning of the majority of the Supreme Court of Canada. It was unfortunate that the Court of Appeal had not been referred to a New Zealand Court of Appeal case where the court had unanimously reached the opposite conclusion (see [74], [53]-[59], [64], [66], [67] of the judgment).

To impose vicarious liability in the present case was based on a close analysis of the legislation and practice in force at the relevant time, and a balancing of the relevant factors arising from that analysis. Applying the same approach, vicarious liability would not have been imposed if the abuse had been perpetrated by the child's parents, if the child had been placed with them, since the parents would not have stood in a relationship with the local authority of the kind described in *Cox*: even if their care of the child might be described as having been approved by the local authority, and had been subject to monitoring and might be terminated, nevertheless they would not have been recruited, selected or trained by the local authority so as to enable it to discharge its child care functions. They would have been carrying on an activity (raising their own child) that was much more clearly distinguishable from, and independent of, the child care services carried on by the local authority than the care of unrelated children by foster parents recruited for that purpose (see [71] of the judgment).

The idea that the imposition of vicarious liability might discourage authorities from placing children in care with foster parents, and encourage them instead to place them in residential homes, was difficult to accept, even if one granted the premise that authorities might be deterred by financial considerations from performing their statutory duty to promote the welfare of the children in their care. Local authorities were accordingly vicariously liable for the abuse of children by those whom they employ in residential care homes (see [68] of the judgment).

Cox v Ministry of Justice [2016] All ER (D) 25 (Mar) applied; *S v Walsall Metropolitan Borough Council* [1985] 3 All ER 294 considered; *McDonnell v Congregation of Christian Brothers Trustees (formerly Irish Christian Brothers)* [2003] All ER (D) 97 (Dec) considered.

Decision of Court of Appeal, Civil Division [2015] All ER (D) 126 (Nov) reversed.

Christopher Melton QC and Philip Davy (instructed by Uppal Taylor Solicitors, Nottingham) for the claimant.

Steven Ford QC and Adam Weitzman (instructed by Browne Jacobson LLP, Nottingham) for the authority.

Secure accommodation

25 Use of accommodation for restricting liberty

Page 510.

By virtue of the Children and Social Work Act 2017, s 10, Sch 1, para 2, in the Children Act 1989, s 25 is to extend also to Scotland and is amended as follows:

- in subsection (1), 'or local authority in Wales' is substituted by 'in England or Wales' and after 'accommodation in England' there is inserted 'or Scotland';
- in subsection (2), in paras (a)(i) and (ii) and (b), after 'secure accommodation in England' there is inserted 'or Scotland' and in para (c) 'or local authorities in Wales' is substituted by 'in England or Wales';
- after subsection (5), there is inserted a new subsection (5A);
- in subsection (7), in para (c), after 'secure accommodation in England' there is inserted 'or Scotland';
- after that paragraph, there is inserted a new paragraph (d); and
- After subsection (8), there is inserted a new subsection (8A).

Section 25 is thereby amended to read:

25 Use of accommodation for restricting liberty

(1) Subject to the following provisions of this section, a child who is being looked after by a local authority in England or Wales may not be placed, and, if placed, may not be kept, in accommodation in England or Scotland provided for the purpose of restricting liberty ('secure accommodation') unless it appears –

    (a)   that –

        (i)   he has a history of absconding and is likely to abscond from any other description of accommodation; and

        (ii)   if he absconds, he is likely to suffer significant harm, or

    (b)   that if he is kept in any other description of accommodation he is likely to injure himself or other persons.

(2) The Secretary of State may by regulations –

    (a)   specify a maximum period –

        (i)   beyond which a child may not be kept in secure accommodation in England or Scotland without the authority of the court; and

        (ii)   for which the court may authorise a child to be kept in secure accommodation in England or Scotland;

    (b)   empower the court from time to time to authorise a child to be kept in secure accommodation in England or Scotland for such further period as the regulations may specify; and

    (c)   provide that applications to the court under this section shall be made only by local authorities in England or Wales.

(3) It shall be the duty of a court hearing an application under this section to determine whether any relevant criteria for keeping a child in secure accommodation are satisfied in his case.

(4) If a court determines that any such criteria are satisfied, it shall make an order authorising the child to be kept in secure accommodation and specifying the maximum period for which he may be so kept.

(5) On any adjournment of the hearing of an application under this section, a court may make an interim order permitting the child to be kept during the period of the adjournment in secure accommodation.

(5A) Where a local authority in England or Wales are authorised under this section to keep a child in secure accommodation in Scotland, the person in charge of the accommodation may restrict the child's liberty to the extent that the person considers appropriate, having regard to the terms of any order made by a court under this section.

(6) No court shall exercise the powers conferred by this section in respect of a child who is not legally represented in that court unless, having been informed of his right to apply for the provision of representation under Part 1 of the Legal Aid, Sentencing and Punishment of Offenders Act 2012 and having had the opportunity to do so, he refused or failed to apply.

(7) The Secretary of State may by regulations provide that –

    (a) this section shall or shall not apply to any description of children specified in the regulations;

    (b) this section shall have effect in relation to children of a description specified in the regulations subject to such modifications as may be so specified;

    (c) such other provisions as may be so specified shall have effect for the purpose of determining whether a child of a description specified in the regulations may be placed or kept in secure accommodation in England or Scotland.

    (d) a child may only be placed in secure accommodation that is of a description specified in the regulations (and the description may in particular be framed by reference to whether the accommodation, or the person providing it, has been approved by the Secretary of State or the Scottish Ministers).

(8) The giving of an authorisation under this section shall not prejudice any power of any court in England and Wales or Scotland to give directions relating to the child to whom the authorisation relates.

(8A) Sections 168 and 169(1) to (4) of the Children's Hearings (Scotland) Act 2011 (enforcement and absconding) apply in relation to an order under subsection (4) above as they apply in relation to the orders mentioned in section 168(3) or 169(1)(a) of that Act.

(9) This section is subject to section 20(8).

Commencement date: 27 April 2017.

Independent reviewing officers

25C   Referred cases

Page 514.

By virtue of Social Services and Well-being (Wales) Act 2014 (Consequential Amendments) Regulations 2017, reg 2, in Children Act 1989, s 25C(2), subsection (2) (referred cases, regulations in respect of Wales) is disapplied in relation to Wales. Commencement date 1 December 2017.

PART IV
CARE AND SUPERVISION

General

31 Care and supervision orders

Page 520.
By virtue of Children and Social Work Act 2017, s 8, in Children Act 1989, s 31, subsection (3B) is substituted. Section 31 is thereby amended to read:

31 Care and supervision orders

(1) On the application of any local authority or authorised person, the court may make an order –

(a) placing the child with respect to whom the application is made in the care of a designated local authority; or

(b) putting him under the supervision of a designated local authority.

(2) A court may only make a care order or supervision order if it is satisfied –

(a) that the child concerned is suffering, or is likely to suffer, significant harm; and

(b) that the harm, or likelihood of harm, is attributable to –

(i) the care given to the child, or likely to be given to him if the order were not made, not being what it would be reasonable to expect a parent to give to him; or

(ii) the child's being beyond parental control.

(3) No care order or supervision order may be made with respect to a child who has reached the age of seventeen (or sixteen, in the case of a child who is married).

(3A) A court deciding whether to make a care order –

(a) is required to consider the permanence provisions of the section 31A plan for the child concerned, but

(b) is not required to consider the remainder of the section 31A plan, subject to section 34(11).

(3B) For the purposes of subsection (3A), the permanence provisions of a section 31A plan are –

(a) such of the plan's provisions setting out the long-term plan for the upbringing of the child concerned as provide for any of the following –

(i) the child to live with any parent of the child's or with any other member of, or any friend of, the child's family;

(ii) adoption;

(iii) long-term care not within sub-paragraph (i) or (ii);

(b) such of the plan's provisions as set out any of the following –

(i) the impact on the child concerned of any harm that he or she suffered or was likely to suffer;

(ii) the current and future needs of the child (including needs arising out of that impact);

(iii) the way in which the long-term plan for the upbringing of the child would meet those current and future needs.

(3C) The Secretary of State may by regulations amend this section for the purpose of altering what for the purposes of subsection (3A) are the permanence provisions of a section 31A plan.

(4) An application under this section may be made on its own or in any other family proceedings.

(5) The court may –

    (a)   on an application for a care order, make a supervision order;

    (b)   on an application for a supervision order, make a care order.

(6) Where an authorised person proposes to make an application under this section he shall –

    (a)   if it is reasonably practicable to do so; and

    (b)   before making the application,

consult the local authority appearing to him to be the authority in whose area the child concerned is ordinarily resident.

(7) An application made by an authorised person shall not be entertained by the court if, at the time when it is made, the child concerned is –

    (a)   the subject of an earlier application for a care order, or supervision order, which has not been disposed of; or

    (b)   subject to –

        (i)   a care order or supervision order;

        (ii) a youth rehabilitation order within the meaning of Part 1 of the Criminal Justice and Immigration Act 2008; or

        (iii) a supervision requirement within the meaning of Part II of the Children (Scotland) Act 1995.

(8) The local authority designated in a care order must be –

    (a)   the authority within whose area the child is ordinarily resident; or

    (b)   where the child does not reside in the area of a local authority, the authority within whose area any circumstances arose in consequence of which the order is being made.

(9) In this section –

'authorised person' means –

    (a)   the National Society for the Prevention of Cruelty to Children and any of its officers; and

    (b)   any person authorised by order of the Secretary of State to bring proceedings under this section and any officer of a body which is so authorised;

'harm' means ill-treatment or the impairment of health or development including, for example, impairment suffered from seeing or hearing the ill-treatment of another;

'development' means physical, intellectual, emotional, social or behavioural development;

'health' means physical or mental health; and

'ill-treatment' includes sexual abuse and forms of ill-treatment which are not physical.

(10) Where the question of whether harm suffered by a child is significant turns on the child's health or development, his health or development shall be compared with that which could reasonably be expected of a similar child.

(11) In this Act –

'a care order' means (subject to section 105(1)) an order under subsection (1)(a) and (except where express provision to the contrary is made) includes an interim care order made under section 38; and 'a supervision order' means an order under subsection (1)(b) and (except where express provision to the contrary is made) includes an interim supervision order made under section 38.

Commencement date: 31 October 2017.

Re A (A child) (Ward of court: approach by Security Service) [2017] EWHC 1022 (Fam), [2017] All ER (D) 39 (May)

(Family Division, Sir James Munby P, 4 May 2017) Ward of court – Contempt of court in wardship proceedings. The Family Division, in a case where a Security Service officer had approached a ward of court, held that there was not and never had been any principle or rule that judicial consent was required before the police could interview a ward of court. Provided that the requirements of the Police and Criminal Evidence Act 1984 with regard to juveniles were complied with, the duty upon the police was discharged and they had no extra duty to perform.

Digest

A local authority brought proceedings concerning a teenager who was a ward of court in which radicalisation was an issue. The ward was approached by an officer of the Security Service, acting in the course of that officer's exercise of functions as an officer of the Security Service. When the authority became aware of what had happened, it wrote to the Security Service, suggesting that the approach should not have taken place without the court's prior authority and that the officer was at serious risk of being in contempt of court. Previously, orders had been made containing a recital to the effect that there was no requirement for the Security Service to obtain the court's permission to fulfil its statutory functions insofar as its actions related to the ward. The episode highlighted a lack of clarity in the law that needed to be resolved in the interests of all who might be involved in similar matters in future and in the wider public interest. Although the issue had arisen in the context of the activities of the Security Service, exactly the same point could arise in the context of activities of, for example, police officers, officers of the Immigration Enforcement and officers of other investigatory, enforcement or regulatory agencies.

The issue for determination concerned the intersection of two principles of wardship law. First, that no important or major step in the life of a ward could be taken without first obtaining the approval of the wardship judge. Secondly, as stated in *A v Liverpool City Council and another* [1981] 2 All ER 385 (Liverpool), that the wardship court could not exercise its powers, however wide they might be, so as to intervene on the merits in an area of concern entrusted by law to another public authority. An aspect of the Liverpool principle was the important principle that wardship did not privilege a ward over a child who was not a ward and did not give a ward an immunity not available to other children. Consideration was given to *Re R, Re G (minors)* [1990] 2 All ER 633 (*Re R*), the Police and Criminal Evidence Act 1984 (PACE), and *Practice Direction (Ward: Witness at Trial)* [1987] 1 WLR 1739 and *Practice Direction (Ward: Witness at Trial) (No 2)* [1988] 1 WLR 989 (the 1988 Practice Direction), which had been subsumed by FPR PD12D (PD12D), in particular, para 5.

The court ruled:

Leaving to one side the various practice directions, there was not and never had been any principle or rule that judicial consent was required before the police could interview a ward of court. The asserted principle or rule that judicial consent was required before the police could interview a ward of court was impossible to reconcile either with the Liverpool principle or with the 'no privilege over other children' principle. The reality was that, in very large measure, the asserted principle or rule that judicial consent was required before the police could interview a ward of court had been hollowed out, almost to the point of extinction, first by the 1988 Practice Direction and even more so by subsequent decisions. There was a pressing need for para 5 of PD12D to be considered as a matter of urgency by the Family Procedure Rule Committee. Radical surgery would probably be required. In the meantime, police officers, officers of the Security Service and others in a similar position should follow the guidance given in *Re R*, namely that, provided that the requirements of PACE with regard to juveniles were complied with, the duty upon the police was discharged. They had no extra duty to perform. There was, of course, a duty upon those having the care of the minor to inform the court at the earliest practical opportunity of what had taken place, but there was no further duty upon the police themselves in those circumstances. PACE did not apply to the Security Service. In relation to the Security Service and other agencies to which PACE did not apply, the references to PACE should be read as referring to the relevant legislative framework governing the functions of the Security Service or other agency involved (see [45]-[47], [49], [50] of the judgment).

S (minors), Re [1987] 3 All ER 1076 disapproved; *Arif (Mohamed) (an infant), Re* [1968] Ch 643 applied; *A v Liverpool City Council* [1981] 2 All ER 385 applied; *B (a minor), Re* [1989] Lexis Citation 1992 applied; *R (minors), Re* [1990] 2 All ER 633 applied; *Egeneonu v Egeneonu* [2017] All ER (D) 69 (Jan) applied; *F (a minor), Re* [1977] 1 All ER 114 considered; *W (a minor), Re* [1985] FLR 879 considered; *Practice Direction (Ward: Witness At Trial)* [1987] 1 WLR 1739 considered; *K (minors), Re* [1988] 1 All ER 214 considered; *Practice Direction (Ward: Witness At Trial) (No 2)* [1988] 1 WLR 989 applied; *A (a minor), Re* [1989] 3 All ER 610 considered; *JS (a minor), Re* [1990] 2 All ER 861 considered; *R (a minor), Re* [1991] 2 All ER 193 considered; *R (a minor), Re* [1994] 3 All ER 658 considered; *T (wardship: review of police protection decision) (No 2), Re* [2010] 1 FLR 1026 considered.

Per curiam: 'The local authority has queried what the position would be in relation to a child who is either accommodated by a local authority in accordance with section 20 of the Children Act 1989 or subject to a care order (interim or final) in accordance with section 31 or section 38 of the 1989 Act. This is really a matter for another day, but in principle I cannot see how the fact that the local authority is exercising its statutory powers in either of these ways under the 1989 Act can either privilege the child over a child who is not the subject of such arrangements or prevent another statutory agency such as the police or the Security Service from exercising its powers in precisely the same way as they would in relation to a child who is not the subject of such arrangements. The fact that, in a sense, a local authority may be acting as a corporate, statutory parent, does not, vis-a-vis the police or the Security Service or any other agency, put the local authority in any different or more powerful position than a natural parent. So, unless the legislative framework governing the functions of the relevant agency requires, for example, consultation with or con-sent from a parent (as in *In re A (A Minor) (Wardship: Police Caution)* [1989] Fam 103), a statutory agency is not required to consult with, let alone obtain the consent of, the local authority. It must, as a matter of principle, be for the relevant agency, not the local authority, to decide how it should act.' (see [49] of the judgment).

A v London Borough of Wandsworth and others [2017] EWCA Civ 398, [2017] All ER (D) 21 (Jun)

(Court of Appeal, Civil Division, Sir James Munby P, Hallett and Macur LJJ, 23 May 2017) Practice – Family proceedings. The Court of Appeal, Civil Division allowed a mother's appeal against a decision to make a final care order at an adjourned Issues Resolution Hearing. The court found that the instant proceedings had not been fair to the mother or the children. They had failed to accord to the mother her rights under Art 6 of the European Convention on Human Rights to a fair hearing, and in all the circumstances had fallen short of safeguarding the procedural and substantive rights of the children under Art 8 of the Convention.

Digest

Final care orders were made in respect of J, A and C (aged 16, 14 and 12, respectively) at an adjourned Issues Resolution Hearing (IRH), despite opposition from all parties, including the children's guardians. The judge justified the procedure he adopted since he had 'heard from the mother' and 'given her the opportunity to set out anything in writing which she wishes'. He quoted extensively from the statements of the social worker and contended that all the evidence pointed in one direction. There had been no updated case analysis or legal representation for J and C. A appealed. The Association of Lawyers for Children was given leave to intervene on procedural issues concerning the making of final orders at an IRH.

That issue was whether the judge was wrong in the procedure he adopted to make the substantive orders at the IRH. Consideration was given to Arts 6 and 8 of the European Convention on Human Rights.

The appeal would be allowed.

Although resolution and final determination of applications at a IRH was envisaged in appropriate cases, it was always subject implicitly to the necessary evidence being before the court. A full hearing might not always be necessary; there was no absolute right to cross-examine each witness or to embark upon a 'fishing expedition'. The determination of what procedure to adopt called for the exercise of judicial discretion dependent on the circumstances of the case before the judge. It was impossible to formulate a 'one size fits all' policy. The court would be slow to interfere in that exercise of judgment carefully articulated and soundly based. However, the principles of procedural fairness provided clear guidance to the first instance judge in his/her decision of the appropriate and fair procedure to be adopted at various stages in family proceedings. It was obvious that Arts 6 and 8 of the European Convention on Human Rights would necessarily be engaged at every stage of the process (see [17], [18], [22], [26] of the judgment).

The instant proceedings had not been fair to the mother or the children. They had failed to accord to the mother her Art 6 rights to a fair hearing, and in all the circumstances had fallen short of safeguarding the procedural and substantive Art 8 rights of the children. The judge had not been deterred by the absence of an updated case analysis or legal representation for J and C despite the children's guardian seeking it. In the absence of fresh information or a change in circumstances, it was inappropriate for the judge to have allowed the appeal of his own motion. The real issue, however, was not whether the judge's assessment of the evidence had been wrong but whether the process adopted by the judge had so undermined any objective concept of procedural fairness as to undermine the integrity of the decision. That was regardless of the distinct likelihood that the boys would not be returned to their mother's care in the foreseeable future (see [29], [30], [36], [37] of the judgment).

W (a child)(cross-examination), Re [2010] All ER (D) 27 (Nov) considered; *S-W (Children) (care proceedings: final care order at case management hearing), Re* [2015] All ER (D) 10 (Mar) considered.

J Bazley QC and M Hellens for A.

A Bagchi QC and G Kelly the first respondent.

S Morgan QC and L Sprinz for the second respondent.

D Fottrell QC and S Segal for the Association of Lawyers for Children.

Re X (A Child) (No 2) [2017] EWHC 1585 (Fam), [2017] All ER (D) 49 (Jul)

(Family Division, Sir James Munby (P), 28 June 2017) Family proceedings – Orders in family proceedings. In circumstances where the relevant local authority had not formulated a properly worked-up care plan for X, who was approaching 17 and detained in a secure unit ahead of her release, the Family Division concluded that, due to the nature of X's complex needs, it was likely that a care plan would involve a deprivation of her liberty. A plan of action was approved that would lead to the formulation of a properly worked-up care plan that could be put before the court for approval, exercising the inherent jurisdiction, before X was released from the secure unit.

Digest

The case concerned X, who was born in 2000. Since 2014, X had regularly engaged in anti-social criminal behaviours, having been arrested on numerous occasions and charged with offences of violence, including assaulting a police officer. According to the relevant local authority, X presented a risk to herself through acts of self-harm and, engaging in violent and destructive behaviours towards others, was sentenced to a detention and training order and was detained in a secure unit. Following detention, X's behaviour continued to deteriorate. At the time of the present proceedings, X was approaching 17 and the authority had not been able to articulate any workable care plan for X, let alone identify where she might be accommodated and what services should be made available for her upon her release from the secure unit.

The issues were whether a care order should be made, and what would be the nature and details of the care order.

The court ruled:

The need for a final care order was overwhelming. It was imperative in X's interests that the authority had parental responsibility and she could enjoy, presently and after she left care, all the benefits that would accrue to her if there was a care order. However, there was, at present, no realistic care plan available to be approved, other than a plan of action that it was hoped would lead to the formulation of a proper care plan. However, the ability to make a care order, given X's age, would be gone in a matter of days. That conundrum could properly be solved because: (i) if an appropriate placement for X could be found that properly met her very complex needs, it was likely to involve a deprivation of her liberty requiring judicial sanction; and (ii) that sanction was, in the circumstances, properly a matter for the Family Division. There were extant proceedings in the Family Division available to be used for that purpose. What would be approved, for the purposes of the care order, was a plan of action that would lead to the formulation of a properly worked-up care plan that could be put before the court for approval, exercising the inherent jurisdiction, before X was released from the secure unit (see [26]–[30] of the judgment).

Michael Jones for the authority.

Ginny Whiteley for X's mother.

Rebecca Gregg for X.

Simon Rowbotham for X's guardian.

Re X (A Child) (No 3) [2017] EWHC 2036 (Fam), [2017] All ER (D) 47 (Aug)

(Family Division, Sir James Munby P, 3 August 2017) Family proceedings – Orders in family proceedings. Despite it being identified in an earlier judgment that X was in an urgent need for a care plan to be established for her upon her release from a secure unit in mid-August 2017, no suitable facility had been identified for her that could adequately provide for her mental care needs. Accordingly, the Family Division, adjourned proceedings to allow time to enable further enquiries to be made as to what placements might be available for X on an interim basis. The court expressed deep concern at the lack of proper provision for young people in similar circumstances to X.

Background

The case concerned the future welfare and mental care of X after the conclusion of her stay at ZX, a secure unit for youth offenders. X was 17 years' old. She had made attempts to commit suicide, and it was the opinion of a staff group at ZX that, if she was to be released from ZX, she would commit suicide within 24 to 48 hours of release. The present state of X's care at ZX had been detailed in a previous judgment (see [2017] All ER (D) 49 (Jul)). A care order had previously been made for X despite there being no plan as to what should happen when she was to be released from ZX in mid-August 2017.

Accordingly, the present proceedings concerned such future plans for X.

The court ruled:

Issues and decisions

Whether, and to what extent, an appropriate care plan had been established, including a suitable placement for X in an appropriate facility, ahead of her release from ZX in mid-August 2017.

X was in a dreadful position, which could be summarised as follows: (i) the regime at ZX was not meeting X's needs. The staff there, despite all their efforts, were managing little more than to contain her; (ii) what X needed – as a matter of desperate urgency – was therapy in an appropriate clinical setting; (iii) placement in a psychiatric intensive care unit would not meet X's complex needs; (iv) what X needed as a matter of desperate urgency was placement in a Tier-4 (adolescent) low secure unit for some 18–24 months. That was clearly the best option for her; (v) no such placement had been available anywhere in the country when the hearing had started or when the hearing had concluded, and no such placement had been available when the judgment had been handed down. The only identified placement had a 6-month waiting list for beds; and (vi) as of the date of the judgment, no placement of any kind was available for X when she left ZX, as she had to no later than 15:00 on 14 August 2017 (see [24] of the judgment).

To send her back to any community setting was a suicide mission to a catastrophic level. Staff at ZX did not think it would take more than 24 to 48 hours before they received a phone call stating that X had made a successful attempt on her life. The lack of provision for X was an outrage. It was difficult to read the updates on X and not form the view that her care plan was being primarily determined by a lack of adolescent mental health resources. It was not right that such a vulnerable child with a lengthy documented history of the most extreme and determined self-harm should have her medical care plan dictated by an absence of resource, as opposed to her identified needs (see [25], [27], [31] of the judgment).

The case would be adjourned and fixed for a further hearing for 7 August 2017: (i) to enable further enquiries to be made as to what placements might be available for X on an interim basis, pending a low secure unit placement, in either a medium secure unit, a child and adolescent PICU, or an adult PICU; and (ii) depending upon the outcome of those inquiries, to determine which form of interim placement – none of which would appropriately meet X's needs – ought to be selected as the least worst option (see [34] of the judgment).

Per curiam: 'What this case demonstrates, as if further demonstration is still required of what is a well-known scandal, is the disgraceful and utterly shaming lack of proper provision in this country of the clinical, residential and other support services so desperately needed by the increasing numbers of children and young people afflicted with the same kind of difficulties as X is burdened with. We are, even in these times of austerity, one of the richest countries in the world. Our children and young people are out future. X is part of our future. It is a disgrace to any country with pretensions to civilisation, compassion and, dare one say it, basic human decency, that a judge in 2017 should be faced with the problems thrown up by this case and should have to express himself in such terms' (see [37] of the judgment).

Michael Jones for the local authority.

Rebecca Gregg for X.

Simon Rowbotham for X's guardian.

Mungo Wenban-Smith for the relevant NHS Clinical Commissioning Group.

Elizabeth Wheeler for NHS England.

Re X (A Child) (No 4) [2017] EWHC 2084 (Fam), [2017] All ER (D) 51 (Aug)

(Family Division, Sir James Munby P, 7 August 2017) Family proceedings – Orders in family proceedings. In a number of previous hearings, X's immediate welfare and mental care needs following her imminent release from a secure unit had been addressed without any care plan being made. However, the Family Division, in the imminent proceedings, confirmed, following representations from NHS England, that an appropriate care plan had been established, including a suitable placement for X in an appropriate facility, ahead of her release.

Background

The case concerned the future welfare and mental care of X after the conclusion of her stay at ZX, a secure unit for youth offenders. X was aged 17. The present state of X's care at ZX had been detailed in a previous judgment (see [2017] All ER (D) 49 (Jul)). A care order had previously been made for X despite there being no plan as to what should happen when she was to be released from ZX in mid-August 2017. Despite the urgency of X's situation being acknowledged, there had been no suitable place in any facility in England identified and secured for X upon her pending release from ZX when the matter had come again before the court (see [2017] All ER (D) 47 (Aug)). The present proceedings, being heard less than a week after the last hearing, concerned developments in securing a suitable place for X in order for her care needs to be adequately met.

At the time of the hearing, confirmation had been received from NHS England that X had been accepted for placement on the child and adolescent mental health service (CAMHS) psychiatric intensive care unit (PICU), at the facility, ZZ. An agreement had been made to fund an extra package of care in order for her needs to be met. The package included treatment that would be recommended following a comprehensive assessment. Treatment would also include dedicated staff to support X throughout her admission, therapy and treatment, including psychological and pharmaceutical input.

The court ruled:

Issues and decisions

Whether, and to what extent, an appropriate care plan had been established, including a suitable placement for X in an appropriate facility, ahead of her release from ZX on 14 August 2017.

It was quite clear, and no one had suggested otherwise, that X's interests would be best served by her proposed transfer from ZX to ZZ on 10 August 2017 (see [24] of the judgment).

NHS England would be ordered to file and serve, no later than 1600 on 9 August 2017, all available documentation relating to X's care and treatment plan at ZZ or, to the extent that the documentation was incomplete, an explanation of why that was so (see [25] of the judgment).

Per curiam: 'Conscious of the dangers of falling into the fallacious trap of post hoc ergo propter hoc, I cannot escape the powerful feeling that, but for my judgment, the steps subsequently taken would have been neither as effective nor as speedily effective as appears to have been the case. This, however, is not a matter for congratulation; on the contrary, it is, of itself, yet further cause for concern. The provision of the care that someone like X needs should not be dependent upon judicial involvement, nor should someone like X be privileged just because her case comes before a very senior judge. I emphasise this because a mass of informed, if anecdotal, opinion indicates that X's is not an isolated case and that there are far too many young women in similar predicaments. How are they to be protected?' (see [18] of the judgment).

Michael Jones for the local authority.

Rebecca Gregg for X.

Simon Rowbotham for X's guardian.

Rachael Watkinson for the relevant NHS Clinical Commissioning Group.

Elizabeth Wheeler for NHS England.

A Local Authority v T (Mother) and others (Alere Toxicology and others intervening) [2017] EWFC 64, [2017] All ER (D) 48 (Oct)

(Family Court, Peter Jackson J, 29 September 2017) Family proceedings – Orders in family proceedings. A supervision order concerning an 8-month-old baby would be made in the applicant local authority's favour for 12 months, the mother having been found to have used cocaine at a relatively low and infrequent level during the latter part of 2015 and during 2016, but not recently. The Family Court also gave suggestions as to how the presentation of reports might be developed so as to be most useful to those working in the field of family justice.

Background

The proceedings concerned an 8-month-old baby, H. She was removed from her mother at birth, but returned to her care at the age of 6 weeks under supervision and, since July, had lived with her mother at home.

It was agreed that, although the threshold for intervention was crossed on the basis of the past history and future risk, H would remain in her mother's care with support provided by the applicant local authority, other agencies, the father and the maternal grandmother. The proceedings concerned the type of order to be made.

Issues and decisions

(1) Whether the mother had been using drugs, albeit at a low level, during the past 2 years. The issue required consideration of a body of scientific information from hair-strand tests taken over the 2-year period, which were interpreted by testing organisations as showing low-level cocaine use for at least some of the time.

The authority had made out its case as to the mother's: (i) neglectful parenting of three older children; (ii) longstanding history of drug and alcohol misuse up to July 2015; (iii) continued use of cocaine, albeit at a low and/or infrequent level, between July 2015 and December 2016, including at times when she had been pregnant; and (iv) repeated lying to professionals and the court about her use of cocaine.

The evidence as a whole drove to the conclusion that the mother had used cocaine at a relatively low and infrequent level during the latter part of 2015 and during 2016, and that she had not told the truth about that. There was much weaker scientific evidence of continuing limited cocaine use after H's birth. Given the finding in relation to earlier use, the possibility could not be discounted that the mother was not telling the truth about that either. However, taking the evidence as a whole, it was not established that the authority had proved its case in respect of that period.

Although there was considerable evidence of the mother's attempts to get help and to rid herself of drug use, the almost continuous array of test results showing cocaine and a metabolite of cocaine significantly above the threshold could not adequately be explained by inadvertent disclosure.

It was not established that the authority had made out its case in relation to recent use of cocaine. It followed that, on balance, the mother's evidence that she had been free of drugs since H had been born would be accepted. Those findings did not call into question the decision that H should remain in her mother's care (see [60], [62], [63], [65], [66] of the judgment).

(2) Whether the arrangement should be underpinned by a care or supervision order.

Neither a care order nor a supervision order would be a wrong choice in the present case. On the facts, a care order would not confer benefits that outweighed those arising under a supervision order. Therefore, a supervision order would be made in the authority's favour for 12 months, trusting that it would be reviewed in 9 months to decide whether an extension would be necessary (see [69], [71] of the judgment).

O (a child) (supervision order: future harm), Re [2001] 1 FLR 923 applied.

William Tyler QC and Emily James for the authority.

Hannah Markham QC and Kate Tompkins for the mother.

Paul Hepher for the father.

Timothy Parker and Edward Lamb for the children's guardian.

Tina Cook QC and Damian Woodward-Carlton for Alere Toxicology, as intervener.

Ronan O'Donovan for Lextox, as intervener.

John Tughan QC for DNA Legal, as intervener.

A Local Authority v AMcC and others [2017] EWHC 2435 (Fam), [2017] All ER (D) 49 (Oct)

(Family Division, Hayden J, 3 October 2017) Family proceedings – Orders in family proceedings. Care orders were made for boys aged 13 and 15, as remaining in their present residential care was in their welfare best interests. The Family Division further held that the presumption of capacity of their nearly 18-year-old brother had not been rebutted, but an injunction would be made, not compelling him to live in any particular place, but restraining him from living at his mother's home until the question of capacity and jurisdiction were reconsidered.

Background

The present proceedings concerned three boys aged 13 years, C, 15 years, A, and 17 years (18 in December), J. The claimant local authority contended that the children had suffered neglect, and physical and emotional harm (for the details of the authority's allegations, see [8] of the judgment). It sought care orders in relation to C and A, planning that they remained in residential care and contemplating a regime of contact between the children and their mother, as well as between the siblings.

In the light of J's obvious and pressing needs, the authority sought permission to pursue proceedings on J's behalf in the Court of Protection and, to that end, had undertaken an assessment of mental capacity. The assessment concluded that, due to J's lack of insight and inflexibility of thought, he lacked capacity to make the decision as to where he should live.

Issues and decisions

(1) Whether the threshold criteria were met.

The threshold criteria were met as particularised in the authority's document. However, the circumstances had come about in consequence of the overwhelming challenges faced by a mother with developmental difficulties herself, variously managing four boys, two of whom were on the autistic spectrum and one of whom might also be (see [22] of the judgment).

(2) Whether care orders should be made in relation to C and A.

A's wishes, that he would like to remain in his current placement, should be regarded as effectively determinative, given the careful and reflective way in which they had been articulated. In any event, the evidence as to his welfare interests pointed overwhelmingly to his remaining where he was.

It was very clear that C's best interests lay in remaining where he was, and it was entirely established that the authority's care plan and proposal for contact served his welfare most effectively (see [29], [30], [34] of the judgment).

(3) Whether it should be declared that J lacked capacity, under MCA 2005, s 15.

It would rarely be possible at the outset of proceedings to elicit evidence of the cogency and weight required by MCA 2005, s 15. However, s 48 was a different test with a different and interim objective, rather than a lesser one. Reason to believe that a patient lacked capacity had to be predicated on solid and well-reasoned assessment in which his voice could be heard clearly and in circumstances where his own powers of reasoning had been given the most propitious opportunity to assert themselves (see [69] of the judgment).

The assessment of mental capacity displayed insufficient forensic rigour to justify its conclusion. Nor was its determination that J lacked capacity adequately reasoned. It was not established that the assessors had explained the purpose of the assessment to J. A prerequisite to evaluation of a person's capacity on any specific issue was at very least that they had explained to them the purpose and extent of the assessment itself. That had not happened. It was probably fatal to any conclusion but, in any event, it at least gravely undermined it.

The test was not met in J's case. The purpose of the assessment had not been explained to him. The analysis of the extent of J's understanding of the relevant information was superficial and incomplete. The ultimate reasoning underpinning the conclusions of the assessment was vague and unsatisfactory. It would be entirely disrespectful to J to curtail any aspect of his autonomy on the basis of such unsatisfactory evidence. It was entirely unclear whether J had capacity to decide where he lived or not. Accordingly, even on an interim basis, the presumption of capacity had not been rebutted. The s 48 test was not met (see [46], [47], [49] of the judgment).

S v S; W v Official Solicitor [1970] 3 All ER 107 applied; *F (mental capacity: interim jurisdiction), Re* [2010] 2 FLR 28 considered; *FM and another v SCC and another* [2016] EWCA Civ 645 considered.

(4) Whether the court's declaratory and injunctive powers under its inherent jurisdiction could be exercised on the basis that J was a vulnerable adult, at risk of harm, whose autonomy had been compromised in relation to his decision-making processes and who might be sufficiently protected by that relief.

It would be unconscionable and socially undesirable if, due to the weaknesses of the assessment that had failed satisfactorily to resolve whether there were reasons to believe that J lacked capacity, he was to find himself beyond the reach of judicial protection. He was not. The question that arose was how he could most effectively be protected with the least intrusive and most proportionate curtailment of his autonomy.

The starting point was that a thorough MCA 2003-compliant assessment of capacity be taken immediately. When that report was available, it would be necessary to revisit the question of capacity and, therefore, jurisdiction. The court's inherent jurisdiction permitted J to be protected while those investigations resumed.

To remain in his present unit was in J's best interest. An injunction should be drafted in terms that did not compel J to live in any particular place, but to restrain him from living at his mother's home. It would only endure until the question of capacity and jurisdiction were reconsidered when the detailed capacity assessment had been completed (see [82]–[84], [87], [88] of the judgment).

SA (vulnerable adult with capacity: marriage), Re [2006] 1 FLR 867 considered; *A Local Authority v DL* [2012] 3 All ER 1064 considered.

Julien Foster for the authority.

Rachel Gillman for the mother.

Lucy Sprinz for the children.

PART XII
MISCELLANEOUS AND GENERAL

Jurisdiction and procedure etc

100 Restrictions on use of wardship jurisdiction

Page 630.

Great Ormond Street Hospital for Children NHS Foundation Trust v Yates and others [2017] EWCA Civ 410, [2017] All ER (D) 20 (Jun)

(Court of Appeal, Civil Division, McFarlane, King and Sales LJJ, 23 May 2017) Minor – Medical treatment. The Court of Appeal, Civil Division, dismissed the parents' appeal against the judge's decision that it would not be in Charlie Gard's best interests to undergo nucleoside therapy overseas and that Great Ormond Street Hospital's application to remove him from a ventilator should be granted. On the basis of the judge's findings, there was no viable alternative treatment for Charlie, such that the parents' argument that there was a new category of child medical treatment cases deriving from *Re Aysha King (A Child)* [2014] All ER (D) 47 (Sep) did not arise.

Digest

The present proceedings concerned a 9-month-old boy, C, who suffered from the effects of an extremely rare and grossly debilitating genetic mutation. He had already suffered irreversible brain damage, had been unable to breathe unaided, save for the first 2 months of his life, and medical staff had, for a number of months, been unable to detect him responding to any stimulus. C's current life expectancy was measured in months, unless an alternative treatment could stall or alter the course of his decline. C's parents had identified a resource through which they believed it might be possible for C to receive treatment (nucleoside therapy) which, while not curing his condition, might slow or halt its destructive progress. C's doctors, who had contemplated that alternative treatment when he had first been in their care, had, following a significant decline in the level of his brain functioning, concluded that there was effectively no chance of C benefiting from its effects. C's parents did not agree with the advice that the treating clinicians had given. In the light of the dispute as to C's future treatment, the hospital where he had been an inpatient issued an application, seeking a declaration that it was lawful and in C's best interests for artificial ventilation to be withdrawn, and for his treating clinicians to provide only palliative care for him. They also sought a declaration that it was lawful and in C's best interests not to undergo nucleoside therapy. The judge concluded that it would not be in C's best interests to undergo nucleoside therapy and that, given the parlous nature of his existence and the bleak prognosis for his imminent demise, the hospital's application to remove him from the ventilator should be granted. The parents appealed, seeking declarations that they were entitled to arrange for C to be transferred to a clinic at which he could be provided with nucleoside therapy.

The parents' contentions included that, first, the judge had erred in having made an order that had prevented C from receiving medical treatment by expert physicians in a reputable hospital overseas in circumstances where there was no risk of that treatment causing significant harm to him. That was based on the arguments that cases fell into two categories: (i) category 1 cases, which included all previously reported medical treatment cases, save and except for *Re Aysha King (A Child)* [2014] All ER (D) 47 (Sep) (*King*), involving parents who opposed the course of treatment for which the treating clinicians applied and did not have a viable alternative therapeutic option to put before the court; and (ii) category 2 cases, in which a viable alternative treatment option was put forward by the parents and the court was required to choose between the two. The parents argued that, in category 2 cases, the law afforded both priority and protection to the privileged position of a parent giving or withholding consent to medical treatment for their child, so that the parents preferred treatment option should only be overridden if it was established that the pursuit of that option was likely to cause the child to suffer 'significant harm'. Second, the judge had had no jurisdiction to grant an order on the application of one clinical team, preventing a second clinical team from carrying out a treatment that the latter had offered in the reasonable exercise of its professional judgment.

The appeal would be dismissed.

(1) The statements of principle more than amply encompassed the case where a parent might be objecting to a proposed course of treatment on the basis that they had a preferred alternative course of treatment. Even if such a case might fall at the more favourable end of the spectrum, the court did not evaluate the reasonableness of the parents' case, or introduce any other factor or filter before it embarked upon deciding what was in the best interests of the child. When thoughtful, caring and responsible parents were putting forward a viable option for the care of their child, the court would look keenly at that option, in the same way that a court in family proceedings, when it reached the welfare stage of any case, looked at the realistic options that were before it. The court evaluated the detail of each option from the child's perspective. It did not prefer any particular option simply because it was put forward by a parent or local authority. If one option was favoured by a parent, that might give it weight or incline the court to be influenced by a reflection that, in the last analysis, the best interests of every child included an expectation that difficult decisions affecting the length and quality of its life would be taken for it by the parent to whom its care had been entrusted by nature. Notwithstanding that that was the case, in the end, it was the judge who had to choose the best course for a child. With respect to *King*, there was no indication that the judge had held that a threshold of significant harm applied to the decision as to the choice of treatment. Alternatively, if the judge had intended to state that, where a parent had put forward a viable option for treatment, the court only had jurisdiction to interfere with a parent's choice of that medical treatment if the child was likely to suffer significant harm as a result, such a statement had no foundation as a matter of law, was contrary to established authority and was, therefore, plainly in error. It was neither necessary nor appropriate to import a test that, where there was a viable alternative treatment available, absent the court being satisfied that the carrying out of the treatment would cause the child significant harm, the parents' view had to prevail, even if their proposed course of treatment was not in the child's best interests, or to create a new category of case. There was no justification for it in any previously decided authority, even *King*. It went without saying that, in many cases, all other things being equal, the views of the parents would be respected and were likely to be determinative. However, the sole principle was that the best interests of the child had to prevail and that had to apply even to cases where parents, for the best of motives, held onto some alternative view (see [94]–[96], [102], [105], [110]–[112], [120], [122] of the judgment).

Where, as in the present case, the judge had made clear findings that going overseas for treatment would be futile, would have no benefit and would simply prolong the awful existence that he had found had been the current state of C's life, he had been fully entitled, on the basis of those findings, to conclude as he had. The consequence of that conclusion was that the proposal for nucleoside therapy had not been a viable option before the court. On the facts of the case, the parents' submissions did not even begin to have traction. Their submission was based upon there being a viable alternative form of treatment available. However, the judge had formed a very pessimistic view of the proposed treatment. Those findings completely undermined, on a factual basis, the parents' submissions. There was no viable alternative treatment for C. That was the incontrovertible consequence of the judge's findings. There being no viable alternative treatment, the question of whether, as a matter of law, there was a group of cases labelled 'category 2' simply did not arise for C. Further, it was plain that the judge had not been invited to consider the law in the way put before the present court, let alone the existence of category 2 cases with the need to establish a threshold for significant harm. However, it was clear that, if he had been invited to form a conclusion on whether C had or had not been suffering significant harm presently, that finding would have been made. It had to follow from the unanimous professional and expert evidence that to move C overseas and expose him to treatment there would be likely to expose him to continued pain and suffering. The prospect of significant harm arose, in the context of such treatment, from the judge's finding that it would be of no benefit for C and that he would need to continue with his regime of life-sustaining treatment, which the judge had concluded had not otherwise been in his best interests, so that the nucleoside therapy could be administered (see [97], [113]–[115], [120], [122] of the judgment).

J (a minor), Re [1990] 3 All ER 930 applied; *Z (a minor) (freedom of publication), Re* [1995] 4 All ER 961 applied; *T (a minor) (wardship: medical treatment), Re* [1997] 1 All ER 906 applied; *Aintree University Hospitals NHS Foundation Trust v James* [2014] 1 All ER 573 applied; *Re A (a child) (withdrawal of medical treatment)* [2016] All ER (D) 183 (Jul) applied; *Aysha King (A Child), Re* [2014] 2 FLR 855 considered.

(2) So far as the argument was made that the hospital had been acting outside its legal powers in having brought the application, it was to be recalled that the issue as to alternative

therapy had been one raised by the parents and not by the hospital. The hospital had brought the application before the court on conventional terms, seeking a declaration about its treatment plan for withdrawal of life support and provision limited to palliative care, with no requirement on its part to consider nucleoside therapy. A choice had had to be made by the judge, rather than the hospital, following a full assessment of C's best interests. Therefore, it had fallen to the judge to decide the issue, rather than it having been a matter of the hospital having forced its opinion on the parents and thereafter having sought the court's sanction. The judge had decided the issue on the ordinary best-interests basis and had made an order declaring the result of that determination had been that nucleoside therapy had not been in C's best interests. It was incorrect to cast the process, in so far as it related to prohibiting nucleoside therapy, as having been driven by the hospital. The order resulted from a 100% child-focused, court-led evaluation where the one issue had been whether or not the therapy had been in C's best interests (see [116]–[118], [120], [122] of the judgment).

Decision of Francis J [2017] EWHC 972 (Fam) affirmed.

Richard Gordon QC, Gerard Rothschild and Grant Armstrong for the parents.

Katie Gollop QC and Susanna Rickard for the hospital.

Victoria Butler-Cole and Benjamin Tankel for C.

SCHEDULE 1
FINANCIAL PROVISION FOR CHILDREN

1 Orders for financial relief against parents

Page 644.

Green v Adams [2017] EWFC 24, [2017] All ER (D) 20 (May)

(Family Court, Mostyn J, 3 May 2017) Family provision – Dependant. The Family Court ruled that the mother's application for further capital provision, in the total sum of £20,600, for her son, from the respondent father was manifestly proportionate and reasonable, and properly reflected the considerations in para 4(1) of Sch 1 to the Children Act 1989.

Digest

In March 2001, N was born. In 2002, N's mother and father separated. Since 2003, the mother and father had been involved in protracted litigation following the end of their relationship. In 2013, the mother commenced a claim against the father, which included a claim for periodical payments (for details of the history of the claim in the courts, see [3] of the judgment). The present proceedings focused on the mother's application for capital provision, in the total sum of £20,600 (for details of the breakdown of the capital provision application, see [1] of the judgment).

It fell to be determined whether the mother's application for further capital provision would be granted. Consideration was given to s 3(1) of the Charging Orders Act 1979 (the 1979 Act) and para 4(1) of Sch 1 to the Children Act 1989 (the 1989 Act).

The application would be granted.

The mother's claim of £20,600 was manifestly proportionate and reasonable, and properly reflected the considerations in para 4(1) of Sch 1 to the 1989 Act. It was necessary for the court to take steps to secure the award so as to ensure that it was paid (see [21] of the judgment).

Under s 3(1) of the 1979 Act, the court was empowered to make an immediate absolute order. Such order would be over one of the father's properties in the sum of £20,600, together with any statutory interest (see [21] of the judgment).

Per curiam: 'Finally, I am constrained to mention an extraordinary state of affairs arising from recent amendments to the child support legislation. The tribunal appeals which I have mentioned were in relation to assessments made under the second regime which was introduced by the Child Support, Pensions and Social Security Act 2000. Under that regime there was, as explained above, a facility to seek variation on the grounds that the non-resident parent had "assets". That regime was replaced by the third regime provided for by the Child Maintenance and Other Payments Act 2008. That third regime has been in full force since 26 November 2013. This case was transferred into that regime on 10 October 2015. For reasons which I cannot fathom the "assets" ground of variation has been removed from this latest regime. There-fore, it is possible, as in this case, for a father to live on his capital, which may be very substantial indeed, and to pay no child support at all. The father was only required to pay the pitiful minimum sum of £7 a week from the early part of this year because it was then that he received his state pension. In my opinion the government needs to consider urgently the reinstatement of the "assets" ground of variation' (see [22] of the judgment).

SCHEDULE 2
SUPPORT FOR CHILDREN AND FAMILIES PROVIDED BY LOCAL AUTHORITIES IN ENGLAND

PART II
CHILDREN LOOKED AFTER BY LOCAL AUTHORITIES IN ENGLAND

19 Arrangements to assist children to live abroad

Page 664.
By virtue of the Children and Social Work Act 2017, s 10, Sch 1, para 3, in the Children Act 1989, in para 19(9) of Sch 2, after 'does not apply' there is inserted '– (a) to a local authority placing a child in secure accommodation in Scotland under section 25, or (b) ', so that para 19 reads:

19 Arrangements to assist children to live abroad

(1) A local authority may only arrange for, or assist in arranging for, any child in their care to live outside England and Wales with the approval of the court.

(2) A local authority may, with the approval of every person who has parental responsibility for the child arrange for, or assist in arranging for, any other child looked after by them to live outside England and Wales.

(3) The court shall not give its approval under sub-paragraph (1) unless it is satisfied that –

    (a)   living outside England and Wales would be in the child's best interests;

    (b)   suitable arrangements have been, or will be, made for his reception and welfare in the country in which he will live;

    (c)   the child has consented to living in that country; and

    (d)   every person who has parental responsibility for the child has consented to his living in that country.

(4) Where the court is satisfied that the child does not have sufficient understanding to give or withhold his consent, it may disregard sub-paragraph (3)(c) and give its approval if the child is to live in the country concerned with a parent, guardian, special guardian or other suitable person.

(5) Where a person whose consent is required by sub-paragraph (3)(d) fails to give his consent, the court may disregard that provision and give its approval if it is satisfied that that person –

    (a)   cannot be found;

    (b)   is incapable of consenting; or

    (c)   is withholding his consent unreasonably.

(6) Section 85 of the Adoption and Children Act 2002 (which imposes restrictions on taking children out of the United Kingdom) shall not apply in the case of any child who is to live outside England and Wales with the approval of the court given under this paragraph.

(7) Where a court decides to give its approval under this paragraph it may order that its decision is not to have effect during the appeal period.

(8) In sub-paragraph (7) 'the appeal period' means –

   (a)   where an appeal is made against the decision, the period between the making of the decision and the determination of the appeal; and

   (b)   otherwise, the period during which an appeal may be made against the decision.

(9) This paragraph does not apply –

   (a)   to a local authority placing a child in secure accommodation in Scotland under section 25, or

   (b)   to a local authority placing a child for adoption with prospective adopters.

Commencement date: 27 April 2017.

Domicile and Matrimonial Proceedings Act 1973

5 Jurisdiction of High Court and county courts

Page 827.

B v B [2017] EWHC 1029 (Fam), [2017] All ER (D) 70 (May)

(Family Division, Macdonald J, 9 May 2017) Divorce – Financial provision. The Family Division, among other determinations, stayed the applicant's application to enforce the provisions of an order, entered into by consent, relating to maintenance. That was because the respondent had, prior to the applicant's application, brought proceedings in Italy seeking to vary the maintenance provisions of that order. The court was satisfied that it was obliged, under the terms of Art 12 of Council Regulation (EC) No 4/2009, to stay the application until such time as the jurisdiction of the Italian court was established.

Digest

In 1992, the parties married. In September 1996, the applicant gave birth to twins. In 2009, the parties separated. In 2011, the parties entered into heads of agreement with respect to the matrimonial assets. In October, the consent order, agreed between the parties embodying the terms of their agreement, was approved (the order). The overall scheme embodied within the order provided for the division of the capital assets and the payment by the respondent to the applicant of continuing maintenance. The order provided, among other things, for the applicant to receive a little over half the assets and global maintenance of £84,000 per annum with provision of a top-up if the respondent's income reached a specified level. The order also provided for the establishment of a school fees fund for the children (for relevant details of the order, see [12] of the judgment). The maintenance provisions of the order also provided for an undertaking by the respondent to assign to the applicant his interest in a Zurich policy or, if that was not possible, to pay to the applicant the value of the policy at a time to be agreed between the parties. In 2015, the applicant made an application to enforce the order. The applicant asserted that arrears of global maintenance began to accrue immediately, with the respondent failing to pay the full amount of the maintenance ordered in 2011 and in each of the subsequent years leading up to the application. The applicant also sought the enforcement of the provision with respect to the Zurich policy. The respondent challenged the application on the grounds that 5 months prior to the applicant's application, he had applied in the Italian court to vary the provisions of the order (for details of the Italian proceedings, see [19] of the judgment). Accordingly, the respondent contended that the proceedings in Italy fell within the terms of Art 12(1) of Council Regulation (EC) No 4/2009 of 18 December 2008 (the Maintenance Regulation).

It fell to be determined whether the matter would be stayed pending the decision in the Italian proceedings and whether the enforcement sought would be granted.

The court ruled:

(1) It was plain that there were proceedings ongoing in both England and in Italy in relation to the maintenance provisions of the order and that those proceedings were between the same parties. In the circumstances of the case, the proceedings in Italy and the proceedings in England involved the same cause of action for the purposes of Art 12(1) of the Maintenance Regulation. Both sets of proceedings concerned, at their heart, the applicant's right to maintenance payments under the terms of the order, and the respondent's obligation to pay maintenance under the terms of the order. Both cases would involve consideration of the extent to which those rights and obligations ought to subsist having regard to an alleged change of circumstances. There was a coincidence between the basic facts and the basic claimed rights and obligations in the Italian proceedings and the English proceedings when due allowance was made for the specific form that the proceedings had taken in each of those national jurisdictions. The two sets of proceedings were a mirror image of each other. That conclusion with respect to cause of action could be tested, and demonstrated to be sound, by reference to the cardinal aim of Art 12 of the Maintenance Regulation, namely to avoid irreconcilable decisions between the jurisdictions of different Member States. Having regard to the strong presumption that, absent a clear case of irregularity, the court of first issue was the court first seised, prima facie, the Italian court was the court first seised for the purposes of Art 12(1). It would be entirely wrong for the court to stray into considering the question of whether the Italian court had jurisdiction or not. That was a matter solely for the Italian court (see [70]–[75], [77] of the judgment).

The applicant's application to enforce the provisions of the order relating to maintenance would be stayed until such time as the jurisdiction of the Italian court was established (see [78], [84] of the judgment).

Wermuth v Wermuth [2003] All ER (D) 18 (Feb) applied.

(2) The respondent had accepted that he remained liable to the applicant under the terms of the order that had dealt with the Zurich policy. The assignment to the applicant of the policy being apparently 'impossible' for the purposes of the order, the respondent was now required by the terms of his undertaking to pay to the applicant such sum as was held within the Zurich policy on a date to be agreed between the parties. Such a date not yet having been agreed between the parties, in the circumstances, the appropriate order was an order adjourning the applicant's application to enforce the term concerning the Zurich policy to allow the parties a period of time to agree, pursuant to the terms of the order, the date by which the respondent would pay to the applicant such sum as was held within the Zurich policy and for payment to be made by that agreed date. In the event that the respondent refused to agree a date or failed by the date agreed to make payment to the applicant such sum as was held within the Zurich policy and was thereby in default, then the applicant's application to enforce could be reinstated (see [83] of the judgment).

The applicant's application to enforce the provisions of the order relating to the Zurich policy would be adjourned generally, with liberty to restore (see [84] of the judgment).

The applicant appeared in person with the support of a McKenzie friend.

Brent Molyneux QC for the respondent.

Human Fertilisation and Embryology Act 2008

PART II
PARENTHOOD IN CASES INVOLVING ASSISTED REPRODUCTION

Meaning of 'father'

37 The agreed fatherhood conditions

Page 979.

ARB v IVF Hammersmith Ltd [2017] EWHC 2438 (QB), [2017] All ER (D) 30 (Oct)
(Queen's Bench Division, Jay J, 6 October 2017) Contract – Damages for breach. The claimant had not signed the consent form for thawing of embryos; his signature had been forged by his former partner, who had subsequently had their daughter. The Queen's Bench Division held that, although the defendant clinic had owed the claimant an express obligation not to thaw and replace an embryo if he had not given his written consent, legal policy concerning the unavailability of damages for the upkeep of a healthy child thwarted his claim.

Background

In 2008, the claimant, A, and the third party, R, had IVF treatment at the defendant's clinic. In 2008, a son was born. A number of embryos had been frozen with the parties' consent and they signed agreements on an annual basis for them to remain in storage. In 2010, R handed the clinic a consent to thawing of embryos form, signed by her and purportedly signed by A. On the basis of that document, an embryo was thawed and successfully implanted in R's womb. In 2011, a daughter was born.

A issued proceedings against the clinic in contract for the cost of bringing up the daughter, alleging that the consent form had not been signed by him and had to have been forged by R, as their relationship had broken down. The clinic brought CPR 1998, Pt 20 proceedings against R for an indemnity on the basis of the tort of deceit.

Application dismissed.

Issues and decisions

(1) Whether R had forged A's signature or A had, in fact, consented to the thawing and use of the frozen embryos.

A had not signed the consent form. His signature had been forged by R. A had not, in fact, given his informed consent to the procedure because he had not been given all the necessary information that would have enabled him to provide his consent. He had not been willing to have a child with R at the time and he would not have signed the consent form if R had asked him to do so.

In any event, the issue of what A had consented to was not merely a question of fact. Whatever might be the position under the HFEA 1990, the position at common law was that A's consent to the procedure had been required and he had not provided it (see [209], [210] of the judgment).

Centre for Reproductive Medicine v U [2002] All ER (D) 213 (Apr) applied.

(2) Whether it had been an express term of the parties' contract, in the nature of a warranty or guarantee, that the clinic would secure A's signed written consent to the thawing and use of the frozen embryos or whether there was an implied term to like effect. Further, whether A had failed, in breach of contract, to inform the clinic that he had separated from R.

The clinic had owed an implied obligation to exercise reasonable care in relation to complying with its obligations under HFEA 1990, relevant guidance and its licence conditions at the time the consent had been sought for the thawing and replacement of the embryo. The clinic had owed A an express obligation not to thaw and replace an embryo if he had not given his written consent, and that obligation was strict. Further, on the facts, A's breach did not preclude him from claiming damages for the clinic's breaches (see [262], [272] of the judgment).

Arnold v Britton [2016] 1 All ER 1 applied; *Liverpool City Council v Irwin* [1976] 2 All ER 39 considered; *Thake v Maurice* [1986] 1 All ER 497 considered; *Centre for Reproductive Medicine v U* [2002] All ER (D) 213 (Apr) considered; *R (on the application of Quintavalle) v Human Fertilisation and Embryology Authority (Secretary of State for Health intervening)* [2003] 3 All ER 257 considered; *Evans v Amicus Healthcare Ltd* [2004] 3 All ER 1025 considered.

(3) Whether public policy precluded A's primary or alternative claims for the upkeep of a healthy child.

Rees v Darlington Memorial Hospital NHS Trust ([2003] 4 All ER 987), concerning the unavailability of damages for the upkeep of a healthy child, was not binding authority in the clinic's favour because its ratio was limited to tortious claims. However, the public policy bar would apply to the contractual claim if there were relevant equivalence or congruence with a hypothetical claim in tort brought on the same facts.

The measure of damages was the same, the test for remoteness did not turn on any distinction pertaining to the nature of the underlying obligation and, most particularly, there was no material difference for the purposes of the legal policy between contractual duties of the two types of claim.

Accordingly, the legal policy enunciated in *Rees*, for reasons of principle, logic and policy, applied equally to contractual claims founded on strict obligations in circumstances where the parties had not sought to quantify or liquidate the damages payable in the event of breach. That thwarted A's claim and the clinic's submission, that legal policy precluded all of A's pleaded claims, would be upheld (see [304], [305], [317], [318], [323] of the judgment).

Parsons (H) (Livestock) Ltd v Uttley Ingham & Co Ltd [1978] 1 All ER 525 applied; *Rees v Darlington Memorial Hospital NHS Trust* [2003] 4 All ER 987 applied; *McFarlane v Tayside Health Board* [1999] 4 All ER 961 considered.

Michael Mylonas QC, Susanna Rickard and Jamie Mathieson (instructed by Hughes Paddison Ltd) for A.

Jeremy Hyam QC and Suzanne Lambert (instructed by Hempsons) for the clinic.

Mark McDonald and Christopher Pask (instructed by Axiom Stone Ltd) for R.

Matrimonial and Family Proceedings Act 1984

PART III
FINANCIAL RELIEF IN ENGLAND AND WALES AFTER OVERSEAS DIVORCE ETC

Applications for financial relief

16 Duty of the court to consider whether England and Wales is appropriate venue for application

Page 1127.

Zimina v Zimin [2017] EWCA Civ 1429, [2017] All ER (D) 57 (Oct)

(Court of Appeal, Civil Division, Patten, Floyd and King LJJ, 5 October 2017) Divorce – Financial provision. The husband's application to set aside an order made by the English courts under the Matrimonial and Family Proceedings Act 1984 was allowed, where another order had been made earlier by the Russian court. Following an evaluation of all the relevant factors, the proper conclusion ought to have been that it had not been appropriate for the English court to make the order.

Background

The appellant husband and respondent wife were Russian nationals who moved to England in 2004. In 2008, the marriage having broken down, the husband issued divorce proceedings in Russia. In August 2009, the Russian court made an order. In 2014, the wife made an application under MFPA 1984, Pt III: Financial Relief in England and Wales after Overseas Divorce etc. In July 2016, the judge made an order regarding the wife's application, ordering that the husband should pay her a lump sum of £1,148,480, together with provision for the children of the marriage. The husband appealed. The central issue was whether it had been appropriate for the judge to have made any order at all in the circumstances of the case.

Appeal allowed.

Issues and decisions

(1) What financial provision should be included in the term 'financial benefit' under s 16(2)(d) of MPFA 1984, which required the court to take into account any 'financial benefit received by the applicant or a child of the family'.

Financial benefit meant precisely that, and covered all forms of financial benefit received by the claimant spouse in whatever form. Not only was the wording of the statute clear, but, given the many differing forms of provision made in jurisdictions all over the world, it would be impossible to get a true and fair picture of the provision made for a wife if it was to be limited in such a way. The present case was one such example (see [50], [51] of the judgment).

Radmacher (formerly Granatino) v Granatino (pre-nuptial contract) [2011] 1 All ER 373 considered.

(2) Whether and how the adequacy of the provision should be assessed, either at the date of the order and/or at the date of the trial. Further, in that context, what impact, if any, would the husband's improved financial provision have upon the outcome of the case.

The court would necessarily consider the adequacy of the provision as of the date upon which the Russian order had been made. The judge had been satisfied that it was adequate. Ordinarily, an application made under MPFA 1984, Pt III would be sufficiently proximate to the making of the foreign divorce in question so that an assessment of the adequacy of the provision at the date at which it had been made, followed by a similar assessment conducted by reference to the trial date, would lead to the same outcome. There would, however, be rare cases where there was a significant delay between the divorce and the Pt III proceedings. In those circumstances, the wording of MPFA 1984, s 18 unequivocally required the court to take into account all the circumstances as they were, which necessarily included those at the date of trial (see [61]–[63] of the judgment).

In the present case, it might be thought that features of particular importance were not so much the husband's present financial circumstances as: (i) the form the financial benefit took and the circumstances leading up to it, in particular whether the provision was made pursuant to a binding agreement between the parties; (ii) any relevant change of circumstances of the wife since the making of the order; and (iii) any delay and the reasons for it (see [65] of the judgment).

Radmacher (formerly Granatino) v Granatino (pre-nuptial contract) [2011] 1 All ER 373 applied; *Edgar v Edgar* [1980] 3 All ER 887 considered.

(3) What impact the delay, which had been in part tactical, on the wife's part in issuing the proceedings ought to have had on the outcome of the case.

The court could, in its discretion, conclude that it was inappropriate to make an order where there had been a substantial delay, notwithstanding that, on an objective assessment, the applicant had unmet needs. Where, however, at the date of trial, an outstanding need had been demonstrated to have been generated for the wife by virtue of her relationship with her former husband, then the court could, if it concluded it to be appropriate, make an order in favour of the wife having taken into account all the circumstances including the length of time since the divorce and the reasons for delay in making the application (see [95] of the judgment).

In the circumstances, it would have been within the discretion of the judge to have found that it was inappropriate to make a further order and to have dismissed the application. However, in the circumstances, the judge had been entitled to allow the matter to proceed (see [96] of the judgment).

Following an evaluation of all the relevant factors, the proper conclusion ought to have been that it had not been appropriate to make an order under MPFA 1984, Pt III. Bearing the relevant matters in mind, the appeal would be allowed and the order for a lump sum payment by the husband to the wife would be set aside (see [114] of the judgment).

PART II

Radmacher (formerly Granatino) v Granatino (pre-nuptial contract) [2011] 1 All ER 373 applied; *Wyatt v Vince* [2015] 2 All ER 755 applied.

Lewis Marks QC and Catherine Cowton (instructed by Stewarts Law LLP) for the husband.
Richard Todd QC and Nicholas Yates (instructed by Vardags) for the wife.

Orders for Financial Provision and Property Adjustment

17 Orders for financial provision and property adjustment

Page 1127.

Zimina v Zimin [2017] EWCA Civ 1429, [2017] All ER (D) 57 (Oct)
See MFPA 1984, s 16, above.

Matrimonial Causes Act 1973

PART II
FINANCIAL RELIEF FOR PARTIES TO MARRIAGE AND CHILDREN OF FAMILY

Ancillary relief in connection with divorce proceedings etc

24 Property adjustment orders in connection with divorce proceedings etc

Page 1171.

Quan v Bray and others [2017] EWCA Civ 405, [2017] All ER (D) 99 (Jun)

(Court of Appeal, Civil Division, King, David Richards and Moylan LJJ, 16 June 2017) Charity – Charitable trust. The Court of Appeal, Civil Division held that although the trial judge gave a short judgment in what was a long trial with voluminous evidence, he had made clear and unequivocal findings in relation to the key aspect of the case. There could be no doubt in anyone's mind as to the basis upon which the judge had reached his conclusion. In such a case where there was a mass of complex factual evidence, the judge had to be regarded as having considerable latitude in deciding which of the legion of issues it was necessary for him to deal with.

Digest

The husband and wife had lived together from 1997, and were married in 2001. They shared an interest in saving the Chinese tigers, a highly endangered species. In 2002, a trust was established called Chinese Tigers South Africa Trust (CTSAT). At the relevant time, the assets of CTSAT were worth tens of millions of pounds. The relationship between the parties broke down and, in July 2012, the wife was removed as director of the fourth respondent charitable organisation (SCT). In August, she petitioned for divorce and in due course made a claim for financial relief. As part of the resolution of the matter, the trial judge ordered a hearing to enquire into the circumstances under which the CTSAT was set up and the nature of its underlying purpose. Consideration was to be given to the availability, to either the husband or the wife, of the funds held by the trust by virtue either of variation of a nuptial settlement, or as a 'resource' (pursuant to, among other things, the line of cases from *Thomas v Thomas* [1995] 2 FLR 668) (*Thomas*) which were available to the parties and capable of being utilised to satisfy the wife's claims within her financial remedy proceedings. The principal issue at the hearing was the true function of the CTSAT. The trial judge held that assets held within CTSAT were not, for the purposes of s 25 of the Matrimonial Causes Act 1973, a resource of either the husband or the wife. In the light of these findings of fact, the judge further declared that CTSAT was not a post-nuptial settlement. The wife appealed. She sought to overturn the judge's findings of fact by way of a reasons challenge directed at the judgment.

The main issue was whether the judge had failed to give adequate reasons for his findings, reflected in the fact that he had purportedly analysed inadequately certain critical topics that should have informed his central findings. Had he done so, it was submitted, he would have found that CTSAT was at least in part for the benefit of the parties from inception and therefore a post-nuptial settlement.

The appeal would be dismissed.

Having regard to the established law that the insight gained by a trial judge who had lived with the case for several days, weeks or even months was far deeper that than of an appeal court, the considerations were: (i) was the basis upon which the trial judge had reached his decision clear, and could the parties understand the basis upon which he had reached his decision; (ii) were any or all of the topics raised critical to the decision of the judge or had they fallen within the judge's margin of appreciation as to what issues were critical and what was peripheral to the determination; (iii) if critical, had the judge specifically made findings in respect of the issue/issues in question, would the outcome have been different (see [165] of the judgment).

The critical issue for determination was about the motives behind and the precise purpose of the CTSAT structure. The starting point was the formal written documents identifying the object and purpose of CTSAT. Given that the wife had sought to go behind the terms of the documents, the judge's assessment of the parties' credibility was the single most critical finding. The judge had made clear and unequivocal findings in relation to that key aspect of the case. There could be no doubt in anyone's mind as to the basis upon which the judge had reached his conclusion. In such a case where there was a mass of complex factual evidence, the judge had to be regarded as having considerable latitude in deciding which of the legion of issues it was necessary for him to deal with in his judgment. Having said that, most judges, probably, would have gone into significantly more detail than had the present judge. While economical judgments were to be applauded, it was hard to resist a submission that the judgment, if not actually short of background and of analysis of the surrounding arguments, was perilously close to it. Nonetheless, having heard the submissions and been taken to the documents, the court was satisfied that the judge's finding in respect of the critical issue in relation to the purpose of CTSAT would have been the same even had he dealt specifically with all the issues raised by wife on appeal. The case turned on the credibility of the parties and the judge had been entitled to reach the conclusions he had done. Nothing would entitle the court to regard it as appropriate to undermine the judge's essential conclusions. It followed from that conclusion that in the light of the findings which had not, as a consequence of the appeal, been successfully challenged or undermined, CTSAT had never constituted and did not constitute a disposition that made any form of continuing provision for either of the parties and it was not a post-nuptial settlement. The judge had made no error of law when concluding that CTSAT's assets were not a *Thomas* resource of the husband's, but were available for the Chinese Tiger Project and only for the Chinese Tiger Project (see [166]–[175] of the judgment).

Piglowska v Piglowski [1999] All ER (D) 668 applied; *DB v Chief Constable of Police Service of Northern Ireland (Northern Ireland)* [2017] All ER (D) 05 (Feb) applied; *B (a child) (care order: proportionality: criterion for review), Re* [2013] All ER (D) 103 (Jun) applied; *Fage UK Ltd v Chobani UK Ltd* [2014] All ER (D) 234 (Jan) applied; *Aerospace Publishing Ltd v Thames Water Utilities Ltd* [2007] All ER (D) 02 (Jan) applied; *DB v Chief Constable of Police Service of Northern Ireland (Northern Ireland)* [2017] All ER (D) 05 (Feb) applied.

Decision of Mr Justice Coldridge [2014] All ER (D) 339 (Oct) affirmed.

Richard Todd QC and Lily Mottahedan (instructed by Vardags Solicitors) for the wife.

The husband appeared in person.

The second respondent did not appear and was not represented.

The third respondent did not appear and was not represented.

The fourth respondent appeared in person.

The fifth respondent did not appear and was not represented.

Stewart Leech QC and Sarah Phipps (instructed by Lee and Thompson LLP) for the sixth respondent.

Ruth Hughes (instructed by The Government Legal Department) for the seventh respondent.

PART II

25 Matters to which court is to have regard in deciding how to exercise its powers under ss 23, 24, 24A, 24B and 24E

Page 1177.

Christoforou v Christoforou [2016] EWHC 2988 (Fam), [2016] All ER (D) 190 (Nov)

(Family Division, Moylan J, 22 November 2016) Divorce – Financial provision. The Family Division made a number of determinations in respect of the wife's financial remedy application in divorce proceedings. In addition to the allocation of companies and properties to the parties, the court held that the circumstances of the case did not warrant a departure from the principle of equal division that both parties had individually contended in favour of themselves.

Digest

In 1980, the parties married. The husband was resident in Cyprus. The wife lived in London. In 2014, the marriage came to an end. The parties had two children from the marriage, the eldest son, A, being 35 and the younger son, N, being 33 at the time of the proceedings. An agreed asset schedule had been prepared for the present proceedings. The gross total was in the region of £50/55m. A substantial part of it was held in a number of special purpose onshore and offshore property-owning companies. Some of the shares in those companies were held in the wife's name. It was the husband's case that the wife had held those shares on trust for him. Apart from a joint bank account, with nearly £8m, which was notionally allocated for tax, and the former matrimonial home, valued at £2.7m, the bulk of the rest of the wealth was represented by properties in North London and Cyprus. It was the husband's case that his parents, in particular his late father, had made very substantial contributions both by giving him properties, and by funding the acquisition and development of properties. Based on those factual assertions, it was the husband's case that three of the London properties and all of the Cypriot properties were not marital assets. There was also a dispute between the husband and the children as to the ownership of three properties (for details of the properties and dispute, see [18] of the judgment). The wife applied for financial remedy.

The financial remedy application would be considered in light of the following considerations: (i) whether either party had failed to give full disclosure of their resources; (ii) whether the husband was the beneficial owner of shares, held in the wife's name, in a number of property-owning companies; (iii) whether any resources should be notionally added back; (iv) whether the husband alone should be responsible for tax penalties; (v) whether there was any property that should not be shared equally between the parties, principally on the basis that it was not marital property; (vi) whether the husband should be provided with funds to meet the costs of litigation involving third parties, including the parties' children; (vii) additional matters, including the issue of tax; and (viii) how certain assets, which both parties sought, should be allocated, such consideration applying to both companies and certain individual properties. Consideration was given to s 25 of the Matrimonial Causes Act 1973 (s 25).

The court ruled:

(1) Upon the evidence, it could not be said that the husband had failed to disclose his interest in two companies, as had been contended by the wife. As for the wife, and the husband's claim that she had failed to disclose property in Lebanon, the husband was unable to give any specific details about this property despite claiming that he had been in Lebanon to effect the purchase. Based upon the wife's evidence, it could satisfactorily concluded that she did not own property in Lebanon (see [39], [48], [51], [54] of the judgment).

(2) The wife was the beneficial owner of the shares in her name. The husband's case as to how any trust had arisen had never been clearly articulated. Indeed, the husband had been unable to advance a consistent or plausible case as to the creation of any trust (see [69] of the judgment).

(3) The history of the proceedings between the parties demonstrated that there had already been a significant element of the reattribution of sums spent by the husband and sought by the wife. Contrary to the wife's contentions, the husband's conduct did not justify any add-back, largely because there was no evidence that supported such a conclusion (see [71], [73], [74] of the judgment).

Vaughan v Vaughan [2007] All ER (D) 43 (Nov) applied.

(4) If a party was going to assert the existence of pre-marital assets, then it was incumbent on that party to prove the same by clear documentary evidence. Documentary evidence was not necessary in every such case because the circumstances might be such that, even in the absence of documentary evidence, the court could, and should, make a finding as to the existence of non-matrimonial property (see [77] of the judgment).

Significant aspects of the husband's case had been so opaque and inconsistent that it had to be dismissed. Accordingly, the husband's contention that the circumstances of the present case justified an other than equal sharing of the wealth, on the basis of non-martial contributions, would be rejected. There were no, or no sufficient, non-marital assets and no, or no sufficient, non-marital contributions which, when weighed within the s 25 exercise, merited in fairness the unequal distribution outcome sought by the husband (see [78], [149] of the judgment).

N v F (Financial Orders: Pre-Acquired Wealth) [2011] All ER (D) 96 (Apr) applied.

(5) Concerning litigation costs and other ownership disputes, on the evidence, it would be inequitable and/or unjustifiable for the wife to bear the costs of such proceedings (see [157], [163], [166]–[168] of the judgment).

(6) The same approach would not be taken in respect of tax liabilities due either from the parties or any of the companies they owned. Although it was accepted that the husband had organised the family's financial affairs, that was not conduct for which he alone ought to bear the financial consequences. That included any tax penalties that might be imposed (see [169], [175] of the judgment).

(7) There would be no proposal to add back or allocate an additional £80,000 to the husband, as requested, to 'compensate' him for costs incurred in respect of the transfer by the wife of a sum of money from a joint bank account. The sum was not sufficiently significant, in the context of the case, to justify separate accounting. Further, the wife's actions in undertaking that transfer had not merited the allocation to the husband of that sum having regard to the circumstances of the case generally (see [176] of the judgment).

(8) The parties having agreed about the allocation of some of the companies and other assets, there would be a determination of the allocation of some of the disputed assets, with the other disputed assets to be addressed in a final order subsequently (see [182], [185], [187], [191] of the judgment).

J Southgate QC and M Bradley (instructed by Withers LLP) for the wife.

C Howard QC and A Tatton-Bennett (instructed by Hughes Fowler Chambers) for the husband.

AAZ v BBZ and others [2016] EWHC 3234 (Fam), [2017] All ER (D) 91 (May)

(Family Division, Haddon-Cave J, 15 December 2016) Ancillary relief – Divorce. The Family Division ruled the husband had failed to prove any valid reasons or 'departure points' that would justify the matrimonial property being divided other than equally, 50:50, and that the wife's ancillary financial relief succeeded in the sum of £453,576,152, comprising 41.5% of the total marital assets. Among other things, it held that the husband had failed to prove, by clear documentary evidence, any case on pre-marital assets, and that so-called trust assets were financial resources, under s 25(2)(a) of the Matrimonial Causes Act 1973, from which the husband could pay the wife's financial award in the proceedings.

Digest

The parties married in 1993. In October 2013, the wife issued a divorce petition against the first respondent, the husband. The second respondent, C Ltd, and the third respondent, P Ltd, were joined to the proceedings. The husband was the sole director of C Ltd, a Cypriot-registered company and the trustee of a Bermudian discretionary trust (the trust). P Ltd was a Panamanian company, which the husband contended was within the trust. In December, A decree nisi was granted. The wife applied for financial orders. In November 2016, the trial of the proceedings commenced. The husband failed to appear at the trial in person in breach of various court orders. He was also in breach of other others, including an order to provide documents and reports in his possession, concerning the historic value of an energy company (the Russian company), and any written offers to buy the business. C Ltd and P Ltd were served with the proceedings and notice of the trial, but played no part in the trial.

First, the court considered its power to make ancillary financial orders in divorce, under ss 23-25 of the Matrimonial Causes Act 1973 (the 1973 Act). In that context, the court considered the principles relevant in respect of computation and distribution. The wife submitted that the marriage had lasted 20 years and had only broken down in October 2013, when she had issued her divorce petition, and that it had finally ended in late 2014. She further submitted that the total net marital wealth in the present case was just over £1bn, and that the entire wealth had been acquired and built up during their long marriage, by the parties' equal contributions to the welfare of the family, which, she contended, should be subject to the sharing principle. The husband submitted that the marriage had broken down in 1999 when he had discovered that the wife was having an affair with a younger man, or in 2004, at the latest. The husband also submitted that he had been wealthy before his marriage to the wife in 1993, and that any sharing claim by the wife should be based on wealth generated up to 2004 at the latest, but not thereafter. The question was whether the vast sum realised from the sale of the husband's Russian company shares in November 2012 (US$1.375m) was to be included in the marital assets. The husband submitted in his statement of issues that he had made a special or stellar contribution to the wealth creation, which would justify a departure from a 50:50 division of the assets in his favour. Secondly, the court considered issues concerning the trust (the trust issues). The husband submitted that his wealth from the sale of his Russian company shares was held in a discretionary Bermudian trust (the trust). He contended that, within the trust structure were Panamanian, Cypriot and Isle of Man companies, which each held assets. The wife submitted that: (i) P Ltd was the husband's nominee and held all its assets for him absolutely; (ii) P Ltd's shares were not 'in' the trust; (iii) the disposition of the companies that owned a yacht, plane, helicopter and real property in March 2015 to the trustee (the March 2015 disposition) should be set aside or reversed, under s 37 of the 1973 Act and/or ss 423 to 425 of the Insolvency Act 1986 (the 1986 Act); and (iv) whatever their corporate organisation, the trust assets were all resources available to the husband whenever he pleased. Consideration was given to the distribution of an English property (£2,479,125), an Aston Martin (£350,000) and a modern art collection (estimated value £90,581,865).

The court ruled:

(1) In deciding how assets should be distributed, the court's overall objective was fairness. The concept of fairness was not to be applied in an overly subjective way, but had to be checked against the yardstick of equality. As a general guide, equality should be departed from only if, and to the extent that, there was good reason for doing so. There was no place for discrimination between husband and wife and their respective roles. If, in their different spheres, each had contributed equally to the family, then, in principle, it mattered not which of them had earned the money and built up the assets. The circumstances in which the court might depart from the principle of equal, 50:50, sharing might include: (i) where assets pre-dated the parties' marriage, namely where there was non-matrimonial property; (ii) the receipt of inherited property, or gifts from sources external to the marriage; (iii) special or 'stellar' contributions during the marriage; (iv) post-separation accrual of assets; and (v) post-separation contribution that was unmatched by the other spouse. The date to which property built up during the marriage was measured was usually the date of separation, although there would be circumstances in which post-separation accrual would be treated as matrimonial property. The fact that the parties did not spend every night under the same roof did not mean that there was not a subsisting marriage. Many married couples spent time apart. Being physically apart for much of the year did not mean that a marriage did not exist. The court did not undertake a prurient assessment of the quality of the marriage in considering financial provision. It was settled law that, if, in their different spheres, each party had contributed equally to the family, then, in principle, it mattered not which of them had earned the money and built up the assets. The threshold for relevant conduct in s 25(2)(g) of the 1973 Act was very high. Adultery was immaterial to the amount of financial provision that was ordered and did not compromise conduct that it would be in equitable to disregard, within the meaning of s 25(2)(g). It was axiomatic that, if a party was going to assert pre-marital assets, it was incumbent on them to prove the same by clear documentary evidence. A computation of a party's resources included, not only assets beneficially owned by the party, but assets that he or she was likely to receive from a third party, for example a trustee, if he or she asked for them. Thus, the legal question was: if a discretionary beneficiary were to request the trustee to advance the whole or part of the capital to him, whether the trustee would be likely to do so currently or in the foreseeable future. The question was not one of control of re-sources, it was one of access to them (see [25]-[28], [37], [48], [55] of the judgment).

In the present case, the husband had failed to prove, by clear documentary evidence, any case on pre-marital assets. On the evidence, notwithstanding a temporary hiatus, the husband and wife's marriage had lasted over 20 years from 1993 to October 2013 when the wife had issued her petition; and the marriage had only finally come to an end, after a failed attempt at reconciliation, in late 2014. Applying settled law, any case made by the husband that he had made a special or 'stellar' contribution to the marital assets, such as to justify a departure from the equality principle, was rejected. The husband had failed to prove any valid reasons or 'departure points' that would justify the matrimonial property being divided other than equally, 50:50. In particular, first, the marriage had endured from 1993 until 2013, as the wife had contended. Second, there was no need to consider the husband's case on post-separation accrual because the wealth had been generated during, and not after, the subsisting marriage. Third, all the (considerable) wealth that had been generated during the marriage was matrimonial property. The value of each of the available assets was as listed in the schedule of assets, namely, totalling £1,092,334,626, subject to the trust issues (see [37], [50], [56], [57], [62] of the judgment).

White v White [2000] All ER (D) 1546 applied; *Charman v Charman* [2005] All ER (D) 298 (Dec) applied; *Miller v Miller; McFarlane v McFarlane* [2006] 3 All ER 1 applied; *Charman v Charman* [2007] All ER (D) 425 (May) applied; *Whaley v Whaley* [2011] All ER (D) 240 (May) applied; *Sorrell v Sorrell* [2005] All ER (D) 104 (Oct) considered; *Charman v Charman* [2005] All ER (D) 298 (Dec) considered; *Prest v Petrodel Resources Ltd* [2013] 4 All ER 673 considered; *Cooper-Hohn v Hohn* [2014] All ER (D) 166 (Dec) considered; *Gray v Work* [2015] All ER (D) 302 (Mar) considered.

(2) On the evidence, if a discretionary beneficiary were to request the trustee of the C Ltd trust to advance the whole or part of the capital to him, the trustee would be likely to do so now or in the foreseeable future and any funds held in the trust could be considered to be financial resources to the husband. Accordingly, the so-called trust assets were financial resources under s 25(2)(a) of the 1973 Act available to the husband, from which he could pay the wife's financial award in the proceedings. Further, applying settled law to the facts, P Ltd was the husband's nominee and P Ltd held all its assets absolutely for the husband on a 'bare' trust. Furthermore, the present case was a paradigm case for the application of s 37 of the 1973 Act. Accordingly, the March 2015 disposition would be set aside and an appropriate declaration would be made. The March 2015 disposition had plainly been at an undervalue. The husband had clearly entered into the transaction for the purpose of, either: (i) putting assets beyond the reach of a person who was making, or might at some time make, a claim against him; and/or (ii) otherwise prejudicing the interests of such a person in relation to the claim that was being made or might be made. The wife had formally asserted a claim under s 423 of the 1986 Act against the husband in respect of the March 2015 disposition. The husband's failure to answer that claim also enabled an adverse inference to be drawn against him in relation to his intention behind the disposition. There was no reason in principle why there should not be an equal, 50:50, division of the total marital assets in the present case, namely, £1,092,334,626 (see [74], [84]-[88], [99], [103], [104], [108] of the judgment).

The wife's ancillary financial relief succeeded in the sum of £453,576,152, comprising 41.5% of the total marital assets. The wife already held assets of £10,165,162 in value. An order would be made for the transfer to her of the contents of the English property (£2,479,125), the Aston Martin (£350,000) and the modern art collection (estimated value £90,581,865). Accordingly, to meet the balance, the husband would be ordered to pay to the wife the sum of £350,000,000 and P Ltd would be jointly and severally liable to pay that sum (see [134], [135] of the judgment).

AC v DC (Financial remedy: effect of s 37 avoidance order) [2012] All ER (D) 380 (Jul) applied; *Prest v Petrodel Resources Ltd* [2013] 4 All ER 673 applied; *Abela v Baadarani* [2013] All ER (D) 249 (Jun) considered.

Nigel Dyer QC, Dakis Hagen and Henry Clayton of Counsel (instructed by Payne Hicks Beach) for the wife.

The respondents were not present and were not represented.

WM v HM [2017] EWFC 25, [2017] All ER (D) 89 (May)

(Family Court, Mostyn J, 9 May 2017) Divorce – Financial provision. The Family Court made an award of over £72m to the wife, following divorce proceedings. The award represented half of the product of the matrimonial partnership after the court rejected the husband's contention that there ought to be an unequal division of the same. While making £145m over the course of a long marriage was a highly creditable achievement, the present case was not one of those rare cases that justified an unequal division of the product of the matrimonial partnership.

Digest

In 1949, the husband was born. In 1968, the wife was born. In July 1978, the husband's business XG, was incorporated and started trading. At first, XG was an equal partnership between the husband and a friend. In 1985, the husband and wife began a relationship. In 1986, they commenced cohabitation. In April 1989, the friend was bought out of XG. In September, the husband and wife married after the birth of their second child. The shares in XG were held 99% to the husband and 1% to the wife. The assets obtained by the husband and wife during their marriage were substantial, being worth, net of latent taxes, £182m (for details of those assets, see [27] of the judgment). In May 2015, after a 29-year partnership, the husband and wife separated. Divorce proceedings subsequently commenced and having regard to ss 25 and 25A of the Matrimonial Causes Act 1973, the issue of division of assets arose.

It fell to be determined what present-day value would be attributed to XG for the date when the husband and wife commenced their relationship. It also fell to be determined whether, as the husband contended, there should be an unequal division of the product of the matrimonial partnership based upon the husband's contribution to the same

The court ruled:

A linear time apportionment would suggest that just over 20% of the present value of XG has been accumulated at the time of the marriage. In numeric terms, that was £44.5m. The linear approach was the evaluation which would be made in the present case. It resonated with fairness. It reflected the true latency of the business at the time that the marital partnership had formed and value was, intrinsically, as much a function of time as it was of work or market forces. Therefore, the matrimonial element of the business would be £176,634,650 and the non-matrimonial element would be £44,490,350. The total marital assets were £145,752,969. While making £145m over the course of a long marriage was a highly creditable achievement, it simply was not one of those rare cases that justified an unequal division of the product of the matrimonial partnership. Therefore, the figure of £145,752,969 should be divided equally, giving the wife a target allocation of £72,876,484 (see [18], [20], [22], [27], [28], [30] of the judgment).

Fage UK Ltd v Chobani UK Ltd [2014] All ER (D) 234 (Jan) considered; *Re F (Children)* [2016] All ER (D) 71 (Jun) considered.

Martin Pointer QC, Rebecca Carew Pole and Kyra Cornwall for the wife.

Lewis Marks QC and Katie Cowton for the husband.

Sharp v Sharp [2017] EWCA Civ 408, [2017] All ER (D) 74 (Jun)

(Court of Appeal, Civil Division, McFarlane, McCombe and David Richards LJJ, 13 June 2017) Divorce – Appeal. The Court of Appeal, Civil Division, in an appeal against a decision to divide matrimonial assets on an equal basis held that the appellant wife was correct to contend that the combination of potentially relevant factors, namely, short marriage, no children, dual income and separate finances, was sufficient to justify a departure from the equal sharing principle in order to achieve overall fairness between the parties.

Digest

In 2007, the husband and wife met. That same year, they commenced cohabitation. In November 2008, they purchased their first home, SD, in joint names, with funds provided exclusively by the wife. In June 2009, they married. In October 2012, the parties purchased a second property, LC, in joint names. Although the parties had both worked prior to, and during their relationship, at the time the parties decided to purchase LC the husband took redundancy. In September 2013, they moved to live in LC. By that time, however, the marriage was already facing difficulties. In December, the wife filed for divorce. While it was not an agreed fact that the couple maintained separate finances, several significant unchallenged aspects of their financial arrangements indicated that there was a marked degree of separation. Further, although the husband was aware that the wife received substantial bonuses during the period of the marriage, he was never privy to the details and, in addition to providing the total purchase price of the two houses, the wife fully funded the parties' various holidays and bought the husband three cars. At the time of ancillary relief proceedings, the total assets held by either party amounted to £6.9m, of which LC represented £1.455m, SD represented £1.067m and £4.171m was credited to the wife's bank accounts. The balance was made up with a range of other smaller elements. The figure for matrimonial assets of £5.45m used by the judge, in his final calculation was arrived at by subtracting £1.1m from £6.9m, being the rounded-up value for SD, which the husband had conceded ought to be kept out of the matrimonial asset pot on the basis that it had been acquired by the wife before the couple were married, and further subtracting £350,000 to reflect the balance of other pre-acquired assets. The judge found, among other things that: (i) there lacked any suggestion that there was a deliberate and agreed intention on the parties' part to maintain strict separation of their finances; (ii) there should not be an inroad into the sharing concept to which the parties in effect subscribed to when they married unless they chose to opt out (or attempt to do so) with a pre-nuptial agreement; (iii) the pattern with regard to the parties' finances had been one of open-ended liberality regularly maintained to meet the wishes and even the whims the wife had afforded them both; and (iv) there had been no sufficient reason that had been identified for departing from equality of division. Therefore, the judge held that the principled outcome would be that of the £6.9m of current assets the husband would receive a sufficient amount to leave him with £3.275m, half of the £6.9m, but after deduction of the top of the agreed £350,000. After deducting from the pool of matrimonial property, the judge held that there should be a total payment of £2.725m to the husband. The wife appealed.

The main issue was whether it was inevitably the case that the matrimonial assets of a divorcing couple should be shared between them on an equal basis where the marriage had been short, there were no children, the couple had both worked and maintained separate finances, and where one of them had been paid very substantial bonuses during their time together. Consideration was given to the principles in, and the decision of, *Miller v Miller; McFarlane v McFarlane* [2006] All ER (D) 343 (May) (*Miller*).

The court ruled:

The present case had been one of the very small number of cases that justified the departure from the equal-sharing principle. Insofar as the decision of the judge in the present case had been at odds with the authoritative guidance of the majority in *Miller* and the actual decision of the full court in that case, he had been in error. The judge's holding that the sharing principle had to apply unless the parties had entered into a pre-nuptial agreement was unsustainable and not supported by any authority. It followed that the judge's finding that the conduct of the parties in relation to separate finances had fallen short of supporting a finding akin to a pre-nuptial agreement had to fall away as no longer being relevant. On the facts, the manner in which the couple had arranged their finances had been more than sufficient to establish that the wife had maintained her capital separately in a manner that was compatible with that described in *Miller*. The division of the assets determined by the judge in the present case had not accorded with the approach dictated by the majority of the House of Lords in *Miller*. Further, as a matter of law, the decision of the House in *Miller* had established that departure from the principle of equal sharing might occur in order to achieve the overarching goal of fairness in a particular case. On the facts of the case, the wife was right to contend that the combination of potentially relevant factors (short marriage, no children, dual incomes and separate finances) was sufficient to justify a departure from the equal-sharing principle in order to achieve overall fairness between the parties. In addition to retaining one half-value of the two properties (£1.3m), the husband ought to receive an additional award to reflect a combination of the following three factors: (i) the standard of living enjoyed during the marriage; (ii) the need for a modest capital fund in order to live in the property that he was to retain; and (iii) some share in the assets held by the wife (see [111]–[114] of the judgment).

The judge's order as to the division of capital would be set aside and replaced with a property adjustment order allocating SD to the husband and LC to the wife, with an additional lump sum payment of £900,000 to the husband, with all other aspects of the judge's order to remain unchanged (see [116] of the judgment).

Miller v Miller; McFarlane v McFarlane [2006] All ER (D) 343 (May) applied.

Decision of Sir Peter Singer [2015] All ER (D) 74 (Nov) reversed in part.

Frank Feehan QC and Deepak Nagpal for the wife.

Jonathan Southgate QC and Joseph Switalski for the husband.

Hart v Hart [2017] EWCA Civ 1306, [2017] All ER (D) 14 (Sep)

(Court of Appeal, Civil Division, Lloyd Jones, Beatson and Moylan LJJ, 31 August 2017) Divorce – Financial provision. Having set out the proper approach to non-matrimonial property when determining a financial remedy claim by application of the sharing principle, the Court of Appeal, Civil Division, dismissed the wife's appeal. The judge had not been required to award the wife a half-share because he had been unable to carry out a formulaic approach, in part, because he had been unable to ascertain the true value of the husband's pre-marital wealth, and he had not erred by having awarded her his needs calculation, when all his other calculations had been for higher amounts.

Background

In financial remedy proceedings, the judge undertook what he described as a multi-faceted approach, but awarded the appellant wife approximately £3.5m out of total resources of just under £9.4m, which was equal to the amount he had calculated as being required to meet her needs. The wife appealed.

Appeal dismissed

Issues and decisions

(1) The proper approach to non-matrimonial and matrimonial property when applying the sharing principle.

The court was not required to adopt a formulaic approach either when determining whether the parties' wealth comprised both matrimonial and non-matrimonial property or when it was deciding what award to make. That was not necessary in order to achieve an acceptable degree of consistency or a fair outcome. The principle that was being applied was that the sharing principle applied with force to matrimonial property and with limited or no force to non-matrimonial property.

The proper approach to the application of the principle in practice when the existence of non-matrimonial property was being asserted was, first, a case management decision would need to be made as to whether and, if so what, proportionate factual investigation was required. If the facts clearly demonstrated the existence of a sharp dividing line, the court would use that line for the purposes of determining what award to make. If the inquiry would require an account to be undertaken of the marriage, some other expensive investigation and/or would be of doubtful utility, the court could be expected to decide that such an enquiry was neither proportionate nor required to enable it to achieve a fair outcome. If some further enquiry was warranted, the court would have to determine what degree of particularity or generality was required.

Secondly, the court would need to make such factual decisions as the evidence enabled it to make. There was no reason to limit the form or scope of the evidence by which the existence of such property could be established. The normal evidential rules applied, including the court's ability to draw inferences if they were warranted. The court might decide that the non-marital contribution was not sufficiently material or bore insufficient weight to justify a finding that any property was non-matrimonial. Alternatively, if the evidence established a clear dividing line between matrimonial and non-matrimonial property, the court would apply that differentiation at the next discretionary stage. However, if there was a complicated continuum, it would be neither proportionate nor feasible to seek to determine a clear line. In those circumstances, the court would undertake a broad evidential assessment and leave the specific determination of how the parties' wealth should be divided to the next stage.

The third and final stage of the process was when the court undertook the discretionary exercise under Matrimonial Causes Act 1973, s 25. Even if the court had made a factual determination as to the extent of the parties' wealth which was matrimonial property and that which was not, the court still had to fit that determination into the exercise of the discretion having regard to all the relevant factors in the case. That was not to suggest that, by application of the sharing principle, the court would share the non-matrimonial property, but the court had an obligation to determine that its proposed award was a fair outcome having regard to all the relevant s 25 factors.

If the court had not been able to make a specific factual demarcation, but had come to the conclusion that the parties' wealth included an element of non-matrimonial property, it would also have to fit that determination into the s 25 discretionary exercise. It would have to decide what award of such lesser percentage than 50% made fair allowance for the parties' wealth in part comprising or reflecting the product of non-marital endeavour. In arriving at that determination, the court did not have to apply any particular mathematical or other specific methodology. It had a discretion as to how to arrive at a fair division and could simply apply a broad assessment of the division that would affect overall fairness.

Further, deficiencies in the evidence and/or litigation conduct did not mandate a particular outcome. Even where a respondent had failed to engage at all with the process, a court would still have to make findings, however broad or abbreviated, as to the scale of the resources. That was because, inevitably, the judge would have to determine that the proposed award was one that the respondent could meet and that was fair (see [84], [88]–[96], [101], [102], [113], [114] of the judgment).

N v F (Financial Orders: Pre-Acquired Wealth) [2011] 2 FLR 533 doubted; *Miller v Miller; McFarlane v McFarlane* [2006] 3 All ER 1 applied; *Jones v Jones* [2011] 1 FLR 1723 applied; *Wyatt v Vince* [2015] 2 All ER 755 applied.

(2) Whether the judge's determination that the respondent husband's pre-marital wealth had justified unequal division had been impermissible because, although the husband had been wealthy at the start of the relationship, his litigation misconduct had made it impossible to make necessary findings either as to the true value of his pre-marital wealth or as to what had become of it during the marriage. Accordingly, the judge had been unable to carry out the formulaic approach in *Jones v Jones* ([2011] All ER (D) 231 (Jan)) and he should have awarded the wife a half-share.

On the application of the proper approach, the judge had not been required to seek to follow the formulaic approach used in *Jones*. It also followed that the wife's submission, that the court had to undertake a detailed evidential enquiry whenever the issue of non-matrimonial property was raised, would not be accepted. The extent of the enquiry and the manner in which that factor was taken into account when the court was exercising its discretion could have varying degrees of specificity or generality.

Accordingly, the wife's first ground of appeal would not be accepted. Deficiencies in the evidence and/or litigation conduct did not mandate a particular outcome. The judge had still had to make findings on such evidence as there was, including by having drawn such fair or adverse inferences as might be appropriate, notwithstanding his findings as to the deficiencies in the husband's evidence (see [99], [101], [102], [113], [114] of the judgment).

Jones v Jones [2011] 1 FLR 1723 applied.

(3) Whether, even if a departure from equality in the husband's favour could be justified, notwithstanding the evidential shortcomings he had caused, the decision to base the award on the wife's needs had been arbitrary and had denied her the greater award she would have received had the judge been properly able to quantify the extent of the non-matrimonial and matrimonial property.

The wife's submissions had considerably more force when she questioned why the judge had awarded her his needs calculation when all his other calculations had been for higher amounts. However, the judge had not fallen into error when having awarded the wife £3.5m. The judgment had sufficiently demonstrated that, by not having awarded the wife the amount reached by his other calculations, his decision had not been flawed.

The main reason for that conclusion was that the judge had independently conducted an overview of the case to ensure that his proposed award had been fair. He had expressly performed the alternative approach endorsed in *Jones* and that he had had to perform at some stage of the process he had been seeking to undertake so as to test his other tentative conclusions or as a cross-check (see [106], [107], [110], [113], [114] of the judgment).

Jones v Jones [2011] 1 FLR 1723 applied.

Peter Mitchell (instructed by Irwin Mitchell LLP) for the wife.

Grant Armstrong (instructed by the Law Practice (UK) Ltd) for the husband.

Alireza v Radwan and others [2017] EWCA Civ 1545, [2017] All ER (D) 74 (Oct)

(Court of Appeal, Civil Division, Gloster, Lewison and King LJJ, 12 October 2017) Divorce – Appeal. Although a prospective inheritance that had the certainty brought to it by the laws of forced heirship was capable of being a 'financial resource' when considering matters under MCA 1973, s 25(2)(a), the judge had been in error giving the wife a time-limited occupational interest in two flats, on that basis. The Court of Appeal, Civil Division, held that the judge had lost sight of her own finding that there were very substantial liquid funds available within the family arrangement (to which the husband had an absolute right) together with his substantial earning capacity and £1.6m in funds outside the family arrangement.

Background

The husband and wife, the parties in the case, married and subsequently divorced. The wife applied for financial remedies. The judge ordered, uncontroversially, payment by the husband to the wife of a lump sum of £2m by way of capitalised maintenance, payments of child maintenance and the children's ongoing educational costs, together with a sum for a replacement motor vehicle. In addition, the judge ordered that ongoing provision for housing for the wife (and children during their minority) would be made by giving her a time-limited occupational interest in two flats in South Kensington (the larger of which was the parties' matrimonial home and principal residence, the smaller of which was used for the housing of domestic staff and guests). The wife's right to occupy the staff flat was to come to an end in 3 years' time and in respect of the principal residence upon either the wife's remarriage or the death of her father (due to her future inheritance from her father), whichever be the sooner. The wife appealed.

Appeal allowed.

Issues and decisions

(1) Whether the judge had been right in law to regard the wife's future inheritance from her father as a resource that she was likely to have in the foreseeable future under MCA 1973, s 25(2)(a).

In the ordinary course of events, uncertainties both as to the fact of inheritance and as to the times at which it would occur would make it impossible to hold that an inheritance prospect was property that was 'likely to be had in the foreseeable future' (see [39] of the judgment).

The present case was different as the wife's inheritance prospects occurred under Sharia law and did not have the uncertainly found where a will was made in a country such as the UK, where there was no concept such as forced heirship. A prospective inheritance that had the certainty brought to it by the laws of forced heirship was capable of being a 'financial resource' that the wife 'had or was likely to have in the foreseeable future'. In those circumstances, a court would be entitled to conclude, as the judge had done, that a portion of the father's estate would indeed come to the wife in 16-plus years. All that such a finding did was to conclude that the prospective inheritance was a resource under s 25(2)(a) of the Act; it did not mean that it was inevitably appropriate for the court to make an order whereby the meeting of the needs of the wife was in any way dependant on the prospective inheritance. The fact that the wife's father had a life expectancy of 16-plus years would be a factor for the court to take into account on the facts of the case. The judge had decided that that gap could reasonably be filled by the wife having an occupational interest in respect of the relevant property until such time as she remarried or her father died (see [40]–[43] of the judgment).

Michael v Michael [1986] 2 FLR 389 applied.

(2) Whether the wife's father's wealth was a resource that could and should be made available to the wife.

Prior to making any order, the judge had to consider all the factors in s 25 of the Act in addition, before making an order tying the parties together for many years to come by way of a *Mesher* order (especially where, as here, the money was available to allow for a clean break between the parties). Careful and specific consideration had to be given both to the issues of potential conflict between the parties and also to the wife's past and future contribution to the welfare of the family (see [50] of the judgment).

The findings of the judge had not automatically led to a finding that such support should, once the trial came on and a court considered how the wife's future needs were to be met, morph into a resource upon which the husband could rely. It followed that had the judge answered the question whether the wife's father would have been likely to advance capital immediately or in the foreseeable future – the answer would have been 'no' (see [59]–[62] of the judgment).

Thomas v Thomas [1996] 2 FCR 544 applied; *Charman v Charman* [2007] All ER (D) 425 (May) applied; *Mesher v Mesher and Hall* [1980] 1 All ER 126n considered.

(3) Whether the judge had been wrong in making an order based on a future inheritance granting the wife an occupational interest in the former matrimonial home rather than ordering the husband to pay a lump sum to the wife sufficient to enable her to buy a property of her own.

The judge had been in error in reaching the conclusion that she had. She had allowed herself to focus too greatly on her desire to respect the integrity of the family arrangement and lost sight of her own finding that there were very substantial liquid funds available within the family arrangement (to which the husband had an absolute right) together with his substantial earning capacity and £1.6m in funds outside the family arrangement (see [70], [71] of the judgment).

The judge had omitted, thereafter, to pull all the factors together in such a way as to give her a complete overview of the case with the result that an order was made which had left the wife with no capital of her own for many years to come and had denied the wife any recognition in the form of a capital settlement to reflect her contribution to the marriage. The wife's prospective inheritance was undoubtedly a resource, but according to the actuarial tables, not for 16-plus years. When not only the family arrangement and the wife's inheritance expectations, and other matters were put into the equation, it could not be said that the needs of the wife and the children would be met by them continuing to live in a three bedroom flat, owned by the husband's family, and subject to draconian terms in the event that she wished to move, especially if one took into account the lack of personal security for the wife in the event that she remarried and the absence of recognition of her contribution to the welfare of the family. The appeal would be allowed and the matter remitted for reconsideration of the appropriate lump sum to be paid to the wife in addition to the agreed sum of £2m not challenged by the husband (see [73], [74], [99], [100], [101], [102], [106], [107] of the judgment).

Robert Peel QC and Amber Sheridan (instructed by Payne Hicks Beach) for the appellant.

Richard Todd QC and Max Lewis (instructed by Grosvenor Law) for the first respondent.

The second to fourth respondents were not represented and did not appear.

Variation, discharge and enforcement of certain orders etc

31 Variation, discharge etc of certain orders for financial relief

Page 1198.

Birch v Birch [2017] UKSC 53, [2017] All ER (D) 165 (Jul)

(Supreme Court, Lady Hale DP, Lord Kerr, Lord Wilson, Lord Carnwath and Lord Hughes SCJJ, 26 July 2017) Divorce – Financial provision. There was jurisdiction to hear appellant wife's application to 'vary' her undertaking so as to postpone her obligation to secure the respondent's husband's release from his covenants under a mortgage by reference to the case-law and given its equivalence with an order for sale under s 24A of the Matrimonial Causes Act 1973, variable under s 31(2)(f). Accordingly, the Supreme Court allowed her appeal and remitted the matter to the Family Court to determine whether the jurisdiction should be exercised.

Background

The parties entered into a consent order by which they compromised their claims against each other for financial orders on the basis of a clean break between them. Part of the order provided, by way of property adjustment, that the respondent husband should transfer to the appellant wife his legal and beneficial interests in the matrimonial home subject to a mortgage. The wife undertook that, if the husband had not been released from his mortgage covenants by 30 September 2012, she would secure his release by placing the home on the market for sale and proceeding to sell it.

The wife subsequently applied to 'vary' her undertaking so as to postpone her obligation to secure the husband's release from his mortgage covenants. The judge and Family Court concluded that they had no jurisdiction to hear the wife's application. The Court of Appeal, Civil Division, held that there had been jurisdiction to hear the wife's application, but that it had only been a formal jurisdiction that existed only technically; that scope for its exercise was extremely limited and that there was no basis for its exercise upon the wife's application. Further, it held that the undertaking could not have been framed as an order for the sale of property under s 24A of the Matrimonial Causes Act 1973. Accordingly, it dismissed the appeal and the wife appealed.

Appeal allowed (Lord Hughes dissenting)

Issues and decisions

Whether there had been jurisdiction to hear the wife's application.

An undertaking was a solemn promise that a litigant volunteered to the court. A court had no power to impose any variation of the terms of a voluntary promise. A litigant who wished to cease to be bound by his undertaking should apply for release from, or discharge of, it and often he would accompany his application for release with an offer of a further undertaking in different terms. The court's power was only to grant or refuse the application for release and, although exercise of its power might result in something that looked like a variation of an undertaking, it was the product of a different process of reasoning.

Further, in circumstances in which an undertaking could have been framed as an order, it would be illogical for answers to questions about the existence and exercise of the jurisdiction to grant release from it to be different from answers to questions about the existence and exercise of the jurisdiction to vary any such an order. Parliament had not, in s 31(7) of the Act concerning variation of orders for financial relief or elsewhere, made a change of circumstances a condition for exercise of the jurisdiction to vary an order under s 24A. Nevertheless, unless there had been a significant change of circumstances since the order had been made, grounds for variation of it under s 31 were hard to conceive.

It had been bold for the Court of Appeal in *Omielan v Omielan* ([1996] 2 FLR 306) to hold that, when Parliament had provided an ostensibly unrestricted jurisdiction to vary an order for sale, the jurisdiction was nevertheless restricted and equally bold for it to hold that the jurisdiction was restricted by reference to territories, namely, that it was restricted to the territory of the order for sale, as opposed to the territory of the property adjustment order.

The Court of Appeal in *Omielan* had erred in having determined that appeal by reference to the non-existence of the jurisdiction to vary the order for sale, rather than a refusal to exercise it. Where Parliament had conferred jurisdiction on a court, there was no scope for a court to say that part of it did not exist. Nor could the existence of jurisdiction sensibly be left to a demarcation of territories. The concept of different territories was hard to apply to the terms of a financial order, which were usually interlinked and which, in the case of an order for sale under s 24A could be made only as an accompaniment to an order for property adjustment or lump sum payment. At all events, demarcation of territories within the order was no proper criterion for identifying the existence of a jurisdiction (see [5], [15], [18], [25], [27] of the judgment).

All three lower courts had adopted, without demur, the wife's application of her application as having been to vary her undertaking. However, her description betrayed a conceptual confusion.

Further, the proceedings had been bedevilled by a failure to distinguish between the existence of the court's jurisdiction to release the wife from her undertaking (conditionally, upon her offering a further one in different terms) and the exercise of its jurisdiction. The preliminary issue had related only to its existence with the result that factors relevant to its exercise had not been the subject of investigation or argument. Influenced by *Omielan*, the lower courts had looked over their shoulders at the ostensibly ambitious nature of the wife's application (being one of the factors relevant to the exercise of the jurisdiction) and they had deployed it as a basis for denying the existence of the jurisdiction or, in the Court of Appeal, as a basis for concluding that the jurisdiction had been no more than formal and technical (which was tantamount to a conclusion that, for practical purposes, the jurisdiction did not exist).

By reference only to the case-law, it could confidently be concluded that there had been a full jurisdiction to hear the wife's application for release, albeit that its exercise in her favour would be likely to attract lively debate. However, there was a completely different line of reasoning that neatly led to the same conclusion, although it had led the courts below to the opposite conclusion.

The equivalence of the wife's undertaking with an order for sale under s 24A, variable under s 31(2)(f), clearly confirmed the exercise of the court's jurisdiction to hear the application for release from it. The part of the Court of Appeal's reasoning in which it had held that the undertaking could not have been framed as an order for sale could not be defended.

Accordingly, the wife's appeal would be allowed, as jurisdiction existed to hear the wife's appeal and the matter would be remitted to the Family Court for inquiry into whether the jurisdiction should be exercised. In the light of the equivalence of the wife's undertaking with an order for sale, its inquiry would be conducted in accordance with s 31(7). It would give first consideration to the welfare of the children while minors, but it was a consideration that might be outweighed by other factors. It would have regard to all relevant circumstances, including in particular whether the wife could establish a significant change of circumstances since her undertaking had been given and whether, and if so to what extent, the husband had suffered, and was likely to continue to suffer, prejudice by remaining liable under his mortgage covenants (see [5], [6], [12], [13], [17], [29] of the judgment).

Omielan v Omielan [1996] 2 FLR 306 overruled; *Russell v Russell* [1956] 1 All ER 466 applied; *Kensington Housing Trust v Oliver* [1997] Lexis Citation 3304 applied; *Mid Suffolk District Council v Clarke* [2006] All ER (D) 190 (Feb) applied; *L v L* [2008] 1 FLR 26 applied.

Decision of Court of Appeal, Civil Division [2015] All ER (D) 34 (Aug) reversed.

Stephen Hockman QC and Jane Campbell (instructed by Alison Fielden & Co, Cirencester) for the wife.

John Wilson QC, Paul Infield and Julia Shillingford (instructed through by Goodman Ray Solicitors LLP) for the husband.

PART II

Consent

33A   Consent orders for financial provision or property adjustment

Page 1205.

CH v WH [2017] EWHC 2379 (Fam), [2017] All ER (D) 25 (Oct)

(Family Court, Mostyn J, 28 September 2017) Practice – Civil litigation. Judges in the Family Court had made a basic mistake by assuming their powers were confined to the Matrimonial Causes Act 1973. The Family Court, in approving a consent order concluding the financial remedy proceedings between the parties, confirmed that the Family Court had the powers to approve the consent order in question, as it had all the powers of the High Court.

Background

In February 2017, the husband and wife submitted to the Family Court a draft final consent order concluding the financial remedy proceedings between them. However, the order had not been made after it was refused for approval twice by a district judge and that refusal confirmed by a different district judge, on the ground that certain of its provisions were outside the power of the court to order, which related to circumstances where each party would have to provide an indemnity to the other (for details of the relevant provisions, see [3]–[5] of the judgment).

The wife referred the matter for the present proceedings.

Issues and decisions

Whether the judges had erred in refusing to approve the court order and, subsequently, upholding that refusal.

It was elementary that the court could not make orders outside of its powers. However, the basic mistake made by the judges had been to assume that their powers had been confined to the four corners of the Matrimonial Causes Act 1973. The Family Court had all the powers of the High Court. The High Court unquestionably had the power, as part of its equitable jurisdiction, to order an indemnity. If awarded, that represented a legal right in favour of the person so indemnified. The court could award an injunction in support of a legal right. To order someone who had been ordered to indemnify the other party in respect of a mortgage to use his best endeavours to keep up the payments on that mortgage was of the nature of an injunction in support of a legal right. That provision was squarely within the power of the High Court to order and was, therefore, within the power of the Family Court (see [8], [9] of the judgment).

The consent order would be approved (see [2] of the judgment).

Livesey (formerly Jenkins) v Jenkins [1985] 1 All ER 106 applied.

Preventing and Combating Violence Against Women and Domestic Violence (Ratification of Convention) Act 2017

Commencement—The Preventing and Combating Violence Against Women and Domestic Violence (Ratification of Convention) Act 2017 (set out below) came into force on 27 June 2017.

1 The timetable for ratification of the Istanbul Convention

(1) The Secretary of State shall lay a report before each House of Parliament setting out –

    (a)   the steps required to be taken to enable the United Kingdom to ratify the Istanbul Convention; and

    (b)   the timescale within which the Secretary of State would expect the United Kingdom to be able to ratify the Convention.

(2) The report at subsection (1) must be laid as soon as reasonably practicable after this Act comes into force.

(3) When the Secretary of State has determined that the United Kingdom is compliant with the Istanbul Convention, the Secretary of State shall make a statement to each House of Parliament –

    (a)   of the determination, and

    (b)   the date by which the Secretary of State would expect the Convention to be ratified.

2 Reports on progress

(1) The Secretary of State shall each year until ratification lay before each House of Parliament a report on the following –

    (a)   if a report has been laid under section 1(1), any alteration in the timescale specified in that report in accordance with subsection (1)(b) and the reasons for its alteration;

    (b)   the administrative measures taken by Her Majesty's Government to enable the United Kingdom to ratify the Istanbul Convention;

    (c)   the legislative proposals brought forward, including those in the Scottish Parliament, the National Assembly for Wales and the Northern Ireland Assembly, to enable the United Kingdom to ratify the Istanbul Convention;

    (d)   the measures to be taken and legislation required to enable the United Kingdom to ratify the Istanbul Convention.

(2) The first annual report shall be laid no later than 1 November 2017.

(3) Subsequent annual reports shall be laid no later than 1 November each year.

Note—The first annual report (dated 1 November 2017) is available at *www.gov.uk/government/ publications/ratification-of-the-council-of-europe-convention-on-combating-violence-against-women- and-domestic-violence*.

3 Short title, commencement and extent

(1) This Act may be cited as the Preventing and Combating Violence Against Women and Domestic Violence (Ratification of Convention) Act 2017.

(2) The provisions of this Act come into force at the end of the period of 2 months beginning with the day on which this Act is passed.

(3) This Act extends to England and Wales, Scotland and Northern Ireland.

PART III

Procedure Rules

Family Procedure Rules 2010, SI 2010/2955

PART 3A
VULNERABLE PERSONS: PARTICIPATION IN PROCEEDINGS AND GIVING EVIDENCE

By virtue of the Family Procedure (Amendment No 3) Rules 2017, as of 27 November 2017, after Part 3 of the Family Procedure Rules 2010 there is inserted a new Part 3A, as set out below:

3A.1 Interpretation

In this Part –

'child' means a person under the age of 18 years whether or not the child is the subject of the proceedings, except that –

    (a)   in adoption proceedings, it also includes a person who is the subject of proceedings and has attained the age of 18 years before the proceedings are concluded; and

    (b)   in proceedings brought under Article 11 of the Council Regulation, the 1980 Hague Convention or the European Convention, it means a person under the age of 16 years who is the subject of proceedings;

'intermediary' means a person whose function is to –

    (a)   communicate questions put to a witness or party;

    (b)   communicate to any person asking such questions the answers given by the witness or party in reply to them; and

    (c)   explain such questions or answers so far as is necessary to enable them to be understood by the witness or party or by the person asking such questions;

'live link' means a live television link or other arrangement whereby a witness or party, while absent from the courtroom or other place where the proceedings are being held, is able to see and hear a person there and to be seen and heard by the judge, legal representatives acting in the proceedings and other persons appointed to assist a witness or party;

'mental disorder' has the meaning given in section 1 of the Mental Health Act 1983; 'participation direction' means –

    (a)   a general case management direction made for the purpose of assisting a witness or party to give evidence or participate in proceedings; or

    (b)   a direction that a witness or party should have the assistance of one or more of the measures in rule 3A.8; and

references to 'quality of evidence' are to its quality in terms of completeness, coherence and accuracy; and for this purpose 'coherence' refers to a witness's or a party's ability in giving evidence to give answers which address the questions put to the witness or the party and which can be understood both individually and collectively.

3A.2 Application of provisions in this Part

(1) Rule 3A.4 does not apply to a party who is a child.

(2) Rules 3A.3 to 3A.5 do not apply to a party who is a protected party.

3A.3 Court's duty to consider vulnerability of a party or witness

(1) When considering the vulnerability of a party or witness as mentioned in rule 3A.4 or 3A.5, the court must have regard in particular to the matters set out in paragraphs (a) to (j) and (m) of rule 3A.7.

(2) Practice Direction 3AA gives guidance about vulnerability.

3A.4 Court's duty to consider how a party can participate in the proceedings

(1) The court must consider whether a party's participation in the proceedings (other than by way of giving evidence) is likely to be diminished by reason of vulnerability and, if so, whether it is necessary to make one or more participation directions.

(2) Before making such participation directions, the court must consider any views expressed by the party about participating in the proceedings.

3A.5 Court's duty to consider how a party or a witness can give evidence

(1) The court must consider whether the quality of evidence given by a party or witness is likely to be diminished by reason of vulnerability and, if so, whether it is necessary to make one or more participation directions.

(2) Before making such participation directions, the court must consider any views expressed by the party or witness about giving evidence.

3A.6 Protected parties

(1) The court must consider whether it is necessary to make one or more participation directions to assist –

    (a) the protected party participating in proceedings; or
    (b) the protected party giving evidence.

(2) Before making such participation directions, the court must consider any views expressed by the protected party's litigation friend about the protected party's participation in the proceedings or that party giving evidence.

> (Part 15 contains rules about representation of a protected party. Practice Direction 15B contains provisions about the ability of a protected party to give evidence.)

3A.7 What the court must have regard to

When deciding whether to make one or more participation directions the court must have regard in particular to –

    (a) the impact of any actual or perceived intimidation, including any behaviour towards the party or witness on the part of –
        (i)   any other party or other witness to the proceedings or members of the family or associates of that other party or other witness; or
        (ii) any members of the family of the party or witness;
    (b) whether the party or witness –
        (i)   suffers from mental disorder or otherwise has a significant impairment of intelligence or social functioning;
        (ii) has a physical disability or suffers from a physical disorder; or
        (iii) is undergoing medical treatment;
    (c) the nature and extent of the information before the court;
    (d) the issues arising in the proceedings including (but not limited to) any concerns arising in relation to abuse;

(e)   whether a matter is contentious;
(f)   the age, maturity and understanding of the party or witness;
(g)   the social and cultural background and ethnic origins of the party or witness;
(h)   the domestic circumstances and religious beliefs of the party or witness;
(i)   any questions which the court is putting or causing to be put to a witness in accordance with section 31G(6) of the 1984 Act;
(j)   any characteristic of the party or witness which is relevant to the participation direction which may be made;
(k)   whether any measure is available to the court;
(l)   the costs of any available measure; and
(m)   any other matter set out in Practice Direction 3AA.

3A.8 Measures

(1) The measures referred to in this Part are those which –

(a)   prevent a party or witness from seeing another party or witness;
(b)   allow a party or witness to participate in hearings and give evidence by live link;
(c)   provide for a party or witness to use a device to help communicate;
(d)   provide for a party or witness to participate in proceedings with the assistance of an intermediary;
(e)   provide for a party or witness to be questioned in court with the assistance of an intermediary; or
(f)   do anything else which is set out in Practice Direction 3AA.

(2) If the family court makes a direction for a measure which is not available where the court is sitting, it may direct that the court will sit at the nearest or most convenient location where the family court sits and the measure is available.

(3) If the High Court makes a direction for a measure which is not available where the court is sitting, it may direct that the court will sit at the nearest or most convenient location where the High Court sits and the measure is available.

(4) Nothing in these rules gives the court power to direct that public funding must be available to provide a measure.

(5) If a direction for a measure is considered by the court to be necessary but the measure is not available to the court, the court must set out in its order the reasons why the measure is not available.

3A.9 When the duties of the court apply and recording reasons for decisions made under this Part

(1) The court's duties under rules 3A.3 to 3A.6 apply as soon as possible after the start of proceedings and continue until the resolution of the proceedings.

(2) The court must set out its reasons on the court order for –

(a)   making, varying or revoking directions referred to in this Part; or
(b)   deciding not to make, vary or revoke directions referred to in this Part, in proceedings that involve a vulnerable person or protected party.

3A.10 Application for directions under this Part

(1) An application for directions under this Part may be made on the application form initiating the proceedings or during the proceedings by any person filing an application notice.

(2) The application form or application notice must contain the matters set out in Practice Direction 3AA.

(3) Subject to paragraph (2), the Part 18 procedure applies to an application for directions made during the proceedings.

(4) This rule is subject to any direction of the court.

3A.11 Procedure where the court makes directions of its own initiative

Where the court proposes to make a participation direction of its own initiative the procedure set out in rule 4.3(2) to (6) applies.

3A.12 Functions of officers of the Service and Welsh family proceedings officers

Nothing in this Part gives the court power to direct that an officer of the Service or a Welsh family proceedings officer should perform any function beyond the functions conferred upon such officers by any other enactment.

To supplement the new FPR 2010, Pt 3A, there is inserted a new PD3AA, which also comes in to force on 27 November 2017:

Practice Direction 3AA –
Vulnerable Persons: Participation in Proceedings and Giving Evidence

This Practice Direction supplements FPR Part 3A.

Preamble and interpretation

1.1 Part 3A FPR makes provision in relation to vulnerable persons (parties and witnesses), including protected parties, in family proceedings.

– Rule 3A.4 FPR places a duty on the court to consider whether a party's participation in the proceedings is likely to be diminished by reason of vulnerability and, if so whether it is necessary to make one or more participation directions (as defined in rule 3A.1 FPR). Rule 3A.4 FPR does not apply to a child or to a party who is a protected party.

– Rule 3A.5 FPR places a duty on the court to consider whether the quality of evidence given by a party or witness is likely to be diminished by reason of vulnerability and, if so whether it is necessary to make one or more participation directions. Rule 3A.5 FPR does not apply to a party who is a protected party.

– Rule 3A.6 FPR places a duty on the court to consider whether it is necessary to make one or more participation directions to assist a protected party in proceedings, or a protected party giving evidence.

1.2 This Practice Direction sets out the procedure and practice to be followed to achieve a fair hearing by providing for appropriate measures to be put in place to ensure that the participation of parties and the quality of the evidence of the parties and other witnesses is not diminished by reason of their vulnerability.

1.3 It is the duty of the court (under rules 1.1(2); 1.2 & 1.4 and Part 3A FPR) and of all parties to the proceedings (rule 1.3 FPR) to identify any party or witness who is a vulnerable person at the earliest possible stage of any family proceedings.

1.4 All parties and their representatives are required to work with the court and each other to ensure that each party or witness can participate in proceedings without the quality of their evidence being diminished and without being put in fear or distress by reason of their vulnerability as defined with reference to the circumstances of each person and to the nature of the proceedings.

1.5 In applying the provisions of Part 3A FPR and the provisions of this Practice Direction, the court and the parties must also have regard to all other relevant rules and Practice Directions and in particular those referred to in the Annex to this Practice Direction.

Factors to which the court has to have regard when considering the vulnerability of a party or witness mentioned: rule 3A.3(1) FPR

2.1 Rule 3A.3 FPR makes clear that when considering the vulnerability of a party or witness for the purposes of rule 3A.4 FPR (the court's duty to consider how a vulnerable party other than a child can participate in the proceedings) or rule 3A.5 FPR (the court's duty to consider how a vulnerable party or witness can give evidence), the court must have regard in particular to the matters set out in paragraphs (a) to (j) and (m) of rule 3A.7 FPR. Where rule 3A.7(d) refers to questions of abuse, this includes any concerns arising in relation to any of the following –

(a)   domestic abuse, within the meaning given in Practice Direction 12J;
(b)   sexual abuse;
(c)   physical and emotional abuse;
(d)   racial and/or cultural abuse or discrimination;
(e)   forced marriage or so called 'honour based violence';
(f)   female genital or other physical mutilation;
(g)   abuse or discrimination based on gender or sexual orientation; and
(h)   human trafficking.

Guidance about vulnerability: rule 3A.3(2) FPR

3.1 Rule 3A.3 FPR requires the court to have regard in particular to the matters set out in paragraphs (a) to (j) and (m) of rule 3A.7 FPR when considering the vulnerability of a party or witness other than a protected party. The court should require the assistance of relevant parties in the case when considering whether these factors or any of them may mean that the participation of any party or witness in the case is likely to be diminished by reason of vulnerability. When addressing this question, the court should consider the ability of the party or witness to-

(a)   understand the proceedings, and their role in them, when in court;
(b)   put their views to the court;
(c)   instruct their representative/s before, during and after the hearing; and
(d)   attend the hearing without significant distress.

Participation directions: participation other than by way of giving evidence

4.1 This section of the Practice Direction applies where a court has concluded that a party's participation in proceedings (other than by way of giving evidence) is likely to be diminished by reason of vulnerability, including cases where a party might be participating in proceedings by way of asking questions of a witness.

4.2 The court will consider whether it is necessary to make one or more participation directions, as required by rule 3A.4. The court may make such directions for the measures specified in rule 3A.8. In addition, the court may use its general case management powers as it considers appropriate to facilitate the party's participation. For example, the court may decide to make directions in relation to matters such as the structure and the timing of the hearing, the formality of language to be used in the court and whether (if facilities allow for it) the parties should be enabled to enter the court building through different routes and use different waiting areas.

Participation directions: the giving of evidence by a vulnerable party, vulnerable witness or protected party

5.1 This section of the Practice Direction applies where a court has concluded that a vulnerable party, vulnerable witness or protected party should give evidence. In reaching its conclusion as to whether a child should give evidence to the court, the court must apply the guidance from relevant caselaw and the guidance of the Family Justice Council in relation to children giving evidence in family proceedings.

Ground rules hearings

5.2 When the court has decided that a vulnerable party, vulnerable witness or protected party should give evidence there shall be a 'ground rules hearing' prior to any hearing at which evidence is to be heard, at which any necessary participation directions will be given –

 (a)   as to the conduct of the advocates and the parties in respect of the evidence of that person, including the need to address the matters referred to in paragraphs 5.3 to 5.7, and

 (b)   to put any necessary support in place for that person.

The ground rules hearing does not need to be a separate hearing to any other hearing in the proceedings.

5.3 If the court decides that a vulnerable party, vulnerable witness or protected party should give evidence to the court, consideration should be given to the form of such evidence, for example whether it should be oral or other physical evidence, such as through sign language or another form of direct physical communication.

5.4 The court must consider the best way in which the person should give evidence, including considering whether the person's oral evidence should be given at a point before the hearing, recorded and, if the court so directs, transcribed, or given at the hearing with, if appropriate, participation directions being made.

5.5 In all cases in which it is proposed that a vulnerable party, vulnerable witness or protected party is to be cross-examined (whether before or during a hearing) the court must consider whether to make participation directions, including prescribing the manner in which the person is to be cross-examined. The court must consider whether to direct that- –

 (a)   any questions that can be asked by one advocate should not be repeated by another without the permission of the court;

 (b)   questions or topics to be put in cross-examination should be agreed prior to the hearing;

 (c)   questions to be put in cross-examination should be put by one legal representative or advocate alone, or, if appropriate, by the judge; and

 (d)   the taking of evidence should be managed in any other way.

5.6 The court must also consider whether a vulnerable party, vulnerable witness or protected party has previously –

(a) given evidence, and been cross-examined, in criminal proceedings and whether that evidence and cross-examination has been pre-recorded (see sections 27 and 28 of the Youth Justice and Criminal Evidence Act 1999); or

(b) given an interview which was recorded but not used in previous criminal or family proceedings.

If so, and if any such recordings are available, the court should consider their being used in the family proceedings.

5.7 All advocates (including those who are litigants in person) are expected to be familiar with and to use the techniques employed by the toolkits and approach of the Advocacy Training Council. The toolkits are available at www.theadvocatesgateway.org/toolkits. Further guidance for advocates is available from the Ministry of Justice at http://www.justice.gov.uk/guidance.htm.

Matters to be included in an application form for directions: rule 3A.10(2) FPR

6.1 An application for directions under Part 3A FPR should contain the following information, as applicable:

(a) why the party or witness would benefit from assistance;

(b) the measure or measures that would be likely to maximise as far as practicable the quality of that evidence;

(c) why the measure or measures sought would be likely to improve the person's ability to participate in the proceedings; and

(d) why the measure or measures sought would be likely to improve the quality of the person's evidence.

ANNEX

As noted at paragraph 1.5, in applying the provisions of Part 3A FPR and the provisions of this Practice Direction, the court and the parties must also have regard to all other relevant rules and Practice Directions and in particular –

- Part 1 FPR (Overriding Objective);
- Part 4 FPR (General Case Management Powers);
- Part 12 FPR and Practice Direction 12J
- Part 15 FPR (Representation of Protected Parties) and Practice Direction 15B (Adults Who May Be Protected Parties and Children Who May Become Protected Parties in Family Proceedings);
- Part 18 FPR (Procedure for Other Applications in Proceedings);
- Part 22 FPR (Evidence);
- Part 24 FPR (Witnesses, depositions generally and taking of evidence in Member States of the European Union);
- Part 25 FPR (Experts) and the Experts Practice Directions;
- Rule 27.6 FPR and Practice Direction 27A (Court Bundles);
- Part 30 FPR (Appeals) and Practice Direction 30A (Appeals).

PART III

PART 4
GENERAL CASE MANAGEMENT POWERS

4.1 The court's general powers of management

Page 1319.

New commentary has been provided to accompany FPR 2010, r 4.1:

> **'take any other step or make any other order for the purpose … of furthering the overriding objective'** (r 4.1(3((o))—For example, that a party should not be permitted to proceed with a variation application or appeal until he has complied with an existing court order (a '*Hadkinson* Order' (*Hadkinson v Hadkinson* [1952] P 285)). Such an order is draconian in its effect because it goes directly to a litigant's right of access to a court and should be regarded as a case management order of last resort where a litigant is in wilful contempt (*Assoun v Assoun (No 1)* [2017] EWCA Civ 21); and see *Mubarak v Mubarik* [2007] 1 FLR 722, FD, as explained in *Re J (Children)* [2016] 2 FLR 1207, CA, and the cases there cited.

There is also new commentary provided at beginning of the note headed '**a power to vary or revoke**' (r 4.1(6)):

> It has been said that the court's power to alter an order, conferred by MFPA 1984, s 31F(6) and given procedural effect by this rule and r 9.9A, must be exercised circumspectly (*EG v CA* [2017] EWFC 52).

4.4 Power to strike out a statement of case

Page 1322.

The commentary to r 4.4 has been updated and extended, so that it reads:

> **'Except in proceedings to which Parts 12 to 14 apply'** (r 4.4(1))—If a statement of case discloses no reasonable grounds for bringing or defending a claim, or is an abuse of process – for example, 'a strategic [divorce] petition which is filed and left to hibernate for years while the parties carry on with their marriage' (per Mostyn J in *Thum v Thum* [2016] EWHC 2634 (Fam)) – the court is likely to deal with it summarily. The power to strike out a case under this rule does not apply to proceedings concerning children; however, in an appropriate case a civil restraint order may be made (*K v K* [2015] EWHC 1064 (Fam)).

> **'Power to strike out a statement of case'** (r 4.4)—PD4A is self-explanatory. Claims that are incoherent and unintelligible are liable to be struck out even if the applicant is a litigant in person, although normally an opportunity to amend should be given – *Spencer v Barclays Bank plc* [2009] EWHC 2832 (Ch).

> In *K v D and others* [1998] 1 FLR 700 (County Court, and therefore helpful but not binding), an order striking out a claim for ancillary relief was 'plainly intended to afford some protection to the respondent' and while the petitioner did not need leave as such to proceed with her application for ancillary relief, she needed an order reinstating it, and the matters relevant to the question whether she should be granted such an order included the lapse of time, the reasons for not pursuing the original application, the strength of the application and the effects on third parties.

> Whereas the CPR also allow the court to give summary judgment, there is no equivalent power in FPR 2010 and this omission is deliberate. An application has 'no reasonable grounds' for the purposes of r 4.4(1)(a) only if it is not legally recognisable, e g because there has already been a final determination of the proceedings or because the applicant has remarried.

> **'that the statement of case is an abuse of the court's process'** (r 4.4(1)(b))—An application is not to be viewed as an 'abuse of process' falling within r 4.4(1)(b) solely on the basis that it appears to have no real prospect of success (*Wyatt v Vince* [2015] 1 FLR 972, SC); but c f the power to dismiss summarily an application under CA 1989 if it is 'if not groundless, lacking enough merit to justify pursuing the matter': *Re Q (Implacable Contact Dispute)* [2016] 2 FLR 287, CA, per Munby P; or is identical to an application that has already been dismissed (*GN v MA (Child Maintenance: Children Act Sch 1)* [2017] 1 FLR 285, FD); or is an improper collateral attack on a subsisting order of the court (*Veluppillai v Chief Land Registrar & ors* [2017] EWHC 1693 (Fam)).

'**likely to obstruct the just disposal of the proceedings**' (r 4.4(1)(b))—Thus where 'virtually incomprehensible' 168-page particulars of claim were served, seeking damages of over £300 m in a case where at most there might have been a claim for a few hundred pounds, the claim was struck out (*Lilley v Financial Times Ltd* [2017] EWHC 1916 (Ch)).

'**must at the same time consider whether it is appropriate to make a civil restraint order**' (r 4.4(5)(b))—Note, however, that by virtue of Sch 2, Table 2 of FC(CDB)R 2014 even a limited civil restraint order may not be made by a District Judge (cf the position in civil proceedings under CPR PD3C, para 2.1) and if the making of such an order does appear appropriate the matter will have to be referred to a Circuit Judge. How this accords with r 1.1(2)(d),(e) is not immediately apparent.

Veluppillai v Chief Land Registrar and others [2017] EWHC 1693 (Fam), [2017] All ER (D) 170 (Apr)

(Family Division, Mostyn J, 11 April 2017) Action – Dismissal. The claimant husband's claims against the defendants, that he had not brought prior divorce proceedings and had not been married to the wife, were legally impossible and wholly abusive, given the decree nisi. Accordingly, the Family Division struck out his claims and made a general civil restraint order against him.

Background

In October 2013, the claimant husband filed for divorce. In October 2015, in financial remedy proceedings, the judge recorded how one of the properties in dispute between the husband and wife (the property) was held in the husband's sole name, had a value of £1m and had been mortgaged in favour of Halifax, which was owned by the third defendant bank, in the sum of just under £480,000. The property was transferred to the wife, along with other provisions made and the assets divided approximately 50:50. A civil restraint order, against the husband, was also made, to endure until October 2017.

However, in August 2016, the husband issued proceedings, first, against the bank and, secondly, against the first defendant Chief Land Registrar (the registrar), including the wife in those second proceedings.

The husband, claiming identity fraud, contended that he was not the individual mentioned in the financial remedy order, and applied for such steps to be taken against the bank and the registrar to effectively stop the transfer of the property to the wife.

The bank and the registrar applied for the husband's claims to be struck out.

Issue

Whether, given the circumstances of the case, the husbands claims against the bank and the registrar should be struck out.

Decision

The decree nisi amounted to a declaration as to status. It amounted to a declaration that the parties were the people who were pleaded in the divorce petition and that they had been married on the date mentioned in the divorce petition. The husband, having petitioned on that basis, could not later be heard to say that he had not been the person mentioned in the divorce petition. Those were clear declarations as to status that could not later be impugned (see [9] of the judgment).

It could be seen in the light of that that the husband's claims were completely legally impossible and wholly abusive. The husband was estopped from making the claims. It was impossible for the husband to deny that he had indeed been the person who had been the subject of the divorce proceedings and it was further manifestly abusive in that it was a yet further attempt to thwart the implementation of the order made to transfer the property to the wife. The husband had made an improper collateral attack on the financial remedy order (see [20], [31], [32] of the judgment).

JSC BTA Bank v Ablyazov [2011] All ER (D) 81 (May) considered.

Conclusion

The husband's claims would be struck out. A general civil restraint order would be made against the husband to endure for 2 years (see [33], [37]–[39] of the judgment).

The husband appeared in person.

The wife appeared in person.

Raj Kumar Arumugam for the registrar.

Edward Jones for the bank.

PART 7
PROCEDURE FOR APPLICATIONS IN MATRIMONIAL AND CIVIL PARTNERSHIP PROCEEDINGS

Chapter 3
How the Court Determines Matrimonial and Civil Partnership Proceedings

7.20 What the court will do on an application for a decree nisi, a conditional order, a decree of judicial separation or a separation order

Page 1392.

Owens v Owens [2017] EWCA Civ 182, [2017] All ER (D) 23 (Apr)

(Court of Appeal, Civil Division, Sir James Munby P, Hallett and Macur LJJ, 24 March 2017) Divorce – Appeal. The Court of Appeal Civil Division, in dismissing the wife's appeal against a refusal of a divorce, applied the law as it stood and found the judge had not erred in finding that although the marriage had broken down, the wife had failed to prove, within the meaning of s 1(2)(b) of the Matrimonial Causes Act 1973, that her husband 'has behaved in such a way that she could not reasonably be expected to live with him'.

Digest

The husband and wife married in 1987 and separated in 2015. In 2015, the wife filed a petition seeking divorce on the ground that the marriage had irretrievably broken down and alleging that the husband had behaved in such a way that she could not reasonably be expected to live with him. There were 27 separate allegations of irretrievable breakdown (including the airport and the restaurant incidents). The husband defended the petition. The trial judge approached the case on the basis that the agreed approach was not to investigate each and every allegation, but through examination and cross-examination of the history of the marriage and selected incidents to give the overall flavour or complexion of the case and of how personal perspective might have altered reality in terms of the pleaded matters. The trial judge refused to grant the wife a decree nisi of divorce, even though he had, correctly, found as a fact that the marriage had broken down. The petition was dismissed on the basis that the wife had failed to prove, within the meaning of s 1(2)(b) of the Matrimonial Causes Act 1973, that her husband 'has behaved in such a way that [she] cannot reasonably be expected to live with [him].' The wife appealed.

The wife submitted that the process adopted by the trial judge was 'seriously flawed'. Consideration was given to: (i) the law as it was to be applied to the present case; (ii) whether the judge had failed to make essential (core) findings of fact as to what the husband had actually done in relation to the 27 pleaded allegations; (iii) whether the judge had failed to make findings as to the impact of that conduct on the wife; (iv) whether the judge had failed to undertake any proper assessment of the wife's subjective characteristics; (v) whether the judge had failed to undertake any assessment of the cumulative impact and effect on the wife of the husband's behaviour; (vi) whether the judge had failed to consider the wife's rights under Arts 8 and 12 of the European Convention on Human Rights. Consideration was given to the Family Procedure Rules 2010.

The appeal would be dismissed.

(1) It was established law that in divorce proceedings, a court had to evaluate what was proved to have happened: (i) in the context of the particular marriage: (ii) looking at the particular wife and husband; (iii) in the light of all the circumstances; and (iv) having regard to the cumulative effect of all a respondent's conduct. The court then had to ask itself the statutory question: given all that, had a respondent to a divorce petition behaved in such a way

that the petitioner could not reasonably be expected to live with the respondent. If a marriage was unhappy, a particular piece of 'conduct' might have more impact and be less 'reasonable' than exactly the same conduct. What might be regarded as trivial disagreements in a happy marriage could be salt in the wound in an unhappy marriage. Section 1 of the 1973 Act was an 'always speaking' enactment and was to be construed as taking into account changes in the understanding of the natural world, technological changes, changes in social standards and, of particular importance here, changes in social attitudes. So when s 1(2)(b) of the 1973 Act used the words 'cannot reasonably be expected', that objective test had to be addressed by reference to the standards of the reasonable man or woman on the Clapham omnibus (see [37] of the judgment).

Dodd v Dodd [1906] P 189 applied; *R v Ireland, R v Burstow* [1997] 4 All ER 225 applied; *Gollins v Gollins* [1963] 2 All ER 966 considered; *Ash v Ash* [1972] Fam 135 considered; *Livingstone-Stallard v Livingstone-Stallard* [1974] 2 All ER 766 considered; *O'Neill v O'Neill* [1975] 3 All ER 289 considered; *Stevens v Stevens* [1979] 1 WLR 885 considered; *Butterworth v Butterworth* [1997] 2 FLR 336 considered; *Hadjimilitis (Tsavliris) v Tsavliris (divorce: irretrievable breakdown)* [2002] All ER (D) 32 (Jul) considered; *G (children) (education: religious upbringing), Re* [2012] All ER (D) 50 (Oct) considered; *Healthcare at Home Ltd v The Common Services Agency (Scotland)* [2014] 4 All ER 210 considered.

(2) The 'overriding objective' had been spelt out in FPR 2010, r 1.1, which enabled the court to deal with cases justly, expeditiously and fairly; proportionate to the nature, importance and complexity of the issues. Ensuring that the parties were on an equal footing, saving expense and allotting to it an appropriate share of the court's resources, while taking into account the need to allot resources to other cases. FPR 2010, r 1.1 was supplemented by FPR 2010, r 22.1, which conferred on the court extensive powers to control the evidence, including, by FPR 2010, r 22.1(2), the power to exclude admissible evidence (see [61] of the judgment).

In the present case, the parties had wisely and prudently, chosen to conduct the proceedings in a more focused and controlled manner. They had accepted that the final hearing should be listed for only 1 day. Given the way in which the hearing developed before him, and given the terms of FPR 2010, rr 1.1 and 22.1. The judge was entirely justified in proceeding as he had done and for the reasons he had done (see [62] of the judgment).

Griffiths v Griffiths [1974] 1 All ER 932 not followed; *Livingstone-Stallard v Livingstone-Stallard* [1974] 2 All ER 766 considered.

(3) The judge had specifically rejected the wife's case that the pleaded 27 allegations were 'examples' of behaviour that was more widespread. He had made the same point in relation to the airport and restaurant incidents. These were all findings that were plainly open to the judge and that could not be interfered with. Further, it could not be said that the judge had to make specific findings in relation to each of the 27 pleaded allegations. What the judge had to do was to decide whether the husband's conduct as proved by the wife established her case under s 1(2)(b) of the Act. That had not required specific findings in relation to each allegation. The judge had well understood that he had to evaluate the impact on the wife of the events that found proved and his findings were clear as he evaluated the events, he found their impact to be modest at best (see [64], [66], [67] of the judgment).

(4) Although there had not been an explicit reference in the judgment to the cumulative effect on the wife of the husband's conduct, when the judgment was read as a whole and taken in context, it could be seen that the use of the phrases 'a consistent and persistent course of conduct' and 'isolated incidents', among others, showed that the judge had indeed been looking to all the circumstances and to their cumulative effect (see [71], [72] of the judgment).

(5) There was no Convention right to be divorced nor, if domestic law permitted divorce, was there any Convention right to a favourable outcome in such proceedings. Applying established law, if the provisions of the Convention could not be interpreted as guaranteeing a possibility, under domestic law, of obtaining divorce, they could not, a fortiori, be interpreted as guaranteeing a favourable outcome in divorce proceedings instituted under the provision of that law allowing for a divorce (see [77], [80] of the judgment).

Johnston v Ireland (Application 9697/82) [1986] ECHR 9697/82 applied.

Philip Marshall QC (instructed by Payne Hicks Beach) for the wife.

Nigel Dyer QC and Hamish Dunlop (instructed by Hughes Paddison) for the husband.

PART III

PART 8
PROCEDURE FOR MISCELLANEOUS APPLICATIONS

Chapter 6
Application for Permission to Apply for a Financial Remedy after Overseas
Proceedings

8.23 Scope of this Chapter

Page 1424.

By virtue of the Family Procedure (Amendment No 2) Rules 2017, in FPR 2010, r 8.23, following the words in parenthesis, there is inserted:

> (The Family Court (Composition and Distribution of Business) Rules 2014 make provision in relation to the allocation of the proceedings to which this Chapter applies to a specified level of judge in the family court.)

Commencement date: 7 August 2017.

8.25 Application without notice

Page 1425.

By virtue of the Family Procedure (Amendment No 2) Rules 2017, in FPR 2010, r 8.25 is substituted by:

8.25 Application without notice

(1) The application must be made without notice to the respondent.

(2) Subject to paragraph (3), the court must determine the application without notice.

(3) The court may direct that the application be determined on notice to the respondent if the court considers that to be appropriate.

Commencement date: 7 August 2017.

8.28 Direction that application be dealt with by a district judge of the principal registry

Page 1425.

By virtue of the Family Procedure (Amendment No 2) Rules 2017, in FPR 2010, r 8.28 is revoked. Commencement date: 7 August 2017.

PART 9
APPLICATIONS FOR A FINANCIAL REMEDY

Chapter 2
Procedure for Applications

9.5 Where to start proceedings

Page 1432.

By virtue of the Family Procedure (Amendment No 2) Rules 2017, in FPR 2010, r 9.5, para (3) and the words in parenthesis that follow that paragraph are revoked. Commencement date: 7 August 2017.

Chapter 4
Procedure after Filing an Application

9.15 Duties of the court at the first appointment

Page 1438.

By virtue of the Family Procedure (Amendment No 2) Rules 2017, in FPR 2010, r 9.15, para (4) is substituted by:

(4) The court must direct that the case be referred to a FDR appointment unless –

    (a) the first appointment or part of it has been treated as a FDR appointment and the FDR appointment has been effective; or

    (b) there are exceptional reasons which make a referral to a FDR appointment inappropriate.

Commencement date: 7 August 2017.

PART 12
CHILDREN PROCEEDINGS EXCEPT PARENTAL ORDER PROCEEDINGS AND PROCEEDINGS FOR APPLICATIONS IN ADOPTION, PLACEMENT AND RELATED PROCEEDINGS

Chapter 2
General Rules

12.12 Directions

Page 1506.

Re R (Closed Material Procedure: Special Advocates: Funding) [2017] EWHC 1793 (Fam), [2017] All ER (D) 138 (Jul)

(Family Division, Cobb J, 13 July 2017) Legal representation – Funding. The police had wished to disclose sensitive material in closed session in family proceedings and for the disclosure of such material to the parties to be closely and rigorously controlled. The issue arose as to who was to pay for the costs of an instructed special advocate. The Family Court held that the police ought to pay those costs. The police ought to be required to broaden its obligations to ensure that those who were most affected by the information, which included the father, were given the fullest and fairest opportunity to have the case for non-disclosure tested.

Background

Shortly after the birth of their child, R, the parents separated. After the separation, the father was the victim of a life-endangering attack, which he survived (the original crime). It led to a trial, and convictions, of a number of people for the offence of conspiracy to murder. A significant volume of evidence gathered by the police had been disclosed to the parties in the present family proceedings.

There had been three closed material hearings in the case during which the mother had been represented by a special advocate (SA), who had seen the limited undisclosed material. However, the father had not participated in the closed hearings, by SA or at all. The mother's SA had been funded by the police authority that had investigated the original crime. The police had agreed to fund the mother's SA out of pragmatism.

The police had assessed, on information supplied, that there was a second, and continuing, conspiracy to murder the father. That information had been shared with the parties. However, the police had resisted disclosure of a small quantity of information relevant to that continuing conspiracy, arguing that disclosure of the information would materially heighten the risk to the father, to R, and to others, and would unhelpfully expose police operational details.

At a case management hearing, the judge directed that the father should have a SA for future closed material hearings. The order stated, among other things, that the costs occasioned should be borne on the public funding certificate of the father and that justice would only be served if the costs of the SA were met by the Legal Aid Agency.

The circumstances of the proceedings were such that there was a need for at least one further closed material hearing at which the sensitive information from the police would be reviewed. The Attorney General had indicated that he would not instruct a SA for the father without a funding arrangement for the SA and special advocates' support office (SASO) support being in place. No party volunteered to fund the SASO team for the father.

The court ruled:

Issue

The issue was how the costs of an instructed SA should be funded in the family proceedings.

Decision

It appeared that in family cases in which SAs were engaged, there had been no clear or definitive ruling on the question of who ought to fund SAs, nor was there any apparent reliable precedent, or rule. Where SAs had been engaged in family proceedings in the past, either no dispute had arisen about their funding, and a pragmatic solution had been agreed, or the court had taken a pragmatic course and imposed an outcome that no party had sought to challenge (see [25], [26] of the judgment).

In the absence of clear or authoritative steer from statute, guidance or otherwise, and relying on the arguments marshalled by the parties, the agency that held the sensitive material, namely the police, ought to fund the SA for the father. That was in relation to fees already incurred and to be incurred. The police had exclusive ownership of the sensitive material. It wished to ensure that: (i) the court was in possession of that material; and (ii) the court was aware of the reasons why disclosure of that material would be contrary to the public interest. It had proposed that the sensitive information was therefore presented to the court exclusively in closed session, and that its disclosure to the parties ought to be closely and rigorously controlled. Having taken that position, the police ought to be required to broaden its obligations to ensure that those who were most affected by the information were given the fullest and fairest opportunity to have the case for non-disclosure tested (see [28], [29] of the judgment).

Alison Ball QC and Matthew Fletcher for the authority.

Janet Bazley QC and Sharon Segal for the mother.

Ian Bugg for the father.

Mukul Chawla QC and Tom Bullmore as Special Advocate for the mother in closed proceedings.

Ashley Underwood QC as proposed Special Advocate for the father in closed proceedings.

Jeremy Johnson QC for the relevant Police Constabulary.

Doushka Krish for the children's guardian of R.

David Martin for the Ministry of Justice.

Chapter 5
Special Provisions about Inherent Jurisdiction Proceedings

12.36 Where to start proceedings

Page 1542.

Gard and others v United Kingdom (App No 39793/17) [2017] All ER (D) 165 (Jun)

(European Court of Human Rights, Sicilianos (President), Pardalos, Pejchal, Wojtyczek, Harutyunyan, Eicke and Ilievski, 28 June 2017) Human Rights – Right to respect for private and family life. The European Court of Human Rights declared that complaints by Charlie Gard and his parents of violation of their rights under Arts 2, 5, 6 and 8 of the European Convention on Human Rights were inadmissible. Although there had been interference in their Art 8 rights by decisions to withdraw artificial ventilation and provide palliative care to Charlie, contrary to his parents' wishes, it had been in accordance with the law, had pursued a legitimate aim and had been necessary in a democratic society.

Digest

The first applicant child, CG, suffered from a very rare and severe mitochondrial disease. There were no usual signs of normal brain activities, such as responsiveness, interaction or crying. The second and third applicant parents became aware of a form of therapy that had been used on patients with a less severe mitochondrial condition (nucleoside treatment). The hospital treating CG applied for an order, stating that it would be lawful and in CG's best interests for artificial ventilation to be withdrawn and palliative care provided. The judge acceded to that application and also considered that it would not be in CG's best interests to undergo nucleoside treatment in the USA ([2017] EWHC 972 (Fam)). The Court of Appeal, Civil Division, found that the judge was entitled to conclude that the nucleoside treatment option would be futile and would have no benefit, and that to move CG to the US and expose him to treatment would be likely to expose him to continued pain, suffering and distress ([2017] All ER (D) 20 (Jun)). The Supreme Court rejected the applicants' request for permission to appeal. It reiterated the Court of Appeal's finding that, even if the 'best interest' test was replaced with a test of 'significant harm', it was likely that CG would suffer significant harm if his suffering was prolonged without any realistic prospect of improvement. The parents complained, on their own behalf and on CG's behalf, under Arts 2 and 5 of the European Convention on Human Rights. The parents also complained, on their own behalf, under Arts 6 and 8 of the Convention.

First, the applicants contended that the hospital had blocked life-sustaining treatment to CG in violation of the positive obligation under Art 2 of the Convention (Art 2). Secondly, they contended that CG was deprived of his liberty, within the meaning of Art 5 of the Convention (Art 5) by the judge's order. Thirdly, with respect to Art 6 of the Convention (Art 6), the parents complained that the Court of Appeal had concluded that their intended parental decisions would cause CG significant harm without having heard witness evidence on the point. Fourthly, the parents argued that the judge's declaration and subsequent domestic court decisions amounted to a disproportionate interference in their parental rights because they had taken their decisions in the best interests of CG, whereas they should have asked whether there was a likelihood that he was suffering or likely to suffer significant harm. As a result, the interference in their parental rights under Art 8 of the Convention (Art 8) was disproportionate and could not be justified.

The application would be dismissed.

(1) The positive obligations under Art 2 might include the duty to put in place an appropriate legal framework concerning access to experimental treatment, for instance, regulations compelling hospitals to adopt appropriate measures for the protection of their patients' lives. However, Art 2 could not be interpreted as requiring access to unauthorised medicinal products for the terminally ill to be regulated in a particular way. Further, in addressing the

question of the administering or withdrawal of medical treatment, consideration had been given to: (i) the existence in domestic law and practice of a regulatory framework compatible with the requirements of Art 2; (ii) whether account had been taken of the applicant's previously expressed wishes and those of persons close to him, as well as the opinions of other medical personnel; and (iii) the possibility to approach the courts in the event of doubts as to the best decision to take in the patient's interests. In the sphere concerning the end of life, as in that concerning the beginning of life, states had to be afforded a margin of appreciation, not just as to whether or not to permit the withdrawal of artificial life-sustaining treatment and the detailed arrangements governing such withdrawal, but also regarding the means of striking a balance between the protection of patients' right to life and the protection of their right to respect for their private life and their personal autonomy. However, that margin of appreciation was not unlimited and the power to review whether or not the state had complied with its obligations under Art 2 was reserved (see [77], [78], [80], [83], [84] of the judgment).

A regulatory framework governing access to experimental medication was in place and, as Art 2 could not be interpreted as requiring access to unauthorised medicinal products for the terminally ill to be regulated in any particular way, that aspect of the complaint was manifestly ill-founded. Although no argument had been made concerning the withdrawal of life-sustaining treatment, it was also appropriate to analyse the applicants' complaint from that perspective. First, given that the applicants had not raised arguments about the existence of a regulatory framework compatible with the requirements of Art 2, there was no reason to change the court's previous conclusion that the regulatory framework in place had been appropriate. Secondly, while CG could not express his own wishes, the domestic courts had ensured that his wishes had been expressed through his guardian, an independent professional appointed expressly by the domestic courts for that purpose. Further, the opinions of all medical personnel involved had been examined in detail. Thirdly, the hospital had properly applied to the judge under the relevant statute and the court's inherent jurisdiction to obtain a legal decision as to the appropriate way forward. Accordingly, the three elements on withdraw of medical treatment were satisfied. Therefore, that complaint was also manifestly ill-founded (see [87]–[89], [92], [93], [95]–[98] of the judgment).

Glass v United Kingdom (Application 61827/00) [2004] 1 FLR 1019 considered; *Hristozov v Bulgaria* (App. Nos. 47039/11 and 358/12) [2012] ECHR 47039/11 considered; *Lambert v France* (Application No. 46043/14) (2015) 38 BHRC 709 considered.

(2) As to the absence of procedural safeguards concerning detention, on the facts of the case, that element was linked to the availability of a domestic framework and the possibility to apply to the domestic courts, which had already been considered in the context of Art 2. Accordingly, the applicants' complaint under Art 5 added nothing further to their claim from a Convention perspective and that aspect of the complaint was manifestly ill-founded (see [102], [103] of the judgment).

(3) Where there was a conflict between a parent's desire concerning medical care for their child and the opinion of medical professionals treating the child, the decisive issue was whether the fair balance that had to exist between the competing interests at stake, namely, those of the child, of the two parents and of public order, had been struck, within the margin of appreciation afforded to states in such matters, taking into account that the best interests of the child had to be of primary consideration. There was also a broad consensus, including in international law, in support of the idea that, in all decisions concerning children, their best interests had to be paramount (see [107] of the judgment).

The parents' complaint under Art 6 about the manner in which the domestic courts had made their decisions, concerned exclusively the alleged arbitrary interference in their private and family life. Therefore, the complaint would be examined under Art 8 alone. In the light of the case-law, there had been an interference in the Art 8 rights of the applicants. Any such interference constituted a violation of Art 8 unless it was in accordance with the law, pursued an aim or aims that were legitimate, under Art 8(2), and could be regarded as necessary in a democratic society. No reason had been advanced to challenge the court's prior conclusion in respect of the legal framework, such that the interference had been in accordance with the law. The interference had also been aimed at protecting the health or morals, and the rights and freedoms of CG and, therefore, had pursued aims that were legitimate under Art 8(2). Further, it had been appropriate for the hospital to turn to the courts in the event of conflict. The question of the appropriate test, namely, the child's best interests or significant harm, was not decisive in the circumstances of the case. Even if the test of significant harm suggested by the applicants was the appropriate one, the Court of Appeal and the Supreme Court had concluded that there had been a risk of significant harm to CG. Having examined the decisions taken by the domestic courts in the light of the relevant considerations, they had: (i) been meticulous and thorough; (ii) ensured that all those concerned had been represented throughout; (iii) heard extensive and high-quality expert evidence; (iv) accorded weight to all the arguments raised; and (v) been reviewed at three levels of jurisdiction with clear and extensive reasoning, giving relevant and sufficient support for their conclusions at all three levels. Accordingly, no element suggested that those decisions could amount to an arbitrary or disproportionate interference and that part of the complaint was manifestly ill-founded (see [104], [111]–[113], [117]–[119], [124], [125] of the judgment).

Glass v United Kingdom (Application 61827/00) [2004] 1 FLR 1019 considered; *MAK v United Kingdom* (Application Nos 45901/05 and 40146/06) [2010] 2 FLR 451 considered; *Lambert v France* (Application No. 46043/14) (2015) 38 BHRC 709 considered.

NHS Hospital Trust v GM and others [2017] EWHC 1710 (Fam), [2017] All ER (D) 129 (Jul)

(Family Division, Baker J, 30 June 2017) Medical treatment – Withdrawal of treatment. A child's current treatment plan was ordered to be revised, with immediate effect, such that it was lawful, and in the child's best interest, for there to be no further neurosurgical intervention and, in the event of a cardiac arrest, no form of cardiac resuscitation. The Family Division held that the medical evidence was manifestly clear that there was nothing more that could be done for the child by way of neurological intervention.

Background

In March 2017, H was born by Caesarean section at 41 weeks. In May, shortly after his vaccinations, his mother noticed a deterioration in H's condition. Subsequently, H suffered a number of physical and, in particular, neurological difficulties. In addition to other symptoms, he suffered from seizures, significant intracranial bleeding, a left-sided subdural haematoma, right-sided unilateral descending transtentorial herniation and partial effacement of the basal cistern. Further, H had suffered an acute deterioration with a decrease in his level of consciousness and cardiovascular instability. Furthermore, in terms of treatment, H had undergone a number of CT scans, intubation and ventilation (for further details of H's conditions and treatments, see [3]–[10] of the judgment). Two days prior to the present proceedings, there had been a further deterioration in H's condition, which included a very significant drop in the level of his haemoglobin, indicating some form of blood loss, likely an internal bleed and possibly intracranial.

The relevant NHS Trust (the Trust), where H was being treated, applied for an order declaring that it was in the best interests of H that the current treatment plan be revised with immediate effect.

Application allowed.

Issues and decisions

Whether it was in H's best interests that his treatment plan be revised so that it was lawful for there to be no neurological intervention and, in the event of cardiac arrest, there be no form of cardiac resuscitation given to H.

H's life was important, and respect for him, his personal integrity and autonomy required the court to give the very strongest weight to his right to life and to remain alive (see [27] of the judgment).

However, the medical evidence was manifestly clear. There was no benefit to be gained from further neurological intervention, since there was no neurological treatment that could be carried out that would be of benefit to H. Rather, there was a very significant risk that any further attempt at intervention would be harmful to H. There was, in effect, nothing more that could be done for H by way neurological intervention (see [28] of the judgment).

Carrying out the balancing exercise, the balance manifestly came own in favour of allowing the application on behalf of the Trust (see [29] of the judgment).

An order would be made that it was in H's best interest that his current treatment plan be revised with immediate effect so that it was lawful and in his best interests for there to be no further neurological intervention. Further, it was in his best interests that, in the event of a cardiac arrest, there should be no form of cardiac resuscitation (see [29] of the judgment).

Peter Boyce for the Trust.

Edward Devereux QC for the first respondent mother.

Alev Giz for the second respondent father.

Melanie Carew for H by his guardian.

Great Ormond Street Hospital v Yates and others [2017] EWHC 1909 (Fam), [2017] All ER (D) 148 (Jul)

(Family Division, Francis J, 24 July 2017) Minor – Medical treatment. Charlie Gard's parents accepted that his life could not be improved, and that the only remaining course was for him to be given palliative care and to permit him to die with dignity. Accordingly, it was the Family Division's duty to confirm its previous declarations, including that it was lawful and in Charlie's best interests for artificial ventilation to be withdrawn and that he not undergo nucleoside therapy, but the court refused to make a mandatory order.

Background

The court previously made declarations, including that: (i) it was not in the best interests of the third respondent child, C, for artificial ventilation to continue to be provided, and that it was lawful and in his best interests to be withdrawn; (ii) it was in C's best interests for his treating clinicians to provide him with palliative care only; and (iii) it was lawful and in C's best interests not to undergo nucleoside therapy (see [2017] EWHC 972 (Fam)). C's parents' appeals to the Court of Appeal, Civil Division ([2017] All ER (D) 20 (Jun)), the Supreme Court and the European Court of Human Rights ([2017] All ER (D) 165 (Jun)) were unsuccessful.

The first and second respondent parents subsequently contacted the applicant hospital, asserting that the best interests assessment and declaration had been overtaken by events and were potentially unsafe, and that the best interests assessment was weighted significantly in favour of preserving C's life and providing treatment. The hospital asked the court to affirm the declarations, if necessary, after hearing further evidence and to make orders in the same terms to remove any ambiguity. The parents later accepted that C's life could not be improved and that the only remaining course was for him to be given palliative care and to permit him to die with dignity.

Issues and decisions

Whether it was in C's best interests to affirm the declarations and make orders.

The parents had had to face the reality that C was beyond any help, even from experimental treatment and that it was in his best interests for him to be allowed to die. Given the consensus that existed between the parents, the treating doctors and the parents' medical expert, it was the court's duty to confirm the declarations previously made. However, a mandatory order would not be made (see [14] of the judgment).

Katie Gollop QC (instructed by Great Ormond Street Hospital) for the hospital.

Grant Armstrong and Gerard Rothschild (instructed by Harris da Silva) for the parents.

Victoria Butler-Cole (instructed by Cafcass) for the guardian.

Practice Direction 12D – Inherent Jurisdiction (Including Wardship) Proceedings

Criminal Proceedings (para 5)

Page 1603.

President of the Family Division Circular: Amendment to Practice Direction 12D – Interviewing Wards of Court

The president of the Family Division, Sir James Munby, has issued an amendment to FPR PD12D, following his judgment in *Re A (A child)* [2017] EWHC 1022 (Fam) on whether police officers and officers of the Security Service may interview a ward of court without first having obtained the approval of the wardship judge.

The President's Circular is set out below:

(16 June 2017) On 4 May 2017 I handed down judgment *In the matter of a Ward of Court* [2017] EWHC 1022 (Fam). It related to the question whether police officers and officers of the Security Service may interview a ward of court without first having obtained the approval of the wardship judge.

In the course of my judgment I had to consider paras 5.1–5.6 of PD12D (set out in para 40 of the judgment). Para 5.2 of PD12D stated baldly, though the effect was somewhat modified by what followed, that

'Where the police need to interview a child who is already a ward of court, an application must be made for permission for the police to do so.'

For the reasons set out in the judgment, I concluded (para 46) that

'the asserted principle or rule that judicial consent is required before the police can interview a ward of court, is impossible to reconcile [with other established principles].'

I said (para 48) that PD12D

'in significant part is … simply wrong.'

I went on (para 49) to observe that there was

'a pressing need for paragraph 5 of PD12D to be considered as a matter of urgency by the Family Procedure Rule Committee', adding that '[r]adical surgery will probably be required.'

I am grateful for the assistance of the Rule Committee and of the relevant officials, who have acted with commendable speed and diligence in assisting me to decide how PD12D should be amended. I made the necessary amendments on 14 June 2017. They were approved the same day by the Lord Chancellor. They come into effect today, 16 June 2017.

Accordingly, with effect from 16 June 2017, paras 5.1–5.6 of PD12D have been removed in their entirety. Paragraph 5 of PD12D now reads as follows:

5.1 Case law establishes that:

1   There is no requirement for the police or any other agency carrying out statutory powers of investigation or enforcement to seek the permission of the court to interview a child who is a ward of court. The fact that a child is a ward of court does not affect the powers and duties of the police or other statutory agencies in relation to their investigations. Provided that the relevant statutory requirements are complied with, the police or other agencies are under no duty to take any special steps in carrying out their functions in relation to a child who is a ward of court.

2   Where a child has been interviewed by the police in connection with contemplated criminal proceedings and the child is, or subsequently becomes, a ward of court, the permission of the court is not required for the child to be called as a witness in the criminal proceedings.

For a full review of the relevant case law and principles, see *In the matter of a Ward of Court* [2017] EWHC 1022 (Fam).

5.2 Where the police or other statutory agencies take any action in relation to a child who is a ward of court, the person(s) with day to day care and control of the child, or where applicable the local authority, should bring the relevant information to the attention of the court as soon as practicable. Where wardship

PART III

proceedings are continuing, any children's guardian appointed for the child must be informed of the situation by the other parties.'

James Munby
President of the Family Division

Practice Direction 12J – Child Arrangements and Contact Order: Domestic Violence and Harm

Page 1624.
The President of the Family Division has issued a revised FPR PD12J, which is set out below:

Practice Direction 12J – Child Arrangements and Contact Orders: Domestic Abuse and Harm

This Practice Direction supplements FPR Part 12, and incorporates and supersedes the President's Guidance in Relation to Split Hearings (May 2010) as it applies to proceedings for child arrangements orders.

Summary

1 This Practice Direction applies to any family proceedings in the Family Court or the High Court under the relevant parts of the Children Act 1989 or the relevant parts of the Adoption and Children Act 2002 in which an application is made for a child arrangements order, or in which any question arises about where a child should live, or about contact between a child and a parent or other family member, where the court considers that an order should be made.

2 The purpose of this Practice Direction is to set out what the Family Court or the High Court is required to do in any case in which it is alleged or admitted, or there is other reason to believe, that the child or a party has experienced domestic abuse perpetrated by another party or that there is a risk of such abuse.

3 For the purpose of this Practice Direction –

'domestic abuse' includes any incident or pattern of incidents of controlling, coercive or threatening behaviour, violence or abuse between those aged 16 or over who are or have been intimate partners or family members regardless of gender or sexuality. This can encompass, but is not limited to, psychological, physical, sexual, financial, or emotional abuse. Domestic abuse also includes culturally specific forms of abuse including, but not limited to, forced marriage, honour-based violence, dowry-related abuse and transnational marriage abandonment;

'abandonment' refers to the practice whereby a husband, in England and Wales, deliberately abandons or 'strands' his foreign national wife abroad, usually without financial resources, in order to prevent her from asserting matrimonial and/or residence rights in England and Wales. It may involve children who are either abandoned with, or separated from, their mother;

'coercive behaviour' means an act or a pattern of acts of assault, threats, humiliation and intimidation or other abuse that is used to harm, punish, or frighten the victim;

'controlling behaviour' means an act or pattern of acts designed to make a person subordinate and/or dependent by isolating them from sources of support, exploiting their resources and capacities for personal gain, depriving them of the means needed for independence, resistance and escape and regulating their everyday behaviour;

'development' means physical, intellectual, emotional, social or behavioural development;

'harm' means ill-treatment or the impairment of health or development including, for example, impairment suffered from seeing or hearing the ill-treatment of another, by domestic abuse or otherwise;

'health' means physical or mental health;

'ill-treatment' includes sexual abuse and forms of ill-treatment which are not physical; and

'judge' includes salaried and fee-paid judges and lay justices sitting in the Family Court and, where the context permits, can include a justices' clerk or assistant to a justices' clerk in the Family Court.

General principles

4 Domestic abuse is harmful to children, and/or puts children at risk of harm, whether they are subjected to domestic abuse, or witness one of their parents being violent or abusive to the other parent, or live in a home in which domestic abuse is perpetrated (even if the child is too young to be conscious of the behaviour). Children may suffer direct physical, psychological and/or emotional harm from living with domestic abuse, and may also suffer harm indirectly where the domestic abuse impairs the parenting capacity of either or both of their parents.

5 The court must, at all stages of the proceedings, and specifically at the First Hearing Dispute Resolution Appointment ('FHDRA'), consider whether domestic abuse is raised as an issue, either by the parties or by Cafcass or CAFCASS Cymru or otherwise, and if so must –

- identify at the earliest opportunity (usually at the FHDRA) the factual and welfare issues involved;
- consider the nature of any allegation, admission or evidence of domestic abuse, and the extent to which it would be likely to be relevant in deciding whether to make a child arrangements order and, if so, in what terms;
- give directions to enable contested relevant factual and welfare issues to be tried as soon as possible and fairly;
- ensure that where domestic abuse is admitted or proven, any child arrangements order in place protects the safety and wellbeing of the child and the parent with whom the child is living, and does not expose either of them to the risk of further harm; and
- ensure that any interim child arrangements order (i.e. considered by the court before determination of the facts, and in the absence of admission) is only made having followed the guidance in paragraphs 25–27 below.

In particular, the court must be satisfied that any contact ordered with a parent who has perpetrated domestic abuse does not expose the child and/or other parent to the risk of harm and is in the best interests of the child.

6 In all cases it is for the court to decide whether a child arrangements order accords with Section 1(1) of the Children Act 1989; any proposed child arrangements order, whether to be made by agreement between the parties or otherwise must be carefully scrutinised by the court accordingly. The court must not make a child arrangements order by consent or give permission for an application for a child arrangements order to be withdrawn, unless the parties are present in court, all initial safeguarding checks have been obtained by the court, and an officer of Cafcass or CAFCASS Cymru has spoken to the parties separately, except where it is satisfied that there is no risk of harm to the child and/or the other parent in so doing.

7 In proceedings relating to a child arrangements order, the court presumes that the involvement of a parent in a child's life will further the child's welfare, unless there is evidence to the contrary. The court must in every case consider carefully whether the statutory presumption applies, having particular regard to any allegation or admission of harm by domestic abuse to the child or parent or any evidence indicating such harm or risk of harm.

8 In considering, on an application for a child arrangements order by consent, whether there is any risk of harm to the child, the court must consider all the evidence and information available. The court may direct a report under Section 7 of the Children Act 1989 to be provided either orally or in writing, before it makes its decision; in such a case, the court must ask for information about any advice given by the officer preparing the report to the parties and whether they, or the child, have been referred to any other agency, including local authority children's services. If the report is not in writing, the court must make a note of its substance on the court file and a summary of the same shall be set out in a Schedule to the relevant order.

Before the FHDRA

9 Where any information provided to the court before the FHDRA or other first hearing (whether as a result of initial safeguarding enquiries by Cafcass or CAFCASS Cymru or on form C1A or otherwise) indicates that there are issues of domestic abuse which may be relevant to the court's determination, the court must ensure that the issues are addressed at the hearing, and that the parties are not expected to engage in conciliation or other forms of dispute resolution which are not suitable and/or safe.

10 If at any stage the court is advised by any party (in the application form, or otherwise), by Cafcass or CAFCASS Cymru or otherwise that there is a need for special arrangements to protect the party or child attending any hearing, the court must ensure so far as practicable that appropriate arrangements are made for the hearing (including the waiting arrangements at court prior to the hearing, and arrangements for entering and exiting the court building) and for all subsequent hearings in the case, unless it is advised and considers that these are no longer necessary. Where practicable, the court should enquire of the alleged victim of domestic abuse how best she/he wishes to participate.

First hearing/FHDRA

11 At the FHDRA, if the parties have not been provided with the safeguarding letter/report by Cafcass/CAFCASS Cymru, the court must inform the parties of the content of any safeguarding letter or report or other information which has been provided by Cafcass or CAFCASS Cymru, unless it considers that to do so would create a risk of harm to a party or the child.

12 Where the results of Cafcass or CAFCASS Cymru safeguarding checks are not available at the FHDRA, and no other reliable safeguarding information is available, the court must adjourn the FHDRA until the results of safeguarding checks are available. The court must not generally make an interim child arrangements order, or orders for contact, in the absence of safeguarding information, unless it is to protect the safety of the child, and/or safeguard the child from harm (see further paragraphs 25–27 below).

13 There is a continuing duty on the Cafcass Officer/Welsh FPO which requires them to provide a risk assessment for the court under section 16A Children Act 1989 if they are given cause to suspect that the child concerned is at risk of harm. Specific provision about service of a risk assessment under section 16A of the 1989 Act is made by rule 12.34 of the FPR 2010.

14 The court must ascertain at the earliest opportunity, and record on the face of its order, whether domestic abuse is raised as an issue which is likely to be relevant to any decision of the court relating to the welfare of the child, and specifically whether the child and/or parent would be at risk of harm in the making of any child arrangements order.

Admissions

15 Where at any hearing an admission of domestic abuse toward another person or the child is made by a party, the admission must be recorded in writing by the judge and set out as a Schedule to the relevant order. The court office must arrange for a copy of any order containing a record of admissions to be made available as soon as possible to any Cafcass officer or officer of CAFCASS Cymru or local authority officer preparing a report under section 7 of the Children Act 1989.

Directions for a fact-finding hearing

16 The court should determine as soon as possible whether it is necessary to conduct a fact-finding hearing in relation to any disputed allegation of domestic abuse –

(a) in order to provide a factual basis for any welfare report or for assessment of the factors set out in paragraphs 36 and 37 below;

(b) in order to provide a basis for an accurate assessment of risk;

(c) before it can consider any final welfare-based order(s) in relation to child arrangements; or

(d) before it considers the need for a domestic abuse-related Activity (such as a Domestic Violence Perpetrator Programme (DVPP)).

17 In determining whether it is necessary to conduct a fact-finding hearing, the court should consider –

(a) the views of the parties and of Cafcass or CAFCASS Cymru;

(b) whether there are admissions by a party which provide a sufficient factual basis on which to proceed;

(c) if a party is in receipt of legal aid, whether the evidence required to be provided to obtain legal aid provides a sufficient factual basis on which to proceed;

(d) whether there is other evidence available to the court that provides a sufficient factual basis on which to proceed;

(e) whether the factors set out in paragraphs 36 and 37 below can be determined without a fact-finding hearing;

(f) the nature of the evidence required to resolve disputed allegations;

(g)   whether the nature and extent of the allegations, if proved, would be relevant to the issue before the court; and

(h)   whether a separate fact-finding hearing would be necessary and proportionate in all the circumstances of the case.

18 Where the court determines that a finding of fact hearing is not necessary, the order must record the reasons for that decision.

19 Where the court considers that a fact-finding hearing is necessary, it must give directions as to how the proceedings are to be conducted to ensure that the matters in issue are determined as soon as possible, fairly and proportionately, and within the capabilities of the parties. In particular it should consider –

(a)   what are the key facts in dispute;

(b)   whether it is necessary for the fact-finding to take place at a separate (and earlier) hearing than the welfare hearing;

(c)   whether the key facts in dispute can be contained in a schedule or a table (known as a Scott Schedule) which sets out what the applicant complains of or alleges, what the respondent says in relation to each individual allegation or complaint; the allegations in the schedule should be focused on the factual issues to be tried; and if so, whether it is practicable for this schedule to be completed at the first hearing, with the assistance of the judge;

(d)   what evidence is required in order to determine the existence of coercive, controlling or threatening behaviour, or of any other form of domestic abuse;

(e)   directing the parties to file written statements giving details of such behaviour and of any response;

(f)   whether documents are required from third parties such as the police, health services or domestic abuse support services and giving directions for those documents to be obtained;

(g)   whether oral evidence may be required from third parties and if so, giving directions for the filing of written statements from such third parties;

(h)   where (for example in cases of abandonment) third parties from whom documents are to be obtained are abroad, how to obtain those documents in good time for the hearing, and who should be responsible for the costs of obtaining those documents;

(i)   whether any other evidence is required to enable the court to decide the key issues and giving directions for that evidence to be provided;

(j)   what evidence the alleged victim of domestic abuse is able to give and what support the alleged victim may require at the fact-finding hearing in order to give that evidence;

(k)   in cases where the alleged victim of domestic abuse is unable for reasons beyond their control to be present at the hearing (for example, abandonment cases where the abandoned spouse remains abroad), what measures should be taken to ensure that that person's best evidence can be put before the court. Where video-link is not available, the court should consider alternative technological or other methods which may be utilised to allow that person to participate in the proceedings;

(l)   what support the alleged perpetrator may need in order to have a reasonable opportunity to challenge the evidence; and

(m)   whether a pre-hearing review would be useful prior to the fact-finding hearing to ensure directions have been complied with and all the required evidence is available.

20 Where the court fixes a fact-finding hearing, it must at the same time fix a Dispute Resolution Appointment to follow. Subject to the exception in paragraph 31

below, the hearings should be arranged in such a way that they are conducted by the same judge or, wherever possible, by the same panel of lay justices; where it is not possible to assemble the same panel of justices, the resumed hearing should be listed before at least the same chairperson of the lay justices. Judicial continuity is important.

Reports under Section 7

21 In any case where a risk of harm to a child resulting from domestic abuse is raised as an issue, the court should consider directing that a report on the question of contact, or any other matters relating to the welfare of the child, be prepared under section 7 of the Children Act 1989 by an Officer of Cafcass or a Welsh family proceedings officer (or local authority officer if appropriate), unless the court is satisfied that it is not necessary to do so in order to safeguard the child's interests.

22 If the court directs that there shall be a fact-finding hearing on the issue of domestic abuse, the court will not usually request a section 7 report until after that hearing. In that event, the court should direct that any judgment is provided to Cafcass/CAFCASS Cymru; if there is no transcribed judgment, an agreed list of findings should be provided, as set out at paragraph 29.

23 Any request for a section 7 report should set out clearly the matters the court considers need to be addressed.

Representation of the child

24 Subject to the seriousness of the allegations made and the difficulty of the case, the court must consider whether it is appropriate for the child who is the subject of the application to be made a party to the proceedings and be separately represented. If the court considers that the child should be so represented, it must review the allocation decision so that it is satisfied that the case proceeds before the correct level of judge in the Family Court or High Court.

Interim orders before determination of relevant facts

25 Where the court gives directions for a fact-finding hearing, or where disputed allegations of domestic abuse are otherwise undetermined, the court should not make an interim child arrangements order unless it is satisfied that it is in the interests of the child to do so and that the order would not expose the child or the other parent to an unmanageable risk of harm (bearing in mind the impact which domestic abuse against a parent can have on the emotional well-being of the child, the safety of the other parent and the need to protect against domestic abuse including controlling or coercive behaviour).

26 In deciding any interim child arrangements question the court should–

(a) take into account the matters set out in section 1(3) of the Children Act 1989 or section 1(4) of the Adoption and Children Act 2002 ('the welfare check-list'), as appropriate; and

(b) give particular consideration to the likely effect on the child, and on the care given to the child by the parent who has made the allegation of domestic abuse, of any contact and any risk of harm, whether physical, emotional or psychological, which the child and that parent is likely to suffer as a consequence of making or declining to make an order.

27 Where the court is considering whether to make an order for interim contact, it should in addition consider –

    (a)   the arrangements required to ensure, as far as possible, that any risk of harm to the child and the parent who is at any time caring for the child is minimised and that the safety of the child and the parties is secured; and in particular:

        (i)   whether the contact should be supervised or supported, and if so, where and by whom; and

        (ii)   the availability of appropriate facilities for that purpose;

    (b)   if direct contact is not appropriate, whether it is in the best interests of the child to make an order for indirect contact; and

    (c)   whether contact will be beneficial for the child.

The fact-finding hearing or other hearing of the facts where domestic abuse is alleged

28 While ensuring that the allegations are properly put and responded to, the fact-finding hearing or other hearing can be an inquisitorial (or investigative) process, which at all times must protect the interests of all involved. At the fact-finding hearing or other hearing –

- each party can be asked to identify what questions they wish to ask of the other party, and to set out or confirm in sworn evidence their version of the disputed key facts; and
- the judge should be prepared where necessary and appropriate to conduct the questioning of the witnesses on behalf of the parties, focusing on the key issues in the case.

29 The court should, wherever practicable, make findings of fact as to the nature and degree of any domestic abuse which is established and its effect on the child, the child's parents and any other relevant person. The court must record its findings in writing in a Schedule to the relevant order, and the court office must serve a copy of this order on the parties. A copy of any record of findings of fact or of admissions must be sent by the court office to any officer preparing a report under Section 7 of the 1989 Act.

30 At the conclusion of any fact-finding hearing, the court must consider, notwithstanding any earlier direction for a section 7 report, whether it is in the best interests of the child for the court to give further directions about the preparation or scope of any report under section 7; where necessary, it may adjourn the proceedings for a brief period to enable the officer to make representations about the preparation or scope of any further enquiries. Any section 7 report should address the factors set out in paragraphs 36 and 37 below, unless the court directs otherwise.

31 Where the court has made findings of fact on disputed allegations, any subsequent hearing in the proceedings should be conducted by the same judge or by at least the same chairperson of the justices. Exceptions may be made only where observing this requirement would result in delay to the planned timetable and the judge or chairperson is satisfied, for reasons which must be recorded in writing, that the detriment to the welfare of the child would outweigh the detriment to the fair trial of the proceedings.

In all cases where domestic abuse has occurred

32 The court should take steps to obtain (or direct the parties or an Officer of Cafcass or a Welsh family proceedings officer to obtain) information about the facilities available locally (to include local domestic abuse support services) to assist any party or the child in cases where domestic abuse has occurred.

33 Following any determination of the nature and extent of domestic abuse, whether or not following a fact-finding hearing, the court must, if considering any form of contact or involvement of the parent in the child's life, consider –

    (a)   whether it would be assisted by any social work, psychiatric, psychological or other assessment (including an expert safety and risk assessment) of any party or the child and if so (subject to any necessary consent) make directions for such assessment to be undertaken and for the filing of any consequent report. Any such report should address the factors set out in paragraphs 36 and 37 below, unless the court directs otherwise;

    (b)   whether any party should seek advice, treatment or other intervention as a precondition to any child arrangements order being made, and may (with the consent of that party) give directions for such attendance.

34 Further or as an alternative to the advice, treatment or other intervention referred to in paragraph 33(b) above, the court may make an Activity Direction under section 11A and 11B Children Act 1989. Any intervention directed pursuant to this provision should be one commissioned and approved by Cafcass. It is acknowledged that acceptance on a DVPP is subject to a suitability assessment by the service provider, and that completion of a DVPP will take time in order to achieve the aim of risk-reduction for the long-term benefit of the child and the parent with whom the child is living.

Factors to be taken into account when determining whether to make child arrangements orders in all cases where domestic abuse has occurred

35 When deciding the issue of child arrangements the court should ensure that any order for contact will not expose the child to an unmanageable risk of harm and will be in the best interests of the child.

36 In the light of any findings of fact or admissions or where domestic abuse is otherwise established, the court should apply the individual matters in the welfare checklist with reference to the domestic abuse which has occurred and any expert risk assessment obtained. In particular, the court should in every case consider any harm which the child and the parent with whom the child is living has suffered as a consequence of that domestic abuse, and any harm which the child and the parent with whom the child is living is at risk of suffering, if a child arrangements order is made. The court should make an order for contact only if it is satisfied that the physical and emotional safety of the child and the parent with whom the child is living can, as far as possible, be secured before during and after contact, and that the parent with whom the child is living will not be subjected to further domestic abuse by the other parent.

37 In every case where a finding or admission of domestic abuse is made, or where domestic abuse is otherwise established, the court should consider the conduct of both parents towards each other and towards the child and the impact of the same. In particular, the court should consider –

    (a)   the effect of the domestic abuse on the child and on the arrangements for where the child is living;

    (b)   the effect of the domestic abuse on the child and its effect on the child's relationship with the parents;

    (c)   whether the parent is motivated by a desire to promote the best interests of the child or is using the process to continue a form of domestic abuse against the other parent;

    (d)   the likely behaviour during contact of the parent against whom findings are made and its effect on the child; and

PART III

    (e)   the capacity of the parents to appreciate the effect of past domestic abuse and the potential for future domestic abuse.

Directions as to how contact is to proceed

38 Where any domestic abuse has occurred but the court, having considered any expert risk assessment and having applied the welfare checklist, nonetheless considers that direct contact is safe and beneficial for the child, the court should consider what, if any, directions or conditions are required to enable the order to be carried into effect and in particular should consider –

    (a)   whether or not contact should be supervised, and if so, where and by whom;

    (b)   whether to impose any conditions to be complied with by the party in whose favour the order for contact has been made and if so, the nature of those conditions, for example by way of seeking intervention (subject to any necessary consent);

    (c)   whether such contact should be for a specified period or should contain provisions which are to have effect for a specified period; and

    (d)   whether it will be necessary, in the child's best interests, to review the operation of the order; if so the court should set a date for the review consistent with the timetable for the child, and must give directions to ensure that at the review the court has full information about the operation of the order.

Where a risk assessment has concluded that a parent poses a risk to a child or to the other parent, contact via a supported contact centre, or contact supported by a parent or relative, is not appropriate.

39 Where the court does not consider direct contact to be appropriate, it must consider whether it is safe and beneficial for the child to make an order for indirect contact.

The reasons of the court

40 In its judgment or reasons the court should always make clear how its findings on the issue of domestic abuse have influenced its decision on the issue of arrangements for the child. In particular, where the court has found domestic abuse proved but nonetheless makes an order which results in the child having future contact with the perpetrator of domestic abuse, the court must always explain, whether by way of reference to the welfare check-list, the factors in paragraphs 36 and 37 or otherwise, why it takes the view that the order which it has made will not expose the child to the risk of harm and is beneficial for the child.

Commencement date: 2 October 2017.

The fact-finding hearing (para 28)

Page 1628.

H v D (Appeal – Failure of Case Management) [2017] EWHC 1907 (Fam), [2017] All ER (D) 193 (Jul)

(Family Division, Peter Jackson J, 24 July 2017) Family proceedings – Orders in family proceedings. Having made all allowances for the difficult position of the court when an alleged abuser was unrepresented, the mother's appeal against the judge's decision that she was not going to interfere with the allegedly abusive father's right to cross-examine the mother on matters that were not sexual succeeded on all grounds. In particular, the Family Division held that the history showed a chronic failure of judicial case management and allowed the appeal on that ground alone.

Background

The substantive proceedings concerned whether or not the respondent father should have contact with the child. The applicant mother opposed any contact, alleging that she had suffered very serious abuse at the father's hands. However, the father had been acquitted by the criminal court of all charges arising from the mother's allegations. The judge decided that she was not going to interfere with the father's right to cross-examine the mother on matters that were not sexual. The mother appealed.

Appeal allowed

Issues and decisions

Whether the judge: (i) had been wrong to allow any direct cross-examination of the mother by the father; (ii) had been overly lenient to the father in the face of his non-compliance with the orders; (iii) had been wrong to put pressure on the child's solicitor to cross-examine the mother; (iv) should have given further reasons when asked; (v) had properly invited guidance from a higher court; and (vi) whether there had been a general failure of case management.

Having made all allowances for the difficult position of the court when an alleged abuser was unrepresented, the appeal succeeded on all grounds.

The history showed a chronic failure of judicial case management. The court's repeated inability to hold a fact-finding hearing had led to prolonged and indefensible delay in making an important decision for the child. The appeal would be allowed on that ground alone.

Further, the judge had not appreciated her powers under FPRPD 12J, having instead assumed that the father had had the right to cross-examine the mother.

The decision about how the mother was to be cross-examined had effectively been taken by the court earlier and there had been no proper basis for having revisited that plan, particularly as the father himself had not been complaining about it.

Having decided to revisit the issue, the judge had not dealt with it effectively, but instead had havered over it throughout the mother's evidence in a way that had made the hearing unproductive and unfair to the mother, who had been entitled to know how her evidence was to be treated before she had entered the witness box and entitled to expect that she would leave it within some reasonable period.

The judge's decision that the father could cross-examine on some issues but not others had been unprincipled. The basis for taking special measures in such cases was the nature of the relationship between the parties, not the nature of the questions themselves. The decision had also been unworkable, in having expected the court and the father to divide up questions depending on whether they had been sexual or not.

The judge's reasons had been inadequate to justify her conclusions and, having been asked to do so, she should have addressed the substantial issues more fully.

The judge's attempt to delegate the questioning to the child's solicitor had been entirely inappropriate and had been rightly rebuffed. It was wrong, in principle, for the court to expect the child's lawyer to cross-examine the child's own parent, robustly or otherwise, as a way of escaping its responsibility to do that itself (see [18]–[21] of the judgment).

Anna Warters for the mother.

The father appeared in person.

Rachel Early for the child.

PART 17
STATEMENTS OF TRUTH

17.1 Interpretation

Page 1721.

By virtue of the Family Procedure (Amendment No 2) Rules 2017, in FPR 2010, r 17.1, para (a) is revoked. Commencement date: 7 August 2017.

17.2 Documents to be verified by a statement of truth

Page 1722.

By virtue of FPR PD36D (Pilot Scheme: Procedure for Using an Online System to Generate Applications in Certain Proceedings for a Matrimonial Order), where that Practice Direction applies, r 17.2 is modified so that:

- in rule 17.2(6), 'The statement of truth' reads 'Subject to paragraph (6A), the statement of truth', so that rule 17.2(6) reads:

(6) Subject to paragraph (6A), the statement of truth must be signed by –

    (a)   in the case of a statement of case –
        (i)   the party or litigation friend; or
        (ii) the legal representative on behalf of the party or litigation friend; and
    (b)   in the case of a witness statement, the maker of the statement.

and

- after r 17.2(6) there is a new para 6A:

(6A) Where a statement of truth is included in an application for a matrimonial order to which the pilot scheme referred to in Practice Direction 36D applies-

    (a)   the applicant must file with the court an application which includes the name of the person who the online system requires to sign a statement of truth printed underneath the statement of truth; and

    (b)   the court may require the applicant to produce a copy of the application containing the signature of the person referred to in sub-paragraph (a) at a later date.

Commencement date: 7 August 2017.

Practice Direction 17A –
Statements of Truth

Page 1725.

By virtue of FPR PD36D (Pilot Scheme: Procedure for Using an Online System to Generate Applications in Certain Proceedings for a Matrimonial Order), where that Practice Direction applies, FPR PD17A is modified so that:

- paras 1.5 and 2.3 are omitted;
- in the heading to para 3.1 and in paras 3.1, 3.7, 3.8 and 3.10 references to 'sign', 'signs', 'signed' and 'signing' are to be read as references to the name of the person being, or having been, printed under the statement of truth included in an application for a matrimonial order to which the pilot scheme referred to in Practice Direction 36D applies;
- paras 4.1, 4.3(a) and 4.3(e) and the Annex are substituted.

The modified FPR PD17A would therefore read:

Practice Direction 17A – Statements of Truth

Documents to be verified by a statement of truth

1.1 Rule 17.2 sets out the documents which must be verified by a statement of truth.

1.2 If an applicant wishes to rely on matters set out in his application notice as evidence, the application notice must be verified by a statement of truth.

1.3 An expert's report should also be verified by a statement of truth. For the form of the statement of truth verifying an expert's report (which differs from that set out below), see paragraph 9.1(j) of Practice Direction 25B (The Duties of an Expert, The Expert's Report and Arrangements for an Expert to Attend Court).

1.4 In addition, the following documents must be verified by a statement of truth –

    (a)   an application notice for –
        (i)   a third party debt order (CPR Part 72 as modified by rule 33.24);
        (ii) a hardship payment order (CPR Part 72 as modified by rule 33.24); or
        (iii) a charging order (CPR Part 73 as modified by rule 33.25); and
    (b)   a notice of objections to an account being taken by the court, unless verified by an affidavit or witness statement.

1.5 (*omitted*)

1.6 Where the form to be used includes a jurat for the content to be verified by an affidavit, then a statement of truth is not required in addition.

1.7 In this Practice Direction, 'statement of case' has the meaning given to it by rule 17.1.

Form of the statement of truth

2.1 The form of the statement of truth verifying a statement of case or an application notice should be as follows:

    '[I believe] [the (applicant or as may be) believes] that the facts stated in this [name document being verified] are true.'

2.2 The form of the statement of truth verifying a witness statement should be as follows:

    'I believe that the facts stated in this witness statement are true.'

2.3 (*omitted*)

Who may sign the statement of truth

3.1 In a statement of case or an application notice, the statement of truth must be signed by –

    (a)   the party or his litigation friend; or
    (b)   the legal representative of the party or litigation friend.

3.2 A statement of truth verifying a witness statement must be signed by the witness.

3.3 A statement of truth verifying a notice of objections to an account must be signed by the objecting party or his or her legal representative.

3.4 Where a document is to be verified on behalf of a company or corporation, subject to paragraph 3.7 below, the statement of truth must be signed by a person holding a senior position in the company or corporation. That person must state the office or position he or she holds.

3.5 Each of the following persons is a person holding a senior position:

 (a) in respect of a registered company or corporation, a director, the treasurer, secretary, chief executive, manager or other officer of the company or corporation; and

 (b) in respect of a corporation which is not a registered company, in addition to those persons set out in (a), the major, chairman, president, chief executive of a local authority or town clerk or other similar officer of the corporation.

3.6 Where the document is to be verified on behalf of a partnership, those who may sign the statement of truth are –

 (a) any of the partners; or

 (b) a person having the management or control of the partnership business.

3.7 Where a party is legally represented, the legal representative may sign the statement of truth on his or her behalf. The statement signed by the legal representative will refer to the client's belief, not his or her own. In signing he or she must state the capacity in which he or she signs and the name of his or her firm where appropriate.

3.8 Where a legal representative has signed a statement of truth, his or her signature will be taken by the court as his or her statement –

 (a) that the client on whose behalf he or she has signed had authorised him or her to do so;

 (b) that before signing he or she had explained to the client that in signing the statement of truth he or she would be confirming the client's belief that the facts stated in the document were true; and

 (c) that before signing he or she had informed the client of the possible consequences to the client if it should subsequently appear that the client did not have an honest belief in the truth of those facts (see rule 17.6).

3.9 A legal representative who signs a statement of truth must print his or her full name clearly beneath his or her signature.

3.10 The individual who signs a statement of truth must sign in his or her own name and not that of his or her firm or employer.

3.11 The following are examples of the possible application of this practice direction describing who may sign a statement of truth verifying statements in documents other than a witness statement. These are only examples and not an indication of how a court might apply the practice direction to a specific situation.

Managing Agent

An agent who manages property or investments for the party cannot sign a statement of truth. It must be signed by the party or by the legal representative of the party.

Trusts

Where some or all of the trustees comprise a single party one, some or all of the trustees comprising the party may sign a statement of truth. The legal representative of the trustees may sign it.

Companies

Paragraphs 3.4 and 3.5 apply. The word 'manager' will be construed in the context of the phrase 'a person holding a senior position' which it is used to define. The court will consider the size of the company and the importance and nature of the proceedings. It would expect the manager signing the statement of truth to have personal knowledge of the content of the document or to be responsible for those who have that knowledge of the content. A small company may not have a manager, apart from the directors, who holds a senior position. A large company will have many such managers. In a large company with specialist claims, insurance or legal departments the statement may be signed by the manager of such a department if he or she is responsible for handling the claim or managing the staff handling it.

Inability of persons to read or sign documents to be verified by a statement of truth

4.1 Where an application (being an application for a matrimonial order to which the pilot scheme referred to in Practice Direction 36D applies) contains a statement of truth with the printed name of a person who is unable to read or sign the document, the application must be accompanied by a certificate made by an authorised person.

4.2 An authorised person is a person able to administer oaths and take affidavits but need not be independent of the parties or their representatives.

4.3 The authorised person must certify –

  (a) that the content of the online application has been read to the person before completion of the statement of truth required by the online system;
  (b) that the person appeared to understand it and approved its content as accurate;
  (c) that the declaration of truth has been read to that person;
  (d) that that person appeared to understand the declaration and the consequences of making a false declaration; and
  (e) that that person confirmed in the presence of the authorised person that it was their belief that the contents of the application were true.

4.4 The form of the certificate is set out at the Annex to this Practice Direction.

Consequences of failure to verify

5.1 If a statement of case is not verified by a statement of truth, the statement of case will remain effective unless it is struck out, but a party may not rely on the contents of a statement of case as evidence until it has been verified by a statement of truth.

5.2 Any party may apply to the court for an order that unless within such period as the court may specify the statement of case is verified by the service of a statement of truth, the statement of case will be struck out.

5.3 The usual order for the costs of an application referred to in paragraph 5.2 will be that the costs be paid by the party who had failed to verify, in any event and immediately.

Penalty

6 Attention is drawn to rule 17.6 which sets out the consequences of verifying a statement of case containing a false statement without an honest belief in its truth, and to the procedures set out in Chapter 5 of Part 37 and in paragraphs 4.1 to 4.7 of Practice Direction 37A (Applications and proceedings in relation to contempt of court).

ANNEX

Certificate to be used where a person is unable to read or sign an application for a matrimonial order to which the pilot scheme in Practice Direction 36D applies.

> I certify that I [name and address of authorised person] have read the contents of the application and the statement of truth to the person whose name is printed under the statement of truth in the application, who appeared to understand (a) the application and approved its contents as accurate and (b) the statement of truth and the consequences of making a false statement, and orally confirmed that this was the case in my presence.

Commencement date: 7 August 2017.

PART 20
INTERIM REMEDIES AND SECURITIES FOR COSTS

Chapter 1
Interim Remedies

20.2 Orders for interim remedies

Page 1742.

Tobias v Tobias [2017] EWFC 46, [2017] All ER (D) 179 (Jun)

(Family Court, Mostyn J, 29 June 2017) Practice – Pre-trial or post-judgment relief. The Family Court provided guidance in relation to applications for freezing orders. In the present case, the husband's application for a freezing injunction was dismissed as, among other things, his application had been defective procedurally and substantively.

Background

The applicant husband was a tetraplegic and lived in a care home. His wife, the respondent, lived in the former matrimonial home (the property). The property was worth probably £650,000, but it was heavily charged in respect of a number of debts in favour of commercial creditors as well as the local authority for unpaid council tax. It was also subject to a notice of home rights under the Family Law Act 1996, in favour of the husband which was registered in December 2016. It was elementary that the property could not be sold without the consent of the husband while that notice was in place.

However, in May 2017, the husband made an ex parte application for a freezing order to the out-of-hours High Court judge. He was unable to explain what the emergency was that had required the use of that service. The out-of-hours High Court judge declined to make a freezing order. His order, which was headed to have been in the 'High Court of Justice' (but which certainly was not in the High Court of Justice, but was rather in the Family Court), provided that the husband's application for injunctive relief would be listed before the urgent applications judge. The witness statement in support of that application was a defective document in that it failed to specify that the property had already been heavily charged in favour of various creditors (it did, however, state that the husband had had the benefit of the home rights charge).

The urgent applications judge, in treating the husband's application as an application for a freezing order, did not make a freezing order but adjourned the matter to be heard inter partes. His order was also headed to have been in the 'High Court of Justice' (but which certainly was not in the High Court of Justice, but was rather in the Family Court).

At the inter partes hearing, the wife gave an undertaking that she would not dispose of 'any of the marital assets'. In recording that undertaking, the judge directed the matter to be determined finally before the present judge.

Issue and decision

Whether the husband's application for a freezing injunction should be allowed.

The following matters of principle arose:

First, an application for a freezing order should only be determined in the Family Court (see [8]–[9] of the judgment).

Secondly, a freezing order may be made at any level of the Family Court above the lay justices. A freezing injunction may not be granted by a lay justice in the Family Court; it could, therefore, be granted by a district judge, a circuit judge or a High Court judge. However, a search order could only be made by a judge of High Court level; therefore, inferentially, an application for a freezing injunction should ordinarily be heard by a judge of district judge level or, by virtue of an efficient allocation of business, by a judge of circuit judge level (see [9] of the judgment).

Thirdly, where there was power for a High Court judge sitting in the Family Court to hear a freezing injunction, the sort of case that should be heard at that level ought to accord to the criteria set out in the Statement on the Efficient Conduct of Financial Remedy Hearings (1 February 2016). Thus, if the application for a freezing injunction sought to freeze assets in excess of £15m, then it would be appropriate to approach a High Court judge. If the application sought to freeze assets in excess of £7.5m, and it was accompanied by the factors of complexity mentioned in the Efficiency Statement at paras 3(3)–(10), then it would be appropriate to approach a High Court judge. However, if the assets that were sought to be frozen did not, on any view, exceed £7.5m, then it would only be appropriate to approach a High Court judge if the application involved a novel and important point of law (see [10] of the judgment).

Fourthly, in respect of ex parte applications, irrespective of the subject matter of the proceedings or the terms of the order, a without notice application would normally be appropriate only if: (i) there was an emergency or other great urgency so that it was impossible to give any notice, however short or informal; or (ii) there was a real risk that, if alerted to what was proposed, if tipped off, the respondent would take steps in advance of the hearing to thwart the court's order or otherwise to defeat the ends of justice. That was particularly relevant where an application was sought to be made to the emergency out-of-hours judge. In such circumstances, the judge would be hearing the matter by telephone and probably would only have one or two pages of material. It was virtually impossible to conceive of any circumstances in any money case where it would be appropriate to approach the emergency out-of-hours judge for an injunction (see [11], [12] of the judgment).

In the present case, there had been no such urgency because, in effect, the husband had already frozen the property by the imposition of his home rights charge in December 2016. Further, the husband had not satisfied the requirement of full candour when he had made his application. The application had been defective procedurally and substantively; it had been procedurally defective in that it went to the wrong court, at the wrong time, for the wrong reasons. In the future, applications for freezing orders had to be made to the Family Court at district judge level, unless the criteria in the Efficiency Statement had justified it being heard at High Court judge level. There had been nothing in the present case, where the assets on any view were probably no more than half a million pounds, justifying relief from a High Court judge sitting in the Family Court (see [13] of the judgment).

L v K (freezing orders: principles and safeguards) [2013] All ER (D) 277 (Jun) applied.

Application dismissed.

Fitzrene Headley (instructed by JCS Solicitors, Hertfordshire) for the wife.

The husband was self-represented and attended by telephone.

PART III

PART 22
EVIDENCE

Chapter 1
General Rules

22.1 Power of court to control evidence

Page 1761.

Re B (A Child) [2017] EWCA Civ 1579, [2017] All ER (D) 100 (Oct)
(Court of Appeal, Civil Division, Sir James Munby P and King LJ, 18 October 2017) Family
proceedings – Orders in family proceedings. There were serious concerns about the judge's
approach to covert recordings, particularly that his guidance on applying for permission to rely
on covert recordings had not been an exercise appropriately undertaken by a circuit judge.
Accordingly, the Court of Appeal, Civil Division, allowed the appellant father's appeal to the
extent of setting aside the relevant part of the judge's order that his judgment be published
and, in its place, directed that the judgment was not to be made publicly available.

Background

The child was the subject of private law proceedings between her parents. The father, in
support of his case of deliberate alienation by the mother, sought to rely on covert recordings.
The judge admitted the recordings, but concluded that little weight should be given to them.
He made an order dealing with the substantive issues in the case and ordered his judgment be
published on the normal terms. The father appealed against the order for publication.

Issues and decisions

Whether it was appropriate for the judge's views as to the proper approach to covert recording
to be disseminated on the internet, available to the professionals and all those advising
parents, including McKenzie friends.

Broadly speaking, the judge's approach to the covert recordings had been in accordance with
the law as it stood and his reasoning in the ultimately decisive paragraphs dealing with the
present case had been unimpeachable. However, there were a number of serious concerns.

First, the judge's conclusion, that the covert recording of conversations with the intention of
using that material as evidence was the antithesis of transparency and that, as a general
principle, the Family Court should deprecate and strongly discourage such making of covert
recordings, did not necessarily follow from the premise, either as a matter of logic or as a
matter of law. Further, the general principle enunciated was far too sweeping and, expressed
in the unnuanced terms, potentially misleading. A more accurate and nuanced formulation
would require consideration of such matters as who was doing the recording and why, and
who was being recorded.

Secondly, in relation to the part of the judge's judgment concerning applying for permission to
rely on covert recordings, the concerns related to the premise underlying the whole of his
analyses, namely that anyone seeking to rely on such material had to apply to the court for
permission. FPR 2010, r 22.1 undoubtedly empowered the court to control the evidence and to
exclude evidence that would otherwise be admissible. However, that was not the same as
saying that the court's permission was required before lawful, relevant and otherwise
admissible evidence could be adduced. That was a matter that required more detailed
analysis, including of the FPR, before it could safely be concluded that what the judge had
said was correct.

Furthermore, the judge had gone on to set out guidance as to how such an application should
proceed. He had addressed matters that he had not needed to in order to decide the case
before him fairly and justly. He had embarked on the whole exercise in a case where, because
both the parents had appeared in person, he had not had the benefit of sustained, professional
and adversarial argument. Most fundamentally, it had not been an exercise appropriately
undertaken by a circuit judge.

Finally, it had not been an appropriate objective in a case such as the present for the judge to
devote so much time and resource in order to stimulate discussion.

Accordingly, the least inappropriate and unattractive of the alternatives was to direct that the judge's judgment was not to be published (see [19]–[24], [33], [36] of the judgment).

The appeal would be allowed to the extent of setting aside the relevant part of the judge's order and, in its place, directing that the judgment was not to be made publicly available. Further, the Family Justice Council would be invited to consider the whole question of covert recording from a multidisciplinary viewpoint (see [33], [35], [36] of the judgment).

The father appeared in person, assisted by a McKenzie friend.

The mother did not appear and was not represented.

Victoria Clifford for the child's guardian.

PART 33
ENFORCEMENT

Section 1
Enforcement of Orders for the Payment of Money

33.1 Application

Page 1927.

New commentary has been provided to sit at the beginning of the note headed 'an application … to enforce an order made in family proceedings' (r 33.1(1)):

> The undoubted jurisdiction in an appropriately exceptional case to prevent a litigant from proceeding with a variation application or appeal until he has complied with an existing court order, while not directly a form of enforcement, may have that effect (*Mubarak v Mubarak* [2007] 1 FLR 722, FD). Such an order is not a breach of ECHR, Art 6 (*Mubarik v UK* [2009] ECHR 1437).

> Similarly, where a judge, correctly anticipating that a lump sum order would not be complied with, adjourned an application for a pension sharing order and subsequently ordered a larger pension share than he would otherwise have done (on the basis that the corresponding part of the lump sum order would not be enforced), this was an entirely legitimate exercise: *Amin v Amin* [2017] EWCA Civ 1114.

33.3 How to apply

Page 1928.

The note headed 'such means of enforcement as the court may consider appropriate' (r 33.3(2)(b)) has been updated to read:

> 'such means of enforcement as the court may consider appropriate' (r 33.3(2)(b))—This provision will result in an order to attend court for questioning to which certain provisions of CPR 1998, Pt 71 will apply. It should be noted that this provision is separate and distinct from the procedure for obtaining information from judgment debtors, which is also available in family proceedings (see r 33.23). As was pointed out by Thorpe LJ in *Corbett v Corbett* [2003] 2 FLR 385, CA, at [32], the intention of this provision is that it should be 'the issue of an enforcement summons to a … judge who would be empowered to apply whatever power or remedy seemed most likely to yield satisfaction and conclusion'. As it is directed to the court considering what means of enforcement are appropriate, the questioning should take place before a judge, who may make an attachment of earnings order, direct the issue of a warrant of control, or make a charging order or third party debt order (as was done in *Kaur v Randhawa* [2015] EWHC 1592 (Fam) where the interim stage of the normal procedure was dispensed with) without further formality or fee; or before lay justices, who may make an attachment of earnings order. As lay justices cannot issue warrants of control or make charging orders or third party debt orders, the case will need to be reallocated to a District Judge if those remedies are thought appropriate. Note that information secured under compulsion in this way cannot be used as the basis for committal, although disclosed documents can be (*Mohan v Mohan* [2014] 1 FLR 717, CA).

> If the respondent fails to attend, as CPR 1998, r 71.8 is not incorporated into this rule, the most appropriate way of securing attendance is for a notice of hearing to be personally served, with a

warning that the court may invoke its powers to deal with the defaulter as a contemnor. If there is still no attendance, a bench warrant may be issued. As to the power of a Family Court judge (including a bench of lay justices) to issue a bench warrant, consider the analysis of HHJ Birss (as he then was) in *Westwood v Knight* [2012] EWPCC 14, starting at [136], and the commentary in previous editions of this work, as approved by Peter Jackson J in *Re K (REMO – Power of Magistrates to Issue Bench Warrant)* [2017] EWFC 27.

Re K (REMO – Power of Magistrates to Issue Bench Warrant) [2017] EWFC 27, [2017] All ER (D) 156 (May)

(Family Court, Peter Jackson J, 12 May 2017) Minor – Maintenance. The Family Court held that s 31E of the Matrimonial and Family Proceedings Act 1984 authorised magistrates to issue a warrant to secure the attendance of an alleged maintenance defaulter who failed to appear in response to their summons. Magistrates' ability to carry out their work effectively would be stultified if they lacked the power to enforce their own orders for a party to attend before them.

Digest

In 2009, on the application of the mother of their child, the court in Poland ordered the father, K, to make monthly payments. Subsequently, no payments were made. In 2014, the mother, believing K to be living in the UK, made formal application to the relevant Polish authority for the enforcement of the order. That application was transmitted by the Reciprocal Enforcement of Maintenance Orders (REMO) process to the Family Court (the court). A larger number of unsuccessful efforts were made to trace and serve notices of hearings on K. The matter was transferred to the court for clarification of the extent of the magistrates' powers.

It fell to be determined whether magistrates sitting in the Family Court had the power to issue a warrant for the arrest of an alleged maintenance debtor who had failed to obey an order to attend for questioning as to his means. Consideration was given to ss 31E and 38 of the Matrimonial and Family Proceedings Act 1984. Consideration was also given to the decision in *Westwood v Knight* [2012] All ER (D) 189 (May) (*Westwood v Knight*).

The court ruled:

Section 31E of the Act stated, among other things, that in any proceedings in the Family Court, the court might make any order that could be made by the High Court if the proceedings had been in the High Court, or that could be made by the County Court if the proceedings had been in the County Court. In *Westwood v Knight*, the judge concluded that s 38(1) of the Act enabled him to issue a bench warrant after finding the absent defendant to be in contempt. The conclusion to be drawn in the present case was that s 31E of the Act, by analogy with s 38 of the Act, provided all judges of the Family Court with the power to issue a warrant to secure attendance. Section 31E authorised magistrates to issue a warrant to secure the attendance of an alleged maintenance defaulter who had failed to appear in response to their summons. That conclusion harmonised with the reality. Magistrates were full judges of the Family Court, performing an indispensable role, and their powers were subject only to the distribution of cases under the allocation rules. Their ability to carry out their work effectively would be stultified if they lacked the power to enforce their own orders for a party to attend before them (see [15]–[17], [19] of the judgment).

Westwood v Knight [2012] All ER (D) 189 (May) applied.

Practice Direction 36D –
Pilot Scheme: Procedure for Using an Online System to Generate Applications in Certain Proceedings for a Matrimonial Order

Page 1980.

FPR PD36D is amended as follows:

- in para 1.2(e), '28 July' is substituted by '27 October' (Commencement date: 27 July 2017);
- after para 4.2, there is inserted new paras 4A.1 and 4A.2 (Commencement date: 7 August 2017); and
- after para 5.4, there is inserted new paras 6.1–6.5 (Commencement date: 7 August 2017).

FPR PD36D is thereby amended to read:

PART III

Practice Direction 36D –
Pilot Scheme: Procedure for Using an Online System to Generate Applications in Certain Proceedings for a Matrimonial Order

This Practice Direction supplements rule 36.2 FPR (Transitional arrangements and pilot schemes).

Scope and interpretation

1.1 This Practice Direction is made under rule 36.2 FPR and sets up a Pilot Scheme to allow for certain applications to be filled in via an online process.

1.2 The Pilot Scheme applies to applications where all of the following conditions are met:

(a) the application is for a matrimonial order which is a decree of divorce made under section 1 of the 1973 Act;

(b) access to the online system for making such applications is permitted;

(c) all stages of the process provided for in the online system can be fully completed;

(d) the application is started in the family court; and

(e) the application is filed in the period commencing 25 January 2017 and ending 27 October 2017.

1.3 In this Practice Direction, 'the online system' means Her Majesty's Courts and Tribunal Service's online system to allow for specified stages in for matrimonial proceedings to be dealt with online.

Purpose of the Pilot Scheme

2.1 The purpose of this Pilot Scheme is to assess new practices and procedures to allow for certain applications for certain matrimonial orders to be generated via the online system. For the purposes of this Pilot Scheme, once the application has been generated the applicant will need to save or print off the generated application. It will then need to be filed at court, in accordance with the procedure currently provided for in the FPR and Practice Directions. It is intended that future Practice Directions will establish other Pilot Schemes which will allow for later stages in matrimonial proceedings to take place via the online system, for example for making the application online.

Modification of the FPR and Practice Directions during the operation of the Pilot Scheme

3.1 During the operation of the Pilot Scheme, the FPR and the Practice Directions supporting the FPR will apply to cases falling within the Pilot Scheme as modified by paragraphs 4.1 to 5.4.

Modification of Part 5 FPR

4.1 For rule 5.1, substitute –

'5.1 Where the Pilot Scheme referred to in Practice Direction 36D applies, the applicant must –

    (a) complete all sections of the application process set out in the online system referred to in that Practice Direction;

    (b) print or save the resulting application form which is generated by the online system;

    (c) when filing that application, include all of the information, including any additional documents, that the online system requires to be included.'.

4.2 Omit rule 5.2.

Modification of Part 17 FPR

4A.1 In rule 17.2(6), for 'The statement of truth' substitute 'Subject to paragraph (6A), the statement of truth'.

4A.2 After rule 17.2(6) insert –

'(6A) Where a statement of truth is included in an application for a matrimonial order to which the pilot scheme referred to in Practice Direction 36D applies –

    (a) the applicant must file with the court an application which includes the name of the person who the online system requires to sign a statement of truth printed underneath the statement of truth; and

    (b) the court may require the applicant to produce a copy of the application containing the signature of the person referred to in sub-paragraph (a) at a later date.'

Modification of PD7A

5.1 For paragraph 1.1, substitute –

'1.1 Where the pilot scheme referred to in Practice Direction 36D applies, an application for a matrimonial order must be made in the form generated by the online system referred to in that Practice Direction. The online system sets out the documents which must accompany the application.'.

5.2 For paragraph 1.2 substitute –

'1.2 The application must be completed according to the detailed guidance contained in the online system. It is especially important that the particulars provide evidence to show why the applicant is entitled to a decree of divorce. The particulars should, however, be as concise as possible consistent with providing the necessary evidence.'.

5.3 In paragraph 3.1 –

(a)   for the heading and the first sentence of paragraph 3.1 substitute –

'Proof of marriage

3.1 The online system referred to in Practice Direction 36D sets out the documents which must accompany the application for a matrimonial order.';

(b)   in the second sentence of paragraph 3.1 omit 'or civil partnership';
(c)   in sub-paragraph (a)(i) –
    (i)   for 'marriage or civil partnership to' substitute 'marriage to'; and
    (ii) omit 'or civil partnership registration'; and
(d)   in sub-paragraph (a)(ii), omit 'or civil partnership registration'.

5.4 In paragraph 4.1 –

(a)   for 'An applicant for a matrimonial or civil partnership order' substitute –

'Where the pilot scheme referred to in Practice Direction 36D applies, an applicant'; and

(b)   omit 'form'.

Modification of Practice Direction 17A

6.1 Omit paragraphs 1.5 and 2.3.

6.2 In the heading to paragraph 3.1 and in paragraphs 3.1, 3.7, 3.8 and 3.10 references to 'sign', 'signs', 'signed' and 'signing' are to be read as references to the name of the person being, or having been, printed under the statement of truth included in an application for a matrimonial order to which the pilot scheme referred to in Practice Direction 36D applies.

6.3 For paragraph 4.1 substitute –

'4.1 Where an application (being an application for a matrimonial order to which the pilot scheme referred to in Practice Direction 36D applies) contains a statement of truth with the printed name of a person who is unable to read or sign the document, the application must be accompanied by a certificate made by an authorised person.'

6.4 In paragraph 4.3 –

(a)   for sub-paragraph (a) substitute 'that the content of the online application has been read to the person before completion of the statement of truth required by the online system;'; and
(b)   for sub-paragraph (e) substitute 'that that person confirmed in the presence of the authorised person that it was their belief that the contents of the application were true.'

6.5 For the Annex substitute –

'Certificate to be used where a person is unable to read or sign an application for a matrimonial order to which the pilot scheme in Practice Direction 36D applies.

I certify that I [name and address of authorised person] have read the contents of the application and the statement of truth to the person whose name is printed under the statement of truth in the application, who appeared to understand (a) the application and approved its contents as accurate and (b) the statement of truth and the consequences of making a false statement, and orally confirmed that this was the case in my presence.'.

40.5 Interim charging order

Page 2023.

New commentary has been provided to accompany FPR 2010, r 40.5:

'**will initially be dealt with by the court without a hearing**' (r 40.5(1))—However, in *Veluppillai v Veluppillai* [2016] 2 FLR 681, FD and *Green v Adams* [2017] EWFC 24, Mostyn J asserted that he could make a final charging order without notice or any other formality to enforce an order he was making.

Civil Procedure Rules 1998, SI 1998/3132

PART 3
THE COURT'S CASE AND COSTS MANAGEMENT POWERS

Section I
Case Management

3.1 The court's general powers of management

Page 2035.

By virtue of the Civil Procedure (Amendment No 2) Rules 2017, in CPR 1998, r 3.1, after para (2)(b) there is inserted a new sub-para (bb) and after para (3) there is inserted a new para (3A). Rule 3.1 is thereby amended to read:

3.1 The court's general powers of management

(1) The list of powers in this rule is in addition to any powers given to the court by any other rule or practice direction or by any other enactment or any powers it may otherwise have.

(2) Except where these Rules provide otherwise, the court may –

   (a) extend or shorten the time for compliance with any rule, practice direction or court order (even if an application for extension is made after the time for compliance has expired);
   (b) adjourn or bring forward a hearing;
   (bb) require that any proceedings in the High Court be heard by a Divisional Court of the High Court;
   (c) require a party or a party's legal representative to attend the court;
   (d) hold a hearing and receive evidence by telephone or by using any other method of direct oral communication;
   (e) direct that part of any proceedings (such as a counterclaim) be dealt with as separate proceedings;
   (f) stay$^{(GL)}$ the whole or part of any proceedings or judgment either generally or until a specified date or event;
   (g) consolidate proceedings;
   (h) try two or more claims on the same occasion;
   (i) direct a separate trial of any issue;
   (j) decide the order in which issues are to be tried;

(k)   exclude an issue from consideration;

(l)   dismiss or give judgment on a claim after a decision on a preliminary issue;

(ll)   order any party to file and exchange a costs budget;

(m)   take any other step or make any other order for the purpose of managing the case and furthering the overriding objective, including hearing an Early Neutral Evaluation with the aim of helping the parties settle the case.

(3)   When the court makes an order, it may –

(a)   make it subject to conditions, including a condition to pay a sum of money into court; and

(b)   specify the consequence of failure to comply with the order or a condition.

(3A)   Where the court has made a direction in accordance with paragraph (2)(bb) the proceedings shall be heard by a Divisional Court of the High Court and not by a single judge.

(4)   Where the court gives directions it will take into account whether or not a party has complied with the Practice Direction (Pre-Action Conduct) and any relevant pre-action protocol$^{(GL)}$.

(5)   The court may order a party to pay a sum of money into court if that party has, without good reason, failed to comply with a rule, practice direction or a relevant pre-action protocol.

(6)   When exercising its power under paragraph (5) the court must have regard to –

(a)   the amount in dispute; and

(b)   the costs which the parties have incurred or which they may incur.

(6A)   Where a party pays money into court following an order under paragraph (3) or (5), the money shall be security for any sum payable by that party to any other party in the proceedings.

(7)   A power of the court under these Rules to make an order includes a power to vary or revoke the order.

(8)   The court may contact the parties from time to time in order to monitor compliance with directions. The parties must respond promptly to any such enquiries from the court.

Commencement date: 1 October 2017.

PART 7
HOW TO START PROCEEDINGS – THE CLAIM FORM

Practice Direction 7A – How to Start Proceedings – The Claim Form

Page 2042.

As part of CPR Update 92 (NB the PD-making document for Update 92 was only in draft form at the time of going to press), as of 1 October 2017, in PD7A, para 2.5 is substituted by:

2.5   A claim relating to Business and Property work (which includes any of the matters specified in paragraph 1 of Schedule 1 to the Senior Courts Act 1981 and which includes any work under the jurisdiction of the Business and Property Courts, may, subject to any enactment, rule or practice direction, be dealt with in the High

Court or in the County Court. The claim form should, if issued in the High Court, be marked in the top right hand corner 'Business and Property Courts' and, if issued in the County Court, be marked 'Business and Property work' (save, in the County Court, for those areas listed in paragraph 4.2 of the Business and Property Courts Practice Direction as exceptions).

(For the equity jurisdiction of the County Court, see section 23 of the County Courts Act 1984.)

PART 47
PROCEDURE FOR DETAILED ASSESSMENT OF COSTS AND DEFAULT PROVISIONS

Section II
Costs Payable by one Party to Another – Commencement of Detailed Assessment Proceedings

47.6 Commencement of detailed assessment proceedings

Page 2168.

By virtue of the Civil Procedure (Amendment No 2) Rules 2017, in CPR 1998, r 47.6, in para (1) sub-para (b) is substituted and in sub-para (c), 'if a costs management order has been made,' is substituted by 'if required by Practice Direction 47,' and in para (2) 'if a costs management order has been made,' is substituted by 'if required by Practice Direction 47,'. Rule 47.6 is thereby amended to read:

47.6 Commencement of detailed assessment proceedings

(1) Detailed assessment proceedings are commenced by the receiving party serving on the paying party –

    (a)   notice of commencement in the relevant practice form;

    (b)   a copy or copies of the bill of costs, as required by Practice Direction 47; and

    (c)   if required by Practice Direction 47, a breakdown of the costs claimed for each phase of the proceedings.

(Rule 47.7 sets out the period for commencing detailed assessment proceedings)

(2) The receiving party must also serve a copy of the notice of commencement, the bill and, if required by Practice Direction 47, the breakdown on any other relevant persons specified in Practice Direction 47.

(3) A person on whom a copy of the notice of commencement is served under paragraph (2) is a party to the detailed assessment proceedings (in addition to the paying party and the receiving party).

(Practice Direction 47 deals with –
other documents which the party must file when requesting detailed assessment;
the court's powers where it considers that a hearing may be necessary;
the form of a bill; and
the length of notice which will be given if a hearing date is fixed.)

(Paragraphs 7B.2 to 7B.7 of the Practice Direction – Civil Recovery Proceedings contain provisions about detailed assessment of costs in relation to civil recovery orders.)

Commencement date: 1 October 2017.

Practice Direction 47 – Procedure for Detailed Assessment of Costs and Default Provisions

Venue for Detailed Assessment Proceedings: Rule 47.4

Page 2177.

As part of Update 90, as of 9 August 2017, PD47, paragraph 4.2(1) is amended so as to omit the reference to Woolwich. The paragraph now reads:

4.2 (1)   This paragraph applies where the appropriate office is any of the following the County Court hearing centres: Barnet, Brentford, Bromley, Central London, Clerkenwell and Shoreditch, Croydon, Edmonton, Ilford, Kingston, Lambeth, Mayors and City of London, Romford, Uxbridge, Wandsworth and Willesden.

Commencement of Detailed Assessment Proceedings: Rule 47.6

Page 2178.

As part of Update 92 (NB the PD-making document for Update 92 was only in draft form at the time of going to press), as of 1 October 2017, PD47, para 5.1 is substituted by:

5.1 In the circumstances provided for in this paragraph, bills of costs for detailed assessment must be in electronic spreadsheet format and compliant with paragraphs 5.2 to 5.4 ('electronic bills') while in all other circumstances bills of costs may be electronic bills or may be on paper ('paper bills') and compliant with paragraphs 5.12 to 5.26. Precedents A, B, C and D in the Schedule of Costs Precedents annexed to this Practice Direction are model forms of paper bills of costs for detailed assessment. The circumstances in which bills of costs must be electronic bills are that –

(a)   the case is a Part 7 multi-track claim, except –
    (i)   for cases in which the proceedings are subject to fixed costs or scale costs;
    (ii)   cases in which the receiving party is unrepresented; or
    (iii)   where the court has otherwise ordered; and
(b)   the bills of costs relate to costs recoverable between the parties for work undertaken after 6 April 2018 ('the Transition Date').

5.A1 A model electronic bill in pdf format is annexed to this Practice Direction as Precedent S and a link to an electronic spreadsheet version of the same model bill is provided in paragraph 5.3 of this Practice Direction.

5.A2 Electronic bills may be in either the spreadsheet format which can be found online at http://www.justice.gov.uk/courts/procedure-rules/civil or any other spreadsheet format which –

(a)   reports and aggregates costs based on the phases, tasks, activities and expenses defined in Schedule 2 to this Practice Direction;
(b)   reports summary totals in a form comparable to Precedent S;
(c)   allows the user to identify, in chronological order, the detail of all the work undertaken in each phase;
(d)   automatically recalculates intermediate and overall summary totals if input data is changed;
(e)   contains all calculations and reference formulae in a transparent manner so as to make its full functionality available to the court and all other parties.

PART III

5.A3 The provisions of paragraphs 5.7 to 5.21 of this Practice Direction shall apply to electronic bills insofar as they are not inconsistent with the form and content of Precedent S. Where those paragraphs require or recommend division of the bill into parts, electronic bills (unless the format of the bill already provides the requisite information, for example in identifying the costs within each phase) should incorporate a summary in a form comparable to the "Funding and Parts Table" in Precedent S to provide the information that would otherwise be provided by its division into parts.

5.A4 Where a bill of costs otherwise falls within paragraph 5.1(a) but work was done both before and after the Transition Date, a party may serve and file either a paper bill or an electronic bill in respect of work done before that date and must serve and file an electronic bill in respect of work done after that date.

In para 5.1A, the draft PD-making document states that 'When electronic bills are served' to 'hard copy,' is to be substituted by 'Whenever electronic bills are served or filed, they must also be served or filed in hard copy,' and 'Precedent Q' to the end of that sentence is omitted. This does not fit with the pre-existing version of para 5.1A. However, the minutes of the CPR Committee meeting held on 5 May 2017 suggest that para 5.1A, in addition to some renumbering, is to be revised to read:

5.1A When electronic bills are served or filed at the court, they must be served or filed in hard copy, in a manageable paper format as shown in the pdf version of Precedent S. A copy of the full electronic spreadsheet version must at the same time be provided to the paying party and filed at the court by email or other electronic means.

In addition, in para 5.2, 'The receiving party must' is substituted by 'On commencing detailed assessment proceedings, the receiving party must', in sub-para (b), after 'a copy' there is inserted '(or, where paragraph 5.A4 applies, copies)' and para (f) is substituted. Paragraph 5.2 is thereby amended to read:

5.2 On commencing detailed assessment proceedings, the receiving party must serve on the paying party and all the other relevant persons the following documents –

   (a)   a notice of commencement in Form N252;

   (b)   a copy (or, where paragraph 5.A4 applies, copies) of the bill of costs;

   (c)   copies of the fee notes of counsel and of any expert in respect of fees claimed in the bill;

   (d)   written evidence as to any other disbursement which is claimed and which exceeds £500;

   (e)   a statement giving the name and address for service of any person upon whom the receiving party intends to serve the notice of commencement;

   (f)   if a costs management order has been made (and if the same information is not already fully provided in an electronic bill), a breakdown of the costs claimed for each phase of the proceedings. Precedent Q in the Schedule of Costs Precedents annexed to this Practice Direction is a model form of breakdown of the costs claimed for each phase of the proceedings.

And in para 5.6(a), 'the bill of costs' is substituted by 'a paper bill' so that para 5.6 reads:

5.6 Where –

   (a)   a paper bill is capable of being copied electronically; and

   (b)   before the detailed assessment hearing,

a paying party requests an electronic copy of the bill, the receiving party must supply the paying party with a copy in its native format (for example, in Excel or an equivalent) free of charge not more than 7 days after receipt of the request.

Detailed Assessment Hearing: Rule 47.14

Page 2184.
As part of Update 92, as of 1 October 2017, in PD47, in para 13.2 in sub-para (j) after 'giving the name,' there is inserted 'e-mail address,' and in sub-para (l) 'LSC', in each place it appears, is substituted by 'LAA'. (NB the PD-making document for Update 92 was only in draft form at the time of going to press.) Paragraph 13.2 is thereby amended to read:

13.2 The request for a detailed assessment hearing must be in Form N258. The request must be accompanied by –

(a) a copy of the notice of commencement of detailed assessment proceedings;
(b) a copy of the bill of costs,
(c) the document giving the right to detailed assessment (see paragraph 13.3 below);
(d) a copy of the points of dispute, annotated as necessary in order to show which items have been agreed and their value and to show which items remain in dispute and their value;
(e) as many copies of the points of dispute so annotated as there are persons who have served points of dispute;
(f) a copy of any replies served;
(g) copies of all orders made by the court relating to the costs which are to be assessed;
(h) copies of the fee notes and other written evidence as served on the paying party in accordance with paragraph 5.2 above;
(i) where there is a dispute as to the receiving party's liability to pay costs to the legal representatives who acted for the receiving party, any agreement, letter or other written information provided by the legal representative to the client explaining how the legal representative's charges are to be calculated;
(j) a statement signed by the receiving party or the legal representative giving the name, e-mail address, address for service, reference and telephone number and fax number, if any, of –
(i) the receiving party;
(ii) the paying party;
(iii) any other person who has served points of dispute or who has given notice to the receiving party under paragraph 5.5(1)(b) above;
and giving an estimate of the length of time the detailed assessment hearing will take;
(k) where the application for a detailed assessment hearing is made by a party other than the receiving party, such of the documents set out in this paragraph as are in the possession of that party;
(l) where the court is to assess the costs of an assisted person or LAA funded client or person to whom civil legal aid services (within the meaning of Part 1 of the Legal Aid, Sentencing and Punishment of Offenders Act 2012) are provided under arrangement made for the purposes of that Part of that Act –
(i) the legal aid certificate, LAA certificate, the certificate recording the determination of the Direction of Legal Aid Casework and relevant

PART III

amendment certificates, any authorities and any certificates of discharge or revocation or withdrawal;

   (ii)   a certificate, in Precedent F(3) of the Schedule of Costs Precedents;

  (iii)   if that person has a financial interest in the detailed assessment hearing and wishes to attend, the postal address of that person to which the court will send notice of any hearing;

  (iv)   if the rates payable out of the LAA fund or by the Lord Chancellor under Part 1 of the Legal Aid, Sentencing and Punishment of Offenders Act 2012 are prescribed rates, a schedule to the bill of costs setting out all the items in the bill which are claimed against other parties calculated at the legal aid prescribed rates with or without any claim for enhancement: (further information as to this schedule is set out in paragraph 17 of this Practice Direction);

   (v)   a copy of any default costs certificate in respect of costs claimed in the bill of costs;

  (m)   if a costs management order has been made, a breakdown of the costs claimed for each phase of the proceedings.

Provisional Assessment: Rule 47.15

Page 2186.

As part of Update 92, as of 1 October 2017, in PD47, para 14.3(c), 'an additional copy of the bill, including a statement of the costs' is substituted by 'an additional copy of any paper bill and a statement of the costs'. (NB the PD-making document for Update 92 was only in draft form at the time of going to press.) Paragraph 14.3 is thereby amended to read:

14.3 In cases falling within rule 47.15, when the receiving party files a request for a detailed assessment hearing, that party must file –

   (a)   the request in Form N258;

   (b)   the documents set out at paragraphs 8.3 and 13.2 of this Practice Direction;

   (c)   an additional copy of any paper bill and a statement of the costs claimed in respect of the detailed assessment drawn on the assumption that there will not be an oral hearing following the provisional assessment;

   (d)   the offers made (those marked 'without prejudice save as to costs' or made under Part 36 must be contained in a sealed envelope, marked 'Part 36 or similar offers', but not indicating which party or parties have made them);

   (e)   completed Precedent G (points of dispute and any reply).

Detailed Assessment Procedure Where Costs are Payable out of the Community Legal Service Fund or by the Lord Chancellor under Part 1 of the Legal Aid, Sentencing and Punishment of Offenders Act 2012: Rule 47.18

Page 2188.

As part of Update 92, as of 1 October 2017, in PD47, para 17 is amended as follows:

- in para 17.2(1) –
  - in para (f), 'LSC certificates' is substituted by 'LAA certificates'; and
  - in para (g), 'fax number' and 'where available' are omitted;
- in para 17.6—
  - 'LSC', in each place it appears, is substituted by 'LAA'; and
  - 'The schedule should' to the end of the sentence is substituted by:

'If on paper (a "paper schedule") the schedule should follow as closely as possible Precedent E of the Schedule of Costs Precedents annexed to this Practice Direction.

If an electronic bill of costs is served on the other person an electronic schedule may, subject to paragraphs 17.7 and 17.8 below, be prepared and filed as if it were an electronic bill.'

- in para 17.8 –
  - in the first sentence, 'the schedule' is substituted by 'a paper schedule';
  - in the second sentence, 'The schedule' is substituted by 'The paper schedule'; and
  - after 'with any divisions in the bill of costs.' there is inserted:

'If the schedule is an electronic schedule, unless the format of the schedule already provides the requisite information it should incorporate a summary in a form comparable to the "Funding and Parts Table" in Precedent S to provide the information that would otherwise be provided by its division into parts.'.

- in para 17.9 –
  - 'contains additional columns setting' is substituted by 'sets';
  - 'LSC' is substituted by 'LAA'; and
  - 'the additional columns of the bill.' is substituted by 'the bill, shown separately from the costs claimed against other parties.';
- in para 17.10, 'LSC' is substituted by 'LAA'; and
- in para 17.11, 'LSC' is substituted by 'LAA'.

(NB the PD-making document for Update 92 was only in draft form at the time of going to press.) Paragraph 17 is thereby amended to read:

Detailed Assessment Procedure Where Costs are Payable out of the Community Legal Service Fund or by the Lord Chancellor under Part 1 of the Legal Aid, Sentencing and Punishment of Offenders Act 2012: Rule 47.18

17.1 The time for requesting a detailed assessment under rule 47.18 is within 3 months after the date when the right to detailed assessment arose.

17.2

(1) The request for a detailed assessment of costs must be in Form N258A. The request must be accompanied by –

(a) a copy of the bill of costs;

(b) the document giving the right to detailed assessment (see paragraph 13.3 above);

(c) copies of all orders made by the court relating to the costs which are to be assessed;

(d) copies of any fee notes of counsel and any expert in respect of fees claimed in the bill;

(e) written evidence as to any other disbursement which is claimed and which exceeds £500;

(f) the legal aid certificates, LAA certificates, certificates recording the determinations of the Direction of Legal Aid Casework, any relevant amendment certificates, any authorities and any certificates of discharge, revocation or withdrawal and;

(g) a statement signed by the legal representative giving the representative's name, address for service, reference, telephone number, e-mail address and, if the assisted person has a financial interest in the detailed assessment and wishes to attend, giving the postal address of that person, to which the court will send notice of any hearing.

(2) The relevant papers in support of the bill as described in paragraph 13.12 must only be lodged if requested by the costs officer.

17.3 Where the court has provisionally assessed a bill of costs it will send to the legal representative a notice, in Form N253 annexed to this practice direction, of the amount of costs which the court proposes to allow together with the bill itself. The legal representative should, if the provisional assessment is to be accepted, then complete the bill.

17.4 If the solicitor whose bill it is, or any other party wishes to make an application in the detailed assessment proceedings, the provisions of Part 23 applies.

17.5 It is the responsibility of the legal representative to complete the bill by entering in the bill the correct figures allowed in respect of each item, recalculating the summary of the bill appropriately and completing the Community Legal Service assessment certificate (Form EX80A).

Costs Payable by the Legal Services Commission or Lord Chancellor at Prescribed Rates

17.6 Where the costs of an assisted person or LAA funded client or person to whom civil legal services (within the meaning of Part 1 of the Legal Aid, Sentencing and Punishment of Offenders Act 2012) are provided under arrangements made for the purposes of that Part of that Act are payable by another person but costs can be claimed against the LAA or Lord Chancellor at prescribed rates (with or without enhancement), the solicitor of the assisted person or LAA funded client or person to whom civil legal services are provided must file a legal aid/ LAA schedule in accordance with paragraph 13.2(l) above. If on paper (a 'paper schedule') the schedule should follow as closely as possible Precedent E of the Schedule of Costs Precedents annexed to this Practice Direction. If an electronic bill of costs is served on the other person an electronic schedule may, subject to paragraphs 17.7 and 17.8 below, be prepared and filed as if it were an electronic bill.

17.7 The schedule must set out by reference to the item numbers in the bill of costs, all the costs claimed as payable by another person, but the arithmetic in the schedule should claim those items at prescribed rates only (with or without any claim for enhancement).

17.8 Where there has been a change in the prescribed rates during the period covered by the bill of costs, a paper schedule (as opposed to the bill) should be divided into separate parts, so as to deal separately with each change of rate. The paper schedule must also be divided so as to correspond with any divisions in the bill of costs. If the schedule is an electronic schedule, unless the format of the schedule already provides the requisite information it should incorporate a summary in a form comparable to the 'Funding and Parts Table' in Precedent S to provide the information that would otherwise be provided by its division into parts.

17.9 If the bill of costs sets out costs claimed against the LAA or Lord Chancellor only, the schedule may be set out in a separate document or, alternatively, may be included in the bill, shown separately from the costs claimed against other parties.

17.10 The detailed assessment of the legal aid/LAA schedule will take place immediately after the detailed assessment of the bill of costs but on occasions, the court may decide to conduct the detailed assessment of the legal aid/LAA schedule separately from any detailed assessment of the bill of costs. This will occur, for example, where a default costs certificate is obtained as between the parties but that certificate is not set aside at the time of the detailed assessment of the legal aid costs.

17.11 Where costs have been assessed at prescribed rates it is the responsibility of the legal representative to enter the correct figures allowed in respect of each item and to recalculate the summary of the legal aid/LAA schedule.

Detailed Assessment Procedure Where Costs are Payable out of a Fund or by the Lord Chancellor under Part 1 of the Legal Aid, Sentencing and Punishment of Offenders Act 2012: Rule 47.19

Page 2189.

As part of Update 92, as of 1 October 2017, in PD47, para 18.3(a), after 'giving his name,' there is inserted 'e-mail address' and after 'address for service, reference' there is inserted 'and'. (NB the PD-making document for Update 92 was only in draft form at the time of going to press.) Paragraph 18.3 is thereby amended to read:

18.3 The request for a detailed assessment of costs out of the fund should be in Form N258B, be accompanied by the documents set out at paragraph 17.2(1) (a) to (e) and the following –

    (a)   a statement signed by the receiving party giving his name, e-mail address, address for service, reference and telephone number,

    (b)   a statement of the postal address of any person who has a financial interest in the outcome of the assessment; and

    (c)   if a person having a financial interest is a child or protected party, a statement to that effect.

PART 52
APPEALS

Section II
Permission to appeal – General

52.3 Permission to appeal

Page 2194.

By virtue of the Civil Procedure (Amendment No 2) Rules 2017, in CPR 1998, r 52.3(1)(a)(iii), after 'the Children Act 1989' there is inserted 'or section 119 of the Social Services and Well-being (Wales) Act 2014'. Rule 52.3 is thereby amended to read:

52.3 Permission to appeal

(1) An appellant or respondent requires permission to appeal –

    (a)   where the appeal is from a decision of a judge in the County Court or the High Court, or to the Court of Appeal from a decision of a judge in the family court, except where the appeal is against –
        (i)   a committal order;
        (ii)   a refusal to grant habeas corpus; or
        (iii)   a secure accommodation order made under section 25 of the Children Act 1989 or section 119 of the Social Services and Well-being (Wales) Act 2014; or

    (b)   as provided by Practice Directions 52A to 52E.

(Other enactments may provide that permission is required for particular appeals.)

(2) An application for permission to appeal may be made –

    (a)   to the lower court at the hearing at which the decision to be appealed was made; or

    (b)   to the appeal court in an appeal notice.

(Rule 52.12 sets out the time limits for filing an appellant's notice at the appeal court. Rule 52.13 sets out the time limits for filing a respondent's notice at the appeal court.

PART III

Any application for permission to appeal to the appeal court must be made in the appeal notice (see rules 52.12(1) and 52.13(3)).)

(3) Where the lower court refuses an application for permission to appeal –

(a) a further application for permission may be made to the appeal court; and
(b) the order refusing permission must specify –
    (i) the court to which any further application for permission should be made; and
    (ii) the level of judge who should hear the application.

Commencement date: 1 October 2017.

52.4 Determination of applications for permission to appeal to the County Court and High Court

Page 2197.

By virtue of the Civil Procedure (Amendment No 2) Rules 2017, in CPR 1998, r 52.4, in para (1), after 'oral hearing', 'except' is substituted by 'unless the court otherwise directs, or' and in para (4) 'Mercantile' is substituted by 'Circuit Commercial'. Rule 52.4 is thereby amended to read:

52.4 Determination of applications for permission to appeal to the County Court and High Court

(1) Where an application for permission to appeal is made to an appeal court other than the Court of Appeal, the appeal court will determine the application on paper without an oral hearing, unless the court otherwise directs, or as provided for under paragraph (2).

(2) Subject to paragraph (3) and except where a rule or practice direction provides otherwise, where the appeal court, without a hearing, refuses permission to appeal, the person seeking permission may request the decision to be reconsidered at an oral hearing.

(3) Where in the appeal court a judge of the High Court, a Designated Civil Judge or a Specialist Circuit Judge refuses permission to appeal without an oral hearing and considers that the application is totally without merit, the judge may make an order that the person seeking permission may not request the decision to be reconsidered at an oral hearing.

(4) For the purposes of paragraph (3), 'Specialist Circuit Judge' means any Circuit Judge in the County Court nominated to hear cases in the Circuit Commercial, Chancery or Technology and Construction Court lists.

(5) Rule 3.3(5) (party able to apply to set aside, etc, a decision made of court's own initiative) does not apply to an order made under paragraph (3) that the person seeking permission may not request the decision to be reconsidered at an oral hearing.

(6) A request under paragraph (2) must be filed within 7 days after service of the notice that permission has been refused.

Commencement date: 1 October 2017.

Practice Direction 52B – Appeals in the County Court and High Court

Table A: Table of appeal centres for each circuit

Page 2217.

As part of Update 90, as of 9 August 2017, PD74A, entries for Kettering, Bolton, Bury, Kendal, Oldham, Llangefni and Woolwich are omitted so that Table A now reads:

Circuit	Court	Appeal Centre
Midland	Birmingham CJC	Birmingham CJC
	Burton-upon-Trent	Nottingham
	Chesterfield	Nottingham
	Coventry	Coventry
	Derby	Nottingham
	Dudley	Walsall
	Hereford	Worcester
	Kidderminster	Worcester
	Leicester	Leicester
	Lincoln	Lincoln
	Mansfield	Nottingham
	Northampton	Northampton
	Nottingham	Nottingham
	Nuneaton	Coventry
	Redditch	Worcester
	Stafford	Stoke-on-Trent
	Stoke-on-Trent	Stoke-on-Trent
	Telford	Telford
	Walsall	Walsall
	Warwick	Coventry
	Wolverhampton	Walsall
	Worcester	Worcester
North East	Barnsley	Sheffield
	Bradford	Bradford
	Darlington	Teesside
	Doncaster	Sheffield
	Durham	Newcastle-upon-Tyne
	Gateshead	Newcastle-upon-Tyne
	Grimsby	Kingston-Upon-Hull
	Harrogate	Leeds
	Huddersfield	Bradford
	Kingston-Upon-Hull	Kingston-Upon-Hull
	Leeds	Leeds
	Newcastle-upon-Tyne	Newcastle-upon-Tyne
	North Shields	Newcastle-upon-Tyne

PART III

Circuit	Court	Appeal Centre
	Scarborough	Leeds
	Sheffield	Sheffield
	Skipton	Bradford
	South Shields	Newcastle-upon-Tyne
	Sunderland	Newcastle-upon-Tyne
	Teesside	Teesside
	Wakefield	Leeds
	York	Leeds
Northern	Barrow-in-Furness	Carlisle
	Birkenhead	Liverpool
	Blackburn	Preston
	Blackpool	Preston
	Bolton	Manchester CJC
	Burnley	Preston
	Carlisle	Carlisle
	Chester CJC	Chester CJC
	Crewe	Chester CJC
	Lancaster	Preston
	Liverpool	Liverpool
	Manchester CJC	Manchester CJC
	Preston	Preston
	St Helens	Liverpool
	Stockport	Manchester CJC
	West Cumbria	Carlisle
	Wigan	Liverpool
Wales	Aberystwyth	Swansea
	Blackwood	Cardiff CJC
	Caernarfon	Wrexham
	Cardiff	Cardiff CJC
	Carmarthen	Swansea
	Conwy & Colwyn	Wrexham
	Haverfordwest	Swansea
	Llanelli	Swansea
	Merthyr Tydfil	Cardiff CJC
	Mold	Wrexham
	Newport (Gwent)	Cardiff CJC
	Pontypridd	Cardiff CJC
	Port Talbot	Swansea
	Prestatyn	Wrexham
	Swansea	Swansea
	Welshpool & Newtown	Wrexham
	Wrexham	Wrexham

Circuit	Court	Appeal Centre
Western	Aldershot & Farnham	Winchester
	Barnstaple	Barnstaple
	Basingstoke	Winchester
	Bath	Bristol CJC
	Bodmin	Bodmin
	Bournemouth	Bournemouth
	Bristol	Bristol CJC
	Cheltenham	Bristol CJC
	Chippenham	Winchester
	Exeter	Exeter
	Gloucester	Bristol CJC
	Newport (Isle of Wight)	Winchester
	Plymouth	Plymouth
	Portsmouth	Portsmouth
	Salisbury	Winchester
	Southampton	Southampton
	Swindon	Swindon
	Taunton	Bristol CJC
	Torquay & Newton Abbot	Torquay & Newton Abbot
	Trowbridge	Trowbridge
	Truro	Truro
	Weston-Super-Mare	Bristol CJC
	Weymouth & Dorchester	Winchester
	Winchester	Winchester
	Yeovil	Bristol
South East	Banbury	Oxford
	Barnet	Barnet
	Basildon	Southend
	Bedford	Luton
	Brentford	Brentford
	Brighton	Brighton
	Bromley	Bromley
	Bury St Edmunds	Cambridge
	Cambridge	Cambridge
	Canterbury	Canterbury
	Central London CJC	Central London CJC
	Chelmsford	Southend
	Chichester	Chichester
	Clerkenwell & Shoreditch	Clerkenwell & Shoreditch
	Colchester	Southend
	Croydon	Croydon
	Dartford	Dartford
	Eastbourne	Eastbourne

Circuit	Court	Appeal Centre
	Edmonton	Edmonton
	Guildford	Guildford
	Hastings	Hastings
	Hertford	Luton
	High Wycombe	Oxford
	Horsham	Horsham
	Hove	Hove
	Ipswich	Norwich
	Kingston-upon-Thames	Kingston-upon-Thames
	Lambeth	Lambeth
	Lewes	Lewes
	Luton	Luton
	Maidstone	Maidstone
	Mayors and City	Mayors and City
	Medway	Medway
	Milton Keynes	Oxford
	Norwich	Norwich
	Oxford	Oxford
	Peterborough	Cambridge
	Reading	Oxford
	Romford	Romford
	Slough	Oxford
	Southend	Southend
	Staines	Staines
	Thanet	Thanet
	Uxbridge	Uxbridge
	Wandsworth	Wandsworth
	Watford	Watford
	Willesden	Willesden
	Worthing	Worthing

Practice Direction 52C – Appeals to the Court of Appeal

SECTION 2 – STARTING AN APPEAL TO THE COURT OF APPEAL

Filing the Appellant's Notice and accompanying documents

Page 2221.

As part of Update 92, as of 1 October 2017, in CPR PD52C, para 3(2), para (f) is omitted. (NB the PD-making document for Update 92 was only in draft form at the time of going to press.)

SECTION 4 – PROCEDURE WHERE PERMISSION TO APPEAL IS SOUGHT FROM THE COURT OF APPEAL

Appellant in receipt of services funded by the Legal Services Commission applying for permission to appeal

Page 2224.

As part of Update 92, as of 1 October 2017, in CPR PD52C, in para 17, in the heading and in both other places it occurs, 'Legal Services Commission' is substituted by 'Legal Aid Agency'. (NB the PD-making document for Update 92 was only in draft form at the time of going to press.) Paragraph 17 now reads:

Appellant in receipt of services funded by the Legal Aid Agency applying for permission to appeal

17 Where the appellant is in receipt of services funded by the Legal Aid Agency and permission to appeal has been refused by the court without a hearing, the appellant must send a copy of the court's reasons for refusing permission to the Legal Aid Agency as soon as it has been received.

PART III

PART 69
COURT'S POWER TO APPOINT A RECEIVER

Page 2279.

The commentary that appears at the beginning of CPR 1998, Pt 69 has been updated and extended so that it reads:

Note—The appointment of a receiver is a remedy that is occasionally useful (it may enable a judgment creditor to reach interests of the debtor that cannot be taken in execution by other means, such as a right to draw down a lump sum from a pension policy (*(1) Blight (2) Meredith (3) Lewis v Brewster* [2012] BPIR 476, ChD) but the expense means that it is seldom appropriate. Note also that if the application for the appointment of a receiver is made on short notice, the applicant has a duty to make full and candid disclosure: *Re BC Softwear Ltd*, Lawtel 4 May 2017 (HHJ Walden-Smith). See *Civil Court Service* (LexisNexis).

PART 73
CHARGING ORDERS, STOP ORDERS AND STOP NOTICES

73.10C Enforcement of charging order by sale

Page 2298.

The commentary headed 'the court may' (r 73.10C(1)) has been updated and extended so that it reads:

'the court may' (r 73.10C(1))—It sometimes seems to be assumed that a creditor is entitled to an order for sale under this provision as a matter of right, but this is not the case. In the common case where the property concerned is the debtor's home, the debtor's right to respect for his home under ECHR Art 8 must be balanced against the creditor's right to secure payment of his debt, as was emphasised in the ECtHR case of *Zehentner v Austria* [2009] ECHR 1119. The claimant's written evidence should address this issue.

In the case of the debtor's home, it is a draconian step to require a sale to satisfy a simple debt. It is rarely done, except in response to the debtor's contumelious neglect or refusal to pay; even then, the order will often be suspended on terms as to payment. It may be otherwise in the case of investment property. Where the order to be enforced is a maintenance order, the debtor's resources will have been taken into account when it was made and his neglect or refusal may thus be easier to demonstrate.

The fact that the value of the property charged significantly exceeds the judgment debt is not a reason for refusing a sale; it is 'just one of the considerations to be taken into account and not an overriding one'; *Packman Lucas Ltd v (1) Mentmore Towers Ltd (2) Charles Street Holdings Ltd* [2010] EWHC 1037 (TCC). Thus in *Re Shri Guru Ravidass Sabha Southall* [2017] EWHC 1255 (Ch), the sale of three properties worth an estimated £1.3 m was ordered, to satisfy a balance of costs of some £50,000.

PART 83
WRITS AND WARRANTS – GENERAL PROVISIONS

Section III
Writs

83.9 Issue of writs of execution and writs of control

Page 2327.

By virtue of the Civil Procedure (Amendment No 2) Rules 2017, in CPR 1998, r 83.9(5), 'The' is substituted by 'Subject to paragraph (5A), the' and after para (5) there is inserted a new para (5A). Rule 83.9 is thereby amended to read:

83.9 Issue of writs of execution and writs of control

(1) In this rule 'the appropriate office' means –

   (a)   where the proceedings in which execution is to issue are in a District Registry, that Registry;

   (b)   where the proceedings are in the Principal Registry of the Family Division, that Registry;

   (c)   where the proceedings are Admiralty proceedings or commercial proceedings which are not in a District Registry, the Admiralty and Commercial Registry;

   (ca) where the proceedings are in the Chancery Division, Chancery Chambers;

   (d)   in any other case, the Central Office of the Senior Courts.

(2) Issue of a writ of execution or control takes place on its being sealed by a court officer of the appropriate office.

(3) Before a writ is issued a request for its issue must be filed.

(4) The request must be signed –

   (a)   by the person entitled to execution, if acting in person; or

   (b)   by or on behalf of the solicitor of the person entitled to execution.

(5) Subject to paragraph (5A), the writ will not be sealed unless at the time it is presented for sealing –

   (a)   the person presenting the writ produces –

      (i)   the judgment or order on which the writ is to issue, or an office copy of it;

      (ii)   where permission was required for the writ to be issued, the order granting such permission or evidence of the granting of it;

      (iii) where judgment on failure to acknowledge service has been entered against a State, as defined in section 14 of the State Immunity Act 1978, evidence that the State has been served in accordance with rule 40.10 and that the judgment has taken effect; and

   (b)   the court officer authorised to seal it is satisfied that the period, if any, specified in the judgment or order for the payment of any money or the doing of any other act under the judgment or order has expired.

(5A) Where a request is made for a writ of possession to enforce a notice under section 33D of the Immigration Act 2014 (termination of agreement where all occupiers disqualified), a copy of that notice must be filed with the request instead of the judgment or order required by paragraph (5)(a)(i).

(6) Every writ of execution or control will bear the date of the day on which it is issued.

Commencement date: 1 October 2017.

83.13 Enforcement in the High Court of a judgment or order for possession of land

Page 2328.

By virtue of the Civil Procedure (Amendment No 2) Rules 2017, in CPR 1998, r 83.13(2), after 'any land' there is inserted ', or to enforce a notice under section 33D of the Immigration Act 2014,'. Rule 83.13 is thereby amended to read:

83.13 Enforcement in the High Court of a judgment or order for possession of land

(1) A judgment or order for the giving of possession of land may be enforced in the High Court by one or more of the following means –

    (a) writ of possession;

    (b) in a case in which rule 81.4 applies, an order of committal;

    (c) in a case in which rule 81.20 applies, writ of sequestration.

(2) Subject to paragraphs (3), (5) and (6), a writ of possession to enforce a judgment or order for the giving of possession of any land, or to enforce a notice under section 33D of the Immigration Act 2014, will not be issued without the permission of the court.

(3) The court's permission is not required for the issue of a writ of possession in a possession claim against trespassers under Part 55 unless the writ is to be issued after the expiry of three months from the date of the order.

(4) An application for permission under paragraph (3) may be made without notice being served on any other party unless the court orders otherwise.

(5) The courts' permission to issue a writ of restitution in aid of a writ of possession is required whether or not permission was required for the writ of possession.

(6) The court's permission is not required for the issue of a writ of possession to enforce a judgment or order for the giving of possession of any land where the judgment or order was given or made in proceedings in which there is a claim for –

    (a) payment of moneys secured by the mortgage;

    (b) sale of the mortgaged property;

    (c) foreclosure;

    (d) delivery of possession (whether before or after foreclosure or without foreclosure) to the mortgagee by the mortgagor or by any other person who is alleged to be in possession of the property;

    (e) redemption;

    (f) reconveyance of the land or its release from the security; or

    (g) delivery of possession by the mortgagee.

(7) In paragraph (6) 'mortgage' includes a legal or equitable mortgage and a legal or equitable charge, and reference to a mortgagor, a mortgagee and mortgaged land is to be interpreted accordingly.

(8) Permission referred to in paragraph (2) will not be granted unless it is shown –

PART III

121

(a) that every person in actual possession of the whole or any part of the land ('the occupant') has received such notice of the proceedings as appears to the court sufficient to enable the occupant to apply to the court for any relief to which the occupant may be entitled; and

(b) if the operation of the judgment or order is suspended by section 16(2) of the Landlord and Tenant Act 1954, that the applicant has not received notice in writing from the tenant that the tenant desires that the provisions of section 16(2)(a) and (b) of that subsection shall have effect.

(9) A writ of possession may include provision for enforcing the payment of any money adjudged or ordered to be paid by the judgment or order which is to be enforced by the writ.

Commencement date: 1 October 2017.

New commentary has also been added to accompany CPR 1998, r 83.13:

'**such notice of the proceedings as appears to the court sufficient**' (r 83.13(8)(a))—Where there is a sole occupant who is the subject of the possession order and he/she has full knowledge of the possession proceedings, a reminder of the terms of the court order and a request that possession is given up under the order is, generally speaking, sufficient notice within this rule. Where the sole defendant has played no part in the possession proceedings, a letter or other suitable form of communication containing all the above information should ensure that sufficient notice within the rule has been given. Where there are occupants other than the defendant to the possession proceedings known to occupy the property, then a letter addressed to them (if known by name) or to 'the occupants' (if the names are not known) in similar terms to that referred to above is required, it being necessary to include reference to the intention to apply for permission to issue a writ of possession if possession is not delivered up by the date prescribed in the order and that eviction will follow (*Partridge v Gupta* [2017] EWHC 2110 (QB)).

PART 84
ENFORCEMENT BY TAKING CONTROL OF GOODS

Practice Direction 84 – Enforcement by Taking Control of Goods

Page 2346.

As part of Update 90, as of 9 August 2017, PD84, paragraph 2.2, is amended so as the entry for Oldham is substituted with Manchester. The table in paragraph 2.2 now reads:

London	**North-West**	**South-West**
Central London	Birkenhead	Bristol
	Burnley	Plymouth
Midlands	Manchester	Southampton
Birmingham		
Northampton	**South-East**	**Wales**
Nottingham	Brighton	Caernarfon
Worcester	Chelmsford	Cardiff
	Dartford	Swansea
North-East	Hertford	Wrexham
Gateshead	Norwich	
Kingston Upon Hull	Oxford	
Middlesbrough		
York		

PART IV

Statutory Instruments

Child Abduction and Custody (Parties to Conventions) Order 1986, SI 1986/1159

SCHEDULE 1
CONVENTION ON THE CIVIL ASPECTS OF INTERNATIONAL CHILD ABDUCTION, THE HAGUE, 25 OCTOBER 1980

Page 2428.

By virtue of the Child Abduction and Custody (Parties to Conventions) (Amendment) Order 2017, in the Child Abduction and Custody (Parties to Conventions) Order 1986, Sch 1 is substituted by:

SCHEDULE 1
CONVENTION ON THE CIVIL ASPECTS OF INTERNATIONAL CHILD ABDUCTION, THE HAGUE, 25 OCTOBER 1980

Contracting States to the Convention	*Territories specified in Declarations under Article 39 or 40 of the Convention*	*Date of Coming into Force of Convention as between the United Kingdom and the State or Territory*
Albania	—	1 July 2016
Andorra	—	1 July 2016
Argentina	—	1 June 1991
Armenia	—	1 July 2016
Australia	Australian States and mainland Territories	1 January 1987
Austria	—	1 October 1988
The Bahamas	—	1 January 1994
Belarus	—	1 October 2003
Belgium	—	1 May 1999
Belize	—	1 October 1989
Bosnia and Herzegovina	—	1 December 1991
Brazil	—	1 March 2005
Bulgaria	—	1 May 2009
Burkina Faso	—	1 November 1992
Canada	Ontario	1 August 1986
	New Brunswick	1 August 1986
	British Columbia	1 August 1986
	Manitoba	1 August 1986
	Nova Scotia	1 August 1986
	Newfoundland and Labrador	1 August 1986
	Prince Edward Island	1 August 1986
	Quebec	1 August 1986
	Yukon Territory	1 August 1986
	Saskatchewan	1 November 1986
	Alberta	1 February 1987

PART IV

Contracting States to the Convention	Territories specified in Declarations under Article 39 or 40 of the Convention	Date of Coming into Force of Convention as between the United Kingdom and the State or Territory
	Northwest Territories	1 April 1988
	Nunavut	1 January 2001
Chile	—	1 May 1994
China	Hong Kong Special Administrative Region	1 September 1997
	Macau Special Administrative Region	1 March 1999
Columbia	—	1 March 1996
Costa Rica	—	1 May 2009
Croatia	—	1 December 1991
Cyprus	—	1 February 1995
Czech Republic	—	1 March 1998
Denmark	—	1 July 1991
Ecuador	—	1 June 1992
El Salvador	—	1 May 2009
Estonia	—	1 October 2003
Fiji	—	1 October 2003
Finland	—	1 August 1994
France	—	1 August 1986
Georgia	—	1 October 1997
Germany	—	1 December 1990
Greece	—	1 June 1993
Honduras	—	1 March 1994
Hungary	—	1 September 1986
Iceland	—	1 November 1996
Ireland	—	1 October 1991
Israel	—	1 December 1991
Italy	—	1 May 1995
Japan	—	1 April 2014
Kazakhstan	—	1 April 2017
Republic of Korea	—	1 April 2017
Latvia	—	1 October 2003
Lithuania	—	1 March 2005
Luxembourg	—	1 January 1987
Macedonia	—	1 December 1991
Malta	—	1 March 2002
Mauritius	—	1 June 1993
Mexico	—	1 October 1991
Monaco	—	1 February 1993
Montenegro	—	1 December 1991
Morocco	—	1 July 2016
Netherlands	—	1 September 1990

Contracting States to the Convention	Territories specified in Declarations under Article 39 or 40 of the Convention	Date of Coming into Force of Convention as between the United Kingdom and the State or Territory
New Zealand	—	1 October 1991
Norway	—	1 April 1989
Panama	—	1 May 1994
Peru	—	1 October 2003
Poland	—	1 November 1992
Portugal	—	1 August 1986
Romania	—	1 February 1993
Russian Federation	—	1 July 2016
St Kitts and Nevis	—	1 August 1994
San Marino	—	1 June 2011
Serbia	—	1 December 1991
Seychelles	—	1 July 2016
Singapore	—	1 July 2016
Slovakia	—	1 February 2001
Slovenia	—	1 June 1994
South Africa	—	1 October 1997
Spain	—	1 September 1987
Sweden	—	1 June 1989
Switzerland	—	1 August 1986
Turkey	—	1 August 2000
Turkmenistan	—	1 March 1998
Ukraine	—	1 June 2011
United States of America	—	1 July 1988
Uruguay	—	1 October 2003
Uzbekistan	—	1 October 2003
Venezuela	—	1 January 1997
Zimbabwe	—	1 July 1995

PART IV

Commencement date: 20 July 2017.

SCHEDULE 2

EUROPEAN CONVENTION ON RECOGNITION AND ENFORCEMENT OF DECISIONS CONCERNING CUSTODY OF CHILDREN AND ON THE RESTORATION OF CUSTODY OF CHILDREN, LUXEMBOURG, 20 MAY 1980

Page 2430.

By virtue of the Child Abduction and Custody (Parties to Conventions) (Amendment) Order 2017, as of 20 July 2017, in the Child Abduction and Custody (Parties to Conventions) Order 1986, Sch 2 is substituted by:

SCHEDULE 2

EUROPEAN CONVENTION ON RECOGNITION AND ENFORCEMENT OF DECISIONS CONCERNING CUSTODY OF CHILDREN AND ON THE RESTORATION OF CUSTODY OF CHILDREN, LUXEMBOURG, 20 MAY 1980

Contracting States to the Convention	Territories specified in Declarations under Article 24 or 25 of the Convention	Date of Coming into Force of Convention as between the United Kingdom and the State or Territory
Andorra	—	1 July 2011
Austria	—	1 August 1986
Belgium	—	1 August 1986
Bulgaria	—	1 October 2003
Cyprus	—	1 October 1986
Czech Republic	—	1 July 2000
Denmark	—	1 August 1991
Estonia	—	1 September 2001
Finland	—	1 August 1994
France	—	1 August 1986
Germany	—	1 February 1991
Greece	—	1 July 1993
Hungary	—	1 June 2004
Iceland	—	1 November 1996
Ireland	—	1 October 1991
Italy	—	1 June 1995
Latvia	—	1 August 2002
Liechtenstein	—	1 August 1997
Lithuania	—	1 May 2003
Luxembourg	—	1 August 1986
Macedonia	—	1 March 2003
Malta	—	1 February 2000
Moldova	—	1 May 2004
Montenegro	—	6 June 2006
Netherlands	—	1 September 1990
Norway	—	1 May 1989
Poland	—	1 March 1996
Portugal	—	1 August 1986
Romania	—	1 September 2004
Serbia	—	1 May 2002
Slovakia	—	1 September 2001
Spain	—	1 August 1986
Sweden	—	1 July 1989
Switzerland	—	1 August 1986
Turkey	—	1 June 2000
Ukraine	—	1 November 2008

Children (Secure Accommodation) Regulations 1991, SI 1991/1505

Page 2432.

By virtue of the Children and Social Work Act 2017, s 10, Sch 1, para 7, in Children (Secure Accommodation) Regulations 1991, reg 3 is substituted by:

3 Approval by Secretary of State of secure accommodation in a children's home

(1) Accommodation in a children's home shall not be used as secure accommodation unless –

  (a) in the case of accommodation in England, it has been approved by the Secretary of State for that use;

  (b) in the case of accommodation in Scotland, it is provided by a service which has been approved by the Scottish Ministers under paragraph 6(b) of Schedule 12 to the Public Services Reform (Scotland) Act 2010.

(2) Approval by the Secretary of State under paragraph (1) may be given subject to any terms and conditions that the Secretary of State thinks fit.

Commencement date: 27 April 2017.

Justices' Clerks and Assistants Rules 2014, SI 2014/603

SCHEDULE

Page 2499.

By virtue of the Justices' Clerks and Assistants (Amendment) Rules 2017, in the Justices' Clerks and Assistants Rules 2014:

- new entries are inserted for FPR rr 6.14(4) and (6), 6.16(1), 6.19, 6.20, 7.10(3)(a), 7.20(4) and 9.46(2); and
- in the entry for FPR r 7.14(1) the words in the second column are omitted;

The table in the Schedule is thereby amended to read:

FPR rule 3.3		FPR rule 4.3(2)	
FPR rule 3.4		FPR rule 4.3(5)	
FPR rule 3.10		FPR rule 4.7(a) and (b)	
FPR rule 4.1(3)(a)	Except any extensions in public law proceedings that would have the effect that disposal of the application would occur later than the end of twenty-six weeks beginning with the day on which the application was issued.	FPR rule 6.14(4) and (6)	
		FPR rule 6.16(1)	
		FPR rule 6.19	
		FPR rule 6.20	
FPR rule 4.1(3)(b), (c), (d), (f), (h), (j), (k), (n), (o)		FPR rule 6.24(2)	
		FPR rule 6.26(5)	

FPR rule 6.32			FPR rule 9.18	
FPR rule 6.36			FPR rule 9.20	
MCA, section 1(3)	Only in undefended cases		FPR rule 9.26	
MCA, sections 1(4) and 1(5)	Only in undefended cases, and only the making 'absolute' of decrees of divorce		FPR rule 9.46(2)	
			FPR rule 10.3(1)	
MCA, section 6(2)	Only where the parties consent to the adjournment		FPR rule 10.6(2)	
			FPR rule 10.7	
MCA, sections 10A(2) and (3)	Only in an application under section 10A(2) to which the other party consents		FPR rule 12.3(2)	Only where the parties consent to the person being made a respondent and where the person is not a child
MCA, section 17(2)	Only in undefended cases		FPR rule 12.3(3)	Only where the parties consent to the person being made a respondent and where the person is not a child
CPA, section 37(1)(a) and (d)	Only in undefended cases, and only the making 'final' of such orders			
CPA, section 42(3)	Only where the parties consent to the adjournment		FPR rule 12.3(4)	Only where otherwise authorised to add or remove the person as a party
CPA, sections 44(2) and (4)	Only in undefended cases		FPR rule 12.4(5)	Only where the parties consent to the person being made a respondent and where the person is not a child
FPR rule 7.10(3)(a)	Only where the petitioner and respondent agree that a named person should not be made a co-respondent		FPR rule 12.5(1)	
			Children Act 1989, section 32(1)	
FPR rule 7.13(5)(b)	Only in undefended cases		Children Act 1989, section 32(4)	Except that the carrying out of such function must not have the direct or indirect effect of extending the timetable for the proceedings with the effect that the disposal of the application would occur later than the end of twenty-six weeks beginning with the day on which the application was issued
FPR rule 7.13(7)	Only in undefended cases			
FPR rule 7.13(8)	Only in undefended cases			
FPR rule 7.14(1)				
FPR rule 7.20(2)				
FPR rule 7.20(3)				
FPR rule 7.20(4)			FPR rule 12.5(2)	Except at an Issues Resolution Hearing for which Practice Direction 12A makes provision, and except the carrying out of any function that has the direct or indirect effect of extending the timetable for the proceedings with the effect that the disposal of the application would occur later than the end of twenty-six weeks beginning with the day on which the application was issued
FPR rule 7.20(5)				
FPR rule 7.21(3)				
FPR rule 7.30(1)(d)(ii) and (3)	Only where the application under section 10A(2) was made on consent			
FPR 7.32(2)				
FPR rule 8.20(4)	Only where the parties consent to the person being made a respondent and where the person is not a child			

FPR rule 12.6(a)–(c)	
Children Act 1989, section 7(1) and FPR rule 12.6(d)	
FPR rule 12.12	Except at an Issues Resolution Hearing for which Practice Direction 12A makes provision, and except any direction in public law proceedings that has the direct or indirect effect of extending the timetable for the proceedings with the effect that the disposal of the application would occur later than the end of twenty-six weeks beginning with the day on which the application was issued
FPR rule 12.13	Except that in any public law proceedings, the carrying out of such function must not have the direct or indirect effect of extending the timetable for the proceedings with the effect that the disposal of the application would occur later than the end of twenty-six weeks beginning with the day on which the application was issued
FPR rule 12.14(3) and (4)	
FPR rule 12.15	Except any direction in a public law proceeding that has the direct or indirect effect of extending the timetable for the proceedings with the effect that the disposal of the application would occur later than the end of twenty-six weeks beginning with the day on which the application was issued
FPR rule 12.16(6)	
FPR rule 12.16(7)	
FPR rule 12.19(2) and (3)	
FPR rule 12.21(1)	
FPR rule 12.22	
FPR rule 12.73(1)(b)	

Practice Direction 12G, paragraph 1.2	
Practice Direction 12J, paragraph 6, first three bullet points only	
Practice Direction 12J, paragraph 8	
Practice Direction 12J, paragraph 15	
Practice Direction 12J, paragraph 21	
FPR rule 12.24	
FPR rule 12.25(1), (2) and (5)	
FPR rule 12.26	
FPR rule 12.29	
FPR rule 12.30	
Children Act 1989, section 41	
Children Act 1989, sections 10(1) and (2)	Only where – (a) a previous such order has been made in the same proceedings; (b) the terms of the order sought are the same as those of the last such order made; (c) the order is an order in the course of proceedings and does not dispose finally of the proceedings; and (d) a written request for such an order has been made and – (i) the other parties and any children's guardian consent to the request and they or their legal representatives have signed the request; or (ii) at least one of the other parties and any children's guardian consent to the request and they or their legal representatives have signed the request, and the remaining parties have not indicated that they either consent to or oppose the making of the order.

PART IV

Children Act 1989, section 38(1)	Only where – (a) a previous such order has been made in the same proceedings; (b) the terms of the order sought are the same as those of the last such order made; and (c) a written request for such an order has been made and – (i) the other parties and any children's guardian consent to the request and they or their legal representatives have signed the request; or (ii) at least one of the other parties and any children's guardian consent to the request and they or their legal representatives have signed the request, and the remaining parties have not indicated that they either consent to or oppose the making of the order.	FPR rule 14.3(2)	Only where the parties consent to the child being made a respondent
		FPR rule 14.3(3)	Only where the parties consent to the person or body being made a respondent or to a party being removed, as the case may be, and only where the person being made a respondent or being removed as a party is not a child
		FPR rule 14.3(4)	Only where such directions are consequential on directions made under FPR rule 14.3(2) or (3)
		FPR rule 14.5(2)(b) and (3)	
		FPR rule 14.6(1)	
		FPR rule 14.6(2)(a)	
FPR rule 12.31		FPR rule 14.6(2)(b)	
FPR rule 13.3(3)		FPR rule 14.6(3)(b)	
FPR rule 13.3(4)		FPR rule 14.6(4)	
FPR rule 13.3(5)		FPR rule 14.7	
FPR rule 13.5		Adoption and Children Act 2002, section 51B(3)	
FPR rule 13.8			
FPR rule 13.9(1)	Except 13.9(1)(e) and (f)	FPR rule 14.8(1)	Except 14.8(1)(d)
FPR rule 13.9(3)		FPR rule 14.8(4)	
FPR rule 13.9(6)		FPR rule 14.8(6)	
FPR rule 13.9(8)		FPR rule 14.8(7)	
FPR rule 13.9(9)		FPR rule 14.9(4)(b)	
FPR rule 13.11(1)		FPR rule 14.10(2)	
FPR rule 13.14			
FPR rule 13.16		FPR rule 14.14	
FPR rule 13.17		FPR rule 14.16(4) and (7)	
FPR rule 13.21(1)		FPR rule 14.18	
FPR rule 13.21(4)		FPR rule 14.20	
FPR rule 13.22(4)		FPR rule 14.26(1)	
FPR rule 14.2(3)	Only where the applicant consents to the removal	FPR rule 14.27(2)	

Practice Direction 14E, paragraph 1.2	
FPR rule 15.6(3)	
FPR rule 15.6(5)	
FPR rule 15.8(1)(b)	
FPR rule 15.9	
Practice Direction 15B	
FPR rule 16.3(1)	
FPR rule 16.3(2), (3) and (4)	Only in relation to specified proceedings as defined in the Children Act 1989, section 41(6)
FPR rule 16.4	
FPR rule 16.11(3)	
FPR rule 16.11(5) and (6)	
FPR rule 16.21	
FPR rule 16.24	
FPR rule 16.30	
FPR rule 16.33	
FPR rule 16.34	
FPR rule 17.3(2)	
FPR rule 17.4	
FPR rule 17.5	
FPR rule 18.3(1)(c)	Only where the parties consent to the person being made a respondent and where the person being made a respondent is not a child
FPR rule 18.4(2)(b)	
FPR rule 18.5(2)(c)	
FPR rule 18.8(4)	
FPR rule 18.9(1)	Only where authorised by these Rules to deal with the application with a hearing
Practice Direction 18A, paragraph 8.1	

Practice Direction 18A, paragraph 10.1	
Practice Direction 18A, paragraph 11.2	
FPR rule 19.1(3)	
FPR rule 19.4(4)	
FPR rule 19.6(2)	
FPR rule 19.8(1)(b)	
FPR rule 19.8(3)	
FPR rule 19.9(2)	
Practice Direction 19A, paragraphs 4.1 and 4.4	
FPR rule 21.2(3)	Only where the parties consent to the application for disclosure
Practice Direction 21A, paragraph 2.4	
FPR rule 22.1(1)	
FPR rule 22.3	
FPR rule 22.5	
FPR rule 22.7(1)	
FPR rule 22.9	
FPR rule 22.10	
Practice Direction 22A, paragraph 5.3	
FPR rule 23.4(1)	
FPR rule 23.6(8)	
The Act, section 31G(2)	
FPR rule 23.9	
FPR rule 24.3	
FPR rule 24.4(2)	
FPR rule 24.7	
FPR rule 24.8	

PART IV

133

FPR rule 24.9		Practice Direction 25E, paragraph 4.1	
FPR rule 24.10			
FPR rule 24.11(3)		FPR rule 26.3	
FPR rule 24.13		FPR rule 26.4	
Children and Families Act 2014, section 13		FPR rule 27.3	
		FPR rule 27.4	
FPR rule 25.4		FPR rule 27.7	
FPR rule 25.8		FPR rule 29.1	
FPR rule 25.9		FPR rule 29.4	
FPR rule 25.10(2)		FPR rule 29.11	
FPR rule 25.10(3)		FPR rule 29.14	
FPR rule 25.10(4)		FPR rule 29.15	Only where the order in question is one which the justices' clerk or assistant justices' clerk made
FPR rule 25.11			
FPR rule 25.12		FPR rule 29.16	Only where the order in question is one which a justices' clerk or assistant justices' clerk made
FPR rule 25.13			
FPR rule 25.16			
FPR rule 25.17		FPR rule 29.19(5)	
FPR rule 25.18		FPR rule 37.9(3)	
FPR rule 25.19		The Family Court (Composition and Distribution of Business) Rules 2014, rule 20	
Practice Direction 25A, paragraph 2.1			
Practice Direction 25B, paragraphs 10.1 and 10.2			

Commencement date 7 August 2017.

PART V

Practice Guidance

President's Guidance
2 May 2017

Judicial Cooperation with Serious Case Reviews

1 It is apparent that there is widespread misunderstanding as to the extent to which judges (which for this purpose includes magistrates) can properly participate in Serious Case Reviews (SCRs). The purpose of this Guidance is to clarify the position and to explain what judges can and cannot do.

2 This guidance applies to all judges sitting in the Family Division or the Family Court, including Magistrates and, where exercising judicial functions, Legal Advisers.

3 Judges should provide every assistance to SCRs which is compatible with judicial independence. It is, however, necessary to be aware that key constitutional principles of judicial independence, the separation of powers and the rule of law can be raised by SCRs.

Background

4 From time to time, judges are asked to participate in various ways in SCRs following the death of a child where there has been contact with Local Authority Children's Services. SCRs are conducted by Local Safeguarding Children Boards (LSCBs). These are statutory bodies, established by the Children Act 2004, with chairs independent of the Local Authority they scrutinise – usually a senior social work manager from another Local Authority.

5 On occasions LSCBs have written to judges after child deaths to request either an interview or the completion of an Independent Management Review (IMR). An IMR is a detailed review of an agency's involvement with a child and is one of the principal means of capturing information for use in SCRs. Sometimes LSCBs write with a list of specific questions which they invite the judge to answer. Some LSCBs have written to request that judges attend before them to answer questions in evidence sessions.

Position of judges

6 For important constitutional reasons, judicial participation in SCRs must be limited: therefore, judges do not respond to questions from SCRs, or requests from SCRs to complete IMRs, do not attend evidence sessions or other meetings with SCRs and are under no obligation to provide information to SCRs.

7 The judiciary takes this stance, not because it wishes to evade scrutiny or accountability, but in order to protect its independence and the independence of individual judges.

8 Judicial independence is a fundamental principle, of key importance to both the constitutional separation of powers and the rule of law. The judiciary and individual judges must be independent of and protected from potential encroachment by the executive. And individual judges, in the exercise of their judicial functions, must be, and are, free from direction or management by other judges. Thus neither the judiciary nor the senior judiciary nor the relevant Head of Division (in this instance, the President of the Family Division) has any right to intervene in or any responsibility for the decision of a judge in a particular case. The responsibility is, and must be, that of the individual judge, subject of course to review by an appellate court.

9 Sir Mark Potter P took the view that seeking to ask judges to explain their judgments outside the court arena to bodies of officials was incompatible with judicial

independence.[1] If a Local Authority is dissatisfied with a judgment, then its remedy is to appeal. He relied upon the principle that the judgment should speak for itself and that judges should not be asked to explain the reasons why they made their decisions outside the judgment.

1   Sir Mark Potter P, who first established the judicial position in relation to SCRs, expressed the issue in the following terms:
'The question of whether and how far the judiciary can be engaged in the serious case review process needs careful consideration, if only because there are questions of judicial independence involved. Such independence may be put at risk if judges are seen to be participants in a review conducted by a government or local authority agency, which is often based on non-disclosable confidential information, and which deals with far wider questions than those which may have preoccupied the Court at any particular stage.
The role of the judge in the overall history of a case … is a restricted one; its propriety is normally only open to investigation through the appellate or judicial complaints process and not by departmental or local authority review. Further, whether any general guidance to judges is appropriate following a serious case review is a question for the President rather than the department or authority concerned. It is also the case that, outside the confines of the issues before the Court in particular proceedings, it is no part of the duty or function of the judiciary to review or comment upon the actions of social workers or other agencies concerned with safeguarding children. That said, however, while there can be no duty upon the Court to assist if … a judicial decision may have played a material part in the handling and eventual outcome of a case which has ended in tragedy, it is plainly desirable as a general proposition that the review should be acquainted with the course of the proceedings and the material upon which the Court came to its conclusion.'

10 The judiciary is not an agency in the same way that local authorities or the police are agencies. Nor is an individual judge. Judges have a distinct constitutional role and function. It is a fundamental principle that judges do not comment on the decisions of other judges outside the appellate process. This is why it would be inappropriate for an IMR of a judicial decision to be conducted; it would, effectively, be one judge (or group of judges) commenting upon the decisions of another judge outside the proper appellate process. It would be even less appropriate for an official (including for this purpose an official in the Judicial Office or in the Judicial Press Office) to seek to comment on a judicial decision. This principle evolved in order to protect the rule of law – it reinforces the idea that the only way to challenge a judicial decision is to do so in court, not to seek to undermine it outside the court process.

11 This position on SCRs has been followed by Sir Mark's successors, Sir Nicholas Wall P and, in turn, by me.

12 If a LSCB writes to a judge to ask them to participate in a SCR it is important to bring this to the attention of the President's Office immediately.[2] The President's Office will then be in a position to assist and advise and to deal with all correspondence with the LSCB.

2   Contact Alex Clark at Alex.Clark@judiciary.gsi.gov.uk or on 0207 947 7041

Position of HMCTS

13 It is important to note that the judiciary and Her Majesty's Courts and Tribunal Service (HMCTS) are entirely separate and distinct. HMCTS is the administrative arm of the courts and tribunals. It has, and a matter of constitutional principle must have, no involvement in or responsibility for judicial decision-making, which is the exclusive responsibility of the individual judge.

14 For this reason, it is of the highest importance to be clear that where HMCTS decides to complete an IMR as part of a SCR this can be appropriate only in so far as it relates to administrative matters. It can never be appropriate for an IMR to be carried out by HMCTS, or any other officials, of a judicial decision.

Provision of documents

15 In principle, it is appropriate, unless there are highly exceptional reasons why this should not be so, for a SCR to have access to (a) all material that the judge had access to in hearing the case, including all expert reports, (b) transcripts of the proceedings, (c) all court orders and (d) transcripts of all judgments. Therefore, the proper response to any request for information from a LSCB or SCR is to make available copies of all such documents, though not copies of the judge's notes. This can be done either by copying the contents of the court file or, preferably, the judge's trial bundle if still available. Where a transcript has to be prepared, it should be supplied on the payment of any fee required.

16 Documents will be supplied subject to an undertaking that any reporting restrictions in place (for example to protect the identity of any surviving siblings) are to be respected in the final report of the SCR.

Learning lessons

17 The President of the Family Division considers carefully all SCRs that come to his attention. If the President takes the view that the findings of a SCR raise issues for the family judiciary that should be addressed through a President's Practice Direction or President's Guidance, then he will issue an appropriate Practice Direction or Guidance.

Sir James Munby

President of the Family Division

President's Guidance
23 June 2017

Judicial participation in OFSTED inspections of local authority children's services

Some confusion has arisen over the propriety of judges speaking to OFSTED staff conducting inspections of local authority children's services. For the avoidance of doubt, it is perfectly legitimate for judges, should they wish to do so, to speak to OFSTED inspectors about the quality of the preparation of public law cases that the local authority brings before the Family Court. It would not, however, be appropriate for judges to give feedback on the performance of individuals.

It is not, of course, mandatory for judges to contribute their views and they are free to decline.

In most cases, OFSTED will contact the local DFJ to request feedback on the local authority and the DFJ will be the most appropriate judge to provide feedback. However, from time to time, it may be helpful for OFSTED to hear from other judges.

If a DFJ becomes aware that an OFSTED inspection is taking place and has not been contacted for feedback then the DFJ is free to contact OFSTED, on their own initiative, should they feel that they have pertinent feedback to contribute to the inspection.

Sir James Munby

President of the Family Division

President's Guidance
5 July 2017

Settlement Conferences Pilot – training and guidance

Some Designated Family Judge (DFJ) areas are piloting settlement conferences. In a settlement conference, a trained family judge adopts an inquisitorial approach in order to encourage cooperation between parties with a view to reaching an agreement that is in the children's best interests. I know that opinions on settlement conferences are divided but, in my view, it is an approach that is worth piloting in order to inform decisions on whether to take them further.

Settlement conferences are already taking place in a number of DFJ areas. The pilots are supported by an 'action research' evaluation – led by social researchers in the Ministry of Justice – which has already identified important areas of learning for the pilot. Some of this feedback highlighted that family judges would find training and further guidance helpful before participating in the pilot in their area. This feedback has informed the drafting of a package of training and guidance materials.

Further information:

- A training video outlining the settlement conference approach in both public and private law [*https://design102.wistia.com/medias/ijhr2n8b7d*]:
- Case summaries to consider alongside the training video:
  - Carter and Miller case summary [*https://www.judiciary.gov.uk/wp-content/uploads/2017/07/carter-miller-case-summary.pdf*]
  - Brown and Jones case summary [*https://www.judiciary.gov.uk/wp-content/uploads/2017/07/brown-jones-case-summary.pdf*]
- Settlement Conferences Protocol as to Basic Principles with Annexes 1 and 2 [*https://www.judiciary.gov.uk/wp-content/uploads/2017/07/protocols-and-annexes.pdf*]
- Opening for judges conducting settlement conferences [*https://www.judiciary.gov.uk/wp-content/uploads/2017/07/opening-for-judges-conducting.pdf*]
- The strategy for settlement conferences roll-out [*https://www.judiciary.gov.uk/wp-content/uploads/2017/07/strategy-for-set-conf-roll-out.pdf*]
- Settlement conferences draft directions [*https://www.judiciary.gov.uk/wp-content/uploads/2017/07/set-conf-draft-directions.pdf*]
- Information leaflet for parties [*https://www.judiciary.gov.uk/wp-content/uploads/2017/07/leaflet-information-for-parties.pdf*]

This pilot has my full support. I am keen that we understand whether, and how, this approach can lead to appropriate outcomes for children and families in a less adversarial context. I would like to encourage judges to consider adopting the pilot in their areas using these training materials.

The evaluation will continue during the pilot to seek the views and experiences of both judges as well as professional and lay parties. This will ensure lessons learnt and areas of good practice are shared and the settlement conference model is continually reviewed and improved.

Sir James Munby

President of the Family Division

Guidance
1 October 2017

Mr Justice Baker's Guidance of 1 October 2017

On 1 October 2017, Mr Justice Baker, Senior Family Liaison Judge and judge in charge of appeals to the Family Division, wrote to the Family Law Bar Association as follows:

'The rules and PD30A provide that an appeal from a district judge in the family court should normally be heard by a circuit judge except (a) where there is a need for a High Court Judge to hear the appeal on grounds of efficiency, (b) where a Designated Family Judge or judge of High Court level considers that the appeal would raise an important point of practice or principle or (c) where it is an appeal from a PRFD district judge (or deputy) in a financial remedies case, in which case the appeal is to a judge of High Court Judge level.

It has been decided that all financial remedy appeals from PRFD district judges sitting at First Avenue House should be referred in the first instance to one of the s 9 judges sitting there. He or she will decide either (a) that the appeal should remain there, in which case it will be managed in the office there and heard by a s 9 judge, or (b) that it should be heard by a full High Court Judge, in which case it will be referred to the Family Division Appeals Office and managed there and heard by a High Court Judge.

We will consider whether there needs to be any formal guidance to that effect, or an amendment to the Rules, but meanwhile I would be grateful if the FLBA would ensure that its members are aware of the practice as outlined above.'

PART V

PART VI

European Material

Council Regulation (EC) No 2201/2003

CHAPTER II
JURISDICTION

Section 2
Parental responsibility

Article 15

Transfer to a court better placed to hear the case

Page 2784.

FE v MR and others [2017] EWHC 2298 (Fam), [2017] All ER (D) 110 (Oct)

(Family Division, Baker J, 14 September 2017) Child – Practice. The circumstances of the present case supported a request to the Spanish court under European Community Regulation 2201/2003, Art 15 for the transfer of proceedings concerning two children who were habitually resident in England. A transfer of the case could only take place if the Spanish court, as the court of the Member State having jurisdiction as to the substance of the matter, concluded that the three criteria of Art 15 were satisfied. Ultimately, the decision rested with the Spanish court.

Background

In 2002, the parties married in Barcelona, Spain. In October 2003, having moved to Pamplona, their first child, A, was born. In 2006, the parties moved to Kent, England. In December 2006, their youngest child, J, was born. In July 2011, the family moved back to Pamplona but a few weeks later moved to Tenerife. In July 2012, the father moved back to Pamplona, the mother and children remaining in Tenerife. During the course of the following year, the relationship broke down.

In September 2013, the mother commenced divorce proceedings in Spain. Having secured employment in England, the mother applied for interim custody and permission to remove the children from Spain. In December, the Spanish court granted the mother's application and the children moved to England with the mother.

Subsequently, in June 2016, the Spanish courts awarded guardianship and custody of the children to the father and gave directions of visitation and contact with the mother mainly through the school holidays (for details of the June 2016 order, see [5], [6] of the judgment). In September, the mother filed a notice of appeal against the Spanish judge's decision. Subsequently, the Spanish judge ordered the mother to hand over the children to the father's care and pay a daily fine of €100 for each day that passed when she failed to hand the children over to the children.

The matter came before the English and Spanish courts on various occasions (for details of the subsequent hearings, see [7]-[16] of the judgment).

The present proceedings concerned, among other matters, the jurisdiction of the courts of England and Wales to make orders concerning the children, their future care arrangements and the status and continuation of the father's proceedings to recognise and enforce the orders in his favour made in June and September 2016 in the courts of Spain.

Issues and decisions

Whether the proceedings should be transferred to Spain under European Council Regulation 2201/2003, Art 15.

The children had a particular connection with England because they and the mother were, and had been for some time, habitually resident there. Both children had lived in England for the majority of their lives. In all the circumstances, it was manifestly clear that the children and their mother were habitually resident and had a particular connection with the country (see [53] of the judgment).

PART VI

145

A more difficult question was whether the English court was better placed to hear the case, or a specific part thereof. Given the children's strong antipathy to travelling to Spain, and the fact that they would be parties to the proceedings in England and represented by a guardian, the English court was in a better position to evaluate the emotional needs and the wishes and feelings of the children and to carry out a comprehensive analysis of all the issues impinging on the children's welfare (see [54], [60] of the judgment).

For similar reasons, it would be in the best interests of the children for the case to be transferred to the English court. The question at the present stage was whether the transfer of the proceedings was in the children's best interests, not what eventual outcome would be in their best interests. If the proceedings were transferred, the children's wishes and feelings, and their overall welfare needs, could be assessed by professionals and the court in the jurisdiction without the children having to travel to Spain. The immediate consequences of a transfer in the short term would therefore be the lifting of the anxieties in the children's minds that they would be sent to Spain before a thorough analysis of the issues relevant to the decision as to the future care arrangements, including their own wishes and feelings (see [61] of the judgment).

The circumstances of the case justified the court submitting a request to the Spanish court under Art 15. As required under Art 15(2), that request was supported by one of the parties, namely the mother. The criteria that had to be satisfied in order for the transfer under Art 15 to take place were satisfied in the present case (see [62] of the judgment).

A transfer of the case could only take place if the Spanish court, as the court of the Member State having jurisdiction as to the substance of the matter, concluded that the three criteria of Art 15 were satisfied. Ultimately, the decision rested with the Spanish court. Whatever the conclusion of the Spanish court on that matter, it was imperative that the judges of the two courts worked together to resolve the unhappy dispute that had blighted the lives of the children for too long. It was therefore proposed that the judgment, and the consequent order, would be sent to the International Family Justice Office for England and Wales for onward transmission to the Spanish network judge, with a view to facilitating communications between the two courts in accordance with a duty to cooperate imposed by Art 15 (see [63], [64] of the judgment).

The mother and father appeared in person.

Alistair Perkins for the children by their guardian.

CHAPTER III
RECOGNITION AND ENFORCEMENT

Section 6
Other provisions

Article 48

Practical arrangements for the exercise of rights of access

Page 2796.

Re M (Children) [2017] EWCA Civ 891, [2017] All ER (D) 79 (Jul)

(Court of Appeal, Civil Division, Black, Treacy and Simon LJJ, 29 June 2017) Family proceedings – Orders in family proceedings. Council Regulation (EC) 2201/2003 (Brussels IIA) and United Kingdom domestic law had not provided any means for enforcing the interim contact order made by the Estonian court in circumstances where the relevant government organisations were not willing to supervise contact as required by the order. The Court of Appeal, Civil Division held that despite the acknowledged importance of the need to enforce foreign judgments in relation to it with the greatest possible expedition wherever feasible, Brussels IIA did not require a court it to abandon its domestic law concerning enforcement.

Digest

The father obtained an interim contact order from the Estonian county court (the Estonian order) in respect of his two daughters. The daughters lived in the United Kingdom with their mother. The order specified that contact between the father and the children in the UK was to be in the presence of a competent child welfare authority. The relevant children's services, following an assessment, refused to supervise contact on the basis that it was neither safe nor in the children's best interests.

The father applied to enforce the interim contact order in the UK under Council Regulation (EC) 2201/2003 (Brussels IIA). Chapter III of Brussels IIA dealt with recognition and enforcement. The material provisions were contained in s 4 of Ch III (Arts 40–45), which applied by virtue of Art 40(1)(a) (see [11]–[13] of the judgment). The effect of the various provisions was that the Estonian order was to be treated as if it were a judgment given by the domestic courts in the UK and 'enforced in the same conditions' as a domestic judgment with there being no interference with the substance of the decision.

The matter came before the court. The judge rejected the argument that supervision by the local authority or Cafcass could be ordered under the various provisions proposed on behalf of the father (see [16] of the judgment) and concluded that the Estonian order could not practically be enforced in its current terms.

He further concluded that it was not for him to explore alternative forms of contact or to consider whether it was for the Estonian court to undertake that or to consider the issue of contact more generally. The father appealed.

Appeal dismissed.

First issue

Whether the judge should have concluded that Art 48 of Brussels IIA, taken together with Arts 41 and 47, required the court to 'make it happen' and that the scope of Art 48 permitted an implementation or phasing-in process of the Estonian order.

Decision

The terms of Arts 26, 47 and 48, and the general scheme of Brussels IIA in relation to access judgments meant that the domestic court was not entitled to vary the 'essential elements' of the judgment it was requested to enforce. An essential element of the interim contact order was the provision for contact to be supervised by a 'competent child welfare authority' albeit that that competent child welfare authority might assign someone to do the supervision. A local authority was obviously a 'competent child welfare authority' and Cafcass was too. Someone assigned by either of those two bodies to do the supervision would come within the terms of the Estonian order.

However, the supervision element of the Estonian order would not be respected if the court were to permit an independent social worker to be instructed directly by the parties or to entrust the supervision to the Anna Freud Centre, without the centre being assigned to the task by the local authority or Cafcass.

The order required supervision by a government agency, the enforcing court should be very cautious about doing anything other than taking that requirement at face value (see [24]–[28] of the judgment).

Second issue

How supervision of contact was provided for in domestic law by a local authority or CAFCASS and whether a family assistance order under s 16 of the Children Act 1989 was of any assistance.

Decision

The general advising, assisting and befriending which was referred to in s 16 of the 1989 Act did not obviously translate into 'supervising'. Further, s 16 of the 1989 Act was to be considered as part of the whole scheme of the 1989 Act and there would be considerable ramifications for local authorities if they faced a significant number of orders requiring them to supervise contact, even if only for 12 months (the maximum period under s 16(5)). Supervising contact was likely to require resources in terms of accommodation and of personnel, both to be present during contact and probably also to write up notes of the session.

Under the 1989 Act, it was for local authorities to determine how to fulfil their duties to children in need and in respect of child protection. They had to take strategic decisions as to how to make their limited funds and staff stretch to cover all the demands upon them. If it had been intended to place upon them the significant burden on carrying out contact supervision, at whatever frequency the court might order, that would have been spelled out expressly in the 1989 Act (see [34] of the judgment).

Third issue

Whether ss 11A–11P of the 1989 Act which included provisions enabling the court to make an 'activity direction' could be used to require CAFCASS to set up supervision of contact.

Decision

Sections 11A–11P of the 1989 Act could not be used in the manner suggested. It was the individuals involved in the child's life who were the primary target of the provisions of ss 11A–11P; they could be required to participate in activities. In so far as the provisions imposed obligations on Cafcass, those obligations were as to monitoring and reporting. There was nothing in the sections that would entitle the court to oblige Cafcass (or indeed a local authority) either to provide supervised contact or itself to supervise contact (see [45] of the judgment).

Fourth issue

Whether the inherent jurisdiction of the court could be used to require supervision to be provided.

Decision

Although there were examples of courts drawing upon the inherent jurisdiction to supplement statutory schemes, there was no case in which a local authority had been ordered to supervise contact. That was revealing given the difficulties in obtaining supervision for contact sessions.

It was impossible to contemplate introducing, by the route of the inherent jurisdiction, what might prove to be a significant additional obligation on the child welfare agencies (see [46], [48] of the judgment).

Fifth issue

Whether there was any practical way to enforce the Estonian order

Decision

Despite the acknowledged importance of the need to enforce foreign judgments with the greatest possible expedition wherever feasible, Brussels IIA did not require a court it to abandon its domestic law concerning enforcement. The trial judge had been right to have reached the decision that he had and it had not been incumbent on him to explore further the Anna Freud and independent social worker options, those possibilities strayed too far from the essence of the Estonian order. The process contemplated was a different one.

Nor was it for the Estonian court to reconsider and decide whether it would be appropriate to involve an independent social worker, or an organisation such as the Anna Freud Centre to assist (see [70], [72], [73] of the judgment).

David Williams QC and Hassan Khan (instructed by Dawson Cornwell) for the appellant.

Frank Feehan QC (instructed on a direct access basis) and Andrea Watts (instructed on a Pro Bono basis) for the respondent.

Jennifer Perrins and Mike Hinchliffe (instructed by Cafcass) for the second respondent children.

Council Regulation (EC) No 4/2009

CHAPTER II
JURISDICTION

Article 13
Related actions

Page 2869.

B v B [2017] EWHC 1029 (Fam), [2017] All ER (D) 70 (May)

(Family Division, Macdonald J, 9 May 2017) Divorce – Financial provision. The Family Division, among other determinations, stayed the applicant's application to enforce the provisions of an order, entered into by consent, relating to maintenance. That was because the respondent had, prior to the applicant's application, brought proceedings in Italy seeking to vary the maintenance provisions of that order. The court was satisfied that it was obliged, under the terms of art 12 of Council Regulation (EC) 4/2009, to stay the application until such time as the jurisdiction of the Italian court was established.

Digest

In 1992, the parties married. In September 1996, the applicant gave birth to twins. In 2009, the parties separated. In 2011, the parties entered into heads of agreement with respect to the matrimonial assets. In October, the consent order, agreed between the parties embodying the terms of their agreement, was approved (the order). The overall scheme embodied within the order provided for the division of the capital assets and the payment by the respondent to the applicant of continuing maintenance. The order provided, among other things, for the applicant to receive a little over half of the assets and global maintenance of £84,000 per annum with provision of a top-up if the respondent's income reached a specified level. The order also provided for the establishment of a school fees fund for the children (for relevant details of the order, see [12] of the judgment). The maintenance provisions of the order also provided for an undertaking by the respondent to assign to the applicant his interest in a Zurich policy or, if that was not possible, to pay to the applicant the value of the policy at a time to be agreed between the parties. In 2015, the applicant made an application to enforce the order. The applicant asserted that arrears of global maintenance began to accrue immediately, with the respondent failing to pay the full amount of the maintenance ordered in 2011 and in each of the subsequent years leading up the application. The applicant also sought the enforcement of the provision with respect to the Zurich policy. The respondent challenged the application on the grounds that five months prior to the applicant's application, he had applied in the Italian court to vary the provisions of the order (for details of the Italian proceedings, see [19] of the judgment). Accordingly, the respondent contended that the proceedings in Italy fell within the terms of art 12(1) of Council Regulation (EC) 4/2009 of 18 December 2008 (the Maintenance Regulation).

It fell to be determined whether the matter would be stayed pending the decision in the Italian proceedings and whether the enforcement sought would be granted.

The court ruled:

(1) It was plain that there were proceedings ongoing in both England and in Italy in relation to the maintenance provisions of the order and that those proceedings were between the same parties. In the circumstances of the case, the proceedings in Italy and the proceedings in England involved the same cause of action for the purposes of art 12(1) of the Maintenance Regulation. Both sets of proceedings concerned, at their heart, the applicant's right to maintenance payments under the terms of the order, and the respondent's obligation to pay maintenance under the terms of the order. Both cases would involve consideration of the extent to which those rights and obligations ought to subsist having regard to an alleged change of circumstances. There was a coincidence between the basic facts and the basic claimed rights and obligations in the Italian proceedings and the English proceedings when due allowance was made for the specific form that the proceedings had taken in each of those national jurisdictions. The two sets of proceedings were a mirror image of each other. That

conclusion with respect to cause of action could be tested, and demonstrated to be sound, by reference to the cardinal aim of art 12 of the Maintenance Regulation, namely to avoid irreconcilable decisions between the jurisdictions of different member states. Having regard to the strong presumption that, absent a clear case of irregularity, the court of first issue was the court first seised, prima facie, the Italian court was the court first seised for the purposes of art 12(1). It would be entirely wrong for the court to stray into considering the question of whether the Italian court had jurisdiction or not. That was a matter solely for the Italian court (see [70]–[75], [77] of the judgment).

The applicant's application to enforce the provisions of the order relating to maintenance would be stayed until such time as the jurisdiction of the Italian court was established (see [78], [84] of the judgment).

Wermuth v Wermuth [2003] All ER (D) 18 (Feb) applied.

(2) The respondent had accepted that he remained liable to the applicant under the terms of the order that had dealt with the Zurich policy. The assignment to the applicant of the policy being apparently 'impossible' for the purposes of the order, the respondent was now required by the terms of his undertaking to pay to the applicant such sum as was held within the Zurich policy on a date to be agreed between the parties. Such a date not yet having been agreed between the parties, in the circumstances, the appropriate order was an order adjourning the applicant's application to enforce the term concerning the Zurich policy to allow the parties a period of time to agree, pursuant to the terms of the order, the date by which the respondent would pay to the applicant such sum as was held within the Zurich policy and for payment to be made by that agreed date. In the event that the respondent refused to agree a date or failed by the date agreed to make payment to the applicant such sum as was held within the Zurich policy and was thereby in default, then the applicant's application to enforce could be reinstated (see [83] of the judgment).

The applicant's application to enforce the provisions of the order relating to the Zurich policy would be adjourned generally, with liberty to restore (see [84] of the judgment).

The applicant appeared in person with the support of a McKenzie friend.

Brent Molyneux QC for the respondent.

PART VII

Welsh Materials

Introduction

Devolution

(1) The Government of Wales Act 2006 came into force on 25 July 2006 and remains in force to date. It is an Act in six parts. Part 2 of the Act together with Schedule 3 established the Welsh Assembly Government as an entity separate from, but accountable to, the National Assembly for Wales. Part 3 and Schedule 5 of the Act introduced a mechanism that conferred on the Assembly the power to pass a type of subordinate legislation in relation to Wales called 'Measures of the National Assembly for Wales' but usually known as 'Welsh Measures'. The Act also provided a mechanism for conferring greater power on the Assembly. Part 4 and Schedules 6 and 7 provided power for a referendum to be called and for further powers to be granted to the Assembly in the event of the vote on the referendum being favourable. That referendum was held on 3 March 2011 and asked: 'Do you want the Assembly now to be able to make laws on all matters in the 20 subject areas it has powers for?'; 63.49 per cent of the electorate voted in favour. As a consequence of that vote, on 5 May 2011 the Assembly Act provisions of the 2006 Act came into force subject to certain transitional provisions: s 106(2),(3). The Assembly Act provisions are defined in s 158 as ss 107, 108 and 110–115 of the Act. Section 108(4) provides the test for competence by reference to Schedule 7. The effect of the Assembly Act provisions is that the Welsh Parliament is able to pass primary legislation in certain prescribed areas that are devolved.

(2) Whereas family law and family proceedings are not devolved in Wales, significant areas of law that impact on the daily practice of family lawyers are devolved. The following areas of law are among those areas now fully devolved in Wales:

(a) Education and training (Sch 7, para 5)   Educational, vocational, social and physical training and the careers service; promotion of advancement; and application of knowledge. Exception: research councils.
(b) Health and health services (Sch 7, para 9)   Promotion of health; prevention, treatment and alleviation of disease, illness, injury, disability and mental disorder; control of disease; family planning; provision of health services, including medical, dental, ophthalmic, pharmaceutical and ancillary services and facilities; clinical governance and standards of healthcare; organisation and funding of the National Health Service. Exceptions: abortion; human genetics, human fertilisation, human embryology and surrogacy arrangements; xenotransplantation; regulation of health professionals; poisons; misuse of and dealing in drugs; human medicines and medicinal products, including authorisations for use and regulation of prices; standards for, and testing of, biological substances; vaccine damage payments; welfare foods; and Health and Safety Executive and Employment Medical Advisory Service and provisions made by health and safety regulations.
(c) Housing (Sch 7, para 10, as amended)   Encouragement of home energy efficiency and conservation, otherwise than by prohibition and regulation; regulation of rent; homelessness; and residential caravans and mobile homes.
(d) Social Welfare (Sch 7, para 15)   Social Welfare, including social services; protection and well-being of children (including adoption and fostering) and young adults; care of children, young adults, vulnerable persons and older persons, including care standards; badges for display on motor vehicles used by disabled persons. Exceptions: child support; child trust funds subject to certain exceptions; tax credits; child benefit and guardian's allowance; social security; Independent Living Funds; Motability; intercountry adoption, apart from adoption agencies and their functions, and functions of 'the Central Authority' under the Hague Convention on Protection of Children and Co-operation in respect of Inter-Country Adoption; the Children's Commissioner (established under Children Act 2004); family law and proceedings, apart from:
   (i)   welfare advice to courts, representation and provision of information, advice and other support to children ordinarily resident in Wales and their families; and
   (ii)   Welsh family proceedings officers.

(3) Devolution is a dynamic issue in Wales. The Wales Act 2017 has been passed but is not yet in force. When it comes into force, Sch 7 of the 2006 Act will be replaced by Schs 7A and 7B of the 2017 Act. Under the 2017 Act, the above areas will continue to be devolved. Family law and family proceedings will not be devolved under the 2017 Act.

Dealing with devolved issues

(4) The consequence of the devolution settlement is that family law in Wales differs increasingly from family law in England. Munby LJ in *Re X and Y (Executive Summary of Serious Case Review: Reporting Restrictions)* [2013] 2 FLR 628, at [66–67] expressed the view that it would be of great assistance if, in such cases and as a matter of practice, advocates brought to the court's attention the fact that there was such a difference and were able to both identify the corresponding provisions applicable in the other country and, at least, in summary, to indicate the nature of the differences between the two regimes,

namely between the law applicable in Wales and that applicable in England. This practice, he said, was not intended to encourage judges to make pronouncements obiter dicta on legislation that is not before them but it may facilitate understanding of legislation that is under scrutiny. Importantly, it will alert practitioners reading a law report of such a case to appreciate that the law with which they are concerned may not be the same as that in the reported case they are considering. (See also Ryder LJ in *Re W (Care Proceedings: Functions of Court and Local Authority)* [2014] 2 FLR 431, at [29].) Pill LJ in *Re X* (above) agreed with Munby LJ's view, adding that practitioners also need to be aware that primary and secondary legislation in Wales are enacted both in English and Welsh and that those languages are treated as having equal standing. Whereas the need for comparison in practice may be rare, there is a possibility that cannot be excluded in all cases that Welsh words will throw a light on the proper translation of the English words, and vice versa.

Social Services and Well-being (Wales) Act 2014

(5) The Social Services and Well-being (Wales) Act 2014 is primary legislation made under the powers devolved to the Welsh Parliament. It received Royal Assent on 1 May 2014. The majority of the provisions in the 2014 Act came into force on 6 April 2016 (commencement order no 3). However, commencement order no 1 brought into force (on 8 Oct 2014) s 170 of the 2014 Act, which sets out joint arrangements for adoption services, and commencement order no 2 brought in (as of 21 October 2015) the section relating to the new National Independent Safeguarding Board that has been established in Wales.

(6) It is Welsh primary legislation and it applies in Wales.

(7) The 2014 Act and the legislative framework that underpins it repeals or disapplies in Wales:

- CA 1989, Pt III; and
- existing community care legislation.

(8) In Wales, the community care legislation that has been repealed or disapplied includes:

- National Assistance Act 1948, Pts 3 and 4;
- Disabled Persons (Employment) Act 1958, s 3;
- Health Services and Public Health Act 1968, s 45;
- Chronically Sick and Disabled Persons Act 1970, ss 1, 2 and 28A;
- Health and Social Services and Social Security Adjudications Act 1983, s 17;
- Disabled Persons (Services, Consultation and Representation) Act 1986, ss 3, 4 and 8;
- National Health Service and Community Care Act 1990, s 46 (NB s 47 of the 1990 Act is being amended so that it does not apply to assessing and meeting needs for community care services insofar as this is now provided for in the 2014 Act but it will continue to apply to assessing and meeting needs for services under Mental Health Act 1983, s 117);
- Carers (Recognition and Services) Act 1995;
- Carers and Disabled Children Act 2000;
- Health and Social Care Act 2001, ss 49, 50, 54, 56 and 57;
- Community Care (Delayed Discharges etc) Act 2003, s 16;
- Carers (Equal Opportunities) Act 2004;
- National Health Service (Wales) Act 2006, s 192 and Sch 15;
- Personal Care at Home Act 2010;
- Social Care Charges (Wales) Measure 2010; and
- Carers Strategies (Wales) Measure 2010 (NB this is being repealed as a consequence of the provisions in s 14 of the 2014 Act, which require local authorities and local health boards to carry out assessments of the needs of their local population, including the needs of carers).

(9) This is an extensive piece of legislation, being an Act in 11 Parts. Various sections of the Act include enabling legislation, which has resulted in a host of secondary legislation, regulations and statutory guidance, which is provided in a series of Codes made under the Act. The legislative scheme provides the statutory framework that is intended by Welsh Government to integrate social services to support people of all ages, and support people as part of families and communities. The Act introduces the new 'people' approach. The people approach has two principal aspects: (1) voice and control; and (2) seeing the person as an individual regardless of age. Many of the provisions of the Act apply to adults and children alike, although some sections do draw a distinction based on age.

(10) Key to the statutory scheme is the concept of well-being, which has a statutory definition at s 2 of the Act. The focus of the scheme is on meeting well-being outcomes. Well-being outcomes are necessarily subjective; they can be met by the person themselves and by their friends, families and community. Sometimes it is necessary that they are met by social services.

(11) According to the Code to Part 6 (Preamble, para 15), the Act will transform the way social services are delivered, primarily through promoting people's independence to give them a stronger voice and control. It is expected that integration and simplification of the law will provide greater consistency and clarity to people who use social services, their carers, local authority staff and their partner organisation, the court and the judiciary. The stated intention of the Act is to promote equality, improvements in the quality of services and the provision of information people receive. There is to be a shared focus on prevention and early intervention.

(12) The Act affects children in Wales and their families insofar as they are in need of care and support, are carers in need of support and are looked after or accommodated children.

(13) In *Re A (A Child)* [2016] EWFC B101, HHJ G Jones stated that, since the Act came into force, 'A court, therefore, exercising its discretion under the Children Act 1989 in care proceedings or when making other family orders where relevant for children in Wales is now entitled to proceed on the basis that local authorities in Wales acting in good faith will comply with these statutory obligations fully'. See also *Re R (A Child)* [2016] EWFC 60, which is an example of a local authority using its powers under the 2014 Act to provide care and support to a vulnerable mother who had care and support needs in a care case.

Statutes

Social Services and Well-being (Wales) Act 2014

ARRANGEMENT OF SECTIONS

PART 1
INTRODUCTION

PART 2
GENERAL FUNCTIONS

PART VII

PART 6
LOOKED AFTER AND ACCOMMODATED CHILDREN

Interpretation

Accommodation duties

Duties of local authorities in relation to looked after children

Regulations about looked after children

PART VII

Codes of Practice—The Codes to Parts 2, 3, 4 and 6 of the 2014 Act are set out in the online version of *The Family Court Practice*.

PART 1
INTRODUCTION

Overview

1 Overview of this Act

(1) This Act has 11 Parts.

(2) This Part provides an overview of the whole Act and defines some key terms.

(3) Part 2 (general duties) –

    (a) requires persons exercising functions under this Act to seek to promote the well-being of people who need care and support and carers who need support(section 5);

    (b) imposes overarching duties on persons exercising functions under this Act in relation to persons who need or may need care and support, carers who need or may need support, or persons in respect of whom functions are exercisable under Part 6, so as to give effect to certain key principles (section 6);

    (c) requires the Welsh Ministers to issue a statement specifying the well-being outcomes that are to be achieved for people who need care and support and carers who need support and to issue a code to help achieve those outcomes (sections 8 to 13);

    (d) requires local authorities to assess the needs in their areas for care and support, support for carers and preventative services (section 14);

    (e) requires local authorities to provide or arrange for the provision of preventative services (section 15);

PART VII

(f)   requires the promotion by local authorities of social enterprises, co-operatives, user led services and the third sector in the provision in their areas of care and support and support for carers (section 16);

(g)   requires the provision by local authorities of a service providing information and advice relating to care and support and support for carers and assistance in accessing it (section 17);

(h)   requires local authorities to establish and maintain registers of sight-impaired, hearing-impaired and other disabled people (section 18).

(4) Part 3 (assessing the needs of individuals) provides for –

(a)   the circumstances in which a local authority must assess a person's needs for care and support or a carer's needs for support;

(b)   how assessments are to be carried out.

(5) Part 4 (meeting needs) provides for –

(a)   the circumstances in which needs for care and support or support for carers may or must be met by local authorities;

(b)   how needs are to be met.

(6) Part 5 (charging and financial assessment) provides for –

(a)   the circumstances in which local authorities may charge for providing or arranging care and support or support for carers;

(b)   the circumstances in which local authorities may charge for preventative services and the provision of assistance;

(c)   how such charges are to be set, paid and enforced.

(7) Part 6 (looked after and accommodated children) –

(a)   provides for the interpretation of references to a child or young person looked after by a local authority (section 74);

(b)   requires local authorities –

(i)   to secure sufficient accommodation in their areas for the children they look after (section 75), and

(ii)   to accommodate children without parents or who are lost or abandoned or are under police protection, detention or on remand (sections 76 and 77);

(c)   provides for the functions of local authorities in relation to the children they look after (sections 75 to 103, 124 and 125);

(d)   provides for the circumstances in which local authorities may or must provide support for young people –

(i)   leaving, or who have left, local authority care;

(ii)   formerly accommodated in certain establishments;

(iii)   formerly fostered;

(iv)   with respect to whom special guardianship orders are or were in force; (sections 104 to 118);

(e)   provides for limits on the use of secure accommodation for children looked after by local authorities or local authorities in England or children of a description specified in regulations (section 119);

(f)   requires the assessment by local authorities of children who are accommodated by health authorities or education authorities or in care homes or independent hospitals and the provision of visits and services to those children (sections 120 to 123);

(g)   introduces Schedule 1 which makes provision about contributions towards the maintenance of children looked after by local authorities.

(8) Part 7 (safeguarding) –

(a)   requires local authorities to investigate where they suspect that an adult with care and support needs is at risk of abuse or neglect (section 126);

(b) provides for adult protection and support orders to authorise entry to premises (if necessary by force) for the purpose of enabling an authorised officer of a local authority to assess whether an adult is at risk of abuse or neglect and, if so, what to do about it (section 127);

(c) requires local authorities and their relevant partners to report to the appropriate authority where they suspect that people may be at risk of abuse or neglect (sections 128 and 130);

(d) disapplies section 47 of the National Assistance Act 1948 (which enables local authorities to apply for a court order to remove people in need of care and attention from their homes to hospitals or other places) (section 129);

(e) establishes a National Independent Safeguarding Board to provide support and advice in order to ensure the effectiveness of Safeguarding Boards (sections 132 and 133);

(f) provides for Safeguarding Boards for adults and children and for the combination of such boards (sections 134 to 141).

(9) Part 8 (social services functions) –

(a) introduces Schedule 2, which specifies the social services functions of local authorities (section 143);

(b) requires the appointment of directors of social services by local authorities and makes related provision (section 144);

(c) provides for codes about the exercise of social services functions to be made by the Welsh Ministers (sections 145 to 149);

(d) provides for intervention by the Welsh Ministers in the exercise of social services functions where a local authority is failing to exercise them properly (sections 150 to 161).

(10) Part 9 (co-operation and partnership) –

(a) requires local authorities to make arrangements to promote co-operation with their relevant partners and others in relation to adults with needs for care and support, carers and children (sections 162 and 163);

(b) imposes a duty on the relevant partners to co-operate with, and provide information to, the local authorities for the purpose of their social services functions (section 164);

(c) makes provision about promoting the integration of care and support with health services (section 165);

(d) provides for partnership arrangements between local authorities and Local Health Boards for the discharge of their functions (sections 166 to 169);

(e) empowers the Welsh Ministers to direct local authorities to enter into joint arrangements for the provision of an adoption service (section 170).

(11) Part 10 (complaints, representations and advocacy services) has three chapters.

(12) Chapter 1 provides for complaints and representations about social services provided or arranged by local authorities.

(13) Chapter 2 provides for complaints to the Public Services Ombudsman for Wales about private social care and palliative care.

(14) Chapter 3 provides for advocacy services to be made available to people with needs for care and support for purposes relating to their care and support.

(15) Part 11 (miscellaneous and general) –

(a) empowers the Welsh Ministers, local authorities and Local Health Boards to conduct research, and empowers the Welsh Ministers to require information, about matters connected with functions under the Act and other related matters (section 184);

PART VII

(b) makes provision about how this Act applies to persons in prison, youth detention accommodation or bail accommodation etc (sections 185 to 188);

(c) makes provision about the steps to be taken by a local authority where an establishment or agency (within the meaning of the Care Standards Act 2000) becomes unable to meet needs in the authority's area because of business failure (sections 189 to 191);

(d) disapplies section 49 of the National Assistance Act 1948 (which allows a local authority to meet expenses incurred by any of its officers appointed by the Court of Protection as a deputy) (section 192);

(e) makes provision for the recovery of costs between local authorities in certain circumstances (section 193);

(f) provides for the resolution of questions about the ordinary residence of a person for the purposes of this Act (section 194);

(g) contains the definitions that apply for the purposes of this Act generally and an index of defined expressions (section 197);

(h) contains other provisions which apply generally for the purposes of this Act.

(16) There are also provisions about social services in the Acts and Measures listed in Schedule 2.

Key terms

2 Meaning of 'well-being'

(1) This section applies for the purpose of this Act.

(2) 'Well-being', in relation to a person, means well-being in relation to any of the following –

(a) physical and mental health and emotional well-being;
(b) protection from abuse and neglect;
(c) education, training and recreation;
(d) domestic, family and personal relationships;
(e) contribution made to society;
(f) securing rights and entitlements;
(g) social and economic well-being;
(h) suitability of living accommodation.

(3) In relation to a child, 'well-being' also includes –

(a) physical, intellectual, emotional, social and behavioural development;
(b) 'welfare' as that word is interpreted for the purposes of the Children Act 1989.

(4) In relation to an adult, 'well-being' also includes –

(a) control over day to day life;
(b) participation in work.

'Well-being' (s 2(2)–(4))—'Well-being', as defined in this section, is a statutory definition to be used when applying this Act and the statutory scheme that flows from it. In relation to children, the term 'well-being' includes welfare as interpreted by CA 1989 but it is not so limited; it is intended to be a much broader concept. Well-being is subjective: see the Code to Part 2, para 30.

3 Meaning of 'adult', 'child', 'carer' and 'disabled'

(1) This section applies for the purposes of this Act.

(2) 'Adult' means a person who is aged 18 or over.

(3) 'Child' means a person who is aged under 18.

(4) 'Carer' means a person who provides or intends to provide care for an adult or disabled child; but see subsections (7) and (8) and section 187(1).

(5) A person is 'disabled' if the person has a disability for the purposes of the Equality Act 2010, subject to provision made under subsection (6).

(6) Regulations may provide that a person falling within a specified category is or is not to be treated as disabled for the purposes of this Act.

(7) A person is not a carer for the purposes of this Act if the person provides or intends to provide care –

    (a)   under or by virtue of a contract, or

    (b)   as voluntary work.

(8) But a local authority may treat a person as a carer for the purposes of any of its functions under this Act if the authority considers that the relationship between the person providing or intending to provide care and the person for whom that care is, or is to be, provided is such that it would be appropriate for the former to be treated as a carer for the purposes of that function or those functions.

4 Meaning of 'care and support'

Any reference to care and support in this Act is to be construed as a reference to –

    (a)   care;

    (b)   support;

    (c)   both care and support.

PART 2
GENERAL FUNCTIONS

Note—See the Code to Part 2.

Overarching duties

5 Well-being duty

A person exercising functions under this Act must seek to promote the well-being of –

    (a)   people who need care and support, and

    (b)   carers who need support.

Defined terms—'well-being': s 2(2)–(4).

Duty—The duty is owed to **people**, adults and children alike. This overarching duty applies to all persons and bodies exercising functions under this Act. This includes Welsh Ministers, local authorities, local health boards and other statutory agencies (Code to Part 2, para 26).

Promoting well-being means that local authorities must be proactive in seeking to improve the well-being of people who need care and support and carers who need support (Code to Part 2).

In order to discharge this duty, responsibility for well-being must be shared with those who need care and support and carers who need support (Code to Part 2, para 27). It is intended that outcomes are achieved through **co-production**. Agencies and organisations cannot deliver well-being outcomes but they can support those to whom they owe a duty to achieve that outcome (Code to Part 2, para 27). Local authorities must look at what people, their families and their communities can contribute to a care and support plan (Code to Part 2, para 49).

National well-being outcome statements—When seeking to promote well-being of people who need care and support and carers who need support, local authorities must take into account the national well-being outcome statements that underpin the definition of well-being, under each aspect of well-being – see the definition of well-being at s 2(2). The national well-being outcome statements are found in the Code to Part 2.

PART VII

Not all personal outcomes will be achievable and raising hopes and expectations that cannot be met may do more harm than good (Code to Part 2, para 11).

Responses and outcomes—Responses and outcomes, as well as the process that underpins them, must be proportionate and timely (Code to Part 2, para 30).

Grounds for an enquiry—When personal outcomes cannot be achieved through an equal relationship between people and practitioners, consideration must be given to whether the grounds exist for an enquiry under CA 1989, s 47 in relation to a child or under s 126 of the 2014 Act in relation to an adult (Code to Part 2, para 32).

6 Other overarching duties: general

(1) A person exercising functions under this Act in relation to –

    (a)   an individual who has, or may have, needs for care and support,

    (b)   a carer who has, or may have, needs for support, or

    (c)   an individual in respect of whom functions are exercisable under Part 6 (looked after children etc),

must comply with the duties in subsection (2).

(2) The person must –

    (a)   in so far as is reasonably practicable, ascertain and have regard to the individual's views, wishes and feelings,

    (b)   have regard to the importance of promoting and respecting the dignity of the individual,

    (c)   have regard to the characteristics, culture and beliefs of the individual (including, for example, language), and

    (d)   have regard to the importance of providing appropriate support to enable the individual to participate in decisions that affect him or her to the extent that is appropriate in the circumstances, particularly where the individual's ability to communicate is limited for any reason.

(3) A person exercising functions under this Act in relation to an adult falling within subsection (1)(a), (b) or (c) must, in addition, have regard to –

    (a)   the importance of beginning with the presumption that the adult is best placed to judge the adult's well-being, and

    (b)   the importance of promoting the adult's independence where possible.

(4) A person exercising functions under this Act in relation to a child falling within subsection (1)(a), (b) or (c), in addition –

    (a)   must have regard to the importance of promoting the upbringing of the child by the child's family, in so far as doing so is consistent with promoting the well-being of the child, and

    (b)   where the child is under the age of 16, must ascertain and have regard to the views, wishes and feelings of the persons with parental responsibility for the child, in so far as doing so is –

        (i)   consistent with promoting the well-being of the child, and

        (ii) reasonably practicable.

'individual' (s 6(1))—Part 6 of the 2014 Act covers looked-after children, accommodated children and care leavers. 'Individual' includes adults and children: the duty owed under s 6 applies to those who may have needs for care and support or be a carer who may need support, as well as those who have those needs.

Strategic Framework (s 6(2))—Individual includes adults and children: the Code to Part 2 states that for many Welsh speakers language is an integral element of achieving their care and securing their rights and entitlements. The Welsh Government has established a Strategic Framework for Welsh Language Services in Health, Social Services and Social Care, which is available at *http://wales.gov.uk/topics/health/*

publications/health/guidance/words/?lang=en. The Framework outlines six key objectives that all organisations, including local authorities, need to work towards.

'have regard' (s 6(4))—The requirements under s 6(4) are in addition to those under s 6(2). CA 1989, ss 17 and 22 no longer apply in Wales. Well-being is defined in s 2(2). The requirement to 'have regard' in the context of s 6 is similar to a requirement to consider or take into account that matter (Code to Part 2, para 55).

7 Other overarching duties: UN Principles and Convention

(1) A person exercising functions under this Act in relation to an adult falling within section 6(1)(a) or (b) must have due regard to the United Nations Principles for Older Persons adopted by the General Assembly of the United Nations on 16 December 1991.

(2) A person exercising functions under this Act in relation to a child falling within section 6(1)(a), (b) or (c) must have due regard to Part 1 of the United Nations Convention on the Rights of the Child adopted and opened for signature, ratification and accession by General Assembly resolution 44/25 of 20 November 1989 ('the Convention').

(3) For the purposes of subsection (2), Part 1 of the Convention is to be treated as having effect –

    (a)   as set out for the time being in Part 1 of the Schedule to the Rights of Children and Young Persons (Wales) Measure 2011, but

    (b)   subject to any declaration or reservation as set out for the time being in Part 3 of that Schedule.

(4) Subsection (2) does not apply to the Welsh Ministers (see, instead, the Rights of Children and Young Persons (Wales) Measure 2011).

'have due regard' (s 7)—The requirement to 'have due regard' in the context of s 7 is similar to a requirement to consider or take into account that matter (Code to Part 2, para 60). When exercising functions under the Act in relation to disabled persons who need care and support and disabled carers who need support, due regard must be had to the United Nations Convention on the Rights of Disabled People (Code to Part 2, para 63).

Well-being outcomes

8 Duty to issue a statement of the outcomes to be achieved

(1) The Welsh Ministers must issue a statement relating to the well-being of –

    (a)   people in Wales who need care and support, and

    (b)   carers in Wales who need support.

(2) The statement must be issued within 3 years beginning with the date on which this Act receives Royal Assent.

(3) The statement must specify the outcomes that are to be achieved, in terms of the well-being of the people mentioned in subsection (1), by means of –

    (a)   care and support (or, in the case of carers, support) provided by local authorities under this Act, and

    (b)   care and support (or, in the case of carers, support) provided by others which is of a kind that could be provided by local authorities under this Act.

(4) The statement must also specify measures by reference to which the achievement of those outcomes is to be assessed.

(5) The statement may specify different outcomes or measures for different categories of people who need care and support (or, in the case of carers, support).

PART VII

(6) The Welsh Ministers must keep the statement under review and may revise the statement whenever they consider it appropriate to do so.

(7) Before issuing or revising the statement, the Welsh Ministers must consult such persons as they think fit.

(8) The Welsh Ministers must, on issuing or revising the statement –

    (a)   lay a copy of the statement before the National Assembly for Wales, and

    (b)   publish the statement on their website.

9   Power to issue a code to help achieve the outcomes

(1) The Welsh Ministers must issue, and from time to time revise, a code to help achieve the outcomes specified in the statement under section 8.

(2) The code may –

    (a)   give guidance to any person providing care and support (or, in the case of carers, support) of the kind described in section 8(3), and

    (b)   impose requirements on local authorities in relation to provision of that kind.

(3) The following are examples of the matters which may be set out in the code –

    (a)   standards ('quality standards') to be achieved in the provision of care and support (or, in the case of carers, support);

    (b)   measures ('performance measures') by reference to which performance in achieving those quality standards can be assessed;

    (c)   targets ('performance targets') to be met in relation to those performance measures;

    (d)   steps to be taken in relation to those standards, measures and targets.

(4) The code may specify –

    (a)   different quality standards for –

        (i)   different categories of care and support (or, in the case of carers, support);

        (ii)   different categories of people who need care and support (or, in the case of carers, support);

    (b)   different performance measures or performance targets for –

        (i)   different categories of care and support (or, in the case of carers, support);

        (ii)   different categories of persons who provide care and support (or, in the case of carers, support);

    (c)   different quality standards, performance measures or performance targets to apply at different times.

(5) The Welsh Ministers must –

    (a)   publish on their website the code which is for the time being in force, and

    (b)   make available to the public (whether on their website or otherwise) codes which are no longer in force.

10   Local authorities and the code

(1) In exercising its functions under this Act, a local authority must –

    (a)   act in accordance with any relevant requirements imposed upon it by a code issued under section 9, and

    (b)   have regard to any relevant guidance contained in that code.

(2) Where performance measures or performance targets are specified in a code issued under section 9, they are to be treated (so far as they apply to the performance of local

authorities in exercising their functions) as having been specified as performance indicators or performance standards respectively under section 8(1) of the Local Government (Wales) Measure 2009.

11 Issue, approval and revocation of the code

(1) Before issuing or revising a code under section 9, the Welsh Ministers must consult such persons as they think fit on a draft of the code (or revised code).

(2) If the Welsh Ministers wish to proceed with the draft (with or without modifications) they must lay a copy of the draft before the National Assembly for Wales.

(3) If, before the end of the 40 day period, the National Assembly for Wales resolves not to approve the draft, the Welsh Ministers must not issue the code (or revised code) in the form of that draft.

(4) If no such resolution is made before the end of that period –

    (a) the Welsh Ministers must issue the code (or revised code) in the form of the draft, and

    (b) the code (or revised code) comes into force on the date appointed by order of the Welsh Ministers.

(5) The 40 day period –

    (a) begins on the day on which the draft is laid before the National Assembly for Wales, and

    (b) does not include any time during which the National Assembly for Wales is dissolved or is in recess for more than four days.

(6) Subsection (3) does not prevent a new draft of a code (or revised code) from being laid before the National Assembly for Wales.

(7) The Welsh Ministers may revoke a code (or revised code) issued under this section in a further code or by direction.

(8) A direction under subsection (7) must be laid before the National Assembly for Wales.

12 Power to help local authorities to comply with the code's requirements

(1) The Welsh Ministers may do anything which they consider is likely to help a local authority to comply with requirements imposed by a code under section 9.

(2) The power under subsection (1) includes power –

    (a) to enter into arrangements or agreements with any person;

    (b) to co-operate with, or facilitate or co-ordinate the activities of, any person;

    (c) to exercise on behalf of any person any functions of that person;

    (d) to provide staff, goods, services or accommodation to any person.

(3) Unless the Welsh Ministers are exercising the power under subsection (1) in response to a request made under subsection (4), they must, before exercising that power, consult –

    (a) the local authority which they propose to assist by the exercise of the power, and

    (b) those persons who appear to the Welsh Ministers to be key stakeholders affected by the exercise of the power.

(4) If a local authority asks them to do so, the Welsh Ministers must consider whether to exercise their power under subsection (1).

PART VII

13 Publication of information and reports

The Welsh Ministers may publish –

(a) information about the provision of care and support (or, in the case of carers, support) of the kind described in section 8(3), and

(b) reports on the progress made by local authorities and others towards the achievement of –

    (i) the outcomes specified in a statement under section 8;

    (ii) the quality standards and performance targets (if any) specified in a code under section 9.

Local arrangements

14 Assessment of needs for care and support, support for carers and preventative services

(1) A local authority and each Local Health Board any Part of whose area lies within the area of the local authority must, in accordance with regulations, jointly assess –

(a) the extent to which there are people in the local authority's area who need care and support;

(b) the extent to which there are carers in the local authority's area who need support;

(c) the extent to which there are people in the local authority's area whose needs for care and support (or, in the case of carers, support) are not being met (by the authority, the Board or otherwise);

(d) the range and level of services required to meet the care and support needs of people in the local authority's area (including the support needs of carers);

(e) the range and level of services required to achieve the purposes in section 15(2) (preventative services) in the local authority's area;

(f) the actions required to provide the range and level of services identified in accordance with paragraphs (d) and (e) through the medium of Welsh.

(2) Regulations under subsection (1) may, for example, provide for the timing and review of assessments.

(3), (4) (*repealed*)

Amendments—Well-being of Future Generations (Wales) Act 2015, s 46, Sch 4, para 33.

14A Plans following assessments of needs under section 14

(1) In this section, 'relevant body' means a local authority or Local Health Board which has carried out a joint assessment under section 14(1).

(2) Each relevant body must prepare and publish a plan setting out –

(a) the range and level of services the body proposes to provide, or arrange to be provided, in response to the assessment of needs under paragraphs (a) to (c) of section 14(1);

(b) in the case of a local authority, the range and level of services the authority proposes to provide, or arrange to be provided, in seeking to achieve the purposes in section 15(2) (preventative services);

(c) in the case of a Local Health Board, anything the Board proposes to do in connection with its duty under section 15(5) (Local Health Boards to have regard to the importance of preventative action when exercising functions);

(d) how the services set out in the plan are to be provided, including the actions the body proposes to take to provide, or arrange to provide, the services through the medium of Welsh;

(e) any other action the body proposes to take in response to the assessment under section 14(1);

(f) the details of anything the body proposes to do in response to the assessment jointly with another relevant body;

(g) the resources to be deployed in doing the things set out in the plan.

(3) A relevant body's plan may be published by including it within a local well-being plan published under section 39 or 44(5) of the Wellbeing of Future Generations (Wales) Act 2015 (the '2015 Act') by a public services board of which the body is a member.

(4) A local authority and a Local Health Board who have carried out a joint assessment together under section 14(1) may jointly prepare and publish a plan under subsection (2).

(5) Two or more local authorities may jointly prepare and publish a plan under subsection (2); but such a joint plan may be published by including it within a local well-being plan only if each local authority is a member of the public services board (see sections 47 and 49 of the 2015 Act (merging of public services boards)).

(6) A relevant body must submit to the Welsh Ministers –

(a) any part of a plan it has prepared under subsection (2) which relates to the health and well-being of carers;

(b) any other part of such a plan as may be specified by regulations.

(7) Regulations may make provision about plans prepared and published under subsection (2), including provision –

(a) specifying when a plan is to be published;

(b) about reviewing a plan;

(c) about consulting persons when preparing or reviewing a plan;

(d) about the monitoring and evaluation of services and other action set out in a plan.

Amendments—Inserted by Well-being of Future Generations (Wales) Act 2015, s 46, Sch 4, para 34.

15 Preventative services

(1) A local authority must provide or arrange for the provision of a range and level of services which it considers will achieve the purposes in subsection (2) in its area.

(2) The purposes are –

(a) contributing towards preventing or delaying the development of people's needs for care and support;

(b) reducing the needs for care and support of people who have such needs;

(c) promoting the upbringing of children by their families, where that is consistent with the well-being of children;

(d) minimising the effect on disabled people of their disabilities;

(e) contributing towards preventing people from suffering abuse or neglect;

(f) reducing the need for –

(i) proceedings for care or supervision orders under the Children Act 1989,

(ii) criminal proceedings against children,

(iii) any family or other proceedings in relation to children which might lead to them being placed in local authority care, or

(iv) proceedings under the inherent jurisdiction of the High Court in relation to children;

(g) encouraging children not to commit criminal offences;

PART VII

(h)   avoiding the need for children to be placed in secure accommodation within the meaning given in section 119 and in section 25 of the Children Act 1989;

(i)   enabling people to live their lives as independently as possible.

(3) The things that may be provided or arranged in discharging the duty under subsection (1) include, but are not limited to, care and support (or in the case of carers, support) of the kind that must or may be provided under sections 35 to 45.

(4) A local authority must, in the exercise of its other functions, have regard to the importance of achieving the purposes in subsection (2) in its area.

(5) A Local Health Board must, in the exercise of its functions, have regard to the importance of achieving the purposes in subsection (2) in its area.

(6) In discharging its duty under subsection (1) a local authority –

(a)   must identify the services already available in the authority's area which may help in achieving the purposes in subsection (2) and consider involving or making use of those services in discharging the duty;

(b)   may take account of services which the authority considers might reasonably be provided or arranged by other persons in deciding what it should provide or arrange;

(c)   must make the best use of the authority's resources and in particular avoid provision which might give rise to disproportionate expenditure.

(7) Provision is not to be considered as giving rise to disproportionate expenditure only because that provision is more expensive than comparable provision.

(8) Two or more local authorities may jointly discharge the duty under subsection (1) in relation to their combined area; where they do so –

(a)   references in this section to a local authority are to be read as references to the authorities acting jointly, and

(b)   references in this section to a local authority's area are to be read as references to the combined area.

(9) See sections 46 (exception for persons subject to immigration control), 47 (exception for provision of health services), 48 (exception for provision of housing etc) and 49 (restrictions on provision of payments) for an exception to the duty under subsection (1) and limitations on the manner in which the duty may be discharged.

Amendments—SI 2016/413.

'**the purposes in subsection (2)**' (s 15(4))—A local authority must have regard to the importance of achieving these purposes in relation to the exercise of all its functions, not just in relation to social services functions (Code to Part 2, para 149).

16 Promoting social enterprises, co-operatives, user led services and the third sector

(1) A local authority must promote –

(a)   the development in its area of social enterprises to provide care and support and preventative services;

(b)   the development in its area of co-operative organisations or arrangements to provide care and support and preventative services;

(c)   the involvement of persons for whom care and support or preventative services are to be provided in the design and operation of that provision;

(d)   the availability in its area of care and support and preventative services from third sector organisations (whether or not the organisations are social enterprises or co-operative organisations).

(2) In this section –

'care and support' ('*gofal a chymorth*') includes support for carers;

'preventative services' ('*gwasanaethau ataliol*') means services the local authority considers would achieve any of the purposes in section 15(2);

'social enterprise' ('*menter gymdeithasol*') means an organisation whose activities are wholly or mainly activities which a person might reasonably consider to be activities carried on for the benefit of society ('its social objects'), and which –

    (a)   generates most of its income through business or trade,

    (b)   reinvests most of its profits in its social objects,

    (c)   is independent of any public authority, and

    (d)   is owned, controlled and managed in a way that is consistent with its social objects;

'society' ('*y gymdeithas*') includes a section of society;

'third sector organisation' ('*sefydliad trydydd sector*') means an organisation which a person might reasonably consider to exist wholly or mainly to provide benefits for society.

(3) For the purposes of this section, regulations may provide –

    (a)   that activities of a specified description are or are not to be treated as activities which a person might reasonably consider to be activities carried on for the benefit of society;

    (b)   that organisations or arrangements of a specified description are or are not to be treated as –

        (i)   social enterprises,

        (ii)   co-operative organisations or arrangements, or

        (iii) third sector organisations;

    (c)   for what does, does not or may constitute a section of society.

17 Provision of information, advice and assistance

(1) A local authority must secure the provision of a service for providing people with –

    (a)   information and advice relating to care and support, and

    (b)   assistance in accessing care and support.

(2) In subsection (1)(a), 'information' includes, but is not limited to, financial information (including information about direct payments).

(3) The local authority must seek to ensure that the service –

    (a)   is sufficient to enable a person to make plans for meeting needs for care and support that might arise, and

    (b)   provides information, advice and assistance to a person in a manner which is accessible to that person.

(4) The service must include, as a minimum, the publication of information and advice on the following matters –

    (a)   the system provided for by this Act and how the system operates in the authority's area,

    (b)   the types of care and support available in the authority's area,

    (c)   how to access the care and support that is available, and

    (d)   how to raise concerns about the well-being of a person who appears to have needs for care and support.

(5) A Local Health Board or an NHS Trust providing services in the area of a local authority must, for the purposes of this section, provide that local authority with information about the care and support it provides in the local authority's area.

(6) Two or more local authorities may jointly secure the provision of a service under this section for their combined area; and where they do so –

PART VII

(a)   references in this section to a local authority are to be read as references to the authorities acting jointly, and

(b)   references in this section to a local authority's area are to be read as references to the combined area.

(7)   In this section, 'care and support' includes support for carers.

18 Registers of sight-impaired, hearing-impaired and other disabled people

(1)   A local authority must establish and maintain a register of the people ordinarily resident in the authority's area who –

(a)   are sight-impaired or severely sight-impaired,

(b)   are hearing-impaired or severely hearing-impaired, or

(c)   have sight and hearing impairments which, in combination, have a significant effect on their day to day lives.

(2)   The register must identify, in respect of each person included in the register –

(a)   the paragraph in subsection (1) within which that person falls, and

(b)   the person's linguistic circumstances.

(3)   Regulations may specify, for the purposes of subsection (1), categories of people who are, or are not, to be treated as falling within paragraph (a), (b) or (c) of that subsection.

(4)   A local authority must establish and maintain a register of children to whom subsection (6) applies and who are within the local authority's area.

(5)   A local authority may establish and maintain a register of adults to whom subsection (6) applies and who are ordinarily resident in the local authority's area.

(6)   This subsection applies to a person who –

(a)   is disabled,

(b)   is not disabled but has a physical or mental impairment which gives rise, or which the authority considers may in the future give rise, to needs for care and support, or

(c)   comes within any other category of persons the authority considers appropriate to include in a register of persons who have, or who the authority considers may in the future have, needs for care and support.

(7)   A local authority –

(a)   may categorise people included in a register under subsection (4) or (5) as it thinks fit, and

(b)   must identify the linguistic circumstances of those people in the relevant register.

(8)   The registers established and maintained under this section may be used in the exercise of the authority's functions; for example, for the purpose of –

(a)   planning the provision by the authority of services to meet needs for care and support or support for carers, and

(b)   monitoring changes over time in the number of people in the authority's area with needs for care and support and the types of needs they or their carers have.

(9)   Nothing in this section requires a local authority to include any person in a register maintained under this section unless –

(a)   the person has applied to be included in the register, or

(b)   an application to be so included has been made on the person's behalf.

(10) Where a local authority includes a person in a register maintained under this section, the authority –

    (a)   must inform the person that he or she has been so included, and

    (b)   if a request is made by the person or on the person's behalf, must remove from the register any personal data (within the meaning of the Data Protection Act 1998) relating to that person.

PART 3
ASSESSING THE NEEDS OF INDIVIDUALS
Note—See the Code to Part 3.

Assessing adults

19 Duty to assess the needs of an adult for care and support

(1) Where it appears to a local authority that an adult may have needs for care and support, the authority must assess –

    (a)   whether the adult does have needs for care and support, and

    (b)   if the adult does, what those needs are.

(2) The duty under subsection (1) applies in relation to –

    (a)   an adult who is ordinarily resident in the authority's area, and

    (b)   any other adult who is within the authority's area.

(3) The duty under subsection (1) applies regardless of the local authority's view of –

    (a)   the level of the adult's needs for care and support, or

    (b)   the level of the adult's financial resources.

(4) In carrying out a needs assessment under this section, the local authority must –

    (a)   seek to identify the outcomes that the adult wishes to achieve in day to day life,

    (b)   assess whether, and if so, to what extent, the provision of –

        (i)   care and support,

        (ii)   preventative services, or

        (iii) information, advice or assistance,

        could contribute to the achievement of those outcomes or otherwise meet needs identified by the assessment, and

    (c)   assess whether, and if so, to what extent, other matters could contribute to the achievement of those outcomes or otherwise meet those needs.

(5) A local authority, in carrying out a needs assessment under this section, must involve –

    (a)   the adult, and

    (b)   where feasible, any carer that the adult has.

(6) The nature of the needs assessment required by this section is one that the local authority considers proportionate in the circumstances, subject to any requirement in regulations under section 30.

Section 19(1)—The mandatory duty to assess arises if the adult may have a need of care and support.

Note—National Health Service and Community Care Act 1990, s 47(1)(a) has been amended. In Wales, it now only applies to assessments for after-care under MHA 1983, s 117. The duties under ss 6–7 of the 2014 Act are engaged. Due regard must be paid to the UN Principles for Older Persons and the UN Convention on the Rights of Disabled People (Code to Part 3, para 46). The Care and Support (Assessment) (Wales) Regulations 2015 apply.

PART VII

The Code to Part 3 applies. The assessment process is at paras 16–43 and the assessment requirements at paras 43–65. Additional considerations when assessing adults are at paras 66–67. Additional considerations for assessing needs that are met by carers are at paras 80–84.

There is a National Minimum Core Data Set. A key part of the assessment must be to establish whether there is reasonable cause to suspect that the adult is at risk. An adult at risk is defined in s 126 of the 2014 Act. A common recording requirement has been developed. Assessments should be dynamic, timely and proportionate.

20 Refusal of a needs assessment for an adult

(1) If an adult (or, where applicable, an authorised person) refuses a needs assessment under section 19, the duty under that section to assess the adult's needs does not apply.

(2) But a refusal under subsection (1) does not discharge a local authority from its duty under section 19 in the following cases –

CASE 1 – the local authority is satisfied, in the case of a refusal given by the adult, that –

(a) the adult lacks capacity to decide whether to refuse to have the assessment, but

(b) there is an authorised person to make the decision on the adult's behalf;

CASE 2 – the local authority is satisfied, in the case of a refusal given by the adult, that –

(a) the adult lacks capacity to decide whether to refuse to have the assessment,

(b) there is no authorised person to make the decision on the adult's behalf, and

(c) having the assessment would be in the adult's best interests;

CASE 3 – the local authority suspects that the adult is experiencing or at risk of abuse or neglect.

(3) Where a local authority has been discharged from its duty under section 19 by a refusal under this section, the duty is re-engaged if –

(a) the adult (or, where applicable, an authorised person) subsequently asks for an assessment, or

(b) the local authority considers that the adult's needs or circumstances have changed,

(subject to any further refusal under this section).

(4) In this section 'authorised person' means a person authorised under the Mental Capacity Act 2005 (whether in general or specific terms) to decide whether to refuse, or ask for, a needs assessment on the adult's behalf.

Assessing children

21 Duty to assess the needs of a child for care and support

(1) Where it appears to a local authority that a child may need care and support in addition to, or instead of, the care and support provided by the child's family, the authority must assess –

(a) whether the child does need care and support of that kind, and

(b) if the child does, what those needs are.

(2) The duty under subsection (1) applies in relation to –

(a) a child who is ordinarily resident in the authority's area, and

(b) any other child who is within the authority's area.

(3) The duty under subsection (1) applies regardless of the local authority's view of –

(a) the level of the child's needs for care and support, or

(b) the level of the financial resources of the child or any person with parental responsibility for the child.

(4) In carrying out a needs assessment under this section, the local authority must –

(a) assess the developmental needs of the child,

(b) seek to identify the outcomes that –

(i) the child wishes to achieve, to the extent it considers appropriate having regard to the child's age and understanding,

(ii) the persons with parental responsibility for the child wish to achieve in relation to the child, to the extent it considers appropriate having regard to the need to promote the child's well-being, and

(iii) persons specified in regulations (if any) wish to achieve in relation to the child,

(c) assess whether, and if so, to what extent, the provision of –

(i) care and support,

(ii) preventative services, or

(iii) information, advice or assistance,

could contribute to the achievement of those outcomes or otherwise meet needs identified by the assessment,

(d) assess whether, and if so, to what extent, other matters could contribute to the achievement of those outcomes or otherwise meet those needs, and

(e) take account of any other circumstances affecting the child's well-being.

(5) A local authority, in carrying out a needs assessment under this section, must involve –

(a) the child, and

(b) any person with parental responsibility for the child.

(6) The nature of the needs assessment required by this section is one that the local authority considers proportionate in the circumstances, subject to any requirement in regulations under section 30.

(7) For the purposes of subsection (1) a disabled child is presumed to need care and support in addition to, or instead of, the care and support provided by the child's family.

(8) This section does not apply to a child looked after by –

(a) a local authority,

(b) a local authority in England,

(c) a local authority in Scotland, or

(d) a Health and Social Care trust.

Note—CA 1989, s 17 and Sch 2 are repealed.

The duties under ss 6–7 of the 2014 Act are engaged (see above).

Due regard must be paid to the UN Convention on the Rights of the Child and the UN Convention on the Rights of Disabled People (Code to Part 3, para 46). 'Due regard' is similar to a requirement to consider or take into account.

'Due regard' is similar to a requirement to consider or take into account a matter (Code to Part 2, para 55).

The Care and Support (Assessment) (Wales) Regulations 2015 apply.

The Code to Part 3 applies. The assessment process is at paras 16–43 and the assessment requirements are at paras 43–65. Additional considerations when assessing adults are at paras 68–79 and additional considerations for assessing needs that are met by carers are at paras 80–84.

There is a National Minimum Core Data Set.

A key part of the assessment must be to establish whether there is reasonable cause to suspect that the child is at risk. A child at risk is defined in s 130(4). The pace and scope of the assessment may need to

PART VII

change to recognise risk and additional risk to children (Code to Part 3, paras 89–90). Where an assessment produces reasonable cause to suspect that a child is experiencing or is at risk and it has not already done so, a local authority must make enquiries (CA 1989, s 7 applies).

A common recording requirement has been developed as an interim measure while new assessment documents are formulated. The Framework for Assessment (DoH) no longer applies in Wales.

Assessments should be dynamic, proportionate and timely. The maximum timescale for completion of an assessment in relation to a child is 42 working days (Code to Part 3, para 78). Completion of an assessment should not take precedence over an analysis of what is happening in a child's life and what immediate action is needed, however difficult or complex the child's circumstances (Code to Part 3, para 34). A child's safety should not be compromised.

22 Refusal of a needs assessment for a child aged 16 or 17

(1) If a child aged 16 or 17 (or, where applicable, an authorised person) refuses a needs assessment under section 21, the duty under that section to assess the child's needs does not apply.

(2) If a person with parental responsibility for a child aged 16 or 17 refuses a needs assessment for that child under section 21 in circumstances in which the local authority is satisfied that –

    (a)   the child lacks capacity to decide whether to refuse to have the assessment, and

    (b)   there is no authorised person to make the decision on the child's behalf,

the duty under that section to assess the child's needs does not apply.

(3) But a refusal under subsection (1) or (2) does not discharge a local authority from its duty under section 21 in the following cases –

CASE 1 – the local authority is satisfied, in the case of a refusal given by a child, that the child lacks capacity to decide whether to refuse to have the assessment;

CASE 2 – the local authority is satisfied, in the case of a refusal given by a person with parental responsibility for the child, that the person lacks capacity to decide whether to refuse the assessment;

CASE 3 – the local authority is satisfied, in the case of a refusal given by a person with parental responsibility for the child, that not having the assessment would not be in the child's best interests;

CASE 4 – the local authority suspects that the child is experiencing or at risk of abuse, neglect or other kinds of harm.

(4) Where a local authority has been discharged from its duty under section 21 by a refusal under this section, the duty is re-engaged if –

    (a)   the child (or, where applicable, an authorised person) subsequently asks for an assessment,

    (b)   a person with parental responsibility for the child subsequently asks for an assessment in the circumstances described in subsection (2), or

    (c)   the local authority considers that the child's needs or circumstances, or the needs or circumstances of a person with parental responsibility for the child, have changed,

(subject to any further refusal under this section).

(5) In this section 'authorised person' means a person authorised under the Mental Capacity Act 2005 (whether in general or specific terms) to decide whether to refuse, or ask for, a needs assessment on the child's behalf.

23 Refusal of a needs assessment for a child aged under 16

(1) If –

(a)   a child aged under 16 refuses a needs assessment under section 21, and

(b)   the local authority is satisfied that the child has sufficient understanding to make an informed decision about the refusal of the assessment,

the duty under that section to assess the child's needs does not apply.

(2) If a person with parental responsibility for a child aged under 16 refuses a needs assessment for that child under section 21, the duty under that section to assess the child's needs does not apply.

(3) But a refusal under subsection (1) or (2) does not discharge a local authority from its duty under section 21 in the following cases –

CASE 1 – the local authority is satisfied, in the case of a refusal given by a person with parental responsibility for the child, that the person lacks capacity to decide whether to refuse the assessment;

CASE 2 – the local authority is satisfied, in the case of a refusal given by a person with parental responsibility for the child, that the child –

(a)   has sufficient understanding to make an informed decision about the refusal of the assessment, and

(b)   does not agree with the refusal given by the person with parental responsibility for the child;

CASE 3 – the local authority is satisfied, in the case of a refusal given by a person with parental responsibility for the child, that not having the assessment would be inconsistent with the child's well-being;

CASE 4 – the local authority suspects that the child is experiencing or at risk of abuse, neglect or other kinds of harm.

(4) Where a local authority has been discharged from its duty under section 21 by a refusal under this section, the duty is re-engaged if –

(a)   the child subsequently asks for an assessment and the local authority is satisfied that the child has sufficient understanding to make an informed decision about having an assessment,

(b)   a person with parental responsibility for the child subsequently asks for an assessment, or

(c)   the local authority considers that the child's needs or circumstances, or the needs or circumstances of a person with parental responsibility for the child, have changed,

(subject to any further refusal under this section).

Assessing carers

24 Duty to assess the needs of a carer for support

(1) Where it appears to a local authority that a carer may have needs for support, the authority must assess –

(a)   whether the carer does have needs for support (or is likely to do so in the future), and

(b)   if the carer does, what those needs are (or are likely to be in the future).

(2) The duty under subsection (1) applies in relation to a carer who is providing or intends to provide care for –

(a)   an adult or disabled child who is ordinarily resident in the authority's area, or

(b)   any other adult or disabled child who is within the authority's area.

(3) The duty under subsection (1) applies regardless of the authority's view of –

PART VII

- (a)   the level of the carer's needs for support, or
- (b)   the level of the financial resources of the carer or the person for whom the carer provides or intends to provide care.

(4) In carrying out a needs assessment under this section, the local authority must –

- (a)   assess the extent to which the carer is able, and will continue to be able, to provide care for the person for whom the carer provides or intends to provide care,
- (b)   assess the extent to which the carer is willing, and will continue to be willing, to do so,
- (c)   in the case of a carer who is an adult, seek to identify the outcomes that the carer wishes to achieve,
- (d)   in the case of a carer who is a child, seek to identify the outcomes that –
  - (i)   the carer wishes to achieve, to the extent it considers appropriate having regard to the carer's age and understanding,
  - (ii)   the persons with parental responsibility for the carer wish to achieve in relation to the carer, to the extent it considers appropriate having regard to the need to promote the carer's well-being, and
  - (iii) persons specified in regulations (if any) wish to achieve in relation to the carer,
- (e)   assess whether, and if so, to what extent, the provision of –
  - (i)   support,
  - (ii)   preventative services, or
  - (iii) information, advice or assistance,
  could contribute to the achievement of those outcomes or otherwise meet needs identified by the assessment, and
- (f)   assess whether, and if so, to what extent, other matters could contribute to the achievement of those outcomes or otherwise meet those needs.

(5) A local authority, in carrying out a needs assessment under this section, must have regard to –

- (a)   whether the carer works or wishes to do so,
- (b)   whether the carer is participating in or wishes to participate in education, training or any leisure activity, and
- (c)   in the case of a carer who is a child –
  - (i)   the developmental needs of the child, and
  - (ii)   whether it is appropriate for the child to provide the care (or any care) in light of those needs.

(6) A local authority, in carrying out a needs assessment under this section, must involve –

- (a)   the carer, and
- (b)   where feasible, the person for whom the carer provides or intends to provide care.

(7) The nature of the needs assessment required by this section is one that the local authority considers proportionate in the circumstances, subject to any requirement in regulations under section 30.

Note—The duties under ss 5–7 of the 2014 Act are engaged.

Due regard must be paid, as appropriate, depending upon whether the carer being assessed is an adult or a child, to the UN Principles for Older Persons, the UN Convention on the Rights of the Child and the UN Convention on the Rights of Disabled People (Code to Part 3, para 46).

The Care and Support (Assessment) (Wales) Regulations 2015 apply.

The Code to Part 3 applies. The consideration of the assessment of a carer is at para 15, The assessment process is at paras 16–43 and the assessment requirements at paras 43–65. Additional considerations when assessing adults are at paras 66–67. Additional considerations for assessing children are at paras 68–79. Where the carer is a child, consideration should be given to whether the child may have care and support needs of his/her own and be assessed under s 21 of the 2014 Act. If the carer is aged 16–25, any assessment must include an assessment of and have due regard to any current or future transitions the carer is likely to wish to make into further or higher education, employment or training (Code to Part 3, para 15).

There is a National Minimum Core Data Set.

A common recording requirement has been developed.

Assessments should be dynamic, proportionate and timely.

25 Refusal of a needs assessment for an adult carer

(1) If a carer who is an adult (or, where applicable, an authorised person) refuses a needs assessment under section 24, the duty under that section to assess the carer's needs does not apply.

(2) But a refusal under subsection (1) does not discharge a local authority from its duty under section 24 in the following cases –

CASE 1 – the local authority is satisfied, in the case of a refusal given by the carer, that –

    (a) the carer lacks capacity to decide whether to refuse to have the assessment, but

    (b) there is an authorised person to make the decision on the carer's behalf;

CASE 2 – the local authority is satisfied, in the case of a refusal given by the carer, that –

    (a) the carer lacks capacity to decide whether to refuse to have the assessment,

    (b) there is no authorised person to make the decision on the carer's behalf, and

    (c) having the assessment would be in the carer's best interests.

(3) Where a local authority has been discharged from its duty under section 24 by a refusal under this section, the duty is re-engaged if –

    (a) the carer (or, where applicable, an authorised person) subsequently asks for an assessment, or

    (b) the local authority considers that the carer's needs or circumstances have changed,

(subject to any further refusal under this section).

(4) In this section 'authorised person' means a person authorised under the Mental Capacity Act 2005 (whether in general or specific terms) to decide whether to refuse, or ask for, a needs assessment on the carer's behalf.

26 Refusal of a needs assessment for a carer aged 16 or 17

(1) If a carer aged 16 or 17 (or, where applicable, an authorised person) refuses a needs assessment under section 24, the duty under that section to assess the carer's needs does not apply.

(2) If a person with parental responsibility for a carer aged 16 or 17 refuses a needs assessment for the carer under section 24 in circumstances in which the local authority is satisfied that –

    (a) the carer lacks capacity to decide whether to refuse to have the assessment, and

    (b) there is no authorised person to make the decision on the carer's behalf,

the duty under that section to assess the carer's needs does not apply.

PART VII

(3) But a refusal under subsection (1) or (2) does not discharge a local authority from its duty under section 24 in the following cases –

CASE 1 – the local authority is satisfied, in the case of a refusal given by the carer, that the carer lacks capacity to decide whether to refuse to have the assessment;

CASE 2 – the local authority is satisfied, in the case of a refusal given by a person with parental responsibility for the carer, that the person lacks capacity to decide whether to refuse the assessment;

CASE 3 – the local authority is satisfied, in the case of a refusal given by a person with parental responsibility for the carer, that not having the assessment would not be in the carer's best interests.

(4) Where a local authority has been discharged from its duty under section 24 by a refusal under this section, the duty is re-engaged if –

(a)   the carer (or, where applicable, an authorised person) subsequently asks for an assessment,
(b)   a person with parental responsibility for the carer subsequently asks for an assessment in the circumstances described in subsection (2), or
(c)   the local authority considers that the carer's needs or circumstances, or the needs or circumstances of a person with parental responsibility for the carer, have changed,

(subject to any further refusal under this section).

(5) In this section 'authorised person' means a person authorised under the Mental Capacity Act 2005 (whether in general or specific terms) to decide whether to refuse, or ask for, a needs assessment on the carer's behalf.

27 Refusal of a needs assessment for a carer aged under 16

(1) If –

(a)   a carer aged under 16 refuses a needs assessment under section 24, and
(b)   the local authority is satisfied that the carer has sufficient understanding to make an informed decision about the refusal of the assessment,

the duty under that section to assess the carer's needs does not apply.

(2) If a person with parental responsibility for a carer aged under 16 refuses a needs assessment for the carer under section 24, the duty under that section to assess the carer's needs does not apply.

(3) But a refusal under subsection (1) or (2) does not discharge a local authority from its duty under section 24 in the following cases –

CASE 1 – the local authority is satisfied, in the case of a refusal given by a person with parental responsibility for the carer, that the person lacks capacity to decide whether to refuse the assessment;

CASE 2 – the local authority is satisfied, in the case of a refusal given by a person with parental responsibility for the carer, that the carer –

(a)   has sufficient understanding to make an informed decision about the refusal of the assessment, and
(b)   does not agree with the refusal given by the person with parental responsibility for the carer;

CASE 3 – the local authority is satisfied, in the case of a refusal given by a person with parental responsibility for the carer, that not having the assessment would be inconsistent with the carer's well-being.

(4) Where a local authority has been discharged from its duty under section 24 by a refusal under this section, the duty is re-engaged if –

(a)   the carer subsequently asks for an assessment and the local authority is satisfied that the carer has sufficient understanding to make an informed decision about having an assessment,

(b)   a person with parental responsibility for the carer subsequently asks for an assessment, or

(c)   the local authority considers that the carer's needs or circumstances, or the needs or circumstances of a person with parental responsibility for the carer, have changed,

(subject to any further refusal under this section).

Supplementary

28 Combining needs assessments for a carer and a cared for person

(1) Where a person who appears to need care and support has a carer, a local authority may combine –

(a)   the person's needs assessment under section 19 or 21, and

(b)   the carer's needs assessment under section 24,

but this is subject to subsections (2) to (4).

(2) A local authority may not combine a needs assessment for an adult (whether under section 19 or 24) with a needs assessment for another person unless –

(a)   the adult (or, where applicable, an authorised person) gives valid consent, or

(b)   the requirement for valid consent may be dispensed with.

(3) A local authority may not combine a needs assessment for a child aged 16 or 17 (whether under section 21 or 24) with a needs assessment for another person unless –

(a)   the child (or, where applicable, an authorised person) gives valid consent,

(b)   a person with parental responsibility for the child gives valid consent in circumstances in which the local authority is satisfied that –

(i)   the child lacks capacity to decide whether to consent to the combining of the needs assessments, and

(ii)   there is no authorised person to make the decision on the child's behalf, or

(c)   the requirement for valid consent may be dispensed with.

(4) A local authority may not combine a needs assessment for a child aged under 16 (whether under section 21 or 24) with a needs assessment for another person unless –

(a)   the child or a person with parental responsibility for the child gives valid consent, or

(b)   the requirement for valid consent may be dispensed with.

(5) Consent given under subsection (2), (3) or (4) is valid except in the following cases –

CASE 1 – the local authority is satisfied, in the case of consent given by an adult or a child aged 16 or 17, that the adult or child lacks capacity to consent to the combination of the needs assessments;

CASE 2 – the local authority is satisfied, in the case of consent given by a child aged under 16, that the child does not have sufficient understanding to make an informed decision about the combination of the needs assessments;

CASE 3 – the local authority is satisfied, in the case of consent given by a person with parental responsibility for a child aged under 16 in relation to the child's needs assessment, that the child –

PART VII

(a) has sufficient understanding to make an informed decision about the combination of the needs assessments, and

(b) does not agree with the consent given by the person with parental responsibility.

(6) A local authority may dispense with the requirement for valid consent in the following cases –

CASE 1 – the local authority is satisfied, with regard to the needs assessment of an adult, that –

(a) there is no person who may give valid consent, and

(b) combining the needs assessments would be in the adult's best interests;

CASE 2 – the local authority is satisfied, with regard to the needs assessment of a child aged 16 or 17, that –

(a) the child lacks capacity to give valid consent,

(b) there is no authorised person who may give valid consent on the child's behalf, and

(c) combining the needs assessments would be in the child's best interests;

CASE 3 – the local authority is satisfied, with regard to the needs assessment of a child aged under 16, that –

(a) the child does not have sufficient understanding to make an informed decision about the combination of the needs assessments, and

(b) combining the needs assessments would be consistent with the child's well-being.

(7) In this section 'authorised person' means a person authorised under the Mental Capacity Act 2005 (whether in general or specific terms) to decide whether to consent to the combination of the needs assessments on the adult or child's behalf.

Combining needs assessments—Subject to the relevant consents being given, a person's needs assessment may be combined with his or her carer's assessment where it is beneficial to do so.

29 Combining needs assessments and other assessments

(1) Where a person who appears to need support as a carer also appears to have needs for care and support in his or her own right, a local authority may combine a needs assessment for that person under section 24 with a needs assessment for that person under section 19 or 21.

(2) A local authority may carry out a needs assessment for a person at the same time as it or another body carries out another assessment under any enactment in relation to that person.

(3) For the purposes of subsection (2) –

(a) the local authority may carry out the other assessment on behalf of or jointly with the other body, or

(b) if the other body has already arranged for the other assessment to be carried out jointly with another person, the local authority may carry out the other assessment jointly with the other body and that other person.

Duplication—It is intended that duplication of assessments under different legislation should be avoided (Code to Part 3, para 38).

30 Regulations about assessment

(1) Regulations must make provision about carrying out needs assessments.

(2) Regulations under this section must make provision for the review of needs assessments, and may, for example, specify –

    (a)   the persons who may request a review of an assessment (on their own behalf or on behalf of another person);

    (b)   the circumstances in which a local authority –

        (i)   may refuse to comply with a request for a review of an assessment, and

        (ii)   may not refuse to do so.

(3) Regulations under this section may also, for example, provide for –

    (a)   further persons whom a local authority must involve in carrying out an assessment under section 19, 21 or 24;

    (b)   the way in which an assessment is to be carried out, by whom and when;

    (c)   the recording of the results of an assessment;

    (d)   the considerations to which a local authority is to have regard in carrying out an assessment;

    (e)   powers to provide information for the purposes of assessment.

Regulations—The relevant regulations are the Care and Support (Assessment) (Wales) Regulations 2015.

31 Part 3: interpretation

In this Part –

    'information, advice or assistance' (*'gwybodaeth, cyngor neu gynhorthwy'*) means information, advice or assistance that may be provided by virtue of section 17;

    'preventative services' (*'gwasanaethau ataliol'*) means services that may be provided by virtue of section 15.

PART 4
MEETING NEEDS

Code of Practice—The relevant Code is the Code to Part 4.

Deciding what to do following needs assessment

32 Determination of eligibility and consideration of what to do to meet needs

(1) Where a local authority is satisfied, on the basis of a needs assessment, that a person has needs for care and support or, if the person is a carer, needs for support, the authority must –

    (a)   determine whether any of the needs meet the eligibility criteria;

    (b)   if the needs do not meet the eligibility criteria, determine whether it is nevertheless necessary to meet the needs in order to protect the person from –

        (i)   abuse or neglect or a risk of abuse or neglect (if the person is an adult);

        (ii)   abuse or neglect or a risk of abuse or neglect, or other harm or a risk of such harm (if the person is a child);

    (c)   determine whether the needs call for the exercise of any function it has under this Act or Parts 4 or 5 of the Children Act 1989, in so far as the function is relevant to that person;

    (d)   consider whether the person would benefit from the provision of anything that may be provided by virtue of section 15 (preventative services) or 17 (information, advice and assistance) or anything else that may be available in the community.

PART VII

(2) If a local authority determines that any needs must be met, or are to be met, under sections 35 to 45, the authority must –

   (a)   consider what could be done to meet those needs;

   (b)   consider whether it would impose a charge for doing those things, and if so, determine the amount of that charge (see Part 5).

(3) Regulations must make provision about the discharge of the duty under subsection (1)(a).

(4) Needs meet the eligibility criteria if they –

   (a)   are of a description specified in regulations, or

   (b)   form Part of a combination of needs of a description so specified.

(5) The regulations may, for example, describe needs by reference to –

   (a)   the effect that the needs have on the person concerned;

   (b)   the person's circumstances.

Regulations—The relevant regulations are the Care and Support (Eligibility) (Wales) Regulations 2015.

'needs' (s 32(1))—This section applies to people, adults and children alike. 'needs assessment' is an assessment under s 19 of the Act for adults, s 21 for children and s 24 for carers.

If, after a needs assessment, a person has needs for care and support or a carer has need for support, the local authority must determine and consider each of the matters set out in s 32(1)(a)–(d).

Meeting the needs—Where needs meet the eligibility criteria, s 32 requires a local authority to consider what could be done to meet those needs and whether it should impose a charge under Pt 5 of the Act.

Where the eligibility criteria are not met, a local authority must determine whether it is necessary to meet the assessed needs for protective reasons defined in s 32(1).

'eligibility criteria' (s 32(1)(a))—The Care and Support (Eligibility) (Wales) Regulations 2015 set out the eligibility criteria to be applied to adults (regs 2(1), 3 and 6), children (regs 2(2), 4 and 6) and carers (regs 2(3), 5 and 6). In each case, the eligibility criteria include a requirement to establish the need, whether it relates to one of the well-being-related factors, whether or not the need can be met by the person alone or with assistance, and whether or not a person is likely to achieve personal outcomes without the provision of care and support by the local authority. Regulation 6 provides that, for the purpose of judging whether or not a person is able to meet one of their needs, whether with assistance or without it, the person should be regarded as unable to do so even if they can in fact meet the need but only by enduring significant pain, anxiety or distress, by endangering him or herself or another person, or by taking a significantly longer time than would normally be expected.

A local determination of eligibility must support a move away from the deficit model of care and seek to emphasise strengths, capacities and capabilities. The eligibility must be outcome-based and relate closely to the national outcomes framework. The local authority must determine whether the provision of care and support or support for a carer will assist the person to meet their personal outcomes within the framework of well-being (see s 2). The local authority must be clear about what matters to a person and what the person can do to maximise their own well-being. Eligibility status is conferred on the person's well-being need, not on the person (Code to Part 4, paras 6–21). If the provision of care and support cannot help the person achieve their own outcomes, the question of eligibility does not arise. It is not the purpose of the eligibility criteria to draw local authority care and support services into challenges they cannot address (Code to Part 4, para 29).

Examples of the application of the eligibility criteria are given in the Code to Part 4, Annex 1.

Outcome—The outcome of any assessment and eligibility assessment must be recorded on the assessment and eligibility tool (Code to Part 4, paras 24 and 33).

Disagreement—Where a person disagrees with the local authority's decision that their needs do not meet the requisite eligibility criteria, the individual will be informed of their right to access the complaints process and be supported through that process (Code to Part 4, para 51).

33 Procedure for regulations under section 32

(1) Before making regulations under section 32(3) or (4), the Welsh Ministers must carry out the following steps.

(2) The Welsh Ministers must consult –

(a) such persons as appear to them likely to be affected by the regulations,

(b) such organisations as appear to them to represent the interests of persons likely to be affected by the regulations, and

(c) such other persons as they consider appropriate,

on the proposed draft regulations.

(3) The Welsh Ministers must –

(a) allow those persons a period of at least 12 weeks to submit comments on the proposed draft regulations,

(b) consider any comments submitted within that period, and

(c) publish a summary of those comments.

(4) The Welsh Ministers must lay a draft of the regulations before the National Assembly for Wales.

(5) Draft regulations laid under subsection (4) –

(a) must be accompanied by a statement of the Welsh Ministers giving details of any differences between the draft regulations consulted on under subsection (2) and the draft regulations laid under subsection (4), and

(b) may not be approved by a resolution of the National Assembly for Wales in accordance with section 196(6) until after the expiry of the period of 60 days beginning with the day on which the draft regulations are laid.

34 How to meet needs

(1) The following are examples of the ways in which a local authority may meet needs under sections 35 to 45 –

(a) by arranging for a person other than the authority to provide something;

(b) by itself providing something;

(c) by providing something, or by arranging for something to be provided, to a person other than the person with needs for care and support (or, in the case of a carer, support).

(2) The following are examples of what may be provided or arranged to meet needs under sections 35 to 45 –

(a) accommodation in a care home, children's home or premises of some other type;

(b) care and support at home or in the community;

(c) services, goods and facilities;

(d) information and advice;

(e) counselling and advocacy;

(f) social work;

(g) payments (including direct payments);

(h) aids and adaptations;

(i) occupational therapy.

(3) Where a local authority is meeting a person's needs under sections 35 to 45 by providing or arranging care and support at the person's home, the local authority must satisfy itself that any visits to the person's home for that purpose are of sufficient length to provide the person with the care and support required to meet the needs in question.

PART VII

(4) A code issued under section 145 must include guidelines as to the length of visits to a person's home for the purpose of providing care and support.

(5) See sections 47 (exception for provision of health services), 48 (exception for provision of housing etc) and 49 (restrictions on provision of payments) for limitations on what may be provided or arranged to meet needs for care and support and the way in which it may be provided or arranged.

'visits ... are of sufficient length' (s 34(3))—See the Code to Part 4, para 96.

Meeting care and support needs of adults

35 Duty to meet care and support needs of an adult

(1) A local authority must meet an adult's needs for care and support if it is satisfied that conditions 1, 2 and 3 are met (but see subsection (6)).

(2) Condition 1 is that the adult is –

    (a)   ordinarily resident in the local authority's area, or

    (b)   of no settled residence and within the authority's area.

(3) Condition 2 is that –

    (a)   the needs meet the eligibility criteria, or

    (b)   the local authority considers it necessary to meet the needs in order to protect the adult from abuse or neglect or a risk of abuse or neglect.

(4) Condition 3 is that –

    (a)   there is no charge for the care and support needed to meet those needs, or

    (b)   there is a charge for that care and support but –

        (i)   the local authority is satisfied on the basis of a financial assessment that the adult's financial resources are at or below the financial limit,

        (ii)   the local authority is satisfied on the basis of a financial assessment that the adult's financial resources are above the financial limit but the adult nonetheless asks the authority to meet his or her needs, or

        (iii)   the local authority is satisfied that the adult lacks capacity to arrange for the provision of care and support and there is no person authorised to make such arrangements under the Mental Capacity Act 2005 or otherwise in a position to do so on the adult's behalf.

(5) For the meaning of 'financial assessment' and 'financial limit' see Part 5.

(6) The duty under subsection (1) does not apply to an adult's needs to the extent that the local authority is satisfied that those needs are being met by a carer.

'eligibility criteria' (s 35(3)(a))—The relevant eligibility criteria can be found in the Care and Support (Eligibility) (Wales) Regulations 2015.

Preferred accommodation—Where a local authority is going to meet needs under ss 35–38 of the Act by providing or arranging for the provision of accommodation of a specified type for a person and the person concerned has expressed a preference for particular accommodation of that type, the local authority must provide or arrange for the provision of the preferred accommodation. The Care and Support (Choice of Accommodation) (Wales) Regulations 2015 apply to cases where a local authority is meeting care and support needs of adults and children through the provision of care home accommodation.

36 Power to meet care and support needs of adult

(1) A local authority may meet an adult's needs for care and support if the adult is –

    (a)   within the local authority's area, or

    (b)   ordinarily resident in the authority's area, but outside its area.

(2) If a local authority meets the needs of an adult who is ordinarily resident in the area of another local authority under subsection (1), it must notify the local authority in whose area the adult is ordinarily resident that it is doing so.

(3) A local authority has the power to meet needs under this section whether or not it has completed a needs assessment in accordance with Part 3 or a financial assessment in accordance with Part 5.

Note—See the notes to s 35, above. This means that even where the s 35 duty is not owed a local authority may exercise its discretion to provide care and support services. The discretion is broad and can be used to meet urgent one-off care and support needs and longer term needs alike.

Meeting care and support needs of children

37 Duty to meet care and support needs of a child

(1) A local authority must meet a child's needs for care and support if it is satisfied that conditions 1 and 2, and any conditions specified in regulations, are met (but see subsections (5) and (6)).

(2) Condition 1 is that the child is within the local authority's area.

(3) Condition 2 is that –

    (a) the needs meet the eligibility criteria, or

    (b) the local authority considers it necessary to meet the needs in order to protect the child from –

        (i) abuse or neglect or a risk of abuse or neglect, or

        (ii) other harm or a risk of such harm.

(4) If the local authority has been notified about a child under section 120(2)(a) or under section 85(1) of the Children Act 1989 (children accommodated by health authorities and local education authorities), it must treat the child as being within its area for the purposes of this section.

(5) The duty under subsection (1) does not apply to a child's needs to the extent that the local authority is satisfied that those needs are being met by the child's family or a carer.

(6) This section does not apply to a child who is looked after by –

    (a) a local authority,

    (b) a local authority in England,

    (c) a local authority in Scotland, or

    (d) a Health and Social Care trust.

Amendments—SI 2016/413.

'eligibility criteria' (s 37(2)(a))—The relevant eligibility criteria can be found in the Care and Support (Eligibility) (Wales) Regulations 2015. See also the notes to s 35, above.

38 Power to meet care and support needs of a child

(1) A local authority may meet a child's needs for care and support if the child is –

    (a) within the local authority's area, or

    (b) ordinarily resident in the authority's area, but outside its area,

(but see subsection (4)).

(2) If a local authority meets the needs of a child who is ordinarily resident in the area of another local authority under subsection (1), it must notify the local authority in whose area the child is ordinarily resident that it is doing so.

PART VII

(3) A local authority has the power to meet needs under this section whether or not it has completed a needs assessment in accordance with Part 3 or a financial assessment in accordance with Part 5.

(4) This section does not apply to a child who is looked after by –

    (a)   a local authority,
    (b)   a local authority in England,
    (c)   a local authority in Scotland, or
    (d)   a Health and Social Care trust.

Note—See the notes to s 35 and 36, above. This section provides a broad discretion. It enables a local authority to meet the care and support needs of children who are not 'looked after'. It provides a power to meet urgent needs as well as more long terms needs.

39 Duty to maintain family contact

(1) This section applies to a child –

    (a)   who is within the area of a local authority,
    (b)   whom the local authority considers has needs for care and support in addition to the care and support provided by the child's family,
    (c)   who is living apart from the child's family, and
    (d)   who is not looked after by the local authority.

(2) If the local authority considers it necessary in order to promote the well-being of the child, it must take such steps as are reasonably practicable to –

    (a)   enable the child to live with the child's family, or
    (b)   promote contact between the child and the child's family.

Looked-after children—This section does not apply to 'looked after' children.

Meeting support needs of a carer

40 Duty to meet support needs of an adult carer

(1) A local authority must meet the needs for support of a carer who is an adult if it is satisfied that conditions 1, 2 and 3, and any conditions specified in regulations, are met.

(2) Condition 1 is that the person cared for by the carer is –

    (a)   an adult who is –
        (i)   ordinarily resident in the local authority's area, or
        (ii)   of no settled residence and within the authority's area, or
    (b)   a disabled child who is within the authority's area.

(3) Condition 2 is that the carer's needs meet the eligibility criteria.

(4) Condition 3 is that –

    (a)   in so far as meeting the carer's needs involves the provision of support to the carer –
        (i)   there is not a charge under section 59 for meeting those needs, or
        (ii)   in so far as there is a charge, section 41(1) or (2) applies;
    (b)   in so far as meeting the carer's needs involves the provision of care and support to an adult cared for by the carer –
        (i)   there is not a charge under section 59 for meeting those needs and section 41(7), (8) or (9) applies, or
        (ii)   in so far as there is a charge, section 41(3) or (4) applies;
    (c)   in so far as meeting the carer's needs involves the provision of care and support to a disabled child aged 16 or 17 who is cared for by the carer –

    (i)   there is not a charge under section 59 for meeting those needs and section 41(7), (8) or (10) applies, or

    (ii) in so far as there is a charge, section 41(5) or (6) applies;

(d) in so far as meeting the carer's needs involves the provision of care and support to a disabled child aged under 16 who is cared for by the carer –

    (i)   there is not a charge under section 59 for meeting those needs and section 41(12) or (13) applies, or

    (ii) in so far as there is a charge, section 41(5) or (6) applies.

'eligibility criteria' (s 40(3))—The relevant eligibility criteria can be found in the Care and Support (Eligibility) (Wales) Regulations 2015.

41 Duty to meet support needs of an adult carer: supplementary

(1) This subsection applies if the local authority is satisfied on the basis of a financial assessment that the carer's financial resources are at or below the financial limit.

(2) This subsection applies if –

(a) the local authority is satisfied on the basis of a financial assessment that the carer's financial resources are above the financial limit, and

(b) the carer nonetheless asks the authority to meet the needs in question.

(3) This subsection applies if –

(a) the local authority is satisfied on the basis of a financial assessment that the financial resources of the adult cared for by the carer are at or below the financial limit, and

(b) subsection (7), (8) or (9) applies.

(4) This subsection applies if –

(a) the local authority is satisfied on the basis of a financial assessment that the financial resources of the adult cared for by the carer are above the financial limit, and

(b) subsection (7), (8) or (9) applies.

(5) This subsection applies if –

(a) in respect of an adult upon whom the local authority thinks it would impose a charge for the provision of care and support to the disabled child cared for by the carer, the local authority is satisfied on the basis of a financial assessment that it would not be reasonably practicable for the adult to pay any amount for the care and support, and

(b) either –

    (i)   subsection (7), (8) or (10) applies, in the case of a disabled child aged 16 or 17, or

    (ii) subsection (12) or (13) applies, in the case of a disabled child aged under 16.

(6) This subsection applies if –

(a) in respect of an adult upon whom the local authority thinks it would impose a charge for the provision of care and support to the disabled child cared for by the carer, the local authority is satisfied on the basis of a financial assessment that it would be reasonably practicable for the adult –

    (i)   to pay the standard charge for the care and support, or

    (ii) to pay any other amount for the care and support,

(b) the adult does not object to the provision of the care and support, and

(c) either –

    (i)   subsection (7), (8) or (10) applies, in the case of a disabled child aged 16 or 17, or

(ii)   subsection (12) or (13) applies, in the case of a disabled child aged under 16.

(7)   This subsection applies if –

(a)   the local authority is satisfied that the person cared for by the carer has capacity to decide whether to have the needs in question met by the provision of care and support to that person, and

(b)   the person agrees to have those needs met in that way.

(8)   This subsection applies if an authorised person agrees, on behalf of the person cared for by the carer, to have the needs in question met by the provision of care and support to that person.

(9)   This subsection applies if –

(a)   the local authority is satisfied that the adult cared for by the carer lacks capacity to decide whether to have the needs in question met by the provision of care and support to that adult,

(b)   there is no authorised person to make the decision on the adult's behalf, and

(c)   the local authority is satisfied that it is in the adult's best interests to have those needs met in that way.

(10)   This subsection applies if –

(a)   the local authority is satisfied that the disabled child cared for by the carer lacks capacity to decide whether to have the needs in question met by the provision of care and support to that child,

(b)   there is no authorised person to make the decision on the child's behalf, and

(c)   no objection has been made by a person with parental responsibility for the child to having those needs met in that way.

(11)   The local authority may disregard an objection for the purposes of subsection (10)(c) if it is satisfied that it would not be in the disabled child's best interests.

(12)   This subsection applies if –

(a)   the local authority is satisfied that the disabled child cared for by the carer has sufficient understanding to make an informed decision about having the needs in question met by the provision of care and support to that child, and

(b)   the child agrees to have those needs met in that way.

(13)   This subsection applies if –

(a)   the local authority is satisfied that the disabled child cared for by the carer does not have sufficient understanding to make an informed decision about having the needs in question met by the provision of care and support to that child, and

(b)   no objection has been made by a person with parental responsibility for the child to having those needs met in that way.

(14)   The local authority may disregard an objection for the purposes of subsection (13)(b) if it is satisfied that it would not be consistent with the disabled child's well-being.

(15)   In this section –

'authorised person' (*'person awdurdodedig'*) means a person authorised under the Mental Capacity Act 2005 (whether in general or specific terms) to decide on behalf of the person cared for by the carer whether to have the needs in question met by the provision of care and support to that person;

'standard charge' (*'ffi safonol'*) has the meaning given by section 63(3).

(16)   For the meaning of 'financial assessment' and 'financial limit' see Part 5.

42 Duty to meet support needs of a child carer

(1) A local authority must meet the needs for support of a carer who is a child if it is satisfied that conditions 1, 2 and (where applicable) 3, and any conditions specified in regulations, are met.

(2) Condition 1 is that the person cared for by the carer is –

  (a) an adult who is –

    (i)   ordinarily resident in the local authority's area, or

    (ii) of no settled residence and within the authority's area, or

  (b) a disabled child who is within the authority's area.

(3) Condition 2 is that the carer's needs meet the eligibility criteria.

(4) Condition 3 is that –

  (a) in so far as meeting the carer's needs involves the provision of care and support to an adult cared for by the carer –

    (i)   there is not a charge under section 59 for meeting those needs and section 43(5), (6) or (7) applies, or

    (ii) in so far as there is a charge, section 43(1) or (2) applies;

  (b) in so far as meeting the carer's needs involves the provision of care and support to a disabled child aged 16 or 17 who is cared for by the carer –

    (i)   there is not a charge under section 59 for meeting those needs and section 43(5), (6) or (8) applies, or

    (ii) in so far as there is a charge, section 43(3) or (4) applies;

  (c) in so far as meeting the carer's needs involves the provision of care and support to a disabled child aged under 16 who is cared for by the carer –

    (i)   there is not a charge under section 59 for meeting those needs and section 43(10) or (11) applies, or

    (ii) in so far as there is a charge, section 43(3) or (4) applies.

Amendments—Regulation and Inspection of Social Care (Wales) Act 2016, s 185, Sch 3, para 62.

43 Duty to meet support needs of a child carer: supplementary

(1) This subsection applies if –

  (a) the local authority is satisfied on the basis of a financial assessment that the financial resources of the adult cared for by the carer are at or below the financial limit, and

  (b) subsection (5), (6) or (7) applies.

(2) This subsection applies if –

  (a) the local authority is satisfied on the basis of a financial assessment that the financial resources of the adult cared for by the carer are above the financial limit, and

  (b) subsection (5), (6) or (7) applies.

(3) This subsection applies if –

  (a) in respect of an adult upon whom the local authority thinks it would impose a charge for the provision of care and support to the disabled child cared for by the carer, the local authority is satisfied on the basis of a financial assessment that it would not be reasonably practicable for the adult to pay any amount for the care and support, and

  (b) either –

    (i)   subsection (5), (6) or (8) applies, in the case of a disabled child aged 16 or 17, or

(ii)   subsection (10) or (11) applies, in the case of a disabled child aged under 16.

(4) This subsection applies if –

(a)   in respect of an adult upon whom the local authority thinks it would impose a charge for the provision of care and support to the disabled child cared for by the carer, the local authority is satisfied on the basis of a financial assessment that it would be reasonably practicable for the adult –
(i)   to pay the standard charge for the care and support, or
(ii)   to pay any other amount for the care and support,
(b)   the adult does not object to the provision of the care and support, and
(c)   either –
(i)   subsection (5), (6) or (8) applies, in the case of a disabled child aged 16 or 17, or
(ii)   subsection (10) or (11) applies, in the case of a disabled child aged under 16.

(5) This subsection applies if –

(a)   the local authority is satisfied that the person cared for by the carer has capacity to decide whether to have the needs in question met by the provision of care and support to that person, and
(b)   the person agrees to have those needs met in that way.

(6) This subsection applies if an authorised person agrees, on behalf of the person cared for by the carer, to have the needs in question met by the provision of care and support to that person.

(7) This subsection applies if –

(a)   the local authority is satisfied that the adult cared for by the carer lacks capacity to decide whether to have the needs in question met by the provision of care and support to that adult,
(b)   there is no authorised person to make the decision on the adult's behalf, and
(c)   the local authority is satisfied that it is in the adult's best interest to have those needs met in that way.

(8) This subsection applies if –

(a)   the local authority is satisfied that the disabled child cared for by the carer lacks capacity to decide whether to have the needs in question met by the provision of care and support to that child,
(b)   there is no authorised person to make the decision on the child's behalf, and
(c)   no objection has been made by a person with parental responsibility for the child to having those needs met in that way.

(9) The local authority may disregard an objection for the purposes of subsection (8)(c) if it satisfied that it would not be in the disabled child's best interests.

(10) This subsection applies if –

(a)   the local authority is satisfied that the disabled child cared for by the carer has sufficient understanding to make an informed decision about having the needs in question met by the provision of care and support to that child, and
(b)   the child agrees to have those needs met in that way.

(11) This subsection applies if –

(a)   the local authority is satisfied that the disabled child cared for by the carer does not have sufficient understanding to make an informed decision about having the needs in question met by the provision of care and support to that child, and

(b) no objection has been made by a person with parental responsibility for the child to having those needs met in that way.

(12) The local authority may disregard an objection for the purposes of subsection (11)(b) if it is satisfied that it would not be consistent with the disabled child's well-being.

(13) In this section –

'authorised person' (*'person awdurdodedig'*) means a person authorised under the Mental Capacity Act 2005 (whether in general or specific terms) to decide on behalf of the person cared for by the carer whether to have the needs in question met by the provision of care and support to that person;

'standard charge' (*'ffi safonol'*) has the meaning given by section 63(3).

(14) For the meaning of 'financial assessment' and 'financial limit' see Part 5.

44 Supplementary provision about the duties to meet carer's needs

(1) This section applies in relation to the duties under sections 40 and 42.

(2) Meeting some or all of a carer's needs for support may involve the provision of care and support to the person cared for by the carer, even where there would be no duty to meet the person's needs for that care and support under section 35 or 37.

(3) Where a local authority is required by section 40 or 42 to meet some or all of a carer's needs for support, but it does not prove feasible for it to do so by providing care and support to the person cared for by the carer, it must, so far as it is feasible to do so, identify some other way in which to do so.

45 Power to meet support needs of a carer

(1) A local authority may meet a carer's needs for support if the person cared for by the carer is –

(a) within the local authority's area, or

(b) ordinarily resident in the authority's area, but outside its area.

(2) A local authority has the power to meet needs under this section whether or not it has completed a needs assessment in accordance with Part 3 or a financial assessment in accordance with Part 5.

Meeting needs: exceptions and restrictions

46 Exception for persons subject to immigration control

(1) A local authority may not meet the needs for care and support of an adult to whom section 115 of the Immigration and Asylum Act 1999 ('the 1999 Act') (exclusion from benefits) applies and whose needs for care and support have arisen solely –

(a) because the adult is destitute, or

(b) because of the physical effects, or anticipated physical effects, of being destitute.

(2) For the purposes of subsection (1), section 95(2) to (7) of the 1999 Act applies but with the references in section 95(4) and (5) of that Act to the Secretary of State being read as references to the local authority in question.

(3) But, until the commencement of section 44(6) of the Nationality, Immigration and Asylum Act 2002, subsection (2) is to have effect as if it read as follows –

PART VII

'(2) For the purposes of subsection (1), section 95(3) and (5) to (8) of, and paragraph 2 of Schedule 8 to, the 1999 Act apply but with references in section 95(5) and (7) and that paragraph to the Secretary of State being read as references to the local authority in question.'

(4) The reference in subsection (1) to meeting an adult's needs for care and support includes a reference to doing so in order to meet a carer's needs for support.

47 Exception for provision of health services

(1) A local authority may not meet a person's needs for care and support (including a carer's needs for support) under sections 35 to 45 by providing or arranging for the provision of a service or facility which is required to be provided under a health enactment, unless doing so would be incidental or ancillary to doing something else to meet needs under those sections.

(2) A local authority may not secure services or facilities for a person under section 15 (preventative services) that are required to be provided under a health enactment, unless doing so would be incidental or ancillary to securing another service or facility for that person under that section.

(3) Regulations may specify –

   (a)   types of services or facilities which may, despite subsections (1) and (2), be provided or arranged by a local authority, or circumstances in which such services or facilities may be so provided or arranged;

   (b)   types of services or facilities which may not be provided or arranged by a local authority, or circumstances in which such services or facilities may not be so provided or arranged;

   (c)   services or facilities, or a method for determining services or facilities, the provision of which is, or is not, to be treated as incidental or ancillary for the purposes of subsection (1) or (2).

(4) A local authority may not meet a person's needs for care and support (including a carer's needs for support) under sections 35 to 45 by providing or arranging for the provision of nursing care by a registered nurse.

(5) A local authority may not secure the provision of nursing care by a registered nurse in discharging its duty under section 15.

(6) But a local authority may, despite subsections (1), (2), (4) and (5), arrange for the provision of accommodation together with nursing care by a registered nurse –

   (a)   if the authority has obtained consent for it to arrange for the provision of the nursing care from –
       (i)   whichever Local Health Board regulations require, in the case of accommodation in Wales, Scotland or Northern Ireland, or
       (ii) whichever English health body regulations require, in the case of accommodation in England, or

   (b)   in an urgent case and where the arrangements are temporary.

(7) In a case to which subsection (6)(b) applies, the local authority must seek to obtain the consent mentioned in subsection (6)(a) as soon as is feasible after the temporary arrangements are made.

(8) Regulations may require a local authority –

   (a)   to make arrangements in connection with the resolution of disputes between the authority and a health body about whether or not a service or facility is required to be provided under a health enactment;

(b) to be involved in the manner specified in processes for assessing a person's needs for health care and deciding how those needs should be met.

(9) Nothing in this section affects what a local authority may do under the National Health Service (Wales) Act 2006, including entering into arrangements under regulations made under section 33 of that Act (arrangements with NHS bodies).

(10) In this section –

an 'English health body' ('*corff iechyd Seisnig*') means –
  (a) a clinical commissioning group;
  (b) the National Health Service Commissioning Board;
a 'health body' ('*corff iechyd*') means –
  (a) a Local Health Board;
  (b) a clinical commissioning group;
  (c) the National Health Service Commissioning Board;
  (d) a Health Board constituted under section 2 of the National Health Service (Scotland) Act 1978;
  (e) a Special Health Board constituted under that section;
  (f) a Health and Social Care trust;
a 'health enactment' ('*deddfiad iechyd*') means –
  (a) the National Health Service (Wales) Act 2006;
  (b) the National Health Service Act 2006;
  (c) the National Health Service (Scotland) Act 1978;
  (d) the Health and Personal Social Services (Northern Ireland) Order 1972;
  (e) the Health and Social Care (Reform) Act (Northern Ireland) 2009;
'nursing care' ('*gofal nyrsio*') means a service which involves either the provision of care or the planning, supervision or delegation of the provision of care, but does not include a service which, by its nature and in the circumstances in which it is to be provided, does not need to be provided by a registered nurse.

'Regulations' (s 47(3))—The relevant regulations are the Care and Support (Provision of Health Services) (Wales) Regulations 2015.

'Regulations' (s 47(8))—Care and Support (Provision of Health Services) (Wales) Regulations 2015, reg 4 requires a local authority to make arrangements in connection with the resolution of disputes between the authority and the health body.

48   Exception for provision of housing etc

A local authority may not meet an adult's needs for care and support (including a carer's needs for support) under sections 35 to 45 or discharge its duty under section 15 by doing anything which that authority or another local authority is required to do under –
  (a) the Housing (Wales) Act 2014, or
  (b) any other enactment specified in regulations.

Amendments—Housing (Wales) Act 2014, s 100, Sch 3, para 22.

49   Restrictions on provision of payments

(1) A local authority may not provide payments to meet a person's needs for care and support or a carer's needs for support under sections 35 to 45 unless –
  (a) the payments are direct payments (see sections 50 to 53),
  (b) the authority considers –
    (i) that the person's needs are urgent, and
    (ii) that it would not be reasonably practicable to meet those needs in any other way,
  (c) the payments are provided under or by virtue of a contract, or

    (d)   the payments are provided in circumstances specified in regulations.

(2) A local authority may not provide payments in the discharge of its duty under section 15(1) unless –

    (a)   the authority considers –
        (i)   that the payments would achieve one or more of the purposes mentioned in section 15(2), and
        (ii) that it would not be reasonably practicable to achieve that purpose or those purposes in any other way,
    (b)   the payments are provided under or by virtue of a contract which relates to the provision of services for the authority's area, or
    (c)   the payments are provided in circumstances specified in regulations.

Direct payments

50 Direct payments to meet an adult's needs

(1) Regulations may require or allow a local authority to make payments to a person towards the cost of meeting an adult's needs for care and support under section 35 or 36.

(2) But regulations under subsection (1) may not require or allow such payments to be made unless condition 1 or 2 is met.

(3) Condition 1 is that –

    (a)   the payments are to be made to the adult who has needs for care and support ('A'),
    (b)   A has, or the local authority believes that A has, capacity to consent to the making of the payments,
    (c)   the local authority is satisfied that –
        (i)   making the payments is an appropriate way of meeting A's needs, and
        (ii) A is capable of managing the payments (either by himself or herself or with the support that is available to A), and
    (d)   A has consented to the making of the payments.

(4) Condition 2 is that –

    (a)   the adult who has needs for care and support ('A') does not have, or the local authority believes that A does not have, capacity to consent to the making of the payments,
    (b)   the payments are to be made to a person ('P') other than A,
    (c)   P is a suitable person,
    (d)   the local authority is satisfied that –
        (i)   making the payments is an appropriate way of meeting A's needs,
        (ii) P is capable of managing the payments (either by himself or herself or with the support that is available to P), and
        (iii) P will act in A's best interests in managing the payments, and
    (e)   the necessary consent has been obtained to make the payments to P.

(5) For the purposes of subsection (4)(c), P is a 'suitable person' –

    (a)   if P is authorised under the Mental Capacity Act 2005 (whether in general or specific terms) to make decisions about A's needs for care and support,
    (b)   where P is not authorised as mentioned in paragraph (a), if a person who is so authorised agrees with the local authority that P is suitable to receive payments towards the cost of meeting A's needs for care and support, or
    (c)   where P is not authorised as mentioned in paragraph (a) and there is no person who is so authorised, if the local authority considers that P is suitable to receive payments of that kind.

(6) For the purposes of subsection (4)(e), the 'necessary consent' means –

(a)   the consent of P, and

(b)   where P is a suitable person by virtue of subsection (5)(b), the consent of a person authorised under the Mental Capacity Act 2005 (whether in general or specific terms) to make decisions about A's needs for care and support.

(7) A payment under this section is referred to in this Act as a 'direct payment'.

51   Direct payments to meet a child's needs

(1) Regulations may require or allow a local authority to make payments to a person towards the cost of meeting a child's needs for care and support under section 37, 38 or 39.

(2) But regulations under subsection (1) may not require or allow payments to be made unless conditions 1 to 4 are met.

(3) Condition 1 is that the payments are to be made to a person ('P') who is –

(a)   a person with parental responsibility for a child who has needs for care and support, or

(b)   a child who has needs for care and support.

(4) Condition 2 is that –

(a)   where P is an adult or a child aged 16 or 17, P has, or the local authority believes that P has, capacity to consent to the making of the payments;

(b)   where P is a child aged under 16, the local authority is satisfied that P has sufficient understanding to make an informed decision about receiving direct payments.

(5) Condition 3 is that the local authority is satisfied that –

(a)   making the payments is an appropriate way of meeting the child's needs,

(b)   the well-being of the child will be safeguarded and promoted by the making of the payments, and

(c)   P is capable of managing the payments (either by himself or herself or with the support that is available to P).

(6) Condition 4 is that P has consented to the making of the payments.

(7) A payment under this section is referred to in this Act as a 'direct payment'.

52   Direct payments to meet a carer's needs

(1) Regulations may require or allow a local authority to make payments to a person towards the cost of meeting a carer's needs for support under section 40, 42 or 45.

(2) But regulations under subsection (1) may not require or allow payments to be made unless conditions 1 to 4 are met.

(3) Condition 1 is that the payments are to be made to the carer who has needs for support ('C').

(4) Condition 2 is that –

(a)   where C is an adult or a child aged 16 or 17, C has, or the local authority believes that C has, capacity to consent to the making of the payments;

(b)   where C is a child aged under 16, the local authority is satisfied that C has sufficient understanding to make an informed decision about receiving direct payments.

(5) Condition 3 is that the local authority is satisfied that –

(a)   making the payments is an appropriate way of meeting C's needs, and

PART VII

  (b)   C is capable of managing the payments (either by himself or herself or with the support that is available to C).

(6) Condition 4 is that C has consented to the making of the payments.

(7) A payment under this section is referred to in this Act as a 'direct payment'.

53 Direct payments: further provision

(1) Regulations under section 50, 51 or 52 may also make provision about the following matters (among other matters) –

  (a)   the manner in which the amounts of the direct payments are to be determined;

  (b)   the making of direct payments as gross payments or alternatively as net payments;

  (c)   the determination of –

     (i)   the financial resources of specified persons, and

     (ii)   the amount (if any) that it would be reasonably practicable for those persons to pay by way of reimbursement (in the case of gross payments) or contribution (in the case of net payments);

  (d)   matters to which a local authority may or must have regard when making a decision of a specified type about direct payments;

  (e)   conditions which a local authority may or must attach, and conditions which it must not attach, in relation to direct payments;

  (f)   steps which a local authority may or must take before, or after, making a decision of a specified type about direct payments;

  (g)   support which a local authority must provide or arrange for persons to whom it makes direct payments;

  (h)   cases or circumstances in which a local authority may act as an agent on behalf of a person to whom direct payments are made;

  (i)   conditions subject to which, and the extent to which, a local authority's duty or power to meet a person's needs for care and support or a carer's needs for support is displaced by the making of direct payments;

  (j)   cases or circumstances in which a local authority must not, or is allowed not to, make payments to a person or in relation to a person;

  (k)   cases or circumstances in which a person who no longer lacks, or who the local authority believes no longer lacks, capacity to consent to the making of direct payments must or may nonetheless be treated for the purposes of sections 50 to 52 as lacking capacity to do so;

  (l)   cases or circumstances in which a local authority making direct payments may or must review the making of those payments;

  (m)   cases or circumstances in which a local authority making direct payments may or must –

     (i)   terminate the making of those payments;

     (ii)   require the repayment of the whole or Part of a direct payment;

  (n)   the recovery of any amount due to a local authority in connection with the making of direct payments.

(2) In subsection (1)(b) and (c) –

'gross payments' means direct payments –

  (a)   which are made at a rate that the local authority estimates to be equivalent to the reasonable cost of securing the provision of the care and support (or, in the case of carers, the support) in respect of which the payments are made, but

  (b)   which may be made subject to the condition that a person specified in regulations pays to the authority, by way of reimbursement, an amount or amounts determined under the regulations;

'net payments' means direct payments –

(a) which are made on the basis that a person specified in regulations will pay an amount or amounts determined under the regulations by way of contribution towards the cost of securing the provision of the care and support (or, in the case of carers, the support) in respect of which the payments are made, and

(b) which are accordingly made at a rate below the rate the local authority estimates to be equivalent to the reasonable cost of securing the provision of that care and support (or, in the case of carers, that support) so as to reflect the contribution to be made by that person.

(3) Regulations under section 50, 51 or 52 may make provision in relation to direct payments which corresponds to the provision which is made by, or may be made under, sections 59 to 67 or section 73.

(4) For the purposes of subsection (3), provision corresponds to that which is made by or under sections 59 to 67 or section 73 if it makes, in relation to reimbursements or contributions, provision which is in the opinion of the Welsh Ministers equivalent in effect to the provision made by or under those sections in relation to charges for providing or arranging the provision of care and support (or, in the case of carers, support) to meet a person's needs.

(5) Regulations under section 50, 51 or 52 must require a local authority to take specified steps to enable relevant persons to make informed choices about the use of direct payments.

(6) In subsection (5) 'relevant persons' means persons whose consent must be obtained to the making of direct payments under regulations made under section 50, 51 or 52.

(7) Regulations under section 51 must specify that where direct payments are made to a person who receives a benefit falling within a specified category, the payments –

(a) must be made at a rate that the local authority estimates to be equivalent to the reasonable cost of securing the provision of the care and support in respect of which the payments are made, and

(b) must not be made subject to any condition that requires a person to pay any amount to the authority by way of reimbursement.

(8) In subsection (7) 'benefit' includes any allowance, payment, credit or loan.

(9) A person to whom a local authority makes a direct payment may, subject to regulations made under section 50, 51 or 52, use the payment to purchase care and support (or, in the case of a carer, support) from any person (including, among others, the authority which made the payment).

(10) A local authority may impose a reasonable charge for the provision of care and support (or, in the case of a carer, support) to meet needs in respect of which a direct payment has been made.

(11) The ways in which a local authority may discharge its duty under section 117 of the Mental Health Act 1983 include by making direct payments; and for that purpose Schedule A1 (which includes modifications of sections 50 and 51 and this section) has effect.

Amendments—Care Act 2014, s 75(8); SI 2016/413.

PART VII

Plans

54 Care and support plans and support plans

(1) Where a local authority is required to meet the needs of a person under section 35 or 37, it must prepare and maintain a care and support plan in relation to that person.

(2) Where a local authority is required to meet the needs of a carer under section 40 or 42, it must prepare and maintain a support plan in relation to that carer.

(3) A local authority must keep under review the plans that it maintains under this section.

(4) Where a local authority is satisfied that the circumstances of the person to whom a plan relates have changed in a way that affects the plan, the authority must –

(a) carry out such assessments as it considers appropriate, and
(b) revise the plan.

(5) Regulations must make provision about –

(a) how plans under this section are to be prepared;
(b) what a plan is to contain;
(c) the review and revision of plans.

(6) Regulations under subsection (5)(c) must specify, in particular –

(a) the persons who may request a review of a plan (on their own behalf or on behalf of another person);
(b) the circumstances in which a local authority –
(i)   may refuse to comply with a request for a review of a plan, and
(ii) may not refuse to do so.

(7) When preparing, reviewing or revising a plan under this section, a local authority must involve –

(a) in the case of a care and support plan relating to an adult, the adult and, where feasible, any carer that the adult has;
(b) in the case of a care and support plan relating to a child, the child and any person with parental responsibility for the child;
(c) in the case of a support plan relating to a carer, the carer and, where feasible, the person for whom the carer provides or intends to provide care.

(8) The local authority may –

(a) prepare, review or revise a plan under this section at the same time as it or another body is preparing, reviewing or revising another document in the case of the person concerned, and
(b) include the other document in the plan.

Care and support plans—The Care and Support (Care Planning) (Wales) Regulations 2015 make further provision about care and support plans. Regulation 2 provides for the training and expertise of persons who prepare, maintain or revise plans. Regulation 3 sets out mandatory requirements in relation to the content of the care and support plan. Regulation 4 provides for the mandatory review of a care and support plan and regulation 5 sets out when a person may request a review of a care and support plan. The action to be taken following a review is set out in regulation 6. Regulations 7 and 8 deal with the distribution of care and support plans and the written record of any relevant decisions together with the reasons.

The Code to Part 4 is relevant. Chapter 2 of the Code specifically deals with care and support planning. The format for the plan is specifically dealt with at paras 76–80 and the Code gives statutory guidance on its contents at paras 81–89.

Overlapping duties with other plans including a Care and Treatment Plan under the Mental Health (Wales) Measure 2010, a care plan under CA 1989, s 31A and an Adoption Support plan are considered at paras 97–101.

Code to Part 4, paras 113–123 give guidance on reviewing care and support plans. Care and support plans can only be closed following a review of the plan in question (Code to Part 4, paras 124–127).

55 Regulations about care and support plans and support plans

Regulations under section 54(5) may, for example –

(a) require plans to be in a specified form;
(b) require plans to contain specified things;
(c) make provision about further persons whom a local authority must involve in the preparation, review or revision of plans;
(d) require plans to be prepared, reviewed or revised by specified persons;
(e) confer functions on persons specified in the regulations in connection with the preparation, review or revision of plans;
(f) specify persons to whom written copies of a plan must be provided (including, in specified cases, the provision of copies without the consent of the person to whom the plan relates);
(g) specify further circumstances in which plans must be reviewed.

Regulations—The relevant regulations are the Care and Support (Care Planning) (Wales) Regulations 2015.

Supplementary

56 Portability of care and support

(1) Where a local authority ('the sending authority') is notified by or on behalf of a person in respect of whom it has a duty under section 35 or 37 to meet needs for care and support that the person is going to move to the area of another local authority ('the receiving authority'), and it is satisfied that the move is likely to happen, it must –

(a) notify the receiving authority that it is so satisfied, and
(b) provide the receiving authority with –
    (i) a copy of the care and support plan prepared for the person, and
    (ii) such other information relating to the person and, if the person has a carer, such other information relating to the carer as the receiving authority may request.

(2) Where the receiving authority is notified by or on behalf of a person in respect of whom the sending authority has a duty under section 35 or 37 to meet needs for care and support that the person is going to move to the receiving authority's area, and the receiving authority is satisfied that the move is likely to happen, it must –

(a) notify the sending authority that it is so satisfied,
(b) provide the person and, if the person has a carer, the carer with such information as it considers appropriate,
(c) if the person is a child, provide the persons with parental responsibility for the child with such information as it considers appropriate, and
(d) assess the person under section 19 (if the person is an adult) or 21 (if the person is a child), having regard in particular to any change in the person's needs for care and support arising from the move.

(3) If, on the day the person moves to its area, the receiving authority has yet to carry out the assessment required by subsection (2)(d), or has done so but has yet to carry out the other steps required by this Part or Part 5, it must meet the person's needs for care and support in accordance with the care and support plan prepared by the sending authority, in so far as that is reasonably practicable.

PART VII

(4) In carrying out the assessment required by subsection (2)(d), the receiving authority must have regard to the care and support plan provided under subsection (1)(b).

(5) The receiving authority is subject to the duty under subsection (3) until it has –

    (a)   carried out the assessment required by subsection (2)(d), and

    (b)   taken the other steps required under this Part or Part 5.

(6) Regulations may –

    (a)   specify steps which a local authority must take to satisfy itself in respect of the matters mentioned in subsections (1) and (2);

    (b)   specify matters to which a receiving authority must have regard in deciding how to comply with the duty under subsection (3);

    (c)   specify cases in which the duties under subsection (1), (2) or (3) do not apply.

(7) A reference in this section to moving to an area is a reference to moving to that area with a view to becoming ordinarily resident there.

Note—See the Code to Part 4, paras 109–112. The portability arrangements are intended to ensure that where a person in receipt of care and support moves across the borders of Welsh authorities, that person's care and support plan together with the information in the assessment travels with them and is 'immediately' available to the receiving authority. The receiving authority is obliged to meet the care and support needs in that plan until the receiving authority is able to make its own assessment of need.

The portability arrangements do **not** apply where the sending authority is providing care and support under its statutory powers rather than in accordance with its duties. In those circumstances, there will still be a duty on the receiving authority to carry out new assessments under s 19 or s 21 of the Act.

57 Cases where a person expresses preference for particular accommodation

(1) Regulations may provide that where –

    (a)   a local authority is going to meet needs under sections 35 to 38 or sections 40 to 45 by providing or arranging for the provision of accommodation of a specified type for a person,

    (b)   the person concerned, or a person of a specified description, expresses a preference for particular accommodation of that type, and

    (c)   specified conditions are met,

the local authority must provide or arrange for the provision of the preferred accommodation.

(2) The regulations may require the person concerned or a person of a specified description to pay some or all of the additional cost (if any) of the preferred accommodation in specified cases or circumstances.

(3) In subsection (2) 'additional cost' means the difference between –

    (a)   the cost of providing or arranging the provision of the preferred accommodation, and

    (b)   the cost that the local authority would usually expect to incur in providing or arranging the provision of suitable accommodation of that type to meet the needs of the person concerned.

Care home accommodation—The Care and Support (Choice of Accommodation) (Wales) Regulations 2015 apply to cases where a local authority is meeting care and support needs of adults and children through the provision of care home accommodation.

58 Protecting property of persons being cared for away from home

(1) This section applies where –

(a)   a person is having needs for care and support met under section 35, 36, 37 or 38 in a way that involves the provision of accommodation, is admitted to hospital (or both), and

(b)   it appears to a local authority that there is a danger of loss or damage to movable property of the person's in the authority's area because –

  (i)   the person is unable (whether permanently or temporarily) to protect or deal with the property, and

  (ii)   no suitable arrangements have been or are being made.

(2) The local authority must take reasonable steps to prevent or mitigate the loss or damage.

(3) For the purpose of discharging that duty, the local authority –

(a)   may at all reasonable times and on reasonable notice enter any premises which the person was living in immediately before being provided with accommodation or admitted to hospital, and

(b)   may take any other steps which it considers reasonably necessary for preventing or mitigating loss or damage.

(4) The local authority must ensure that the following requirements are satisfied before taking any steps under subsection (3)(a) or (b) –

CASE 1 – where the local authority is satisfied that the person is –

(a)   an adult or a child aged 16 or 17 who has capacity to consent to the taking of the steps, or

(b)   a child aged under 16 who has sufficient understanding to make an informed decision about whether to consent to the taking of the steps,

the local authority must obtain the person's consent to the taking of the steps;

CASE 2 – where the local authority is satisfied that the person is an adult who lacks capacity to consent to the taking of the steps –

(a)   the local authority must obtain consent to the taking of the steps from a person authorised under the Mental Capacity Act 2005 (whether in general or specific terms) to give consent on the adult's behalf, if any person is so authorised, or

(b)   if there is no person so authorised, the local authority must be satisfied that the taking of the steps would be in the adult's best interests;

CASE 3 – where the local authority is satisfied that the person is a child aged 16 or 17 who lacks capacity to consent to the taking of the steps –

(a)   the local authority must obtain consent to the taking of the steps from a person authorised under the Mental Capacity Act 2005 (whether in general or specific terms) to give consent on the child's behalf, if any person is so authorised, or

(b)   if there is no person so authorised, the local authority must obtain consent to the taking of the steps from a person with parental responsibility for the child;

CASE 4 – where the local authority is satisfied that the person is a child aged under 16 who does not have sufficient understanding to make an informed decision about whether to consent to the taking of the steps, the local authority must obtain consent to the taking of the steps from a person with parental responsibility for the child.

(5) The local authority must take reasonable steps to obtain any consent which may be needed under subsection (4).

(6) Where the local authority is unable to ensure that the requirements in subsection (4) are satisfied, the local authority's duty under subsection (2) ceases to apply.

(7) Where a local authority is proposing to exercise the power under subsection (3)(a) or (b), the officer it authorises to do so must, upon request, produce valid documentation setting out the authorisation to do so.

(8) A person who, without reasonable excuse, obstructs the exercise of the power under subsection (3)(a) or (b) –

    (a)   commits an offence, and

    (b)   is liable on summary conviction to a fine not exceeding level 4 on the standard scale.

(9) A local authority may recover whatever reasonable expenses it incurs under this section in relation to an adult's movable property from that adult.

(10) An amount recoverable under subsection (9) is recoverable summarily as a civil debt (but this does not affect any other method of recovery).

Amendments—SI 2016/413.

****

PART 6
LOOKED AFTER AND ACCOMMODATED CHILDREN

Regulations—The relevant regulations are the Care Planning, Placement and Case Review (Wales) Regulations 2015 (the CPPCR Regulations).

Code—The relevant code is the Code to Part 6. This is a statutory Code issued under s 145 of the 2014 Act. Local authorities must act in accordance with the requirements of this Code. In addition, local authorities must have regard to the guidelines it contains.

Note—The principle duty of a local authority to a looked-after child is set out and described in s 78 of the Act (see below).

The overall purpose of Pt 6 is to safeguard and promote the well-being of looked-after and accommodated children and care leavers, and to enable each child or young person to achieve recovery and healing from past harm (Code to Part 6, para 29). It also aims to promote resilience and achievement of personal well-being outcomes. In general, the well-being outcomes will relate to the national well-being outcomes as well as those specific to the individual in question. The child or young person's views, wishes and feelings and (where appropriate) those of the parents, will be crucial in determining what those personal outcomes are and how they can be best met. The extent to which a child or young person can participate in defining and achieving those outcomes depends on their age and understanding. It is intended that children and young people should be supported to participate in the process (see Code to Part 6, para 29). Section 178 of the Act maintains the existing duties on local authorities to make arrangements for the provision of assistance to looked-after children, former looked-after children and specified others who fall to make representations that fall within ss 174, 176 and 177 of the Act. There is a dedicated Code on advocacy (Code to Part 10).

The Act places clear duties on individuals and local authorities when carrying out their functions in relation to looked-after and accommodated children and young people.

Persons exercising functions under this part of the Act **must** have regard to the overarching duties under ss 6 and 7 of the Act (see above). Having 'regard' in this context is similar to a requirement to consider or take into account that matter (Code to Part 2, para 55).

In addition, when exercising functions under this Part of the Act a person must take into account the requirements of the Human Rights Act 1998 and the Articles in Sch 1 of that Act.

The United Nations Convention on the Rights of Disabled People may also apply.

Nothing within Pt 6 is intended to undermine a local authority's duty to safeguard a looked-after child. Nothing within Pt 6 of the Act dilutes or amends s 130 of the Act or CA 1989, s 47.

Interpretation

74 Child or young person looked after by a local authority

(1) In this Act, a reference to a child who is looked after by a local authority is a reference to a child who is –

    (a) in its care, or

    (b) provided with accommodation by the authority in the exercise of any functions which are social services functions, apart from functions under section 15, Part 4, or section 109, 114 or 115.

(2) In subsection (1), 'accommodation' means accommodation which is provided for a continuous period of more than 24 hours.

(3) In this Part, a reference to a young person being looked after by a local authority is a reference to a young person being looked after by the authority while he or she is or was a child.

Note—By s 15 of the 2014 Act, a local authority must provide or arrange for preventative services in accordance with that section. Part 4 of the Act deals with meeting the need for care and support or a carer's need for support. Sections 109, 114 and 115 are references to the sections of the Act that form part of the new leaving care arrangements in Wales. Under the new scheme, specific provision is made in relation to six categories of children and young people as defined by s 104 of the Act. Section 109 relates to a category 2 young person. Sections 114 and 115 apply to category 5 and former category 5 young people and category 6 and former category 6 young people. Sections 109, 114 and 115 relate to children aged over 16. Under section 109, a local authority must provide that person with accommodation unless that person's well-being does not require it. Under sections 114 and 115, if certain conditions are met, a local authority may provide that person with accommodation.

Part 2 of the CPPCR Regulations apply to arrangements for looked after children. See also the notes to s 83, below.

Accommodation duties

75 General duty of local authority to secure sufficient accommodation for looked after children

(1) A local authority must take steps that secure, so far as reasonably practicable, that the local authority is able to provide the children mentioned in subsection (2) with accommodation that –

    (a) is within the authority's area, and

    (b) meets the needs of those children.

(2) The children referred to in subsection (1) are those –

    (a) that the local authority is looking after,

    (b) in respect of whom the authority is unable to make arrangements under section 81(2), and

    (c) whose circumstances are such that it would be consistent with their well-being for them to be provided with accommodation that is in the authority's area.

(3) In discharging its duty under subsection (1), the local authority must have regard to the benefit of having –

    (a) a number of accommodation providers in its area that is, in the authority's opinion, sufficient to discharge its duty, and

    (b) a range of accommodation in its area capable of meeting different needs that is, in its opinion, sufficient to discharge its duty.

(4) In this section 'accommodation providers' means –

    (a) local authority foster parents, and

PART VII

(b)   children's homes.

'within the authority's area' (s 75(1)(a))—In discharging this duty, the local authority must have regard to the benefit of having a number of accommodation providers in their area that is sufficient to discharge its duty, and the benefit of having a range of accommodation in its area capable of meeting different needs. The aim is to improve the quality and choice of placements and minimise the likelihood of suitable placements not being available for looked-after children in their local area (Code to Part 6, para 123). See also the notes to s 81, below.

'well-being' (s 75(2)(c))—This has the statutory meaning provided by s 2(2) of the Act. It is a wider definition than welfare within the meaning of CA 1989.

76 Accommodation for children without parents or who are lost or abandoned etc

(1) A local authority must provide accommodation for any child within its area who appears to the authority to require accommodation as a result of –

(a)   there being no person who has parental responsibility for the child,

(b)   the child being lost or having been abandoned, or

(c)   the person who has been caring for the child being prevented (whether or not permanently, and for whatever reason) from providing the child with suitable accommodation or care.

(2) Where a local authority provides accommodation under subsection (1) for a child who is ordinarily resident in the area of another local authority, that other local authority may take over the provision of accommodation for the child within –

(a)   three months of being notified in writing that the child is being provided with accommodation, or

(b)   such other longer period as may be specified.

(2A) Where a local authority in England provides accommodation under section 20(1) of the Children Act 1989 (provision of accommodation for children: general) for a child who is ordinarily resident in the area of a local authority in Wales, that local authority in Wales may take over the provision of accommodation for the child within –

(a)   three months of being notified in writing that the child is being provided with accommodation, or

(b)   such other longer period as may be specified.

(3) A local authority must provide accommodation for any child within its area who has reached the age of 16 and whose well-being the authority considers is likely to be seriously prejudiced if it does not provide the child with accommodation.

(4) A local authority may not provide accommodation under this section for any child if any person objects who –

(a)   has parental responsibility for the child, and

(b)   is willing and able to –

(i)   provide accommodation for the child, or

(ii)   arrange for accommodation to be provided for the child.

(5) Any person who has parental responsibility for a child may at any time remove the child from accommodation provided by or on behalf of a local authority under this section.

(6) Subsections (4) and (5) do not apply while any person –

(a)   in whose favour a child arrangements order is in force with respect to the child,

(b)   who is a special guardian of the child, or

(c)   who has care of the child by virtue of an order made in the exercise of the High Court's inherent jurisdiction with respect to children, agrees to the child being looked after in accommodation provided by or on behalf of the local authority.

(7) Where there is more than one such person as is mentioned in subsection (6), all of them must agree.

(8) Subsections (4) and (5) do not apply where a child who has reached the age of 16 agrees to being provided with accommodation under this section.

Amendments—SI 2016/413; SI 2017/1025.

'well-being' (s 76(3))—This section replaces CA 1989, s 20, which has been repealed in Wales. Well-being in s 76(3) of the 2014 Act has the statutory meaning provided by s 2(2) of that Act.

Accommodating a looked-after child—In deciding how best to accommodate and maintain a looked-after child, a local authority must always be guided by its principal duty under s 78. The options for placing a looked-after child are set out in s 81 (Code to Part 6, para 125).

Ordinary residence—Ordinary residence is the key concept in determining which local authority has a duty to assess and meet the care and/or support needs of an individual under Pts 3, 4 and 6 of the 2014 Act. Regulations made under Pt 11 of the 2014 Act contain additional provisions on ordinary residence, relating to specified accommodation and dispute resolution. Part 2 of the Code to Part 11 of the Act details how disputes should be resolved. In particular, Pt 2 of the Code to Part 11 states that under s 76 of the 2014 Act a local authority is responsible for providing accommodation for any child within its area who meets the criteria in s 76(1). However, where a local authority provides accommodation under this section for a child who was (immediately before the local authority began to look after the child) ordinarily resident within the area of another local authority, it may recover from that other local authority any reasonable expenses incurred by it in providing the accommodation and maintaining the child (see s 193 of the 2014 Act). Section 194(6) provides that in determining the ordinary residence of a child for the purposes of the 2014 Act, the child's residence in the following places is to be disregarded:

- a school or other institution;
- a place in which the child is placed in accordance with the requirements of a supervision order under CA 1989 or in accordance with the requirements of a youth rehabilitation order under Criminal Justice and Immigration Act 2008, Pt 1;
- accommodation provided by or on behalf of a local authority in Wales (or a local authority in England).

This means that where a local authority is providing accommodation for a child under s 76 and is seeking to recover the costs of providing that accommodation from the local authority in whose area the child was ordinarily resident immediately before it began to look after the child, the question of where the child was ordinarily resident is to be determined without regard to their actual place of residence at that time, if this is one of the places listed in s 194(6). Where a looked-after child is the subject of a care order, the local authority responsible for providing accommodation for the child will be the authority that is designated by the court at the time the care order was made. The designated local authority is the authority within whose area the child is ordinarily resident or, where the child does not reside in the area of a local authority, the authority within whose area any circumstances arose in consequence of which the order is being made (see CA 1989, s 31(8)). CA 1989, s 105(6) will apply where there is any question of where a child was ordinarily resident for the purpose of deciding which authority is the designated local authority under s 31(8). Section 105(6) of the 1989 Act makes similar provision to that contained in s 194(6) of the 2014 Act, such that the child's residence in specific places is disregarded when determining the child's ordinary residence for this purpose.

77 Accommodation for children in police protection or detention or on remand etc

(1) A local authority must make provision for the reception and accommodation of children who are removed or kept away from home under Part 5 of the Children Act 1989.

(2) A local authority must receive, and provide accommodation for, children –

    (a)   in police protection whom it is requested to receive under section 46(3)(f) of the Children Act 1989;

- (b) whom it is requested to receive under section 38(6) of the Police and Criminal Evidence Act 1984;
- (c) with respect to whom it is the designated authority and who are –
    - (i)   remanded to accommodation provided by or on behalf of a local authority by virtue of paragraph 4 of Schedule 1 or paragraph 6 of Schedule 8 to the Powers of Criminal Courts (Sentencing) Act 2000 (breach etc of referral orders and reparation orders);
    - (ii)   remanded to accommodation provided by or on behalf of a local authority by virtue of paragraph 21 of Schedule 2 to the Criminal Justice and Immigration Act 2008 (breach etc of youth rehabilitation orders);
    - (iii) remanded to accommodation provided by or on behalf of a local authority by virtue of paragraph 10 of the Schedule to the Street Offences Act 1959 (breach of orders under section 1(2A) of that Act);
    - (iv)   the subject of a youth rehabilitation order imposing a local authority residence requirement or a youth rehabilitation order with fostering.

(3) In subsection (2), the following terms have the same meanings as in Part 1 of the Criminal Justice and Immigration Act 2008 (see section 7 of that Act) –

'local authority residence requirement';
'youth rehabilitation order';
'youth rehabilitation order with fostering'.

(4) Subsection (5) applies where –

- (a) a child has been –
    - (i)   removed under Part 5 of the Children Act 1989, or
    - (ii)   detained under section 38 of the Police and Criminal Evidence Act 1984, and
- (b) the child is not being provided with accommodation –
    - (i)   by a local authority or local authority in England, or
    - (ii)   in a hospital vested in the Welsh Ministers, an NHS Trust, an NHS Foundation Trust or the Secretary of State, or otherwise made available pursuant to arrangements made by a Local Health Board, an NHS Trust, an NHS Foundation Trust, the Welsh Ministers, the Secretary of State, the National Health Service Commissioning Board or a clinical commissioning group.

(5) Any reasonable expenses of accommodating the child are recoverable from the local authority or local authority in England in whose area the child is ordinarily resident.

Amendments—SI 2016/413.

Duties of local authorities in relation to looked after children

78 Principal duty of a local authority in relation to looked after children

(1) A local authority looking after any child must –

- (a) safeguard and promote the child's well-being, and
- (b) make such use of services available for children cared for by their own parents as appears to the authority reasonable in the child's case.

(2) The duty of a local authority under subsection (1)(a) to safeguard and promote the well-being of a child looked after by it includes, for example –

- (a) a duty to promote the child's educational achievement;
- (b) a duty –
    - (i)   to assess from time to time whether the child has care and support needs which meet the eligibility criteria set under section 32, and

(ii)   if the child has needs which meet the eligibility criteria, to at least meet those needs.

(3) Before making any decision with respect to a child whom it is looking after, or proposing to look after, a local authority must (in addition to the matters set out in sections 6(2) and (4) and 7(2) (other overarching duties)) have regard to –

(a)   the views, wishes and feelings of any person whose views, wishes and feelings the authority considers to be relevant;

(b)   the child's religious persuasion, racial origin and cultural and linguistic background.

(4) If it appears to a local authority that it is necessary, for the purpose of protecting members of the public from serious injury, to exercise its powers with respect to a child whom it is looking after in a manner which may not be consistent with its duties under this section or section 6, it may do so.

79   Provision of accommodation for children in care

When a child is in the care of a local authority, the authority must provide the child with accommodation.

80   Maintenance of looked after children

A local authority must maintain a child it is looking after in other respects apart from the provision of accommodation.

81   Ways in which looked after children are to be accommodated and maintained

(1)   This section applies where a local authority is looking after a child ('C').

(2)   The local authority must make arrangements for C to live with a person who falls within subsection (3), but this is subject to subsections (4) and (11).

(3)   A person ('P') falls within this subsection if –

(a)   P is a parent of C,

(b)   P is not a parent of C but has parental responsibility for C, or

(c)   in a case where C is in the care of the local authority and there was a child arrangements order in force with respect to C immediately before the care order was made, P was a person in whose favour the child arrangements order was made.

(4)   Subsection (2) does not require the local authority to make arrangements of the kind mentioned in that subsection if doing so –

(a)   would not be consistent with C's well-being, or

(b)   would not be reasonably practicable.

(5)   If the local authority is unable to make arrangements under subsection (2), it must place C in the placement that is, in its opinion, the most appropriate placement available (but this is subject to subsection (11)).

(6)   In subsection (5) 'placement' means –

(a)   placement with an individual who is a relative, friend or other person connected with C and who is also a local authority foster parent,

(b)   placement with a local authority foster parent who does not fall within paragraph (a),

(c)   placement in a children's home, or

PART VII

(d) subject to section 82, placement in accordance with other arrangements that comply with any regulations made for the purposes of this section.

(7) In determining the most appropriate placement for C under subsection (5), the local authority must, subject to the other provisions of this Part (in particular, to its duties under section 78) –

(a) give preference to a placement falling within paragraph (a) of subsection (6) over placements falling within the other paragraphs of that subsection,

(b) comply, so far as is reasonably practicable in all the circumstances of C's case, with the requirements of subsection (8), and

(c) comply with subsection (9) unless it is not reasonably practicable to do so.

(8) The local authority must ensure that the placement is such that –

(a) it allows C to live near C's home;

(b) it does not disrupt C's education or training;

(c) if C has a sibling for whom the local authority is also providing accommodation, it enables C and the sibling to live together;

(d) if C is disabled, the accommodation provided is suitable to C's particular needs.

(9) The placement must be such that C is provided with accommodation within the local authority's area.

(10) Subsection (11) applies where –

(a) the local authority is satisfied that C ought to be placed for adoption and proposes to place C for adoption with a particular prospective adopter ('A'),

(b) an adoption agency has determined that A is suitable to adopt a child, and

(c) the local authority is not authorised to place C for adoption.

(11) The local authority must place C with A, unless in its opinion it would be more appropriate –

(a) to make arrangements for C to live with a person falling within subsection (3), or

(b) to place C in a placement of a description mentioned in subsection (6).

(12) For the purposes of subsection (10) –

(a) 'adoption agency' has the meaning given by section 2 of the Adoption and Children Act 2002;

(b) a local authority is authorised to place C for adoption only if it has been authorised to do so under –

(i) section 19 of that Act (placing children with parental consent), or

(ii) a placement order made under section 21 of that Act.

(13) The local authority may determine –

(a) the terms of any arrangements it makes under subsection (2) in relation to C (including terms as to payment), and

(b) the terms on which it places C with a local authority foster parent under subsection (5) or with a prospective adopter under subsection (11) (including terms as to payment but subject to any order made under section 49 of the Children Act 2004).

Amendments—SI 2017/1025.

Definitions—'looked-after child': s 74; 'well-being': s 2(2).

Placing a child—The Code to Part 6, Ch 2 applies. In deciding how best to accommodate and maintain a looked-after child, a local authority must always be guided by its principal duty under s 78. The options for placing a child are contained in s 81 (Code to Part 6, para 125).

Before making arrangements in accordance with s 81, or if that is not practicable, within 5 working days of making that placement, a local authority must include within the child's care and support plan details of the placement plan and comply with the other requirements of reg 10 of the CPPCR Regulations.

Before making any placement that will have the effect of disrupting a child's education, the requirements of reg 11 of the CPPCR Regulations must be followed.

The placement must be such that the child is accommodated within the local authority's area. A local authority may only make an out-of-area placement if the requirements of reg 12 of the CPPCR Regulations are complied with. Welsh local authorities that border England are specifically dealt with in the Code to Part 6, para 186.

Placements outside England and Wales—These must be made in accordance with s 124.

A person falling within s 81(3)—If it is consistent with the child's well-being, and it is reasonably practicable to do so, a local authority should make arrangements for a looked-after child to live with a person who falls within s 81(3) (s 81(2),(4),(11) applied). A person falls within s 81(3) if he or she is a parent, has parental responsibility for the child and held a residence order or child arrangement order before the child came into care. The CPPCR Regulations specify that a placement should not be made with a parent unless the placement safeguards and promotes the child's well-being and meets their needs as set out in their Pt 6 Care and Support Plans.

A child must not be placed back with a parent etc if to do so would be incompatible with any court order (Code to Part 6, para 139).

The requirements of Pt 4, Ch 1 of the CPPCR Regulations must be complied with when deciding whether to place a child with a parent, a person who has parental responsibility for him etc in accordance with s 81(2). Regulation 20 of CPPCR Regulations sets out the circumstances in which a child may be so placed before a local authority has completed the assessment necessary under reg 18. Where a child is placed under s 81(2) of the Act, a local authority must provide such services and support to the parent, person with parental responsibility etc as is necessary to safeguard and promote the child's well-being (CPPCR Regulations, reg 21).

'a relative, friend or other person connected with C' (s 81(6))—Where it is not possible to place a child with a person falling within the definition in s 81(3), preference should be given to placement with a relative, friend or other person connected with the child. CPPCR Regulations Pt 4, Ch 2 applies to such placements. Where the child is in care – under an interim or final care order – that person will need to be registered as a foster carer. The CPPCR Regulations allow a local authority to make a temporary placement with that person while approval is sought as a foster carer (CPPCR Regulations, regs 26–27). Temporary placements may initially be up to 16 weeks and can be extended in accordance with the Regulations for a further 8 weeks.

Where the child is accommodated on a voluntary basis, and is being discharged into the care of a relative, friend or connected person (with parental consent and because the assessment and review of the child's case has concluded that is the best option for the child), the child will cease to be looked after (Code to Part 6, para 127).

Other placements—If it is not possible to place a looked-after child with a parent or a relative, friend or connected person, according to the Code to Part 6, para 128, the local authority must consider which of the following is the most appropriate:

- placement with an unconnected foster carer;
- placement with a prospective adopter;
- placement in a children's home; or
- placement in accordance with other arrangements, e g supporting young people aged 16 or over to live independently.

Part 4, Chapters 2 and 3 of the CPPCR Regulations apply.

'the terms of any arrangements' (s 81(13))—Local authorities have the power under s 81(3) to determine the terms of any arrangements they make to place a looked-after child with a parent, foster carer (connected or unconnected) or prospective adopter, including terms as to any payments (subject to any order made under CA 2004, s 49).

'Foster to Adopt' (s 81(10)–(13))—These subsections make provision for a child to be placed with prospective adopters provided the local authority has made the 'ought to be placed' decision, the prospective adopters have been matched with the child and a placement order has not been made. In those circumstances, a local authority must place the child with the prospective adopters, unless it considers

PART VII

that it would be more appropriate to place the child elsewhere until the placement order is made. 'Foster to Adopt' arrangements are different from concurrent planning arrangements in England. The CPPCR Regulations, ss 25 and 28 apply.

82 Review of child's case before making alternative arrangements for accommodation

(1) Where a local authority is providing accommodation for a child ('C') other than in accordance with arrangements falling within section 81(6)(d), it must not make such arrangements for C unless it has decided to do so in consequence of a review of C's case carried out in accordance with regulations made under section 102 (review of cases and inquiries into representations).

(2) But subsection (1) does not prevent a local authority making arrangements for C under section 81(6)(d) if it is satisfied that in order to safeguard C's well-being it is necessary –

   (a)   to make such arrangements, and
   (b)   to do so as a matter of urgency.

83 Care and support plans

(1) Where a child becomes looked after by a local authority, any care and support plan prepared under section 54 in relation to that child must be –

   (a)   reviewed, and
   (b)   maintained under this section.

(2) Where a child who does not have a care and support plan under section 54 becomes looked after by a local authority, the local authority must prepare and maintain a care and support plan in relation to that child.

(3) A local authority must keep under review the plans that it maintains under this section.

(4) Where a local authority is satisfied that the circumstances of the child to whom a plan relates have changed in a way that affects the plan, the authority must –

   (a)   carry out such assessments as it considers appropriate, and
   (b)   revise the plan.

(5) Regulations must make provision about –

   (a)   how plans under this section are to be prepared;
   (b)   what a plan is to contain;
   (c)   the review and revision of plans.

(6) Regulations under subsection (5)(c) must specify, in particular –

   (a)   the persons who may request a review of a plan (on their own behalf or on behalf of another person);
   (b)   the circumstances in which a local authority –
       (i)   may refuse to comply with a request for a review of a plan, and
       (ii)   may not refuse to do so.

(7) When preparing, reviewing or revising a plan under this section, a local authority must involve the child to whom the plan relates and any person with parental responsibility for the child.

(8) The local authority may –

   (a)   prepare, review or revise a plan under this section at the same time as it or another body is preparing, reviewing or revising another document in the case of the child concerned, and

(b)   include the other document in the plan.

(9) Any Part of a plan maintained under this section which meets the requirements imposed by or under section 31A of the Children Act 1989 may be treated for the purposes of that Act as a plan prepared under section 31A of that Act.

Timescale—All looked-after children, except those to whom CA 1989, s 31A applies, must have a care and support plan before they are first placed or, if that is not reasonably practicable, within 10 working days thereafter (CPPCR Regulations, reg 4). Where a child was first placed before 6 April 2016 (the date the Act came into force), the care and support plan must be prepared as soon as reasonably practicable (CPPCR Regulations, reg 4(8)).

Content—The content of the care and support plan required under Pt 2 of the CPPCR Regulations is prescribed in regs 5 and 10 of those Regulations. It must be kept under review in accordance with reg 6.

'the requirements ... under section 31A of the Children Act 1989' (s 83(9))—Where a care and support plan prepared in accordance with Pt 2 of the CPPCR Regulations satisfies the requirements for a CA 1989, s 31A care plan, it may be treated as a s 31A care plan (CPPCR Regulations, reg 4(7)).

84 Regulations about care and support plans

Regulations under section 83 may, for example –

(a)   require plans to be in a specified form;

(b)   require plans to contain specified things;

(c)   make provision about further persons whom a local authority must involve in the preparation, review or revision of plans;

(d)   require plans to be prepared, reviewed or revised by specified persons;

(e)   confer functions on persons specified in the regulations in connection with the review or revision of plans;

(f)   specify persons to whom written copies of a plan must be provided (including, in specified cases, the provision of copies without the consent of the person to whom the plan relates);

(g)   specify further circumstances in which plans must be reviewed.

Regulations—The relevant regulations are the Care Planning, Placement and Case Review (Wales) Regulations 2015.

85 Contributions towards maintenance of looked after children

Schedule 1 makes provision about contributions towards the maintenance of children looked after by local authorities.

86 Children's homes provided, equipped and maintained by the Welsh Ministers or Secretary of State

Where a local authority places a child it is looking after in a children's home provided, equipped and maintained by the Welsh Ministers or the Secretary of State under section 82(5) of the Children Act 1989, it must do so on such terms and conditions as the Welsh Ministers or the Secretary of State (as the case may be) may from time to time determine.

Amendments—Substituted by SI 2016/413.

Regulations about looked after children

87 Regulations about looked after children

Regulations may make further provision about children looked after by local authorities.

Regulations—The relevant regulations are the Care Planning, Placement and Case Review (Wales) Regulations 2015.

88 Regulations about conditions under which a child in care is allowed to live with a parent etc

Regulations under section 87 may, for example, impose requirements on a local authority as to –

(a) the making of any decision to allow a child in its care to live with any person falling within section 81(3) (including requirements as to those who must be consulted before the decision is made and those who must be notified when it has been made);

(b) the supervision or medical examination of the child concerned;

(c) the removal of the child, in such circumstances as may be specified in regulations, from the care of the person with whom the child has been allowed to live;

(d) the records to be kept by the local authority.

Regulations—The relevant regulations are the Care Planning, Placement and Case Review (Wales) Regulations 2015.

89 Regulations about placements of a kind mentioned in section 81(6)(d)

(1) Regulations under section 87 may, for example, make provision as to placements of the kind mentioned in section 81(6)(d).

(2) Regulations under subsection (1) may, for example, make provision as to –

(a) the persons to be notified of any proposed arrangements;

(b) the opportunities such persons are to have to make representations in relation to the arrangements proposed;

(c) the persons to be notified of any proposed changes in the arrangements;

(d) the records to be kept by local authorities;

(e) the supervision by local authorities of any arrangements made.

Regulations—The relevant regulations are the Care Planning, Placement and Case Review (Wales) Regulations 2015.

90 Regulations about placements out of area

Regulations under section 87 may, for example, impose requirements that a local authority must comply with –

(a) before a child looked after by it is provided with accommodation at a place outside the area of the authority, or

(b) if the child's well-being requires the immediate provision of such accommodation, within such period of the accommodation being provided as may be specified.

Regulations—The relevant regulations are the Care Planning, Placement and Case Review (Wales) Regulations 2015.

91 Regulations about the avoidance of disruption in education

(1) Regulations under section 87 may, for example, impose requirements that a local authority must comply with before making any decision concerning a child's placement if he or she is in the fourth key stage.

(2) A child is 'in the fourth key stage' if the child is a pupil in the fourth key stage for the purposes of Part 7 of the Education Act 2002 (see section 103 of that Act).

92 Regulations about the placing of children with local authority foster parents and prospective adopters

(1) Regulations under section 87 may, for example, make provision –

(a) with regard to the well-being of children placed with local authority foster parents or prospective adopters;

(b) as to the arrangements to be made by local authorities in connection with the health and education of such children;

(c) as to the records to be kept by local authorities;

(d) for securing that where possible the local authority foster parent or prospective adopter with whom a child is to be placed –

    (i) is of the same religious persuasion as the child, or

    (ii) gives an undertaking that the child will be brought up in that religious persuasion;

(e) for securing that children placed with local authority foster parents or prospective adopters, and the premises in which they are accommodated, will be supervised and inspected by a local authority and that the children will be removed from those premises if their well-being appears to require it.

(2) In this section 'prospective adopter' means a person with whom a child is placed under section 81(11).

Regulations—The relevant regulations are the Care Planning, Placement and Case Review (Wales) Regulations 2015.

93 Regulations providing for approval of local authority foster parents

(1) Regulations under section 87 may, for example, make provision –

(a) for securing that a child is not placed with a local authority foster parent unless that person is for the time being approved as a local authority foster parent by such local authority or other persons as may be specified;

(b) establishing a procedure under which any person in respect of whom a qualifying determination has been made may apply to the Welsh Ministers for a review of that determination by a panel constituted by the Welsh Ministers.

(2) A determination is a qualifying determination if –

(a) it relates to the issue of whether a person should be approved, or should continue to be approved, as a local authority foster parent, and

(b) it is of a specified description.

(3) Regulations made under subsection (1)(b) may include provision as to –

(a) the duties and powers of a panel;

(b) the administration and procedures of a panel;

(c) the appointment of members of a panel (including the number, or any limit on the number, of members who may be appointed and any conditions for their appointment);

(d) the payment of fees to members of a panel;

PART VII

(e)   the duties of any person in connection with a review conducted under the regulations;

(f)   the monitoring of any such reviews.

(4) Regulations made by virtue of subsection (3)(e) may impose a duty to pay to the Welsh Ministers such amount as the Welsh Ministers may determine; but such a duty may not be imposed upon a person who has applied for a review of a qualifying determination.

(5) The Welsh Ministers must secure that, taking one financial year with another, the aggregate of the amounts which become payable to them under regulations made by virtue of subsection (4) does not exceed the cost to them of performing their independent review functions.

(6) The Welsh Ministers may make an arrangement with an organisation under which independent review functions are performed by the organisation on their behalf.

(7) If the Welsh Ministers make such an arrangement with an organisation, the organisation must perform their functions under the arrangement in accordance with any general or specific direction given by the Welsh Ministers.

(8) The arrangement may include provision for payments to be made to the organisation by the Welsh Ministers.

(9) Payments made by the Welsh Ministers in accordance with such provision are to be taken into account in determining (for the purpose of subsection (5)) the cost to the Welsh Ministers of performing their independent review functions.

(10) A direction under subsection (7) –

(a)   must be in writing;

(b)   may be varied or revoked by a later direction.

(11) In this section –

'financial year' ('*blwyddyn ariannol*') means a period of twelve months ending with 31 March;

'independent review function' ('*swyddogaeth adolygu annibynnol*') means a function conferred or imposed on the Welsh Ministers by regulations made by virtue of subsection (1)(b);

'organisation' ('*sefydliad*') includes the Secretary of State, a public body and a private or voluntary organisation.

Amendments—SI 2016/413.

94   Regulations about agency arrangements

Regulations under section 87 may, for example, make provision as to the circumstances in which a local authority may make arrangements for duties imposed on it by the regulations to be discharged on its behalf.

Contact and visits

95   Promotion and maintenance of contact between child and family

(1) Where a child is being looked after by a local authority, the authority must, unless it is not reasonably practicable or consistent with the child's well-being, promote contact between the child and –

(a)   the child's parents,

(b)   any person who is not a parent of the child but who has parental responsibility for the child, and

(c)   any relative, friend or other person connected with the child.

(2) Where a child is being looked after by a local authority, the authority must take such steps as are reasonably practicable to secure that the following persons are kept informed of where the child is being accommodated –

(a)   the child's parents;

(b)   any person who is not a parent of the child but who has parental responsibility for the child.

(3) Every person mentioned in subsection (2)(a) or (b) must secure that the authority is kept informed of his or her address.

(4) Where a local authority ('the receiving authority') takes over the provision of accommodation for a child from a local authority or a local authority in England under section 76 ('the transferring authority') –

(a)   the receiving authority must (where reasonably practicable) inform –
(i)   the child's parents, and
(ii) any person who is not a parent of the child but who has parental responsibility for the child,

(b)   subsection (2) applies to the transferring authority, as well as to the receiving authority, until at least one of the persons mentioned in paragraph (a) or (b) of that subsection has been informed of the change, and

(c)   subsection (3) does not require any person to inform the receiving authority of his or her address until that person has been informed under paragraph (a).

(5) Nothing in this section requires a local authority to inform a person of the whereabouts of a child, other than a child aged under 16 who is being accommodated under section 76, if the authority has reasonable cause to believe that informing the person would prejudice the child's well-being.

(6) Any person who fails, without reasonable excuse, to comply with subsection (3) is guilty of an offence and liable on summary conviction to a fine not exceeding level 2 on the standard scale.

Amendments—SI 2016/413.

96   Family visits to or by children: expenses

(1) This paragraph applies where –

(a)   a child is being looked after by a local authority, and

(b)   the conditions mentioned in subsection (4) are satisfied.

(2) The authority may make payments in respect of travelling, subsistence or other expenses incurred by the following persons in visiting the child –

(a)   a parent of the child,

(b)   any person who is not a parent of the child but who has parental responsibility for the child, or

(c)   any relative, friend or other person connected with the child.

(3) The authority may make payments to the child, or to any person on the child's behalf, in respect of travelling, subsistence or other expenses incurred by or on behalf of the child in visiting the persons mentioned in paragraphs (a) to (c) of subsection (2).

(4) The conditions are that –

(a)   it appears to the authority that the visit in question could not otherwise be made without undue financial hardship, and

(b)   the circumstances warrant the making of the payments.

97 Duty of local authority to ensure visits to, and contact with, looked after children and other children

(1) This section applies to –

    (a)   a child looked after by a local authority;

    (b)   a child who was looked after by a local authority but who has ceased to be looked after by the authority as a result of circumstances specified in regulations;

    (c)   a child who falls within a category specified in regulations.

(2) Regulations specifying a category for the purpose of subsection (1)(c) must also specify the local authority which must discharge the duties imposed by or under this section in relation to a child who falls within the specified category.

(3) The local authority must –

    (a)   ensure that a child to whom this section applies is visited by a representative of the authority ('a representative');

    (b)   arrange for appropriate advice and other support to be available to a child to whom this section applies.

(4) The duties imposed by subsection (3) –

    (a)   are to be discharged in accordance with any regulations made for the purposes of this section;

    (b)   are subject to any requirement imposed by or under an enactment applicable to the place in which the child to whom this section applies is accommodated.

(5) Regulations under this section may, for the purposes of subsection (4)(a), make provision about –

    (a)   the frequency of visits;

    (b)   circumstances in which a child to whom this section applies must be visited by a representative;

    (c)   the functions of a representative.

(6) In choosing a representative, a local authority must satisfy itself that the person chosen has the necessary skills and experience to perform the functions of a representative.

Regulations—The relevant regulations are in Care Planning, Placement and Case Review (Wales) Regulations 2015, Pt 5.

98 Independent visitors for looked after children

(1) A local authority looking after a child must appoint an independent person to be the child's visitor if –

    (a)   the child falls within a category specified in regulations, or

    (b)   in any other case, it appears to the authority that it would be in the child's interests to do so.

(2) A person appointed under this section must visit, befriend and advise the child.

(3) A person appointed under this section is entitled to recover from the appointing authority any reasonable expenses incurred by that person for the purposes of that person's functions under this section.

(4) A person's appointment as a visitor in pursuance of this section comes to an end if –

    (a)   the child ceases to be looked after by the local authority,

    (b)   the person resigns the appointment by giving notice in writing to the appointing authority, or

   (c)   the authority gives the person notice in writing that it has terminated the appointment.

(5) The ending of such an appointment does not affect any duty under this section to make a further appointment.

(6) Where a local authority proposes to appoint a visitor for a child under this section, the appointment must not be made if –

   (a)   the child objects to it, and

   (b)   the authority is satisfied that the child has sufficient understanding to make an informed objection.

(7) Where a visitor has been appointed for a child under this section, the local authority must terminate the appointment if –

   (a)   the child objects to its continuing, and

   (b)   the authority is satisfied that the child has sufficient understanding to make an informed objection.

(8) If the local authority gives effect to a child's objection under subsection (6) or (7) and the objection is to having anyone as the child's visitor, the authority does not have to propose to appoint another person under subsection (1) until the objection is withdrawn.

(9) Regulations may provide for the circumstances in which a person is to be regarded for the purposes of this section as being independent of the appointing local authority.

Review of cases

99 Appointment of independent reviewing officer

(1) If a local authority is looking after a child, it must appoint an individual as the independent reviewing officer for that child's case.

(2) The initial appointment under subsection (1) must be made before the child's case is first reviewed in accordance with regulations made under section 102.

(3) If a vacancy arises in respect of a child's case, the local authority must make another appointment under subsection (1) as soon as is practicable.

(4) An appointee must fall within a category of persons specified in regulations.

Regulations—The relevant regulations are in Care Planning, Placement and Case Review (Wales) Regulations 2015, Pt 6.

100 Functions of the independent reviewing officer

(1) The independent reviewing officer must –

   (a)   monitor the performance by the local authority of its functions in relation to the child's case;

   (b)   participate, in accordance with regulations, in any review of the child's case;

   (c)   ensure that any ascertained wishes and feelings of the child concerning the case are given due consideration by the local authority;

   (d)   perform any other function specified in regulations.

(2) An independent reviewing officer's functions must be performed –

   (a)   in such manner as may be specified in regulations, and

   (b)   having regard to such guidance as that authority may issue in relation to the discharge of those functions.

(3) If the independent reviewing officer considers it appropriate to do so, the child's case may be referred by that officer to a Welsh family proceedings officer.

PART VII

(4) If the independent reviewing officer is not an officer of the local authority, it is the duty of the authority –

    (a)   to co-operate with that individual, and

    (b)   to take such reasonable steps as that individual may require to enable that individual's functions under this section to be performed satisfactorily.

Regulations—The relevant regulations are in Care Planning, Placement and Case Review (Wales) Regulations 2015, Pt 6.

101 Referred cases

(1) In relation to children whose cases are referred to Welsh family proceedings officers under section 100(3), the Lord Chancellor may by regulations –

    (a)   extend any functions of the Welsh family proceedings officers in respect of family proceedings (within the meaning of section 12 of the Criminal Justice and Court Services Act 2000) to other proceedings;

    (b)   require any functions of the Welsh family proceedings officers to be performed in the manner specified by the regulations.

(2) The power to make regulations under this section is exercisable only with the consent of the Welsh Ministers.

102 Review of cases and inquiries into representations

(1) Regulations may require the case of each child who is being looked after by a local authority to be reviewed in accordance with the provisions of the regulations.

(2) The regulations may, among other things, make provision –

    (a)   as to the manner in which each case is to be reviewed;

    (b)   as to the considerations to which the local authority is to have regard in reviewing each case;

    (c)   as to the time when each case is first to be reviewed and the frequency of subsequent reviews;

    (d)   requiring the authority, before conducting any review, to seek the views of –

        (i)   the child,

        (ii)   the child's parents,

        (iii) any person who is not a parent of the child but who has parental responsibility for the child, and

        (iv) any other person whose views the authority considers to be relevant,

        including, in particular, the views of those persons in relation to any particular matter which is to be considered in the course of the review;

    (e)   requiring the authority, in the case of a child who is in its care –

        (i)   to keep the plan under section 31A of the Children Act 1989 (care orders: care plans) for the child under review and, if it is of the opinion that some change is required, to revise the plan or make a new plan accordingly, and

        (ii)   to consider whether an application should be made to discharge the care order;

    (f)   requiring the authority, in the case of a child in accommodation provided by or on behalf of the authority –

        (i)   if there is no plan for the future care of the child, to prepare one,

        (ii)   if there is such a plan for the child, to keep it under review and, if it is of the opinion that some change is required, to revise the plan or make a new plan accordingly, and

        (iii) to consider whether the accommodation accords with the requirements of this Part;

(g) requiring the authority to inform the child, so far as is reasonably practicable, of any steps the child may take under this Act or the Children Act 1989;

(h) requiring the authority to make arrangements, including arrangements with other bodies which provide services and which it considers appropriate, to implement any decision which it proposes to make in the course, or as a result, of the review;

(i) requiring the authority to notify details of the result of the review and of any decision taken by it in consequence of the review to –

    (i) the child,

    (ii) the child's parents,

    (iii) any person who is not a parent of the child but who has parental responsibility for the child, and

    (iv) any other person whom it thinks ought to be notified;

(j) requiring the authority to monitor the arrangements which it has made with a view to ensuring that it complies with the regulations.

Regulations—The relevant regulations are in Care Planning, Placement and Case Review (Wales) Regulations 2015, Pt 6.

Leaving care, accommodation and fostering

Regulations—The relevant regulations are the Care Planning, Placement and Case Review (Wales) Regulations 2015, Pt 7 in particular, and the Care Leavers (Wales) Regulations 2015 (the CL Regulations). The relevant Code is the Code to Part 6.

103 Befriending, advising and assisting looked after children

A local authority looking after a child must advise, assist and befriend the child with a view to promoting the child's well-being when it has ceased to look after the child.

104 Young people entitled to support under sections 105 to 115

(1) The categories of young person defined in subsection (2) are entitled to support in accordance with sections 105 to 115.

(2) In this Act –

    'category 1 young person' means a child who –

        (a) is aged 16 or 17,

        (b) is being looked after by a local authority, and

        (c) has been looked after by a local authority or a local authority in England for a specified period, or periods amounting in all to a specified period, which began after the child reached a specified age and ended after the child reached the age of 16;

    'category 2 young person' means a child who –

        (a) is aged 16 or 17,

        (b) is not being looked after by a local authority or a local authority in England, and

        (c) immediately before ceasing to be looked after, was a category 1 young person;

    'category 3 young person' means a person aged 18 or over who –

        (a) has been a category 2 young person (and would continue to be so if he or she were under the age of 18), or

        (b) was being looked after by a local authority when he or she reached the age of 18 and, immediately before ceasing to be looked after, was a category 1 young person;

    'category 4 young person' means a person who –

PART VII

    (a)   is a category 3 young person towards whom the duties under sections 105, 106, 107(3) and (10) and 110 have ceased to apply (see section 111),

    (b)   has informed the responsible local authority that he or she is pursuing, or wishes to pursue, a programme of education or training, and

    (c)   has not reached the age of 25 or any lower age specified;

'category 5 young person' means a person –

    (a)   who has reached the age of 16 but has not yet reached the age of 21,

    (b)   with respect to whom a special guardianship order is in force (or, if the young person has reached the age of 18, was in force when he or she reached that age), and

    (c)   who was, immediately before the making of that order, looked after by a local authority;

'category 6 young person' means a person, other than a category 5 young person, who –

    (a)   at any time after reaching the age of 16 but while still a child was, but is no longer, looked after, accommodated or fostered,

    (b)   if so accommodated or fostered, is now within Wales, and

    (c)   has not yet reached the age of 21.

(3) In the definition of 'category 6 young person', 'looked after, accommodated or fostered' means –

    (a)   looked after by a local authority (without subsequently being looked after by a local authority in England),

    (b)   accommodated by or on behalf of a voluntary organisation,

    (c)   accommodated in a private children's home,

    (d)   accommodated for a consecutive period of at least three months –

        (i)   by or on behalf of a Local Health Board or Special Health Authority,

        (ii)   by or on behalf of a clinical commissioning group or the National Health Service Commissioning Board,

        (iii)   by or on behalf of a local authority in the exercise of education functions,

        (iv)   by or on behalf of a local authority in England in the exercise of education functions,

        (v)   in any care home or independent hospital, or

        (vi)   in any accommodation provided by or on behalf of an NHS Trust or by or on behalf of an NHS Foundation Trust, or

    (e)   privately fostered (within the meaning of section 66 of the Children Act 1989).

(4) Subsection (3)(d) applies even if the period of three months mentioned there began before the child reached the age of 16.

(5) In this Act 'responsible local authority' means –

    (a)   in relation to a category 1 young person, the local authority which looks after the child;

    (b)   in relation to a category 2, category 3 or category 4 young person, the local authority which last looked after that person;

    (c)   in relation to category 5 young person, a local authority determined in accordance with regulations;

    (d)   in relation to a category 6 young person falling within that category by virtue of paragraph (a) of subsection (3), the local authority which last looked after that person;

    (e)   in relation to a category 6 young person falling within that category by virtue of any other paragraph of that subsection, the local authority within whose area the person is.

(6) Regulations may, for the purposes of any of the powers or duties under sections 105 to 115 –

(a)   specify additional categories of persons;

(b)   specify categories of persons who are not to be treated as falling within a category of young person mentioned in subsection (1);

(c)   make provision for determining which local authority is to be the responsible local authority for the purpose of a category specified under paragraph (a).

'**specified period**' (s 104(2)(c))—The prescribed period is 13 weeks and the prescribed age is 14 (CPPCR Regulations, reg 47).

'**category 1 young person**' (s 104(2)(c))—Children falling within CPPCR Regulations, reg 62 ('short-breaks') are not category 1 young people (CPPCR Regulations, reg 47(2)).

Within the Code to Part 6, category 1 young people are known as 'a young person looked after aged 16 or 17'.

A local authority has the same statutory duty to category 1 young people as they do towards any other child looked after by them. In addition, he must have a personal adviser and, within 3 months of a category 1 young person turning 16 or becoming a category 1 young person over the age of 16, the local authority must assess his needs in accordance with s 107(1) and CPPCR Regulations, reg 49 and prepare his Pathway plan in accordance with s 107(3) and CPPCR Regulations, reg 51. The Pathway plan must include his Pt 6 plan and his PEP plan. His Pathway plan must be regularly reviewed.

'**category 2 young person**' (s 104(2)(c))—The duties to a category 2 young person are set out in ss 105–107 and 109. Within the Code to Part 6, category 2 young people are known as care leavers under 18. A local authority's duties and obligations to a care leaver under 18 are summarised in the Code to Part 6, para 395.

A child who has lived with his parent, a person who otherwise holds parental responsibility for him or who lives with someone who held a child arrangements order for him before he was taken into care for a continuous period of 6 months or more shall not be treated as a category 2 child unless those living arrangements break down (CL regulations, reg 3(4),(5))

A child who is aged 16 or 17, not subject to a care order and on attaining the age of 16 was detained or in hospital, and immediately before being detained or admitted to hospital had been looked after by a local authority for a period totalling at least 13 weeks that began after the child reached the age of 14, is a Category 2 young person (CL Regulations, reg 3(1),(2)).

'**category 3 young person**' (s 104(2)(c))—The duties to category 3 young people are defined in ss 105–107 and 110. Within the Code to Part 6, category 3 young people are known as care leavers aged 18 or over. A local authority's duties and obligations to a care leaver aged 18 and over are summarised in the Code to Part 6, para 395. For cessations of the duties owed to category 3 young people, see s 111.

'**category 4 young person**' (s 104(2)(c))—The duties to a category 4 young person are set out in ss 106–107 and 112. Section 111 defines when the duties owed to a category 3 young person cease. A local authority's duties to a category 4 young person are summarised in the Code to Part 6, para 365. Category 4 young people are known in the Code as young people reconnecting to care for education or training. For cessation of duties owed to category 4 young people, see s 113.

'**category 5 young person**' (s 104(2)(c))—The full duties of local authority to a category 5 young person are set out in s 114 and summarised in the Code to Part 6, para 365. The responsible authority is defined by the Special Guardianship (Wales) Regulations 2005, reg 13.

'**category 6 young person**' (s 104(2)(c))—For further refinement of the definition of a category 6 young person, see s 104(3). The duties and powers in relation to category 6 young people are contained in ss 105 and 115. A local authority's duties to a category 6 young person are summarised in the Code to Part 6, para 365.

105 Keeping in touch

(1) The responsible local authority for a category 2 or category 3 young person must take reasonable steps to keep in touch with that person, whether the person is within its area or not.

(2) If the responsible local authority for a category 2 or category 3 young person has lost touch with that person it must –

(a)   consider how to re-establish contact, and

(b)   take reasonable steps to do so.

(3) In the case of a category 2 young person, the responsible local authority must discharge its duty under subsection (2) without delay and continue to take reasonable steps to re-establish contact until it succeeds.

(4) In the case of a category 3 young person, the duties under subsections (1) and (2) are subject to section 111.

(5) The responsible local authority for a category 6 young person falling within that category by virtue of section 104(3)(a) must take reasonable steps to contact the young person at such times as it thinks appropriate with a view to discharging its functions under section 115.

106 Personal advisers

(1) The responsible local authority for a person mentioned in subsection (2) must arrange for that person to have a personal adviser.

(2) The persons are –

(a)   a category 1 young person;

(b)   a category 2 young person;

(c)   a category 3 young person;

(d)   a category 4 young person.

(3) The duty under subsection (1) –

(a)   in the case of a category 3 young person, is subject to section 111;

(b)   in the case of a category 4 young person, is subject to section 113.

(4) Personal advisers appointed under or by virtue of this Part are to have such functions as may be specified in regulations.

Functions of personal advisers—The functions of personal advisers to category 1 children are prescribed by CPPCR Regulations, reg 52. The functions of personal advisers to category 2–4 young people are prescribed by CL Regulations, reg 8.

107 Pathway assessments and plans: general

(1) The responsible local authority for a category 1 young person must carry out an assessment of the young person's needs with a view to determining what advice and other support it would be appropriate for it to provide to the young person under this Part –

(a)   while it is still looking after the young person, and

(b)   after it ceases to look after the young person.

(2) The responsible local authority for a category 2 or category 3 young person who does not already have a pathway plan must carry out an assessment of the young person's needs with a view to determining what advice and other support it would be appropriate for it to provide to the young person under this Part.

(3) After conducting an assessment under subsection (1) or (2), the local authority must prepare a pathway plan and maintain it for as long as the young person falls within category 1, 2 or 3 (but see subsection (12)).

(4) The responsible local authority for a category 4 young person must carry out an assessment of the young person's needs with a view to determining what advice and other support (if any) it would be appropriate for it to provide to the young person under this Part.

(5) In conducting an assessment under subsection (4), the local authority may take into account any duty that it may have to make a payment to the young person under section 112(2).

(6) After conducting an assessment under subsection (4), the local authority must prepare a pathway plan.

(7) A pathway plan is a plan setting out –

    (a)   in the case of a plan for a category 1 young person –

        (i)   the advice and other support which the local authority intends to provide for the young person under this Part, both while it is looking after the young person and later, and

        (ii)   when it might cease to look after the young person;

    (b)   in the case of a plan for a category 2, category 3 or category 4 young person, the advice and other support which the local authority intends to provide for the young person under this Part;

    (c)   such other matters (if any) as may be specified in regulations.

(8) Regulations may make provision as to assessments for the purposes of this section.

(9) The regulations may, for example, make provision about –

    (a)   the persons who are to be consulted in relation to an assessment;

    (b)   the way in which an assessment is to be carried out, by whom and when;

    (c)   the recording of the results of an assessment;

    (d)   the considerations to which the local authority are to have regard in carrying out an assessment.

(10) The local authority must keep the pathway plan under regular review (but see subsections (12) and (13)).

(11) The local authority may carry out an assessment or review under this section at the same time as any other assessment or review of the young person's needs.

(12) In the case of a category 3 young person, the duties under subsections (3) and (10) are subject to section 111.

(13) In the case of a category 4 young person, the duty under subsection (10) is subject to section 113.

Assessing the needs of a category 1 young person (s 107(1))—The assessment must take into account all the considerations in CPPCR Regulations, reg 49(2).

Assessing the needs of a category 2 or 3 young person (s 107(2))—The assessment must comply with the CL Regulations, regs 4 and 5.

Assessing the needs of a category 4 young person (s 107(4))—The assessment must comply with the CL Regulations, regs 4 and 5.

'plan for a category 1 young person' (s 107(7)(a))—The contents of a Pathway plan for a Category 1 young person are further prescribed by CPPCR Regulations, reg 51 and Sch 9.

'plan for a category 2, category 3 or category 4 young person' (s 107(7)(b))—The contents of the Pathway plan for category 2–4 young people are prescribed by the CL Regulations, reg 6 and Sch 1, unless the young person is detained when Sch 2 applies.

'regular review' (s 107(10))—Reviews of category 2–4 young people's pathway plans are regulated by CL Regulations, reg 7.

108 Pathway assessments and plans: post-18 living arrangements

(1) The responsible local authority for a category 1 young person who has been placed with a local authority foster parent must comply with subsection (2) when –

    (a)   carrying out an assessment in relation to the young person under section 107(1),

(b)   preparing and maintaining a pathway plan for the young person under section 107(3), or

(c)   reviewing the young person's pathway plan under section 107(10).

(2) The responsible local authority must ascertain whether the young person and his or her local authority foster parent wish to make a post-18 living arrangement.

(3) A 'post-18 living arrangement' is an arrangement under which –

(a)   a category 3 young person –
    (i)   who is under the age of 21, and
    (ii)   who was being looked after by a local authority when he or she reached the age of 18 and, immediately before ceasing to be looked after, was a category 1 young person, and

(b)   a person (a 'former foster parent') who was the young person's local authority foster parent immediately before he or she ceased to be looked after,

continue to live together after the young person has ceased to be looked after.

(4) Where the young person and his or her local authority foster parent wish to make a post-18 living arrangement, the responsible local authority must provide advice and other support in order to facilitate the arrangement.

(5) Subsection (4) does not apply if the responsible local authority considers that the making of a post-18 living arrangement between the young person and his or her local authority foster parent would not be consistent with the young person's well-being.

(6) Regulations may make provision about –

(a)   the persons to whom information about post-18 living arrangements must be provided;

(b)   the manner in which that information must be provided.

109 Support for category 2 young people

(1) The responsible local authority for a category 2 young person must safeguard and promote that person's well-being and, unless it is satisfied that the person's well-being does not require it, support the person by –

(a)   maintaining the person,

(b)   providing the person with, or maintaining the person in, suitable accommodation, and

(c)   providing support of such other descriptions as may be specified in regulations.

(2) Support under subsection (1) may be in kind or in cash.

(3) Regulations may make provision about the meaning of 'suitable accommodation' and in particular about the suitability of landlords or other providers of accommodation.

(4) Section 78(3) applies in relation to any decision by a local authority for the purposes of this section as it applies in relation to the decisions referred to in that section.

'suitable accommodation' (s 109(3))—This is defined in CL Regulations, reg 9(2).

110 Support for category 3 young people

(1) The responsible local authority for a category 3 young person must support that young person by –

(a)   contributing, to the extent that the young person's well-being requires it, to expenses incurred by the young person in living near the place where he or she is, or will be, employed or seeking employment;

(b)   contributing, to the extent that the young person's well-being and educational or training needs require it, to expenses incurred by the young person in living near the place where he or she is, or will be, receiving education or training;

(c)   making a grant to the young person, to the extent that the young person's well-being and educational or training needs require it, to enable him or her to meet expenses connected with his or her education or training;

(d)   doing anything else it considers appropriate, to the extent that the young person's well-being requires it.

(2) The responsible local authority for a category 3 young person who has a post-18 living arrangement must, in addition –

(a)   monitor the arrangement, and

(b)   if the authority considers that the arrangement is consistent with the young person's well-being, provide advice and other support to the young person and the former foster parent with a view to maintaining the arrangement.

(3) In subsection (2) 'post-18 living arrangement' has the meaning given by section 108 and 'former foster parent' has the same meaning as in that definition.

(4) The support given under subsection (1)(d) and (2)(b) may be in kind or in cash.

(5) Where support is provided to a former foster parent under subsection (2)(b), the support must include financial support.

(6) The responsible local authority for a category 3 young person who pursues higher education in accordance with his or her pathway plan must pay the relevant amount to that young person.

(7) The duty under subsection (6) is in addition to the responsible local authority's duty under subsection (1).

(8) Subsection (9) applies where the responsible local authority for a category 3 young person is satisfied that the young person –

(a)   is in full-time further or higher education,

(b)   is being given support under subsection (1)(b) or (c) or has received a payment under subsection (6), and

(c)   needs accommodation during a vacation because term-time accommodation is not available.

(9) The responsible authority must –

(a)   provide the young person with suitable accommodation during the vacation, or

(b)   pay the young person enough to secure such accommodation.

(10) The duties under this section are subject to section 111.

111 Cessation of duties in relation to category 3 young people

(1) A responsible local authority's duties towards a category 3 young person cease when the young person reaches the age of 21, except in the circumstances set out in subsection (2).

(2) Where the category 3 young person's pathway plan sets out a programme of education or training which extends beyond the date on which he or she reaches the age of 21 –

(a)   the duties under section 110(1)(b) and (c), (6) and (9) continue until the young person ceases to pursue that programme, and

(b)   the duties under sections 105, 106 and 107(3) and (10) continue concurrently with those duties and cease at the same time.

PART VII

(3) For the purposes of subsection (2)(a), the responsible local authority must disregard any interruption in the young person's pursuance of a programme of education or training if it is satisfied that the young person will resume the programme as soon as is reasonably practicable.

112 Support for category 4 young people

(1) The responsible local authority for a category 4 young person must support that young person, to the extent that his or her educational or training needs require it, by –

    (a)   contributing to expenses incurred by the young person in living near the place where he or she is, or will be, receiving education or training;

    (b)   making a grant to the young person to enable him or her to meet expenses connected with his or her education or training.

(2) The responsible local authority for a category 4 young person who pursues higher education in accordance with his or her pathway plan must pay the relevant amount to that young person.

(3) The duty under subsection (2) is in addition to the responsible local authority's duty under subsection (1).

(4) Where the responsible local authority for a category 4 young person is satisfied that the young person is in full-time further or higher education and needs accommodation during a vacation because term-time accommodation is not available, it must –

    (a)   provide the young person with suitable accommodation during the vacation, or

    (b)   pay the young person enough to secure such accommodation.

(5) The responsible local authority for a category 4 young person may take its duty under subsection (2) into account in assessing the young person's need under section 107(4) and in discharging its duties under subsections (1) and (4).

(6) The duties under this section are subject to section 113.

113 Cessation of duties in relation to category 4 young people

(1) A responsible local authority's duties towards a category 4 young person cease when the young person ceases to pursue a programme of education or training in accordance with his or her pathway plan.

(2) For the purposes of subsection (1), the responsible local authority may disregard any interruption in the young person's pursuance of a programme of education or training if it is satisfied that the young person will resume the programme as soon as is reasonably practicable.

114 Support for category 5 young people and former category 5 young people

(1) The responsible local authority for a category 5 young person must consider whether the conditions in subsection (2) are satisfied in relation to the young person.

(2) The conditions are that –

    (a)   the young person needs support of a kind which it can give under this section, and

    (b)   the local authority is satisfied that the person by whom the young person was being looked after does not have the necessary facilities for advising or befriending him or her.

(3) If the conditions are satisfied the local authority must advise and befriend the young person and may give that person support in the manner described in subsection (4).

(4) The support may be given –

(a)   in kind;

(b)   by contributing to expenses incurred by the young person in living near the place where he or she is, or will be, employed or seeking employment;

(c)   by contributing to expenses incurred by the young person in living near the place where he or she is, or will be, receiving education or training;

(d)   by making a grant to the young person to enable him or her to meet expenses connected with his or her education or training;

(e)   by providing accommodation, if support may not be given in respect of the accommodation under paragraphs (b) to (d);

(f)   in cash.

(5) A local authority may also give support in the manner described in paragraphs (c) and (d) of subsection (4) to a young person who –

(a)   is under the age of 25, and

(b)   would be a category 5 young person if he or she were under the age of 21.

(6) Where a local authority is giving support in the manner described in subsection (4)(c) or (d) it may disregard any interruption in the young person's pursuance of a programme of education or training if it is satisfied that the young person will resume the programme as soon as is reasonably practicable.

(7) Where a local authority is satisfied that a young person for whom it may provide support under subsection (4) or (5) is in full-time further or higher education and needs accommodation during a vacation because term-time accommodation is not available, it must –

(a)   provide the person with suitable accommodation during the vacation, or

(b)   pay the person enough to secure such accommodation.

115 Support for category 6 young people and former category 6 young people

(1) The responsible local authority for a category 6 young person must consider whether the conditions in subsection (2) are satisfied in relation to the young person.

(2) The conditions are that –

(a)   the young person needs support of a kind which the local authority can give under this section, and

(b)   where the young person is a category 6 young person by virtue of section 104(3)(b) to (e), the local authority is satisfied that the person by whom the young person was being looked after, accommodated or fostered (within the meaning of that subsection) does not have the necessary facilities for advising or befriending him or her.

(3) If the conditions are satisfied –

(a)   the local authority must advise and befriend the young person, if that person is a category 6 young person by virtue of section 104(3)(a) or (b), and

(b)   in any other case, the local authority may advise and befriend the young person.

(4) Where as a result of this section, a local authority is under a duty, or is empowered, to advise and befriend a young person, it may give that person support in the manner described in subsection (5).

(5) The support may be given –

(a)   in kind;

(b)   where the young person is a category 6 young person by virtue of section 104(3)(a) –

    (i)   by contributing to expenses incurred by the young person in living near
          the place where he or she is, or will be, employed or seeking employment;
    (ii) by contributing to expenses incurred by the young person in living near
          the place where he or she is, or will be, receiving education or training;
    (iii) by making a grant to the young person to enable him or her to meet
          expenses connected with his or her education or training;
(c) by providing accommodation, if support may not be given in respect of the
     accommodation under paragraph (b);
(d) in cash.

(6) A local authority may also give support in the manner described in
subsection (5)(b)(ii) and (iii) to a young person who –

    (a)   is under the age of 25, and
    (b)   if he or she were under the age of 21, would be a category 6 young person by
          virtue of section 104(3)(a).

(7) Where a local authority is giving support in the manner described in
subsection (5)(b)(ii) or (iii) it may disregard any interruption in the young person's
pursuance of a programme of education or training if it is satisfied that the young person
will resume the programme as soon as is reasonably practicable.

(8) Where a local authority is satisfied that a young person for whom it may provide
support under subsection (4) or (6) is in full-time further or higher education and needs
accommodation during a vacation because term-time accommodation is not available, it
must –

    (a)   provide the person with suitable accommodation during the vacation, or
    (b)   pay the person enough to secure such accommodation.

116 Supplementary provision about support for young persons in further or higher education

(1) Regulations may, for the purposes of sections 110(6) and 112(2) –

    (a)   specify the relevant amount;
    (b)   specify the meaning of 'higher education';
    (c)   make provision as to the payment of the relevant amount;
    (d)   make provision as to the circumstances in which the relevant amount (or any
          Part of it) may be recovered by a local authority from a young person to whom
          a payment has been made under those provisions.

(2) Regulations may make provision for the meaning of 'full-time' ('*llawnamser*'),
'further education' ('*addysg bellach*'), 'higher education' ('*addysg uwch*') and 'vacation'
('*gwyliau*') for the purposes of sections 110(8), 112(4), 114(7) and 115(8).

Regulations—The Children Act 1989 (Higher Education Bursary) (Wales) Regulations 2011 apply.

117 Charging for provision under sections 109 to 115

(1) A local authority may impose a charge for support (other than advice) under
sections 109 to 115.

(2) A charge imposed under subsection (1) –

    (a)   may only cover the cost that the local authority incurs in meeting the needs to
          which the charge applies;
    (b)   may be imposed –
          (i)   on the young person who receives the support, if that person has reached
                the age of 18;

(ii)   on a person with parental responsibility for the young person who receives the support, if the young person is under 18 years of age.

(3) A person is not liable to pay a charge under this section during any period when the person is in receipt of a benefit which falls within a category specified in regulations.

(4) In subsection (3) 'benefit' includes any allowance, payment, credit or loan.

(5) The power to make regulations under section 61 or 62 applies to charges under this section in relation to support as it applies to charges under section 59 in relation to care and support.

(6) Regulations may apply any provision made in or under sections 63 to 68 or sections 70 to 73 to charging under this section with or without specified modifications.

118   Information

(1) Where it appears to a local authority that a young person –

(a)   with whom it is under a duty to keep in touch under section 105,

(b)   whom it has been advising and befriending under section 114 or 115, or

(c)   to whom it has been giving other support under section 114 or 115,

proposes to live, or is living, in the area of another local authority or a local authority in England, it must inform that other authority.

(2) Where a child who is accommodated in Wales –

(a)   by a voluntary organisation or in a private children's home,

(b)   by or on behalf of any Local Health Board or Special Health Authority,

(c)   by or on behalf of a clinical commissioning group or the National Health Service Commissioning Board,

(d)   by or on behalf of local authority in the exercise of education functions,

(e)   by or on behalf of a local authority in England in the exercise of education functions,

(f)   in any care home or independent hospital, or

(g)   in any accommodation provided by or on behalf of an NHS Trust or by or on behalf of an NHS Foundation Trust,

ceases to be so accommodated after reaching the age of 16, the person by whom or on whose behalf the child was accommodated or who carries on or manages the home or hospital (as the case may be) must inform the local authority or local authority in England within whose area the child proposes to live.

(3) Subsection (2) only applies by virtue of paragraphs (b) to (g), if the accommodation has been provided for a consecutive period of at least three months.

(4) In a case where a child was accommodated by or on behalf of a local authority, or a local authority in England, in the exercise of education functions, subsection (2) applies only if the authority which accommodated the child is different from the authority within whose area the child proposes to live.

Secure accommodation

119   Use of accommodation for restricting liberty

(1) Subject to the following provisions of this section, a child who is being looked after by a local authority or a local authority in England may not be placed, and if placed, may not be kept, in accommodation in Wales provided for the purpose of restricting liberty ('secure accommodation') unless it appears –

(a)   that the child –

> (i) has a history of absconding and is likely to abscond from any other description of accommodation, and
>
> (ii) is likely to suffer significant harm if the child absconds, or
>
> (b) that if the child is kept in any other description of accommodation, he or she is likely to injure himself or herself or other persons.

(2) The Welsh Ministers may by regulations –

> (a) specify a maximum period –
>
> (i) beyond which a child may not be kept in secure accommodation in Wales without the authority of the court, and
>
> (ii) for which the court may authorise a child to be kept in secure accommodation in Wales;
>
> (b) empower the court from time to time to authorise a child to be kept in secure accommodation in Wales for such further period as the regulations may specify;
>
> (c) provide that applications to the court under this section be made only by a local authority or a local authority in England.

(3) It is the duty of a court hearing an application under this section to determine whether any relevant criteria for keeping a child in secure accommodation are satisfied in the child's case.

(4) If a court determines that any such criteria are satisfied, it must make an order authorising the child to be kept in secure accommodation and specifying the maximum period for which the child may be so kept.

(5) On any adjournment of the hearing of an application under this section, a court may make an interim order permitting the child to be kept during the period of the adjournment in secure accommodation.

(6) No court is to exercise the powers conferred by this section in respect of a child who is not legally represented in that court unless, having been informed of his or her right to apply for the provision of representation under Part 1 of the Legal Aid, Sentencing and Punishment of Offenders Act 2012 and having had the opportunity to do so, the child refused or failed to apply.

(7) The Welsh Ministers may by regulations provide that –

> (a) this section is or is not to apply to any description of children specified in the regulations;
>
> (b) this section has effect in relation to children of a description specified in the regulations subject to modifications specified in the regulations;
>
> (c) other provisions specified in the regulations are to have effect for the purpose of determining whether a child of a description specified in the regulations may be placed or kept in secure accommodation in Wales.

(8) The giving of an authorisation under this section does not prejudice any power of any court in England and Wales to give directions relating to the child to whom the authorisation relates.

(9) The giving of an authorisation under this section does not prejudice the effect of any direction given by a court in Scotland relating to a child to whom the authorisation relates, in so far as the direction has effect in the law of England and Wales.

(10) This section is subject to section 76(5).

(11) An order made under this section in relation to a child, if it would otherwise still be in force, ceases to have effect when the child reaches the age of 18.

Amendments—SI 2016/413.

Regulations—The relevant regulations are the Children (Secure Accommodation) (Wales) Regulations 2015 and the Children (Secure Accommodation) (Wales) (Amendment) Regulations 2016.

The effect of the Regulations is that CA 1989, s 25 still applies when a Welsh authority places a child in secure accommodation in England but s 119 of the 2014 Act applies when a Welsh authority places a child in secure accommodation in Wales.

The 2016 Regulations clarify that where a Welsh authority places a child in secure accommodation, whether in Wales or in England, the Welsh Regulations govern that placement.

No Welsh authority may place a child aged 13 or under in secure accommodation without the prior approval of the Welsh Ministers. Gaining Ministerial approval is dealt with in the Code to Part 6.

A Welsh authority cannot apply under s 119 to place a child in secure accommodation in Scotland: *X Council v Mother* [2016] EWHC B31 (Fam) applying *Re X (A Child), Re Y (A Child)* [2016] EWHC 2271 (Fam).

Children accommodated in certain establishments

120 Assessment of children accommodated by health authorities and education authorities

(1) Subsection (2) applies where a child is provided with accommodation in Wales by a Local Health Board, an NHS Trust or a local authority in the exercise of education functions ('the accommodating authority') –

(a)   for a consecutive period of at least 3 months, or
(b)   with the intention, on the Part of that authority, of accommodating the child for such a period.

(2) The accommodating authority must notify the appropriate officer of the responsible authority –

(a)   that it is accommodating the child, and
(b)   when it ceases to accommodate the child.

(3) In this section, 'the responsible authority' means –

(a)   the local authority or local authority in England appearing to the accommodating authority to be the authority within whose area the child was ordinarily resident immediately before being accommodated, or
(b)   where it appears to the accommodating authority that a child was not ordinarily resident within the area of any local authority or local authority in England, the local authority within whose area the accommodation is situated.

(4) In this section and in sections 121 and 122 'the appropriate officer' means –

(a)   in relation to a local authority, its director of social services, and
(b)   in relation to a local authority in England, its director of children's services.

(5) Where the appropriate officer of a local authority has been notified under this section, or under section 85 of the Children Act 1989 (assessment of children accommodated by health authorities and education authorities), the authority must –

(a)   assess the child under section 21, and
(b)   consider the extent to which (if at all) it should exercise any of its other functions under this Act, or any of its functions under the Children Act 1989, with respect to the child.

(6) The duty under subsection (5)(a) does not apply in relation to a child looked after by –

(a)   a local authority,
(b)   a local authority in England,
(c)   a local authority in Scotland, or
(d)   a Health and Social Care trust.

Amendments—SI 2016/413.

121 Assessment of children accommodated in care homes or independent hospitals

(1) Subsection (2) applies where a child is provided with accommodation in Wales in any care home or independent hospital –

    (a)   for a consecutive period of at least three months, or

    (b)   with the intention, on the Part of the person taking the decision to accommodate the child, of accommodating the child for such period.

(2) The person carrying on the establishment in question must notify the appropriate officer of the local authority within whose area the establishment is carried on –

    (a)   that it is accommodating the child, and

    (b)   when it ceases to accommodate the child.

(3) Where the appropriate officer of a local authority has been notified under this section, the authority must –

    (a)   assess the child under section 21, and

    (b)   consider the extent to which (if at all) it should exercise any of its other functions under this Act, or any of its functions under the Children Act 1989, with respect to the child.

(4) The duty under subsection (3)(a) does not apply in relation to a child looked after by –

    (a)   a local authority,

    (b)   a local authority in England,

    (c)   a local authority in Scotland, or

    (d)   a Health and Social Care trust.

(5) If a person carrying on a care home or independent hospital fails, without reasonable excuse, to comply with this section, the person is guilty of an offence.

(6) A person authorised by a local authority may enter a care home or independent hospital within the authority's area for the purpose of establishing whether the requirements of this section have been complied with.

(7) A person exercising the power of entry must, upon request, produce some duly authenticated document showing authority to do so.

(8) A person who intentionally obstructs a person exercising the power of entry is guilty of an offence.

(9) A person committing an offence under this section is liable on summary conviction to a fine not exceeding level 3 on the standard scale.

122 Visitors for children notified to a local authority

(1) This section applies if the appropriate officer of a local authority –

    (a)   has been notified with respect to a child under section 120(2)(a) or 121(2)(a), or under section 85(1) of the Children Act 1989 (children accommodated by health authorities and local education authorities), and

    (b)   has not been notified with respect to that child under section 120(2)(b) or section 121(2)(b), or under section 85(2) of the Children Act 1989.

(2) The local authority must, in accordance with regulations made under this section, make arrangements for the child to be visited by a representative of the authority ('a representative').

(3) It is the duty of a representative to provide advice and assistance to the local authority on the performance of its duties under this Act in relation to the child.

(4) Regulations under this section may make provision about –

    (a)   the frequency of visits under visiting arrangements;

    (b)   circumstances in which visiting arrangements must require a child to be visited;

    (c)   additional functions of a representative.

(5) In choosing a representative a local authority must satisfy itself that the person chosen has the necessary skills and experience to perform the functions of a representative.

(6) In this section 'visiting arrangements' means arrangements made under subsection (2).

Amendments—SI 2016/413.

123 Services for children notified to a local authority

(1) A local authority must provide such services as it considers appropriate for children in respect of whom it receives notification under section 120 or 121, or under section 85 of the Children Act 1989 (children accommodated by health authorities and local education authorities).

(2) The services provided under this section must be provided with a view to promoting contact between each child in respect of whom the local authority receives notification and the child's family.

(3) The services may include anything the authority may provide or arrange under Part 4.

(4) Nothing in this section affects the duty imposed by section 39.

Amendments—SI 2016/413.

Moving looked after children to live outside the jurisdiction

124 Arrangements to assist children to live outside England and Wales

(1) A local authority may only arrange for, or assist in arranging for, a child in its care to live outside England and Wales with the approval of the court.

(2) A local authority may, with the approval of every person who has parental responsibility for the child arrange for, or assist in arranging for, any other child looked after by it to live outside England and Wales.

(3) The court must not give its approval under subsection (1) unless it is satisfied that –

    (a)   living outside England and Wales would be in the child's best interests,

    (b)   suitable arrangements have been, or will be, made for the child's reception and well-being in the country in which he or she will live,

    (c)   the child has consented to living in that country, and

    (d)   every person who has parental responsibility for the child has consented to the child living in that country.

(4) Where the court is satisfied that the child does not have sufficient understanding to give or withhold consent, it may disregard subsection (3)(c) and give its approval if the child is to live in the country concerned with a parent, guardian, special guardian, or other suitable person.

(5) Where a person whose consent is required by subsection (3)(d) fails to give consent, the court may dispense with that person's consent if it is satisfied that –

    (a)   the person cannot be found or lacks capacity to give consent, or

    (b)   the well-being of the child requires the consent to be dispensed with.

PART VII

(6) Section 85 of the Adoption and Children Act 2002 (which imposes restrictions on taking children out of the United Kingdom) does not apply in the case of a child who is to live outside England and Wales with the approval of the court given under this section.

(7) Where a court decides to give its approval under this section, it may order that its decision is not to have effect during the appeal period.

(8) In subsection (7) 'the appeal period' means –

(a)   where an appeal is made against the decision, the period between the making of the decision and the determination of the appeal, and

(b)   otherwise, the period during which an appeal may be made against the decision.

(9) This section does not apply to a local authority placing a child for adoption with prospective adopters.

Note—See *Re E (A Child) (Care Proceedings: Placement Outside Jurisdiction)* [2017] EWHC B11 (Fam), which highlights perceived difficulties with para 124 of the Code to Part 6, which states in the context of a placement with a foster carer outside the British Islands, the 'placement should only be agreed where the stay overseas is for a definite and limited period'.

Death of a looked after child

125 Death of children being looked after by local authorities

(1) If a child who is being looked after by a local authority dies, the authority –

(a)   must notify the Welsh Ministers,

(b)   must, so far as is reasonably practicable, notify the child's parents and every person who is not a parent of the child but who has parental responsibility for the child,

(c)   may, with the consent (so far as it is reasonably practicable to obtain it) of every person who has parental responsibility for the child, arrange for the child's body to be buried or cremated, and

(d)   may, if the conditions mentioned in subsection (2) are satisfied, make payments to any person who has parental responsibility for the child, or any relative, friend or other person connected with the child, in respect of travelling, subsistence or other expenses incurred by that person in attending the child's funeral.

(2) The conditions are that –

(a)   it appears to the authority that the person concerned could not otherwise attend the child's funeral without undue financial hardship, and

(b)   that the circumstances warrant the making of the payments.

(3) Subsection (1) does not authorise cremation where it does not accord with the practice of the child's religious persuasion.

(4) Where a local authority has exercised its power under subsection (1)(c) with respect to a child who was under 16 when the child died, it may recover from any parent of the child any expenses incurred by it.

(5) Any amounts so recoverable are, without prejudice to any other method of recovery, recoverable summarily as a civil debt.

(6) Nothing in this section affects any enactment regulating or authorising the burial, cremation or anatomical examination of the body of the deceased person.

Jurisdiction and procedure

Amendments—Heading inserted by SI 2016/413.

125A Jurisdiction of courts

For the purposes of this Part 'court' ('*llys*') means the High Court or a family court.

Amendments—Inserted by SI 2016/413.

125B Rules of court

(1) An authority having power to make rules of court may make such provision for giving effect to –

(a)   this Part, or

(b)   the provisions of any statutory instrument made under this Part, as it appears to that authority to be necessary or expedient.

(2) Section 93 of the Children Act 1989 (rules of court) applies to rules made in accordance with this section as it applies to rules made in accordance with that section.

The rules may, in particular, make provision –

(a)   with respect to the procedure to be followed in any relevant proceedings (including the manner in which any application is to be made or other proceedings commenced);

(b)   as to the persons entitled to participate in any relevant proceedings, whether as parties to the proceedings or by being given the opportunity to make representations to the court;

(c)   for children to be separately represented in relevant proceedings;

(d)   with respect to the documents and information to be furnished, and notices to be given, in connection with any relevant proceedings;

(e)   with respect to preliminary hearings;

(f)   enabling the court, in such circumstance as may be prescribed, to proceed on any application even though the respondent has not been given notice of the proceedings.

(3) In subsection (2) –

'notice of proceedings' ('*hysbysiad o achos*') means a summons or such other notice of proceedings as is required; and

'given' ('*rhoi*') in relation to a summons, means 'served' ('*cyflwyno*');

'prescribed' ('*a ragnodir*') means prescribed by the rules; and

'relevant proceedings' ('*achos perthnasol*') means any application made, or proceedings brought, under any of the provisions mentioned in paragraphs (a) to (c) of subsection (1) and any part of such proceedings.

(4) This section and any other power in this Act to make rules of court are not to be taken as in any way limiting any other power of the authority in question to make rules of court.

(5) When making any rules under this section an authority will be subject to the same requirement as to consultation (if any) as apply when the authority make rules under its general rule making power.

Amendments—Inserted by SI 2016/413.

125C Privacy for children involved in proceedings under this Part

Section 97 of the Children Act 1989 (privacy for children involved in certain proceedings) applies in relation to children involved in any proceedings under this Part as it applies in relation to children involved in any proceedings under that Act.

Amendments—Inserted by SI 2016/413.

Note—This section ensures that the privacy afforded to children involved in certain proceedings applies to children involved in proceedings under this Act. See the CA 1989, s 97 and the notes thereunder in the main work. In practice, the only applications in relation to children likely to be brought before the Family Court under the 2014 Act are applications under ss 119 and 124 of the Act.

125D (1) A person must not publish to the public at large or any section of the public any material which is intended, or likely, to identify –

    (a)   any child which is being involved in any proceedings before the High Court or the family court in which any power under this Act may be exercised by the court with respect to any child; or

    (b)   an address or school as being that of a child involved in any such proceedings.

(2) In any proceedings for an offence under this section it is a defence for the accused to prove that he or she did not know, and had no reason to suspect, that the published material was intended, or likely, to identify the child.

(3) The court or the Lord Chancellor may, if satisfied that the welfare of the child requires it and, in the case of the Lord Chancellor, if the Lord Chief Justice agrees, by order dispense the requirements of subsection (1) to such extent as may be specified in the order.

(4) For the purposes of this section –

    'material' (*'deunydd'*) includes any picture or representation; and

    'publish' (*'cyhoeddi'*) includes –

        (a)   include in a programme service (within the meaning of the Broadcasting Act 1990);

        (b)   cause material to be published.

(5) Any person who contravenes this section is guilty of an offence and liable, on summary conviction, to a fine not exceeding level 4 on the standard scale.

(6) The Lord Chief Justice may nominate a judicial office holder (as defined in section 109(4) of the Constitutional Reform Act 2005) to exercise his or her functions under subsection (3).

Amendments—Inserted by SI 2016/413.

PART 7
SAFEGUARDING
****

128 Duty to report adults at risk

(1) If a relevant partner of a local authority has reasonable cause to suspect that a person is an adult at risk and appears to be within the authority's area, it must inform the local authority of that fact.

(2) If the person that the relevant partner has reasonable cause to suspect is an adult at risk appears to be within the area of a local authority other than one of which it is a relevant partner, it must inform that other local authority.

(3) If a local authority has reasonable cause to suspect that a person within its area at any time is an adult at risk and is living or proposing to live in the area of another local authority (or a local authority in England), it must inform that other authority.

(4) For the purpose of this section a relevant partner of a local authority is a person who is a relevant partner of the authority for the purposes of section 162.

129 Abolition of local authority's power to remove persons in need of care and attention

Section 47 of the National Assistance Act 1948 (which enables local authorities to apply for a court order to remove persons in need of care and attention from home to hospitals or other places) ceases to apply to persons in Wales.

Children at Risk

130 Duty to report children at risk

(1) If a relevant partner of a local authority has reasonable cause to suspect that a child is a child at risk and appears to be within the authority's area, it must inform the local authority of that fact.

(2) If the child that the relevant partner has reasonable cause to suspect is a child at risk appears to be within the area of a local authority other than one of which it is a relevant partner, it must inform that other local authority.

(3) If a local authority has reasonable cause to suspect that a child within its area at any time is a child at risk and is living or proposing to live within the area of another local authority (or a local authority in England), it must inform that other authority.

(4) In this section, 'a child at risk' is a child who –

    (a)   is experiencing or is at risk of abuse, neglect or other kinds of harm, and

    (b)   has needs for care and support (whether or not the authority is meeting any of those needs).

(5) For the purposes of this section a relevant partner of a local authority is –

    (a)   a person who is a relevant partner of the local authority for the purposes of section 162;

    (b)   a youth offending team for an area any part of which falls within the area of the authority.

(6) For provision about a local authority's duty to investigate children at risk, see section 47 of the Children Act 1989.

'duty to investigate children at risk' (s 130(6))—Nothing within the 2014 Act repeals, disapplies, diminishes or alters in any way the duty to make enquiries under CA 1989, s 47 (see the notes to s 47 in the main work). CA 1989, Pts 4 and 5 still apply in Wales.

Guidance

131 Guidance about adults at risk and children at risk

(1) The following must, in exercising their functions under sections 126 to 128 and 130, have regard to any guidance given to them for the purpose by the Welsh Ministers –

    (a)   a local authority;

    (b)   a person who is an authorised officer for the purposes of section 127;

    (c)   a constable or other specified person accompanying an authorised officer in accordance with an adult protection and support order made under section 127;

    (d)   a person who is a relevant partner for the purposes of section 128 or 130.

(2) The Welsh Ministers must consult the Secretary of State before giving guidance under subsection (1).

****

PART VII

PART 9
CO-OPERATION AND PARTNERSHIP
****

164 Duty to co-operate and provide information in the exercise of social services functions

(1) If a local authority requests the co-operation of a person mentioned in subsection (4) in the exercise of any of its social services functions, the person must comply with the request unless the person considers that doing so would –

    (a)   be incompatible with the person's own duties, or

    (b)   otherwise have an adverse effect on the exercise of the person's functions.

(2) If a local authority requests that a person mentioned in subsection (4) provides it with information it requires for the purpose of the exercise of any of its social services functions, the person must comply with the request unless the person considers that doing so would –

    (a)   be incompatible with the person's own duties, or

    (b)   otherwise have an adverse effect on the exercise of the person's functions.

(3) A person who decides not to comply with a request under subsection (1) or (2) must give the local authority which made the request written reasons for the decision.

(4) The persons are –

    (a)   a relevant partner of the local authority making the request;

    (b)   a local authority, a Local Health Board or an NHS Trust which is not a relevant partner of the local authority making the request;

    (c)   a youth offending team for an area any part of which falls within the area of the local authority making the request.

(5) A local authority and each of those persons mentioned in subsection (4) must in exercising their functions under this section have regard to any guidance given to them for the purpose by the Welsh Ministers.

(6) The Welsh Ministers must consult the Secretary of State before giving guidance under subsection (5).

(7) For the purpose of this section a relevant partner of a local authority is a person who is a relevant partner of the authority for the purposes of section 162.

Amendments—SI 2016/413.

164A Duty of other persons to co-operate and provide information

(1) If a local authority requests the co-operation of a person mentioned in subsection (4) in the exercise of its functions mentioned in subsection (5), the person must comply with the request unless the person considers that doing so would –

    (a)   be incompatible with the person's own duties, or

    (b)   otherwise have an adverse effect on the exercise of the person's functions.

(2) If a local authority requests that a person mentioned in subsection (4) provides it with information it requires for the purpose of the exercise of any of its functions mentioned in subsection (5), the person must comply with the request unless the person considers that doing so would –

    (a)   be incompatible with the person's own duties, or

    (b)   otherwise have an adverse effect on the exercise of the person's functions.

(3) A person who decides not to comply with a request under subsection (1) or (2) must give the local authority which made the request written reasons for the decision.

(4) The persons are –

    (a)   a local authority in England;

    (b)   a local housing authority in England;

    (c)   the National Health Service Commissioning Board;

    (d)   any clinical commissioning group, Special Health Authority, NHS Foundation Trust, or NHS trust in England established under section 25 of the National Health Service Act 2006;

    (e)   any other persons –

        (i)   as regulations may specify, or

        (ii) of a description as regulations may specify.

(5) The functions are –

    (a)   the local authority's functions under section 14F of the Children Act 1989 (special guardianship support services);

    (b)   any of the local authority's functions in relation to safeguarding and promoting the well-being of children and young persons, in particular those with needs for care and support, and their families and others;

    (c)   any of the local authority's functions in relation to looked-after and accommodated children;

    (d)   any of the local authority's functions in relation to young persons entitled to support under sections 105 to 115.

(6) Regulations under subsection (4)(e) may not specify the following persons without consent of the Secretary of State –

    (a)   a Minister of the Crown, or

    (b)   the governor of a prison or secure training centre (or in the case of a contracted out prison or secure training centre, its director).

(7) In this section 'local housing authority' (*'awdurdod tai lleol'*) means a local housing authority within the meaning of the Housing Act 1985.

Amendments—Inserted by SI 2016/413.

****

PART 11
MISCELLANEOUS AND GENERAL
****

197 General interpretation and index of defined expressions

(1) In this Act –

    'abuse' (*'camdriniaeth'*, *'cam-drin'*) means physical, sexual, psychological, emotional or financial abuse (and includes abuse taking place in any setting, whether in a private dwelling, an institution or any other place), and 'financial abuse' (*'camdriniaeth ariannol'*) includes –

        (a)   having money or other property stolen;

        (b)   being defrauded;

        (c)   being put under pressure in relation to money or other property;

        (d)   having money or other property misused;

    'adult' (*'oedolyn'*) has the meaning given by section 3;

    'approved premises' (*'mangre a gymeradwywyd'*) is defined for the purposes of section 185 to 187 by section 188(1);

'bail in criminal proceedings' ('*mechnïaeth mewn achos troseddol*') is defined for the
   purposes of sections 185 to 187 by section 188(1);

'care and support' ('*gofal a chymorth*') has the meaning given by section 4;

'care home' ('*cartref gofal*') has the same meaning as in the Care Standards
   Act 2000;

'carer' ('*gofalwr*') has the meaning given by section 3;

'child' ('*plentyn*') has the meaning given by section 3;

'children's home' ('*cartref plant*') means, except in section 86, a children's home
   within the meaning of the Care Standards Act 2000 in respect of which a person
   is registered under Part 2 of that Act

'community home' ('*cartref cymunedol*') and 'controlled community home' ('*cartref
   cymunedol a reolir*') have the meanings given by section 53 of the Children
   Act 1989;

'disabled' ('*anabl*') has the meaning given by section 3;

'education functions' ('*swyddogaethau addysg*') has the meaning given by
   section 579(1) of the Education Act 1996;

'eligibility criteria' ('*meini prawf cymhwystra*') means criteria set under section 32;

'enactment' ('*deddfiad*') means –

   (a)   except in sections 140(2)(b), 172(7) and 198(2)(b), a provision contained
         in any of the following (whenever enacted or made) –
         (i)   an Act of Parliament;
         (ii)   an Act or Measure of the National Assembly for Wales;
         (iii)   an Act of the Scottish Parliament;
         (iv)   Northern Ireland legislation (within the meaning of the Interpretation
                 Act 1978);
         (v)   subordinate legislation made under an enactment falling within
                 sub-paragraphs (i) to (iv);

   (b)   in sections 140(2)(b), 172(7) and 198(2)(b), a provision contained in any
         of the following (whenever enacted or made) –
         (i)   an Act of Parliament;
         (ii)   an Act or Measure of the National Assembly for Wales;
         (iii)   subordinate legislation made under an enactment falling within
                 sub-paragraph (i) or (ii);

'family' ('*teulu*'), in relation to a child, includes (but is not limited to) any person
   who has parental responsibility for the child and any other person with whom the
   child has been living;

'financial assessment' ('*asesiad ariannol*') has the meaning given by section 63;

'financial limit' ('*terfyn ariannol*') has the meaning given by section 66(5);

'function' ('*swyddogaeth*') means power or duty;

'harm' ('*niwed*'), in relation to a child, means abuse or the impairment of –

   (a)   physical or mental health, or
   (b)   physical, intellectual, emotional, social or behavioural development, and
         where the question of whether harm is significant turns on the child's
         health or development, the child's health or development is to be
         compared with that which could reasonably be expected of a similar child;

'Health and Social Care trust' ('*ymddiriedolaeth Iechyd a Gofal Cymdeithasol*')
   means a Health and Social Care trust established under the Health and Personal
   Social Services (Northern Ireland) Order 1991);

'hospital' ('*ysbyty*') has the meaning given by section 206 of the National Health
   Service (Wales) Act 2006;

'independent hospital' ('*ysbyty annibynnol*') –

   (a)   in relation to Wales, has the meaning given by section 2 of the Care
         Standards Act 2000, and

(b) in relation to England, means a hospital as defined by section 275 of the National Health Service Act 2006 that is not a health service hospital as defined by that section;

'local authority' (*'awdurdod lleol'*) means the council of a county or county borough in Wales;

'local authority foster parent' (*'rhiant maeth awdurdod lleol'*) means a person authorised as such in accordance with regulations made by virtue of –

(a) sections 87 and 93;

(b) paragraph 12F of Schedule 2 to the Children Act 1989 (regulations providing for approval of local authority foster parents);

'local authority in England' (*'awdurdod lleol yn Lloegr'*) means –

(a) a county council in England,

(b) a district council for an area in England for which there is no county council,

(c) a London borough council, or

(d) the Common Council of the City of London;

'local authority in Scotland' (*'awdurdod lleol yn yr Alban'*) means a council constituted under section 2 of the Local Government etc (Scotland) Act 1994;

'Local Health Board' (*'Bwrdd Iechyd Lleol'*) means a Local Health Board established under section 11 of the National Health Service (Wales) Act 2006;

'National Board' (*'Bwrdd Cenedlaethol'*) is defined for the purposes of Part 7 by section 142;

'National Health Service Commissioning Board' (*'Bwrdd Comisiynu'r Gwasanaeth Iechyd Gwladol'*) means the body established under section 1H of the National Health Service Act 2006;

'needs assessment' (*'asesiad o anghenion'*) means an assessment under Part 3;

'neglect' (*'esgeulustod'*) means a failure to meet a person's basic physical, emotional, social or psychological needs, which is likely to result in an impairment of the person's well-being (for example, an impairment of the person's health or, in the case of a child, an impairment of the child's development);

'NHS Foundation Trust' (*'Ymddiriedolaeth Sefydledig GIG'*) has the meaning given by section 30 of the National Health Service Act 2006;

'NHS Trust' (*'Ymddiriedolaeth GIG'*) means a National Health Service trust established under section 18 of the National Health Service (Wales) Act 2006;

'parental responsibility' (*'cyfrifoldeb rhiant'*) has meaning given by section 3 of the Children Act 1989;

'prison' (*'carchar'*) is defined –

(a) for the purposes of sections 185 to 187 by section 188(1),

(b) for the purposes of section 134, by section 134(11), and

(c) for the purposes of section 162, by section 162(11);

'private children's home' (*'cartref plant preifat'*) means a children's home which is not –

(a) a community home, or

(b) a voluntary home (within the meaning given by section 60 of the Children Act 1989);

'regulations' (*'rheoliadau'*), other than in relation to section 101, means regulations made by the Welsh Ministers;

'relative' (*'perthynas'*), in relation to a child, means a step-parent, grandparent, brother, sister, uncle or aunt (including any person who is in that relationship by virtue of a marriage or civil partnership or an enduring family relationship);

'Safeguarding Board' (*'Bwrdd Diogelu'*) is defined for the purposes of Part 7 by section 142;

'Safeguarding Board area' ('*ardal Bwrdd Diogelu*') is defined for the purposes of Part 7 by section 142;

'Safeguarding Board partner' ('*partner Bwrdd Diogelu*') is defined for the purposes of Part 7 by section 142;

'services' ('*gwasanaethau*') includes facilities;

'special guardian' ('*gwarcheidwad arbennig*') and 'special guardianship order' ('*gorchymyn gwarcheidiaeth arbennig*') have the meaning given by section 14A of the Children Act 1989;

'Special Health Authority' ('*Awdurdod Iechyd Arbennig*') means a Special Health Authority established under section 22 of the National Health Service (Wales) Act 2006 or section 28 of the National Health Service Act 2006;

'specified' ('*penodedig*', '*a bennir*', '*a bennwyd*') and related expressions, unless the context otherwise requires, means specified in regulations;

'standard charge' ('*ffi safonol*') is defined for the purposes of Part 5 by section 63(3);

'upbringing' ('*magwraeth*'), in relation to a child, includes the care of the child but not the child's maintenance;

'voluntary organisation' ('*sefydliad gwirfoddol*') means a body (other than a public or local authority) whose activities are not carried on for profit;

'well-being' ('*llesiant*') has the meaning given by section 2;

'Welsh family proceedings officer' ('*swyddog achosion teuluol Cymru*') has the meaning given by section 35 of the Children Act 2004;

'youth detention accommodation' ('*llety cadw ieuenctid*') is defined for the purposes of sections 185 to 187 by section 188;

'youth offending team' ('*tîm troseddwyr ifanc*') means a team established under section 39 of the Crime and Disorder Act 1998.

(2) In this Act –

   (a) a reference to a child looked after by a local authority has the meaning given by section 74;

   (b) a reference to a child looked after by a local authority in England has the same meaning as a reference in section 22 of the Children Act 1989 to a child who is looked after by a local authority in England;

   (c) a reference to a child looked after by a local authority in Scotland has the same meaning as a reference in Chapter 1 of Part 2 of the Children (Scotland) Act 1995 to a child who is 'looked after' by a local authority (see section 17(6) of that Act);

   (d) a reference to a child looked after by a Health and Social Care trust has the same meaning as a reference in the Children (Northern Ireland) Order 1995 to a child who is looked after by an authority (see article 25 of that Order).

(3) A reference in this Act to a child who is in the care of a local authority is a reference to a child who is in its care by virtue of a care order (within the meaning given by the Children Act 1989).

(4) A reference in this Act to accommodation provided by or on behalf of a local authority is a reference to accommodation so provided in the exercise of functions of that authority or any other local authority which are social services functions.

(5) A reference in this Act to a person having, or lacking, capacity in relation to a matter is to be interpreted as a reference to a person having, or lacking, capacity within the meaning of the Mental Capacity Act 2005 in relation to that matter.

(6) A reference in this Act to being authorised under the Mental Capacity Act 2005 is a reference to being authorised as –

   (a) a donee of a lasting power of attorney created under that Act, or

   (b) a deputy appointed by the Court of Protection under section 16(2)(b) of that Act.

(7) The Welsh Ministers may by regulations provide that the Council of the Isles of Scilly is to be treated as a local authority in England for the purposes of this Act, or for the purposes of specified provisions of this Act, with such modifications as may be specified.

Amendments—Regulation and Inspection of Social Care (Wales) Act 2016, s 185, Sch 3, para 65; SI 2016/413.

****

Statutory Instruments

Care and Support (Assessment) (Wales) Regulations 2015, SI 2015/1305

1 Title, commencement, application and interpretation

(1) The title of these Regulations is the Care and Support (Assessment) (Wales) Regulations 2015.

(2) These Regulations come into force on 6 April 2016 and apply in relation to Wales.

(3) In these Regulations –

'assessment' (*'asesiad ac asesu'*) means an assessment which is carried out by a local authority under section 19, 21 or 24 of the Act;
'personal outcomes' (*'canlyniadau personol'*) means the outcomes which have been identified in relation to a person in accordance with section 19(4)(a), 21(4)(b) or 24(4)(c) or (d) of the Act;
'the Act' (*'y Ddeddf'*) means the Social Services and Well-being (Wales) Act 2014.

2 Co-ordination

The local authority responsible for carrying out an assessment must ensure that there is a named individual whose function is to co-ordinate the carrying out of the assessment.

3 Training, expertise and consultation

(1) A local authority must ensure that any person carrying out an assessment –

(a)   has the skills, knowledge and competence to carry out the assessment in question, and
(b)   has received training in the carrying out of assessments.

(2) When carrying out an assessment, a local authority must consider whether the nature of the person's needs calls for the involvement of a person who has specialist skills, knowledge or expertise.

(3) If the local authority decides that such involvement is called for, it must either consult with a person who it considers will be able to provide those skills or that knowledge or expertise or arrange for the assessment to be carried out by a person with the required specialist skills, knowledge or expertise.

PART VII

4 Considerations to which the local authority must have regard

In carrying out an assessment, a local authority must –

  (a) assess and have regard to the person's circumstances,
  (b) have regard to the personal outcomes,
  (c) assess and have regard to any barriers to achieving those outcomes,
  (d) assess and have regard to any risks to the person or to other persons if those outcomes are not achieved, and
  (e) assess and have regard to the person's strengths and capabilities.

5 Written records of assessments

(1) When an assessment has been completed, the local authority must make a written record of the results of the assessment and the matters to which the authority has had regard in carrying out the assessment.

(2) If, in the course of carrying out the assessment, the local authority considers that the provision of preventative services, the provision of information, advice or assistance or other matters could contribute to the achievement of the personal outcomes or otherwise meet needs identified in the assessment, the written record must –

  (a) include details of that provision or those matters, and
  (b) include details of how that provision or those matters could contribute to the achievement of the personal outcomes or otherwise meet needs identified in the assessment.

6 Copies of records

(1) Where the assessment is of an adult's needs (including the needs of an adult carer), the local authority must offer to give a copy of the record to –

  (i)   the adult,
  (ii) any person authorised to act on behalf of the adult, and
  (iii) where the adult lacks capacity to be able to request a person to act on their behalf and there is no person authorised to act on their behalf, any person who the local authority considers to be acting in the best interests of the adult.

(2) Where the assessment is of a child's needs (including the needs of a child carer), the local authority must offer to give a copy of the record to –

  (i)   the child,
  (ii) any person with parental responsibility for the child, unless doing so would be inconsistent with the child's well-being,
  (iii) any person authorised to act on behalf of the child, and
  (iv) where the child lacks capacity or is not competent to request a person to act on their behalf and there is no person authorised to act on their behalf, any person who the local authority considers to be acting in the best interests of the child.

(3) In this regulation and in regulation 7, a person is authorised to act on behalf of an adult or a child if –

  (a) the adult or the child has requested the person to act on their behalf, or
  (b) the adult or child lacks capacity and the person is authorised under the Mental Capacity Act 2005 (whether in general or in specific terms) to make decisions about the assessment of the person's needs.

7 Reviews

(1) A local authority must review an assessment if it appears to it that there has been a significant change in the person's circumstances or in their personal outcomes.

(2) The following persons may request a review of an assessment –

    (a)   where the assessment is of an adult's needs (including the needs of an adult carer) –

        (i)   the adult;

        (ii)   any person authorised to act on behalf of the adult;

    (b)   where the assessment is of a child's needs (including the needs of a child carer) –

        (i)   the child;

        (ii)   any person with parental responsibility for the child;

        (iii)   any person authorised to act on behalf of the child.

(3) The local authority must comply with the request if it is satisfied that there has been a significant change in the person's circumstances or in their personal outcomes.

(4) The local authority may refuse to comply with the request if it is satisfied that there has not been any significant change in the person's circumstances or in their personal outcomes since the assessment was completed.

Care and Support (Care Planning) (Wales) Regulations 2015, SI 2015/1335

1 Title, commencement, application and interpretation

(1) The title of these Regulations is The Care and Support (Care Planning) (Wales) Regulations 2015.

(2) These Regulations come into force on 6 April 2016 and apply in relation to Wales.

(3) In these Regulations –

'the Act' ('*y Ddeddf*') means the Social Services and Well-being (Wales) Act 2014.

'care and support plan' ('*cynllun gofal a chymorth*') means a plan which a local authority is required to prepare and maintain under section 54(1) of the Act;

'eligible needs' ('*anghenion cymwys*') in relation to a person means those needs which the local authority is required to meet under section 35, 37, 40 or 42 of the Act;

'the Partnership Regulations' ('*y Rheoliadau Partneriaeth*') means the Partnership Arrangements (Wales) Regulations 2015;

'family' ('*teulu*'), in relation to a person who is part of a family which is receiving support from an IFS team, has the meaning given in regulation 18(3) of the Partnership Regulations;

'IFS team' ('*tîm integredig cymorth i deuluoedd*') means an integrated family support team established by a partnership body in accordance with the Partnership Regulations;

'parent' ('*rhiant*'), in relation to a child who is part of a family which is receiving support from an IFS team, has the meaning given in regulation 18(5) of the Partnership Regulations;

'partnership body' ('*corff partneriaeth*') has the meaning given in regulation 1(4) of the Partnership Regulations;

'personal outcomes' ('*canlyniadau personol*') means the outcomes which have been identified in relation to a person in accordance with an assessment under section 19, 21 or 24 of the Act;

'support plan' ('*cynllun cymorth*') means a plan which a local authority is required to prepare and maintain under section 54(2) of the Act.

Amendments—SI 2017/713.

2 Training and skills

A local authority must ensure that any person responsible for preparing, reviewing or revising a care and support plan or support plan –

  (a) has the skills, knowledge and competence to do so, and

  (b) has received appropriate training.

3 Content of plans

(1) A care and support plan and a support plan must contain a description of –

  (a) the person's eligible needs,

  (b) the personal outcomes,

  (c) the actions to be taken by the local authority and the actions to be taken by other persons to help the person achieve the personal outcomes or to otherwise meet their eligible needs,

  (d) the arrangements for monitoring the extent to which the personal outcomes have been achieved, and

  (e) the arrangements for the review of the plan.

(2) Where some or all of the person's needs are to be met by making direct payments, a care and support plan and a support plan must also contain a description of –

  (a) the eligible needs which are to be met by direct payments, and

  (b) the amount and frequency of the direct payments.

(3) Where enquiries have been made by the local authority in accordance with its duty under section 126(1) of the Act (adults at risk), the care and support plan for the individual who is the subject of those enquiries must contain a record of the conclusion of the enquiries.

4 Review of plans

(1) The local authority must review a care and support plan or a support plan if it appears to the authority that the plan is not meeting the eligible needs of the person to whom the plan relates.

(1A) The local authority must review a care and support plan or a support plan if the person to whom the plan relates is part of a family whose case has been referred to an IFS team and the family has been notified that their case will be supported by that team.

(2) Where the plan contains details of direct payments in accordance with regulation 3(2), the plan must be reviewed at the same time as any review of the direct payments in accordance with regulations under section 53(1).

(3) The considerations to which the local authority must have regard when reviewing a person's care and support plan or support plan where the person is part of a family which is being supported by an IFS team are set out in the Schedule.

Amendments—SI 2017/713.

5 Requests for review of plans

(1) The following persons may request a review of a care and support plan or support plan (as the case may be) –

(a) where the plan relates to meeting the needs of an adult (including the needs of an adult carer) –
(i) the adult, and
(ii) any person authorised to act on behalf of the adult;
(b) where the plan relates to meeting the needs of a child (including the needs of a child carer) –
(i) the child,
(ii) any person with parental responsibility for the child, and
(iii) any person authorised to act on behalf of the child.

(2) The local authority must comply with the request if it is satisfied that the plan is not meeting the eligible needs of the person to whom the plan relates.

(3) The local authority may refuse to comply with the request if it is satisfied that the plan is meeting the eligible needs of the person to whom the plan relates.

(4) In this regulation, and in regulations 7 and 8, a person is authorised to act on behalf of an adult or a child if –

(a) the adult or the child has requested the person to act on their behalf, or
(b) the adult or child lacks capacity and the person is authorised under the Mental Capacity Act 2005 (whether in general or in specific terms) to make decisions about how the person's needs are to be met.

6 Action following review

(1) Following the review, the local authority must consider whether to confirm, revise or close the care and support plan or support plan (as the case may be).

(2) In deciding whether to confirm, revise or close the plan, the local authority must have regard in particular to the following –

(a) any changes to the personal outcomes or the person's circumstances,
(b) any changes to the person's eligible needs,
(c) whether the actions taken by the authority or other persons are helping the person to achieve the personal outcomes or to otherwise meet their eligible needs, and
(d) whether there are other ways in which the local authority or other persons can help the person to achieve the personal outcomes or to otherwise meet their eligible needs.

(3) If the local authority decide to confirm the plan, the authority must record the decision and the reasons for the decision.

(4) If the local authority decide to revise the plan, the authority must prepare a revised plan.

(5) If the local authority decide to close the plan, the authority must prepare a closure statement.

(6) A closure statement is a document which contains the following information –

(a) the reasons for the closure of the plan,
(b) an evaluation of the extent to which the personal outcomes were achieved, and
(c) where the local authority is still satisfied that the person to whom the plan relates has needs for care and support, confirmation that the authority is

PART VII

satisfied that the person's needs can be met by the provision of information, advice or assistance, preventative services or anything else that may be available in the community.

7 Copies of care and support plans etc

(1) The local authority must give a copy of the care and support plan to the persons described in paragraph (5).

(2) If, following a review of a care and support plan, the local authority decides to revise the plan it must give a copy of the revised plan to the persons described in paragraph (5).

(3) If, following a review of a care and support plan, the local authority decides to confirm the plan it must give a copy of the record of the decision and the reasons for the decision to the persons described in paragraph (5).

(4) If, following a review of a care and support plan, the local authority decides to close the plan, it must give a copy of the closure statement to the persons described in paragraph (5).

(5) For the purposes of paragraphs (1) to (4) the persons are –

    (a) if the care and support plan has been prepared for an adult –
        (i)   the adult for whom the plan has been prepared,
        (ii) any person authorised to act on behalf of the adult, and
        (iii) where the adult lacks capacity to be able to request a person to act on their behalf and there is no person authorised to act on their behalf, any person who the local authority considers to be acting in the best interests of the adult;
    (b) if the care and support plan has been prepare for a child –
        (i)   the child for whom the plan has been prepared,
        (ii) any person with parental responsibility for the child, unless this would be inconsistent with the child's well-being,
        (iii) any person authorised to act on behalf of the child, and
        (iv) where the child lacks capacity or is not competent to request a person to act on their behalf and there is no person authorised to act on their behalf, any person who the local authority considers to be acting in the best interest of the child.

8 Copies of support plans etc

(1) The local authority must give a copy of the support plan to the persons described in paragraph (5).

(2) If, following a review of a support plan, the local authority decides to revise the plan it must give a copy of the revised plan to the persons described in paragraph (5).

(3) If, following a review of a support plan, the local authority decides to confirm the plan it must give a copy of the record of the decision and the reasons for the decision to the persons described in paragraph (5).

(4) If, following a review of a support plan, the local authority decides to close the plan, it must give a copy of the closure statement to the persons described in paragraph (5).

(5) For the purposes of paragraphs (1) to (4) the persons are –

    (a) if the support plan has been prepared for an adult carer –
        (i)   the adult carer for whom the plan has been prepared,
        (ii) any person authorised to act on behalf of the adult carer, and
        (iii) where the adult carer lacks capacity to be able to request a person to act on

their behalf and there is no person authorized to act on their behalf, any person who the local authority considers to be acting in the best interests of the adult carer;

(b) if the support plan has been prepared for a child carer –
    (i) the child carer for whom the plan has been prepared,
    (ii) any person with parental responsibility for the child carer, unless this would be inconsistent with the child carer's wellbeing,
    (iii) any person authorised to act on behalf of the child carer, and
(iv) where the child carer lacks capacity or is not competent to request a person to act on their behalf and there is no person authorised to act on their behalf, any person who the local authority considers to be acting in the best interest of the child carer.

SCHEDULE
CONSIDERATIONS TO WHICH A LOCAL AUTHORITY MUST HAVE REGARD WHEN REVIEWING A PLAN WHERE AN IFS TEAM IS INVOLVED

1 Details of any care plan or health treatment plan of a parent.

2 Details of any support or services provided to a parent by any person.

3 Any changes to the parenting capacity of a parent as a result of the health or social care services provided, or as a result of any other factors.

4 Any changes in the family circumstances since the last review.

5 Any significant events outside the family which are relevant.

6 Any difficulties which the family may have had in engaging with the IFS team.

7 Whether there is any conflict between the needs of the child and the needs of a parent, or any other family member and how this can be resolved.

8 The need to prepare for the ending of the involvement of the IFS team.

Amendments—Schedule inserted by SI 2017/713.

Care and Support (Choice of Accommodation) (Wales) Regulations 2015, SI 2015/1840

1 Title, commencement, application and interpretation

(1) The title of these Regulations is the Care and Support (Choice of Accommodation) (Wales) Regulations 2015.

(2) These Regulations come into force on 6 April 2016 and apply in relation to Wales.

(3) In these Regulations –

'the Act' ('*y Ddeddf*') means the Social Services and Well-being (Wales) Act 2014;
'care home accommodation' ('*lletty cartref gofal*') means –
    (a) accommodation in a care home within the meaning given by section 3 of the Care Standards Act 2000 where the accommodation is in Wales or England;
    (b) accommodation in a care home service within the meaning given by paragraph 2 of Schedule 12 to the Public Services Reform (Scotland) Act 2010 where the accommodation is in Scotland; or
    (c) accommodation in a residential care home within the meaning given by article 10 of the Health and Personal Social Services (Quality,

Improvement and Regulation) (Northern Ireland) Order 2003 where the accommodation is in Northern Ireland;

'preferred accommodation' ('*llety sy'n cael ei ffafrio*') means the accommodation for which a person for whom it is to be provided expresses a preference in accordance with regulation 2(b).

2 Choice of accommodation

Where –

    (a) a local authority is going to meet needs under sections 35 to 38 of the Act by providing or arranging for the provision of care home accommodation in the United Kingdom;

    (b) the person for whom the accommodation is to be provided expresses a preference for a particular care home; and

    (c) the conditions in regulation 3 are met,

the local authority must provide or arrange for the provision of the preferred accommodation in accordance with these Regulations.

3 Conditions for provision of preferred accommodation

(1) The following conditions must be met for the provision of preferred accommodation under regulation 2 –

    (a) the care and support plan for the person specifies that the person's needs can be met by the provision of care home accommodation;

    (b) the preferred accommodation is suitable to the person's needs;

    (c) the preferred accommodation is available; and

    (d) where the preferred accommodation is not provided by the local authority, the provider of the accommodation agrees to provide the accommodation to the person on the local authority's terms.

(2) If the cost to the local authority of providing or arranging for the provision of the preferred accommodation is greater than the cost that the local authority would usually expect to incur in providing or arranging the provision of care home accommodation to meet the needs of the person concerned, the additional cost condition in regulation 4 must also be met.

4 The additional cost condition

(1) The additional cost condition is met if –

    (a) the local authority is satisfied that the payer is able and willing to pay the additional cost of the preferred accommodation for the period during which the local authority expects to meet the person's needs by providing or arranging for the provision of that accommodation; and

    (b) the payer enters into a written agreement with the local authority in which the payer agrees to pay the additional cost.

(2) The local authority must provide the payer with access to sufficient information and advice to enable the payer to understand the terms of the proposed written agreement before entering into it.

(3) The written agreement must include –

    (a) the additional cost;

    (b) the cost the local authority would usually expect to incur in providing or arranging the provision of care home accommodation to meet the needs of the person concerned;

(c) the frequency of payments;

(d) the details of the person to whom the payments are to be made;

(e) provision for review of the agreement;

(f) provisions about the matters specified in paragraph (4).

(4) The specified matters are –

(a) he consequences of ceasing to make payments;

(b) the effect of increases in charges made by the provider of the preferred accommodation; and

(c) the effect of changes in the payer's financial circumstances.

(5) For the purposes of this regulation, 'the payer' ('*y talwr*') means –

(a) a person other than the person for whom the accommodation is to be provided; or

(b) in a case to which paragraph (6) applies, the person for whom the accommodation is to be provided.

(6) The local authority may not agree with the person for whom the accommodation is to be provided for that person to pay the additional cost unless –

(a) paragraph 2 of Schedule 2 to the Care and Support (Financial Assessment) (Wales) Regulations 2015 (capital to be disregarded in first 12 weeks) applies to that person; or

(b) the person and the local authority agree or have agreed to enter into a deferred payment agreement in accordance with section 68 of the Act.

(7) For the purposes of this regulation, the additional cost that is to be paid by the payer may be less than the full amount of the additional cost referred to in section 57(3) of the Act, if the local authority agrees that a lesser amount should be paid.

5 Refusal to provide preferred accommodation

Where a local authority refuses to provide or arrange for the provision of preferred accommodation it must provide a statement in writing setting out which of the conditions in regulation 3(1) or regulation 4(1) is not met and specifying the reasons.

Care and Support (Direct Payments) (Wales) Regulations 2015, SI 2015/1815

1 Title, commencement, application and interpretation

(1) The title of these Regulations is the Care and Support (Direct Payments) (Wales) Regulations 2015.

(2) These Regulations come into force on 6 April 2016.

(3) These Regulations apply in relation to Wales.

(4) In these Regulations –

'the Act' ('*y Ddeddf*') means the Social Services and Well-being (Wales) Act 2014;

'A' ('*A*') is used to refer to a person whose care and support needs or support needs are being or will be met by making direct payments;

'P' ('*P*') is used to refer to a person who is, or who it is proposed, will be a recipient of direct payments and who is a 'suitable person' for the purposes of section 50(4) of the Act or a person with parental responsibility for A to whom direct payments may be made for the benefit of A under section 51 of the Act;

'direct payment' ('*taliad uniongyrchol*') is defined in sections 50(7), 51(7) and 52(7) of the Act;

'relative' ('*perthynas*') means –

    (a)   a spouse or civil partner;

    (b)   a person who lives with a person as if a spouse or civil partner;

    (c)   parent, parent-in-law or step-parent,

    (d)   son or daughter;

    (e)   son-in-law or daughter-in-law;

    (f)   stepson or stepdaughter;

    (g)   brother or sister;

    (h)   aunt or uncle;

    (i)   grandparent; or

    (j)   the spouse or civil partner of any person specified in sub-paragraphs (c) to (i).

(5) In these Regulations references to a person's needs 'for care and support' are to be read as a person's 'needs for support' where the person is a carer.

2 Duty to make direct payments

Where –

    (a)   a local authority –

        (i)   is under a duty to meet a person's needs for care and support under section 35, 37, 39, 40 or 42 of the Act; or

        (ii)   has decided to meet the needs of a person for care and support under section 36 or 38 of the Act or support in relation to a carer under section 45 of the Act; and

    (b)   the conditions in section 50, 51 or 52 of the Act (as the case may be) are met,

a local authority must make direct payments towards the cost of meeting that person's needs for care and support unless the person is a person to whom regulation 14 applies.

3 Effect of making payments

Where a local authority makes direct payments to a person, the making of the payments displaces the local authority's duty or power to provide, directly or indirectly, to meet the needs, or that aspect of the needs, in relation to which the payments are made and for the duration of the period for which payments are made.

4 Steps to enable informed choices about direct payments

(1) When a local authority –

    (a)   decides that it will meet the needs of A for care and support, and

    (b)   determines that making direct payments is an appropriate way of meeting A's needs, it must provide information to A to ensure that A is able to make an informed choice about whether or not to consent to the making of payments.

(2) The information which a local authority provides must include –

    (a)   how it proposes to meet those needs if the needs are not met by the making of direct payments;

    (b)   confirmation of whether, in the local authority's view, direct payments are an appropriate way of meeting A's needs;

    (c)   information about the nature and the purpose of direct payments;

    (d)   information about different ways of managing direct payments;

(e) the amount of any payments which the person would be entitled to if a choice was made to have a direct payment and how the amount of the payment would be calculated;

(f) information about the support which is available to assist people to manage direct payments whether from the local authority or from any other person;

(g) information about the effect of financial assessment and whether, in the case of the needs in question any direct payments would be likely to be made as gross payments or net payments.

(3) Where A is an adult who does not have capacity, the local authority must instead provide the information to any person authorised under the Mental Capacity Act 2005 to make decisions about A.

(4) Where A is a child aged 16 or 17 who does not have capacity, or is a child below the age of 16 who does not have sufficient understanding to make an informed decision, the local authority must instead provide the information to a person with parental responsibility for A.

5 Duty to consult and take other steps for persons without capacity

Before considering whether direct payments are an appropriate way of meeting the needs of A where A is an adult without capacity, a local authority must –

(a) consult –

    (i) anyone named by A as someone to be consulted on the issue;

    (ii) anyone engaged in caring for A or with a significant interest in A's welfare;

    (iii) P; and

    (iv) a person authorised under the Mental Capacity Act 2005 (whether in general or specific terms) to make decisions about A's needs for care and support;

(b) where A is an adult who previously had capacity, consider, so far as reasonably practicable –

    (i) A's past and present views, wishes and feelings and, in particular, any relevant written statement made by A while still with capacity;

    (ii) the beliefs and values which would be likely to influence A's decision; and

    (iii) any other relevant factors that A would in the local authority's view be likely to consider, if able to do so; and

(c) obtain an enhanced criminal record certificate issued under section 113B of the Police Act 1997 in respect of P where P is an individual but is neither a relative of A nor a friend of A who is involved in A's care.

6 Conditions about using direct payments to pay relatives

(1) A local authority may authorise the use of direct payments to pay a relative of A who is living in the same household if it considers that it is necessary to promote the well-being of A.

(2) Payments may be authorised to pay the relative either –

(a) for provision of care and support to A; or

(b) for help to A in managing the payments.

(3) In considering whether it is necessary to promote the well-being of A in accordance with paragraph (1) a local authority must take into account the views of A and the other persons mentioned in regulation 11(3).

(4) Where a local authority does not consider that it is necessary to promote A's well-being, it must impose a condition that direct payments are not to be used to pay a relative of A who is living in the same household.

7 Conditions requiring vetting

(1) Where a local authority makes direct payments under section 50 of the Act to P because A lacks capacity, it must impose conditions as set out in this regulation.

(2) The conditions are that P –

    (a)   acts in the best interests of A when securing the provision of care and support; and

    (b)   notifies the local authority if P believes that A no longer lacks capacity.

(3) Where the circumstances in paragraph (4) apply the local authority must also impose a condition that P obtains –

    (a)   an enhanced criminal record certificate issued under section 113B of the Police Act 1997 including suitability information relating to vulnerable adults (within the meaning of section 113BB of that Act) or children (within the meaning of section 113BA of that Act); or

    (b)   verification that a satisfactory certificate of that sort has been obtained, in respect of any person from whom a service is secured being a service for which the direct payments are made.

(4) The circumstances in which a local authority must impose the condition in paragraph (3) are that P is not –

    (a)   a relative of A; or

    (b)   a friend of A who is involved in the provision of care for A.

8 Further conditions which a local authority may apply to the making of direct payments

(1) A local authority may make a direct payment subject to further conditions.

(2) Conditions imposed under paragraph (1) may, for example, include a requirement that –

    (a)   the needs in respect of which payment is being made may not be met by a particular person;

    (b)   the recipient of the payments must provide information reasonably required by the local authority for the purposes of ensuring that direct payments are an appropriate way of meeting A's needs.

(3) A condition imposed under paragraph (2)(a) must not require that A's needs may only be met by a particular person.

9 Net payments or gross payments

(1) When a local authority decides to make direct payments, whether under regulation 2 or regulation 14 of these Regulations, it must decide whether to make them as net payments or gross payments.

(2) In deciding whether to make net payments or gross payments a local authority must take into account the effect on A having regard to A's financial circumstances.

10 Repayment of direct payments

A local authority may terminate its arrangements for making direct payments and may require repayment of all or part of the direct payments which it has made if it is satisfied either –

    (a) that the payments have not been used to meet the need to which they relate; or

    (b) that a condition imposed under regulation 6, 7, 8 or 14 has not been complied with.

11 Reviews

(1) A local authority must review the arrangements for the making of direct payments and the use which is being made of them –

    (a) at intervals which the local authority determines appropriate at the point of starting to make direct payments to A, having regard to the circumstances in A's case;

    (b) when A or P call for a review;

    (c) when the local authority calls for a review either because –

        (i) it is concerned that the use being made of the direct payments is not meeting the needs of A;

        (ii) it is concerned that a condition attached to the making of the payments is not being complied with; or

        (iii) there is a significant change in A or P's circumstances; and

    (d) in any event, at intervals not greater than –

        (i) 6 months after the first payment is made; and

        (ii) 12 months following the first review.

(2) Where A, P or the local authority call for a review under paragraph (1)(b) or (c), the period before the next review is due will be extended accordingly.

(3) When carrying out a review the local authority must involve –

    (a) A;

    (b) P (where payments are made to P);

    (c) any carer of A;

    (d)

        (i) any person whom A asks the local authority to involve;

        (ii) if A is an adult who lacks the capacity to decide who to involve, any person authorised under the Mental Capacity Act 2005 to make decisions about A's needs for care and support;

        (iii) if A is a child aged 16 or 17 who does not have capacity to decide who to involve –

            (aa) any person authorised to make decisions about A's needs for care and support under the Mental Capacity Act 2005; or

            (bb) a person with parental responsibility for A;

        (iv) if A is a child below the age of 16, A's parent or other person in a parental role; and

    (e) any other person who the local authority considers to have sufficient involvement in the care or support arrangements for A.

(4) The requirement to involve a parent or other person in a parental role in a review under paragraph (3)(d)(iv) does not apply where, in the view of the local authority, involving that person would not be consistent with the child's well-being.

(5) In this regulation 'person in a parental role' (*'person mewn rôl rhiant'*) includes a parent, a person with parental responsibility or other person who is looking after the child.

12 Direct payments for a child

(1) Where A is a child and a local authority makes direct payments under section 51 of the Act towards the cost of meeting that child's care and support needs, if the condition in paragraph (2) is met then the local authority must meet the requirements of paragraph (3).

(2) The condition in this paragraph is that either A or P are in receipt of –

  (a) income support under Part 7 of the Social Security Contributions and Benefits Act 1992;

  (b) any element of child tax credit other than the family element;

  (c) working tax credit;

  (d) income-based jobseeker's allowance;

  (e) income-related employment and support allowance; or

  (f) universal credit.

(3) The requirements in this paragraph are that the local authority –

  (a) must make the payments at the rate which it estimates to be the reasonable cost of provision to meet the care and support needs in respect of which the payments are made; and

  (b) must not make the payments subject to any condition requiring either the child A or, the recipient of the payment P, to pay any amount to the authority by way of reimbursement.

(4) In this regulation –

  (a) 'child tax credit' (*'credyd treth plant'*) is construed in accordance with section 8 of the Tax Credits Act 2002 and 'family element' (*'elfen deuluol'*) has the same meaning as in section 9(3) of that Act;

  (b) 'working tax credit' (*'credyd treth gwaith'*) is construed in accordance with sections 10 to 12 of the Tax Credits Act 2002;

  (c) 'income-based jobseeker's allowance' (*'lwfans ceisio gwaith yn seiliedig ar incwm'*) has the meaning given in section 1(4) of the Jobseeker's Act 1995;

  (d) 'income-related employment and support allowance' (*'lwfans cyflogaeth a chymorth yn seiliedig ar incwm'*) means an income-related allowance under Part 1 of the Welfare Reform Act 2007 (employment and support allowance);

  (e) 'universal credit' (*'credyd cynhwysol'*) is construed in accordance with Part 1 of the Welfare Reform Act 2012.

13 Direct payments for an adult who no longer has capacity

(1) A local authority need not terminate the making of direct payments under section 50 of the Act in relation to A where A is an adult to whom paragraph (2) applies and one of the circumstances in paragraph (3) applies.

(2) This paragraph applies where A is an adult in relation to whom condition 1 in subsection (3)(b) of section 50 of the Act was met because A had capacity to consent to the making of payments at the time the arrangement started, but who subsequently loses capacity.

(3) This paragraph applies where either –

  (a) the local authority is satisfied that A's loss of capacity to consent to the making of payments is temporary and either –

    (i) the period or periods of loss of capacity are not likely to affect A's ability to manage the payments; or

    (ii) another person who appears to the authority to be capable of managing the payments is prepared to accept and manage the payments on behalf of A during the periods of A's incapacity; or

(b)   condition 2 in subsection (4) of section 50 of the Act is met.

14 Persons subject to requirements imposed in relation to drug or alcohol use

(1) This regulation applies to persons listed in the Schedule.

(2) A local authority may make a direct payment to a person to whom this regulation applies but only if it attaches conditions in the terms set out in paragraph (3) and the further condition in paragraph (4) is met.

(3) The conditions which must be attached are –

    (a)   that A agrees and remains in agreement that the payments are made to a person ('B') to manage on A's behalf; and

    (b)   that B agrees and remains in agreement to receive the payments and to manage the payments to meet A's needs for care and support.

(4) The further condition is that the local authority is satisfied that B is an appropriate person to receive and manage payments on A's behalf.

15 Section 117 of the Mental Health Act 1983

(1) Where a local authority is under a duty to provide after-care services for a person under section 117 of the Mental Health Act 1983 and the conditions in sections 50, 51 and 52 of the Act (as modified by Schedule A1) are met, then it must make direct payments to discharge its duty.

(2) These Regulations apply to direct payments made in discharge of a local authority's duty under section 117 of the Mental Health Act 1983 with the following modifications.

(3) References in this regulation to 'after-care' ('*ôlofal*') or 'after-care services' ('*gwasanaethau ôlofal*') are to be construed in accordance with section 117 of the Mental Health Act 1983.

(4) In regulation 3 remove the words 'meet the needs, or that aspect of the needs' and substitute 'discharge its duty under section 117 of the Mental Health Act 1983 or that aspect of the duty'.

(5) (a)   In regulation 4(1)(a) remove the words 'meet the needs of A for care and support,' and substitute 'provide after-care services under section 117 of the Mental Health Act 1983';

    (b)   in regulation 4(1)(b) remove the words 'meeting A's needs' and substitute 'discharging its duty under section 117 of Mental Health Act 1983';

    (c)   in regulation 4(2)(a) remove the words 'meet those needs' and substitute 'discharge its duty'; and

    (d)   omit regulation 4(2)(g).

(6) In regulation 5 remove the words 'meeting the needs of' and substitute 'discharging its duty towards'.

(7) In regulation 6(2)(a) remove the words 'care and support' and substitute 'after-care'.

(8) In regulation 7(2)(a) remove the word 'care and support' and substitute 'after-care services'.

(9) (a)   In regulation 8(2)(a) remove the words 'needs in respect of which payment is being made may not be met' and substitute 'after-care services in respect of which payments are made may not be provided';

    (b)   in regulation 8(2)(b) remove the words 'meeting A's needs' and substitute 'discharging its duty towards A'; and

    (c)   in regulation 8(3) remove 'A's needs can only be met' and substitute 'after-care services may only be provided'.

(10) Omit regulation 9.

(11) In regulation 10(a) remove the words 'meet the need' and substitute 'provide the after-care service'.

(12)

    (a)   In regulation 11(1)(c)(i) remove the words 'meeting the needs of' and substitute 'discharging its duty towards';

    (b)   in regulation 11(3)(d)(ii) remove the words 'care and support' and substitute 'after-care'.

(13) Omit regulation 12.

(14) In regulation 14(3)(b) remove the words 'meet A's needs for care and support' and substitute 'provide after-care services for A'.

SCHEDULE

ADULTS WHOSE NEEDS THE LOCAL AUTHORITY MAY MEET BY MAKING DIRECT PAYMENTS SUBJECT TO CERTAIN CONDITIONS

This Schedule applies to a person if they are –

    (a)   subject to a drug rehabilitation requirement, as defined by section 209 of the Criminal Justice Act 2003, imposed by a community order within the meaning of section 177 of that Act, or by a suspended sentence of imprisonment, within the meaning of section 189 of that Act;

    (b)   subject to an alcohol treatment requirement as defined by section 212 of the Criminal Justice Act 2003, imposed by a community order within the meaning of section 177 of that Act, or by a suspended sentence of imprisonment, within the meaning of section 189 of that Act;

    (c)   released on licence under Part 2 of the Criminal Justice Act 1991, Chapter 6 of Part 12 of the Criminal Justice Act 2003 or Chapter 2 of the Crime (Sentences) Act 1997, subject to a non standard licence condition requiring the offender to undertake offending behaviour work to address drug or alcohol related behaviour;

    (d)   required to submit to treatment for their drug or alcohol dependency by virtue of a community rehabilitation order within the meaning of section 41 of the Powers of Criminal Courts (Sentencing) Act 2000 or a community punishment and rehabilitation order within the meaning of section 51 of that Act;

    (e)   subject to a drug treatment and testing order imposed under section 52 of the Powers of Criminal Courts (Sentencing) Act 2000;

    (f)   required to submit to treatment for their drug or alcohol dependency by virtue of a requirement of a probation order within the meaning of sections 228 to 230 of the Criminal Procedure (Scotland) Act 1995 or subject to a drug treatment and testing order within the meaning of section 234B of that Act; or

    (g)   released on licence under section 22 or 26 of the Prisons (Scotland) Act 1989 or under section 1 or 1AA of the Prisoners and Criminal Proceedings (Scotland) Act 1993 and subject to a condition that they submit to treatment for their drug or alcohol dependency.

Care and Support (Disputes about Ordinary Residence, etc) (Wales) Regulations 2015, SI 2015/1494

1 Title, commencement, application and interpretation

(1) The title of these Regulations is The Care and Support (Disputes about Ordinary Residence, etc) (Wales) Regulations 2015.

(2) These Regulations come into force on 6 April 2016 and apply to Wales.

(3) In these Regulations –

'the Act' (*'y Ddeddf*') means the Social Services and Well-being (Wales) Act 2014;
'the appropriate person' (*'y person priodol*') means the person by whom a dispute is to be determined pursuant to section 195 of the Act;
'dispute' (*'anghydfod*') means a dispute –
>   (a)   between local authorities about where a person is ordinarily resident in Wales for the purposes of the Act,
>   (b)   between a sending and receiving local authority under section 56 of the Act (portability of care and support) about the application of that section, or
>   (c)   between local authorities about the application of section 189 of the Act (provider failure: temporary duty on local authority);

'the lead authority' (*'yr awdurdod arweiniol*') means, in relation to a dispute, the local authority which (as a result of regulation 2 or otherwise) –
>   (a)   is meeting the needs of the person to whom the dispute relates, or a carer of that person, as at the date on which the dispute arises, or
>   (b)   if no local authority is meeting those needs at that date, is required to do so by regulation 2(3);

'referred' (*'atgyfeirir', yn cael ei atgyfeirio*') means referred for determination by the appropriate person, and 'refer' (*'atgyfeirio*') and 'referral' (*'atgyfeiriad*') are to be construed accordingly.

(4) References in these Regulations to the date on which a dispute arises are references to the first date on which a written communication is sent by one of the local authorities ('the first authority') to another of the local authorities ('the second authority') which (as the case may be) –

>   (a)   asserts that, in the first authority's view, the person to whom the dispute relates is not ordinarily resident in its area for the purposes of the Act, or that the person is ordinarily resident in the second authority's area for those purposes,
>   (b)   raises an issue about the application of section 56 of the Act, or
>   (c)   raises an issue about the application of section 189 of the Act.

(5) In these Regulations, a reference to 'the authorities' is a reference to the authorities who are parties to a dispute and includes (where different) a reference to the lead authority in relation to that dispute.

2 Responsibility for meeting needs whilst dispute is unresolved

(1) The authorities must not allow the existence of the dispute to prevent, delay, interrupt or otherwise adversely affect the meeting of the needs of the person to whom the dispute relates or a carer of that person.

(2) The local authority which is meeting the needs of the person or carer on the date on which the dispute arises must continue to meet those needs until the dispute is resolved.

(3) If no local authority is meeting the needs on the date on which the dispute arises –

(a)   the local authority in whose area the person to whom the dispute relates is living, or

(b)   if the person to whom the dispute relates is not living in the area of any local authority, the local authority in whose area that person is present

must, until the dispute is resolved, perform the duties under the Act in respect of the person and any carer of that person as if the person was ordinarily resident in its area.

(4) If the duty under paragraph (3) falls to be discharged by a local authority ('A') which is not one of the authorities already a party to the dispute, those authorities must, without delay, bring to A's attention –

(a)   A's duty under that paragraph, and

(b)   A's status as the lead authority for the purposes of these Regulations.

(5) A is not under the duties in these Regulations until the date on which it is aware of, or could reasonably be expected to have been aware of, its status as the lead authority.

(6) Where the dispute is about the application of section 56 (portability of care and support), the authorities must perform the duties under that section notwithstanding the existence of the dispute.

3 Steps to be taken prior to referral of a dispute

(1)   The authorities must, prior to the referral of the dispute, take the steps specified in this regulation.

(2) As soon as reasonably practicable after the date on which the dispute arises –

(a)   the lead authority must seek to identify all the other authorities concerned in the dispute and co-ordinate discussions between those authorities in an attempt to resolve the dispute, and

(b)   each of the authorities must nominate an individual who will act as the point of contact within that authority in relation to the dispute, and provide the other authorities with the contact details of that individual.

(3) The lead authority must –

(a)   co-ordinate the discharge, by the authorities, of their duties under this regulation,

(b)   take steps to obtain from the other authorities information which may be relevant to the determination of the dispute,

(c)   disclose that information to any other authority, and

(d)   disclose to the other authorities any information the lead authority itself holds that may help to resolve the dispute.

(4) The authorities must –

(a)   take all reasonable steps to resolve the dispute between themselves, and

(b)   co-operate with each other in the discharge of their duties under this regulation.

(5) Each of the authorities must –

(a)   engage in a constructive dialogue with the other authorities, with a view to bringing about the speedy resolution of the dispute,

(b)   comply, without delay, with any reasonable request for relevant information made by the lead authority, and

(c)   keep the other authorities informed of any developments which appear to it to be relevant to the determination of the dispute.

(6) The lead authority must provide to the persons to whom paragraph (7) applies such information as appears to it to be appropriate about progress in resolving the dispute.

(7) This paragraph applies to the following persons –

    (a)   the person to whom the dispute relates,

    (b)   the carer of that person (if the dispute is about which authority is to meet the needs of a carer), and

    (c)   a representative of the person or carer.

(8) If the authorities cannot resolve the dispute between themselves within four months of the date on which it arose, the lead authority must refer it to the appropriate person.

4 Referral: disputes about ordinary residence or portability of care and support

(1) The referral must include the following documents –

    (a)   a letter signed by the lead authority in relation to the dispute,

    (b)   a statement of facts signed on behalf of each of the authorities which includes the information specified in paragraph (2), and

    (c)   copies of all correspondence between the authorities which relates to the dispute.

(2) The specified information is –

    (a)   an explanation of the nature of the dispute,

    (b)   a chronology of the events leading up to the referral of the dispute, including the date on which the dispute arose,

    (c)   details of the needs of the person to whom the dispute relates ('the relevant person') from the beginning of the period to which the dispute relates,

    (d)   if the dispute is about which authority is to meet the needs of a carer, details of the needs of the carer from the beginning of the period to which the dispute relates,

    (e)   a statement as to which authority has met those needs since the beginning of the period to which the dispute relates, how those needs have been met and the statutory provisions under which they have been met,

    (f)   details of the relevant person's place of residence, and of any former places of residence which are relevant to the dispute,

    (g)   in a case where the relevant person's capacity to decide where to live is relevant to the dispute, either –

        (i)   a statement that the authorities agree that the person has, or lacks, such capacity, or

        (ii)   information which appears to any of the authorities to be relevant to the question of whether the person has, or lacks, such capacity,

    (h)   a statement as to any other steps taken by the authorities in relation to the relevant person or carer of that person, and which may be relevant to the dispute,

    (i)   details of the steps that the authorities have taken to resolve the dispute between themselves, and

    (j)   any other information which appears to any of the authorities to be relevant to the determination of the dispute.

(3) The authorities must submit any legal arguments they rely on in relation to the dispute within 14 days of the date on which the dispute is referred.

(4) If an authority submits legal arguments, it must –

    (a)   send a copy of those arguments to the other authorities, and

    (b)   provide evidence to the appropriate person that it has done so.

(5) If the appropriate person asks any of the authorities to provide further information, the local authority to which this request is made must comply without delay.

(6) This regulation does not apply to a case to which regulation 5 or 6 applies.

PART VII

5 Referral: disputes about co-operation under section 189 (provider failure: temporary duty on local authority)

(1) This regulation applies to a dispute which is solely about the application of section 189(7)(a) or (b) of the Act (duty to co-operate).

(2) The referral must include the following documents –

    (a)   a letter signed by the lead authority in relation to the dispute, stating that the dispute is being referred,

    (b)   a statement of facts signed on behalf of each of the authorities which includes the information specified in paragraph (3), and

    (c)   copies of all correspondence between the authorities which relates to the dispute.

(3) The specified information is –

    (a)   an explanation of the nature of the dispute,

    (b)   a chronology of the events leading up to the referral of the dispute, including the date on which the dispute arose,

    (c)   details of the steps that the authorities have taken to resolve the dispute between themselves, and

    (d)   any other information which appears to any of the authorities to be relevant to the determination of the dispute.

(4) The authorities must submit any legal arguments they rely on in relation to the dispute within 14 days of the date on which the dispute is referred.

(5) If an authority submits legal arguments it must –

    (a)   send a copy of those arguments to the other authorities, and

    (b)   provide evidence to the appropriate person that it has done so.

(6) If the appropriate person asks any of the authorities to provide further information, the local authority to which this request is made must comply without delay.

6 Referral: disputes about costs incurred under section 189 (provider failure: temporary duty on local authority)

(1) This regulation applies to a dispute which is solely about the application of section 189(7)(c) of the Act (recovery of costs).

(2) The referral must include the following documents –

    (a)   a letter signed by the lead authority in relation to the dispute, stating that the dispute is being referred,

    (b)   a statement of facts signed on behalf of each of the authorities which includes the information specified in paragraph (3), and

    (c)   copies of all correspondence between the authorities which relates to the dispute.

(3) The specified information is –

    (a)   an explanation of the nature of the dispute,

    (b)   a chronology of the events leading up to the referral of the dispute, including the date on which the dispute arose,

    (c)   details of the needs of the person to whom the dispute relates ('the relevant person') from the beginning of the period to which the dispute relates,

    (d)   if the dispute is about which authority is to meet the needs of a carer, details of the needs of the carer from the beginning of the period to which the dispute relates,

    (e)   a statement as to which authority has met those needs since the beginning of the period to which the dispute relates, how those needs have been met and the statutory provisions under which they have been met,

(f) information about the costs being sought to be recovered, including a breakdown of those costs,

(g) details of the steps that the authorities have taken to resolve the dispute between themselves, and

(h) any other information which appears to any of the authorities to be relevant to the determination of the dispute.

(4) The authorities must submit any legal arguments they rely on in relation to the dispute within 14 days of the date on which the dispute is referred.

(5) If an authority submits legal arguments it must –

(a) send a copy of those arguments to the other authorities, and

(b) provide evidence to the appropriate person that it has done so.

(6) If the appropriate person asks any of the authorities to provide further information, the local authority to which this request is made must comply without delay.

7 Review of determinations

(1) An authority may make a request to the Welsh Ministers to review the determination.

(2) Any such request must be made within three months of the date of the determination.

(3) A review may be carried out by the Welsh Ministers (whether in response to a request or otherwise).

(4) The Welsh Ministers may confirm the determination or substitute a different determination.

8 Substituted determinations

(1) Where –

(a) a review of a determination has been carried out in accordance with regulation 7 and a different determination substituted,

(b) in consequence of the first determination a local authority ('A') has paid an amount to another local authority ('B'), and

(c) the effect of the second determination is that some or all of the amount paid by A to B was not required to have been paid,

B must repay to A the sum that was not required to have been paid.

Care and Support (Eligibility) (Wales) Regulations 2015, SI 2015/1578

PART VII

1 Title, commencement, application and interpretation

(1) The title of these Regulations is the Care and Support (Eligibility) (Wales) Regulations 2015.

(2) These Regulations come into force on 6 April 2016 and apply in relation to Wales.

(3) In these Regulations –

'the Act' ('*y Ddeddf*') means the Social Services and Well-being (Wales) Act 2014;
'carer' ('*gofalwr*') has the meaning given in section 3 of the Act;

'eligibility determination' ('*dyfarniad cymhwystra*') means a determination under
   section 32(1)(a) of the Act;

'personal outcomes' ('*canlyniadau personol*') means the outcomes which have been
   identified in relation to a person by an assessment under sections 19, 21, or 24 of
   the Act;

'self-care' ('*hunanofal*') means tasks that a person carries out as part of daily life
   including –
   (i)   eating and drinking;
   (ii) maintaining personal hygiene;
   (iii) getting up and getting dressed;
   (iv) moving around the home;
   (v)   preparing meals;
   (vi) keeping the home clean, safe and hygienic.

2 Eligibility determinations

(1) When the local authority is making an eligibility determination in relation to an adult
who has been assessed under section 19 of the Act as having one or more needs for care
and support, any one of those needs meets the eligibility criteria if it is of a description
specified in regulation 3.

(2) When a local authority is making an eligibility determination in relation to a child
who has been assessed under section 21 of the Act as having one or more needs for care
and support, any one of those needs meets the eligibility criteria if it is of a description
specified in regulation 4.

(3) When a local authority is making an eligibility determination in relation to a carer
who has been assessed under section 24 of the Act as having one or more needs for
support, any one of those needs meets the eligibility criteria if it is of a description
specified in regulation 5.

3 Needs which meet the eligibility criteria – adults with needs for care and support

The need of an adult referred to in regulation 2(1) meets the eligibility criteria if –

   (a) the need arises from the adult's physical or mental ill-health, age, disability,
        dependence on alcohol or drugs, or other similar circumstances;
   (b) the need relates to one or more of the following –
        (i)   ability to carry out self-care or domestic routines;
        (ii)   ability to communicate;
        (iii) protection from abuse or neglect;
        (iv)   involvement in work, education, learning or in leisure activities;
        (v)   maintenance or development of family or other significant personal
               relationships;
        (vi)   development and maintenance of social relationships and involvement in
               the community; or
        (vii) fulfilment of caring responsibilities for a child;
   (c) the need is such that the adult is not able to meet that need, either –
        (i)   alone;
        (ii)   with the care and support of others who are willing to provide that care
               and support; or
        (iii) with the assistance of services in the community to which the adult has
               access; and
   (d) the adult is unlikely to achieve one or more of the adult's personal outcomes
        unless –

      (i)   the local authority provides or arranges care and support to meet the need; or

      (ii)   the local authority enables the need to be met by making direct payments.

4 Needs which meet the eligibility criteria – children with needs for care and support

(1) The need of a child referred to in regulation 2(2) meets the eligibility criteria if –

  (a) either –

      (i)   the need arises from the child's physical or mental ill-health, age, disability, dependence on alcohol or drugs, or other similar circumstances; or

      (ii)   the need is one that if unmet is likely to have an adverse effect on the child's development;

  (b) the need relates to one or more of the following –

      (i)   ability to carry out self-care or domestic routines;

      (ii)   ability to communicate;

      (iii) protection from abuse or neglect;

      (iv) involvement in work, education, learning or in leisure activities;

      (v)   maintenance or development of family or other significant personal relationships;

      (vi) development and maintenance of social relationships and involvement in the community; or

      (vii) achieving developmental goals;

  (c) the need is one that neither the child, the child's parents nor other persons in a parental role are able to meet, either –

      (i)   alone or together,

      (ii)   with the care and support of others who are willing to provide that care and support, or

      (iii) with the assistance of services in the community to which the child, the parents or other persons in a parental role have access; and

  (d) the child is unlikely to achieve one or more of the child's personal outcomes unless –

      (i)   the local authority provides or arranges care and support to meet the need; or

      (ii)   the local authority enables the need to be met by making direct payments.

(2) In this regulation –

      (i)   references to a child's development include the physical, intellectual, emotional, social and behavioural development of that child;

      (ii)   'other persons in a parental role' (*'personau eraill mewn rôl rhiant'*) includes persons with parental responsibility or relatives who play a role in looking after the child;

      (iii) 'relative' (*'perthynas'*) has the meaning given in section 197 of the Act.

5 Needs which meet the eligibility criteria – carers with needs for support

The need of a carer referred to in regulation 2(3) meets the eligibility criteria if –

  (a) the need arises as a result of providing care for either –

      (i)   an adult who has needs which fall within Regulation 3 (a) and (b), or

      (ii)   a disabled child;

  (b) the need relates to one or more of the following –

      (i)   ability to carry out self-care or domestic routines;

      (ii)   ability to communicate;

(iii)   protection from abuse or neglect;

(iv)   involvement in work, education, learning or in leisure activities;

(v)   maintenance or development of family or other significant personal relationships;

(vi)   development and maintenance of social relationships and involvement in the community; or

(vii) in the case of an adult carer, fulfilment of caring responsibilities for a child;

(viii) in the case of a child carer, achieving developmental goals;

(c)   the carer cannot meet the need whether –

(i)   alone;

(ii)   with the support of others who are willing to provide that support; or

(iii) with the assistance of services in the community to which the carer has access; and

(d)   the carer is unlikely to achieve one or more of their personal outcomes unless –

(i)   the local authority provides or arranges support to the carer to meet the carer's need;

(ii)   the local authority provides or arranges care and support to the person for whom the carer provides care, in order to meet the carer's need; or

(iii) the local authority enables the need to be met by making direct payments.

6 Ability to meet need

For the purposes of regulations 3(c), 4(1)(c) and 5(c), a person who is able to meet the need, alone or with the assistance of others is to be regarded as unable to meet the need if doing so –

(a)   causes significant pain, anxiety or distress to that person;

(b)   endangers or is likely to endanger the health or safety of that person or another person;

(c)   takes that person significantly longer than would normally be expected.

Care and Support (Ordinary Residence) (Specified Accommodation) (Wales) Regulations 2015,
SI 2015/1499

1 Title, commencement, application and interpretation

(1) The title of these Regulations is the Care and Support (Ordinary Residence) (Specified Accommodation) (Wales) Regulations 2015.

(2) These Regulations come into force on 6 April 2016 and apply to Wales.

(3) In these Regulations –

'the Act' ('*y Ddeddf*') means the Social Services and Well-being (Wales) Act 2014;

'care home accommodation' ('*llety cartref gofal*') means accommodation in a care home within the meaning given by section 3 of the Care Standards Act 2000.

2 Specified types of accommodation

(1) For the purposes of section 194(1) of the Act (ordinary residence), care home accommodation is accommodation of a specified type.

Care and Support (Provision of Health Services) (Wales) Regulations 2015, SI 2015/1919

1 Title, commencement and application

(1) The title of these Regulations is the Care and Support (Provision of Health Services) (Wales) Regulations 2015 and they come into force on 6 April 2016.

(2) These Regulations apply in relation to Wales.

2 Interpretation

In these Regulations –

'the 2014 Act' ('*Deddf 2014*') means the Social Services and Well-being (Wales) Act 2014;

'A' ('*A*') means a person who has need for care and support under sections 35 to 45 of the 2014 Act;

'Continuing NHS Healthcare' ('*Gofal Iechyd Parhaus y GIG*') means a package of care arranged and funded solely by the health service for a person aged 18 or over where it has been assessed that the person's primary need is a health need;

'health body' ('*corff iechyd*') has the same meaning as in section 47(10) of the 2014 Act;

'health service' ('*gwasanaeth iechyd*') means the health service continued under section 1(1) of the National Health Service (Wales) Act 2006.

3 The specified health body for the purposes of section 47(6) of the 2014 Act

(1) Where a local authority, in reliance on section 47(6) of the 2014 Act, is making arrangements for the provision of accommodation together with nursing care by a registered nurse, the health body from which the local authority must obtain consent is –

    (a) where the local authority proposes to accommodate A in Wales, the Local Health Board for the area in which the accommodation is provided;

    (b) where the local authority proposes to accommodate A in Scotland or Northern Ireland, the Local Health Board for the area in which that local authority is located;

    (c) where the local authority proposes to accommodate A in England, the responsible clinical commissioning group.

(2) For the purposes of this regulation, the responsible clinical commissioning group in respect of any person is the clinical commissioning group which has responsibility for arranging for the provision of nursing care by a registered nurse in respect of that person, pursuant to the provisions of section 3(1), (1A) and (1E) of the National Health Service Act 2006 and any regulations made under section 3(1B) or (1D) of that Act.

4 Arrangements for the resolution of disputes for the purposes of section 47(8) of the 2014 Act

(1) A local authority must make arrangements in connection with the resolution of disputes between the authority and a health body about whether or not a service or facility is required to be provided under a health enactment.

(2) Such arrangements must include arrangements in connection with the resolution of disputes about –

    (a) decisions as to a person's eligibility for Continuing NHS Healthcare;

   (b)   the contribution of a health body or local authority to a joint package of care for a person who is not eligible for Continuing NHS Healthcare.

(3) The arrangements must include –

   (a)   a procedure for resolving such disputes which has been agreed with the health body;

   (b)   provision for meeting the needs of the person to whom the dispute relates pending the resolution of the dispute;

   (c)   a requirement that any dispute does not prevent, delay, interrupt or otherwise adversely affect the meeting of the needs of the person to whom the dispute relates.

Care Leavers (Wales) Regulations 2015, SI 2015/1820

PART 1
GENERAL

1 Title, commencement and application

(1) The title of these Regulations is the Care Leavers (Wales) Regulations 2015 and they come into force on 6 April 2016.

(2) These Regulations apply in relation to Wales.

2 Interpretation

In these Regulations –

    'the Act' ('*y Ddeddf*') means the Social Services and Well-being (Wales) Act 2014;

    'category 2 young person' ('*person ifanc category 2*') has the meaning given in section 104(2) of the Act and regulation 3;

    'category 3 young person' ('*person ifanc category 3*') and 'category 4 young person' ('*person ifanc category 4*') have the meanings given in section 104(2) of the Act;

    'detained' ('*dan gadwad*') means –

        (a)   in relation to a child or a category 2 young person who, having been convicted of an offence, is –

            (i)   detained in prison or in youth detention accommodation,

            (ii)   residing in approved premises, or

            (iii) residing in any other premises because a requirement to do so has been imposed on the child as a condition of the grant of bail in criminal proceedings,

    but does not include a remand to such accommodation or premises

        (b)   in relation to a category 3 or 4 young person, the young person is –

            (i)   detained in prison or in youth detention accommodation,

            (ii)   residing in approved premises, or

            (iii) residing in any other premises because a requirement to do so has been imposed on the child as a condition of the grant of bail in criminal proceedings;

    'former foster parent' ('*cyn-riant maeth*') has the meaning given in section 108(3) of the Act;

    'personal adviser' ('*cynghorydd personol*') means the person appointed in accordance with section 106 of the Act for a category 1, category 2, category 3, or category 4 young person;

    'placement' ('*lleoliad*') has the meaning given in section 81(6) of the Act;

'post-18 living arrangement' (*'trefniant byw ôl-18'*) has the meaning given in section 108(3) of the Act;

'prison' (*'carchar'*), 'youth detention accommodation' (*'llety cadw ieuenctid'*), and 'approved premises' (*'mangre a gymeradwywyd'*) have the meanings given in section 188(1) of the Act;

'responsible local authority' (*'awdurdod lleol cyfrifol'*) has the meaning set out in section 104(5) of the Act.

3 Category 2 young persons

(1) For the purposes of section 104(6)(a) of the Act, children falling within paragraph (2) are an additional category of category 2 young person.

(2) Subject to paragraph (3), a child falls within this paragraph if –

    (a)   the child is aged 16 or 17,

    (b)   the child is not subject to a care order, and

    (c)   on attaining the age of 16 the child was detained, or in hospital, and immediately before being detained or admitted to hospital had been looked after by a local authority for a period or periods amounting in total to at least 13 weeks, which began after the child attained the age of 14.

(3) In calculating the period of 13 weeks referred to in paragraph (2)(c), no account is to be taken of any period in which the child was looked after by a local authority or a local authority in England in the course of a pre-planned series of short-term placements, none of which individually exceeded four weeks, where at the end of the each such placement the child returned to the care of their parent or a person who is not a parent but who has parental responsibility for them.

(4) Subject to paragraph (5), a child who has lived for a continuous period of six months or more (whether that period commenced before or after they ceased to be looked after) with –

    (a)   their parent,

    (b)   someone who is not their parent but who has parental responsibility for them, or

    (c)   where they were in care and there was a child arrangements order in force immediately before the care order was made, a person named in the child arrangements order as the person with whom they were to live,

is not to be treated as a category 2 young person despite falling within the definition set out in section 104(2) of the Act.

(5) Where living arrangements described in paragraph (4) break down and the child ceases to live with the person concerned, the child is to be treated as a category 2 young person.

(6) For the purposes of paragraph (4), a child arrangements order is one that consists of, or includes, arrangements relating to either or both of the following –

    (a)   with whom the child is to live, and

    (b)   when the child is to live with any person.

(7) For the purposes of this regulation –

'child arrangements order' (*'gorchymyn trefniadau plentyn'*) has the meaning given in section 8(1) of the Children Act 1989; and

'hospital' (*'ysbyty'*) has the same meaning as in the Mental Health Act 1983.

PART VII

PART 2
ASSESSMENTS OF NEED AND PATHWAY PLANS

4 Involvement of the young person

(1) In carrying out an assessment of needs under regulation 5, and in preparing or reviewing a pathway plan under regulation 6 or 7, the responsible local authority must, unless it is not reasonably practicable –

(a) seek and have regard to the views of the category 2, category 3 or category 4 young person (the relevant young person) to whom the assessment or pathway plan relates, and

(b) take all reasonable steps to enable the relevant young person to attend and participate in any meeting at which their case is to be considered.

(2) The responsible local authority must as soon as practicable provide the relevant young person with copies of –

(a) the results of the assessment,

(b) the pathway plan,

(c) each review of the pathway plan,

and must ensure that the contents of each document are explained to the relevant young person having regard to their level of understanding, unless it is not reasonably practicable to do so.

(3) The responsible local authority must ensure that a written record is kept of the view obtained under paragraph (1)(a).

5 Assessment of needs

(1) The responsible local authority must assess the needs of each category 2 and 4 young person and each category 3 young person who does not already have a pathway plan, in accordance with this regulation.

(2) The assessment of needs must be completed –

(a) in the case of a category 2 young person not more than 3 months after the date on which the young person became a category 2 young person,

(b) in the case of a category 3 young person who does not already have a pathway plan, not more than 3 months after the date on which young person became a category 3 young person, and

(c) in the case of a category 4 young person, not more than 3 months after the date on which the responsible local authority is informed that the category 4 young person is pursuing, or wishes to pursue, a programme of education or training.

(3) The responsible local authority must ensure that a written record is kept of –

(a) the identity of the persons whose views have been sought for the purpose of carrying out the assessment,

(b) the information obtained in the course of the assessment,

(c) the deliberations at any meeting held in connection with any aspect of the assessment, and

(d) the results of the assessment.

(4) In carrying out an assessment of the needs of a category 2 young person, or a category 3 young person, who does not already have a pathway plan, the responsible local authority must –

(a) take into account –

(i) whether the young person is detained,

      (ii)   where the young person is a category 3 young person, whether he or she has a post-18 living arrangement,

      (iii) the young person's health and development,

      (iv) the young person's needs for education, training and employment,

      (v)   the support available to the young person from members of their family and other persons,

      (vi) the young person's financial needs,

      (vii) the extent to which the young person possesses the practical and other skills necessary for independent living, and

      (viii) the young person's needs for advice and other support; and

  (b)   unless it is not reasonably practicable or appropriate to do so, seek and take into account the views of –

      (i)   the young person's parents,

      (ii)   any person who is not the young person's parent but who has parental responsibility for the young person,

      (iii) any person who on a day-to-day basis cares for, or provides accommodation for, the young person,

      (iv) any school, college or institution within the further education sector attended by the young person,

      (v)   the local authority or local authority in England for the area in which the young person lives where that is different from the responsible local authority,

      (vi) any person providing health care or treatment for the young person,

      (vii) where the young person is detained, the director, governor or registered manager (as the case may be), of the prison or youth detention accommodation,

      (viii) where the young person is a category 3 young person who has a post-18 living arrangement, the young person's former foster parent,

      (ix) any person by whom assistance by way of representation is provided to the young person under section 178 of the Act,

      (x)   the young person's personal adviser, and

      (xi) any other person whose views the responsible local authority, or the young person, consider may be relevant;

  (c)   where the category 2 young person is –

      (i)   a victim, or there is reason to believe that they may be a victim, of trafficking in human beings within the meaning of the Council of Europe Convention on Action against Trafficking in Human Beings,

      (ii)   an 'unaccompanied asylum seeking child' within the meaning of the Immigration Rules and has applied, or has indicated to the responsible local authority an intention to apply, for asylum and has not been granted indefinite leave to remain, take account of the young person's needs as a result of that status.

(5) In carrying out an assessment of the needs of a category 3 young person who has a post-18 living arrangement, the responsible local authority must consider whether the arrangement remains consistent with the well-being of that young person and whether the arrangement should be maintained.

(6) In carrying out an assessment of the needs of a category 4 young person, the responsible local authority must –

  (a)   take into account –

      (i)   whether the category 4 young person is detained,

      (ii)   the category 4 young person's needs for education, training or employment, and

PART VII

      (iii) any other considerations the responsible local authority consider relevant, and

   (b) unless it is not reasonably practicable to do so, seek and take into account the views of –

      (i)   the personal adviser,

      (ii) where the category 4 young person is detained, the director, governor or registered manager (as the case may be), of the prison or youth detention accommodation, and

      (iii) any other person whose views the responsible local authority, or the category 4 young person considers may be relevant.

(7) In this regulation –

   'Immigration Rules' ('*Rheolau Mewnfudo*') means the rules for the time being laid down by the Secretary of State as mentioned in section 3(2) of the Immigration Act 1971; and

   'institution within the further education sector' ('*sefydliad yn y sector addysg bellach*') has the meaning given in section 91(3) of the Further and Higher Education Act 1992.

6 Pathway plans

(1) A pathway plan prepared in accordance with section 107(3) or (4) of the Act must be prepared as soon as possible after the assessment of needs referred to in regulation 5 is completed.

(2) The pathway plan must include, in particular –

   (a) in the case of a plan prepared for a category 2 or category 3 young person, the matters referred to in Schedule 1,

   (b) in the case of a plan prepared for a category 2 or 3 young person who is detained, the matters referred to in Schedule 2,

   (c) in the case of a plan prepared for a category 4 young person, the matters referred to in paragraphs 1 to 4 of Schedule 1, and

   (d) in the case of a plan prepared for a category 4 young person who is detained, the matters referred to in paragraphs 1 to 4 of Schedule 2.

(3) The pathway plan must, in relation to each of the matters included in it by virtue of paragraph (2), set out –

   (a) the manner in which the responsible local authority or the staff of a prison or youth detention accommodation (where relevant) proposes to meet the needs of the young person to whom the plan relates, and

   (b) the date by which, and by whom, any action required to implement any aspect of the pathway plan will be carried out.

(4) The pathway plan, any review of the plan and any changes to the plan as a result of such a review must be recorded in writing.

7 Review of Pathway plans

(1) The responsible local authority must review the pathway plan of each category 2, category 3 and category 4 young person in accordance with this regulation.

(2) The responsible local authority must arrange a review –

   (a) if requested to do so by the category 2, category 3 or category 4 young person,

   (b) if the responsible local authority, or the personal adviser, consider a review necessary,

    (c)   if the young person is detained and a review would not otherwise occur before the young person ceases to be so detained, and

    (d)   in any event, at intervals of not more than 6 months.

(3) If the responsible local authority provides the category 2, category 3 or category 4 young person with accommodation in accordance with sections 109, 110 or 112 of the Act, the responsible local authority must also –

    (a)   arrange a review as soon as is practicable after the end of a period of 28 days beginning on the day on which the accommodation is first provided, and

    (b)   on completing a review under sub-paragraph (a), determine at what intervals (not exceeding 3 months) subsequent reviews will be carried out.

PART 3
PERSONAL ADVISERS

8 Functions of personal advisers

(1) A personal adviser has the following functions in relation to the category 2, category 3 or category 4 young person for whom they are appointed –

    (a)   to provide advice (including practical advice) and support,

    (b)   where applicable, to participate in the assessment and the preparation of the pathway plan,

    (c)   to participate in reviews of the pathway plan,

    (d)   to liaise with the responsible local authority in the implementation of the pathway plan,

    (e)   to co-ordinate the provision of services, and to take reasonable steps to ensure that the young person makes use of such services and that they are appropriate to the young person's needs,

    (f)   to remain informed about the young person's progress and well-being, and

    (g)   to keep a written record of the contacts with, and of services provided to, the young person.

(2) In addition, where accommodation is provided for a category 2, category 3 or category 4 young person by the responsible local authority under section 109, 110 or 112 of the Act, the personal adviser must visit the young person at that accommodation –

    (a)   within 7 days of the accommodation first being provided,

    (b)   subsequently, before the pathway plan is reviewed under regulation 7(3), and

    (c)   at subsequent intervals of not more than two months.

PART 4
MISCELLANEOUS

9 Support and accommodation

(1) For the purposes of section 109(1)(c) of the Act, the responsible local authority must provide assistance in order to meet the category 2 young person's needs in relation to education, training or employment as provided for in that young person's pathway plan.

(2) For the purposes of section 109(3), 'suitable accommodation' ('*llety addas*') means accommodation –

    (a)   which so far as reasonably practicable is suitable for the category 2 young person in the light of their needs, including any health needs and any needs arising from any disability,

PART VII

(b)   in respect of which the responsible local authority has satisfied itself as to the character and suitability of the landlord or other provider, and

(c)   in respect of which the responsible local authority has, so far as reasonably practicable, taken into account the category 2 young person's –

(i)   wishes and feelings, and

(ii)   education, training and employment needs.

(3) In determining for the purposes of paragraph (2)(a) whether accommodation is suitable for a category 2 young person, the responsible local authority must have regard to the matters set out in Schedule 3.

(4) For the purposes of sections 110(8), 112(4), 114(7) and 115(8) of the Act –

'further education' ('*addysg bellach*') has the same meaning as in the Education Act 1996 save that for the purposes of this regulation it only includes further education which is provided on a full-time residential basis; and

'higher education' ('*addysg uwch*') means education provided by means of a course of a description referred to in regulations made under section 22 of the Teaching and Higher Education Act 1998.

10 Records

(1) The responsible local authority must establish and maintain a written case record for each category 2, category 3 and category 4 young person ('the case record') ('*y cofnod achos*').

(2) The case record must include the written records required by virtue of regulation 4(3) and regulation 5(3), and the following records ('relevant records') ('*cofnodion perthnasol*') –

(a)   any assessment of needs,

(b)   any pathway plan,

(c)   any review of a pathway plan.

(3) Relevant records must be retained by the responsible local authority until the 75th anniversary of the date of birth of the category 2, category 3, or category 4 young person to whom they relate or, if the young person dies before attaining the age of 18, for a period of 15 years beginning with the date of death.

(4) The requirement in paragraph (1) may be complied with by retaining the original written records or copies of them, or by keeping all or part of the information contained in them in some other accessible form such as a computer record.

(5) Relevant records must be kept securely and may not be disclosed to any person except in accordance with –

(a)   any provision of, or made under or by virtue of, a statute under which access to such records is authorised, or

(b)   any court order authorising access to such records.

11 Revocation of Regulations

The Children (Leaving Care) (Wales) Regulations 2001 are revoked.

SCHEDULE 1

MATTERS TO BE DEALT WITH IN THE PATHWAY PLAN AND REVIEW

1 The level and nature of contact and personal support to be provided, and by whom, to the young person.

2 A detailed plan for the young person's education or training.

3 How the responsible local authority will assist the young person in relation to employment or other purposeful activity or occupation.

4 Contingency plans for action to be taken by the responsible local authority should the pathway plan for any reason cease to be effective.

5 Details of the accommodation the young person is to occupy (including an assessment of its suitability in the light of the young person's needs, and details of the considerations taken into account in assessing that suitability).

6 The support to be provided to enable the young person to develop and sustain appropriate family and social relationships.

7 A programme to develop the practical and other skills necessary for the young person to live independently.

8 The financial support to be provided to the young person, in particular where it is to be provided to meet needs for accommodation and maintenance.

9 The health needs, including any mental health needs, of the young person and how they are to be met.

10 Details of the arrangements made by the responsible local authority to meet the young person's needs in relation to identity with particular reference to their religious persuasion, racial origin and cultural and linguistic background.

11 Where the young person falls within regulation 5(4)(c), whether the young person's needs as a result of that status are being met.

SCHEDULE 2
MATTERS TO BE DEALT WITH IN THE PATHWAY PLAN AND REVIEW WHERE THE YOUNG PERSON IS DETAINED

1 The name and address of the prison or youth detention accommodation.

2 The level and nature of contact and personal support to be provided to the young person by the responsible local authority and by the staff of the prison or youth detention accommodation.

3 The arrangements made by the staff of the prison or youth detention accommodation for the young person's education and training, including the name and address of any educational or training institution the young person was attending, or any other person providing the young person with education or training, immediately before their detention.

4 The details of how the young person's needs will be met when the young person ceases to be detained, in particular –

    (a)   whether the young person will be provided with accommodation or other support by the responsible local authority, another local authority or a local authority in England, and

    (b)   how the responsible local authority will assist the young person in relation to –
        (i)   education or training, or
        (ii)   employment or other purposeful activity or occupation.

5 Arrangements put in place by staff of the prison or youth detention accommodation to support the young person's development of the practical or other skills necessary for the young person to live independently.

6 Details of and arrangements made by staff of the prison or youth detention accommodation to meet the young person's health needs (including any mental health needs).

7 Arrangements made and support to be provided to enable the young person to develop and sustain appropriate family and social relationships.

8 Details of the young person's personal history, religious persuasion, cultural and linguistic background, racial origin and the arrangements put in place by the staff of the prison or youth detention accommodation for meeting the young person's religious, cultural and linguistic needs.

SCHEDULE 3

MATTERS TO BE CONSIDERED IN DETERMINING THE SUITABILITY OF ACCOMMODATION

1 In respect of the accommodation, the –

- (a) facilities and services provided,
- (b) state of repair,
- (c) safety,
- (d) location,
- (e) support,
- (f) tenancy status, and
- (g) the financial commitments involved for the category 2 young person and their affordability.

2 In respect of the category 2 young person, their –

- (a) views of the accommodation,
- (b) understanding of their rights and responsibilities in relation to the accommodation, and
- (c) understanding of funding arrangements.

Care Planning, Placement and Case Review (Wales) Regulations 2015, SI 2015/1818

ARRANGEMENT OF REGULATIONS

PART 1
GENERAL

PART 2
ARRANGEMENTS FOR LOOKING AFTER A CHILD

PART 3
PLACEMENTS – GENERAL PROVISIONS

PART 4
PROVISION FOR DIFFERENT TYPES OF PLACEMENT

Chapter 1
Placement of a child in care with P

Chapter 2
Placement with local authority foster parents

Chapter 3
Other arrangements

PART 5
VISITS BY THE RESPONSIBLE AUTHORITY'S REPRESENTATIVE ETC

PART 6
REVIEWS OF THE CHILD'S CASE

PART 1
GENERAL

1 Title, commencement and application

(1) The title of these Regulations is the Care Planning, Placement and Case Review (Wales) Regulations 2015 and they come into force on 6 April 2016.

(2) These Regulations apply in relation to Wales.

2 Interpretation

(1) In these Regulations –

'the 1989 Act' (*'Deddf 1989'*) means the Children Act 1989;

'the 2012 Act (*'Deddf 2012'*) means the Legal Aid, Sentencing and Punishment of Offenders Act 2012;

'the 2014 Act' (*'Deddf 2014'*) means the Social Services and Well-being (Wales) Act 2014;

'the Fostering Regulations' (*'y Rheoliadau Maethu'*) means the Fostering Services (Wales) Regulations 2003;

'appropriate person' (*'person priodol'*) means –
   (a) P, where C is to live, or lives, with P;
   (b) F, where C is to be placed, or is placed, with F;
   (c) where C is to be placed, or is placed, in a children's home, the person who is registered under Part 2 of the Care Standards Act 2000 in respect of that home; or
   (d) where C is to be placed, or is placed, in accordance with other arrangements under section 81(6)(d) of the 2014 Act, the person who will be responsible for C at the accommodation;

'area authority' (*'awdurdod yr ardal'*) means the local authority or local authority in England for the area in which C is placed, or is to be placed, where this is different from the responsible authority;

'C' (*'C'*) means a child who is looked after by the responsible authority;

'care and support plan' (*'cynllun gofal a chymorth'*) means the plan for the future care and support of C prepared and maintained in accordance with section 83 of the 2014 Act;

'case record' (*'cofnod achos'*) has the meaning given in regulation 63;

'connected person' (*'person cysylltiedig'*) means a relative, friend or other person connected with C;

'detention placement plan' (*'cynllun lleoli dan gadwad'*) has the meaning given in regulation 58;

'director' (*'cyfarwyddwr'*) means the person in charge of a secure training centre;

'F' (*'F'*) means a person who is approved as a local authority foster parent and with whom it is proposed to place C or, as the case may be, with whom C is placed;

'fostering service provider' (*'darparwr gwasanaeth maethu'*) means –

      (a)   a fostering service provider within the meaning given in regulation 2(1) of
           the Fostering Regulations, and

      (b)   a fostering service provider within the meaning given in regulation 2(1) of
           the Fostering Services (England) Regulations 2011;

'full assessment process' (*'proses asesu gyflawn'*) has the meaning given in
    regulation 26(2)(d);

'general practitioner' (*'ymarferydd cyffredinol'*) means a registered medical
    practitioner who –

      (a)   provides primary medical services under Part 4 of the National Health
           Service (Wales) Act 2006, or

      (b)   provides services which correspond to services provided under Part 4 of
           the National Health Service (Wales) Act 2006, otherwise than in
           pursuance of that Act;

'governor' (*'llywodraethwr'*) means the person in charge of a young offender
    institution;

'health care provider' (*'darparwr gofal iechyd'*) means, in the case of a placement in
    Wales, a local health board, or in the case of a placement in a local authority area
    in England, the National Health Service Commissioning Board and any relevant
    clinical commissioning group) and in any other case, the equivalent body in the
    country in which C is placed or is to be placed;

'health plan' (*'cynllun iechyd'*) has the meaning given in regulation 5(1)(b)(i);

'IFS team' (*'tîm integredig cymorth i deuluoedd'*) means an integrated family
    support team established by a partnership body in accordance with the
    Partnership Regulations;

'independent visitor' (*'ymwelydd annibynnol'*) means the independent person
    appointed to be C's visitor under section 98 of the 2014 Act;

'IRO' (*'SAA'*) means the independent reviewing officer appointed for C's case under
    section 99(1) of the 2014 Act;

'LAC Education Co-ordinator' (*'Cydgysylltydd Addysg PDG'*) means the person
    designated by the responsible authority to co-ordinate personal education plans
    and to address the educational needs of looked after children and care leavers
    within the area of the responsible authority;

'lead director for children and young people's services' (*'cyfarwyddwr arweiniol ar
    gyfer gwasanaethau plant a phobl ifanc'*) means the officer of the responsible
    authority appointed for the purposes of section 27 of the Children Act 2004;

'link worker' (*'gweithiwr dolen gyswllt'*) means a member of staff of a children's
    home appointed in accordance with the requirements of the Children's Homes
    (Wales) Regulations 2002 with particular responsibility for protecting and
    promoting the health and educational well-being of a child and for liaison with
    education and health care providers on that child's behalf;

'nominated officer' (*'swyddog enwebedig'*) means the director for social services or
    other senior officer of the responsible authority nominated in writing by the
    director of social services to act on his or her behalf for the purposes of these
    Regulations;

'P' (*'P'*) means –

      (a)   a person who is C's parent;

      (b)   a person who is not C's parent but who has parental responsibility for C;
           or

      (c)   where C is in the care of the responsible authority and there was a child
           arrangements order which regulated C's living arrangements in force
           immediately before the care order was made, a person named in the child
           arrangements order as a person with whom C was to live;

'the Partnership Regulations' (*'y Rheoliadau Partneriaeth'*) means the Partnership
    Arrangements (Wales) Regulations 2015;

'partnership body' ('*corff partneriaeth*') has the meaning given in regulation 1(4) of the Partnership Regulations;

'pathway plan' ('*cynllun llwybr*') has the meaning given in section 107 of the 2014 Act;

'personal adviser' ('*cynghorydd personol*') means the personal adviser arranged for C in accordance with section 106 of the 2014 Act;

'personal education plan' ('*cynllun addysg personol*') has the meaning given in regulation 5(b)(ii);

'placement' ('*lleoliad*') means –

    (a) arrangements made by the responsible authority for C to live with P in accordance with section 81(2) of the 2014 Act, where C is in the care of the responsible authority, or

    (b) arrangements made by the responsible authority to provide for C's accommodation and maintenance by any of the means specified in section 81(6) of the 2014 Act;

'placement plan' ('*cynllun lleoli*') has the meaning given in regulation 10(1)(a) and forms part of C's care and support plan;

'R' ('*R*') means the representative of the responsible authority who visits C in accordance with arrangements made by it under section 97 of the 2014 Act;

'registered dental practitioner' ('*ymarferydd deintyddol cofrestredig*') means a person registered in the dentists register under section 14 of the Dentists Act 1984 who –

    (a) provides primary dental services under Part 5 of the National Health Service (Wales) Act 2006, or

    (b) provides services which correspond to services provided under Part 5 of the National Health Service (Wales) Act 2006, otherwise than in pursuance of that Act;

'responsible authority' ('*awdurdod cyfrifol*') means the local authority that looks after C;

'registered manager' ('*rheolwr cofrestredig*') means the person who is registered under Part 2 of the Care Standards Act 2000 as a manager of a secure children's home;

'remand to local authority accommodation' ('*remánd i lety awdurdod lleol*') has the meaning given in section 91(3) of the 2012 Act;

'remand to youth detention accommodation' ('*remánd i lety cadw ieuenctid*') has the meaning given in s 91(4) of the 2012 Act;

'secure children's home' ('*cartref plant diogel*') has the meaning given in section 102(11) of the 2012 Act;

'secure training centre' ('*canolfan hyfforddi ddiogel*') has the meaning given in section 43(1)(d) of the Prison Act 1952;

'special educational needs' ('*anghenion addysgol arbennig*') and 'special educational provision' ('*darpariaeth addysgol arbennig*') have the meanings given in section 312 of the Education Act 1996;

'temporary approval' ('*cymeradwyaeth dros dro*') has the meaning given in regulation 26(1);

'working day' ('*diwrnod gwaith*') means any day other than –

    (a) a Saturday or Sunday,

    (b) Christmas day or Good Friday, or

    (c) a bank holiday in England and Wales under the Banking and Financial Dealings Act 1971; and

'young offender institution' ('*sefydliad troseddwyr ifanc*') has the meaning given in section 43(1)(aa) of the Prison Act 1952.

(2) In these Regulations any reference to C being 'detained' ('*dan gadwad*') means that C, having been convicted of an offence, is –

PART VII

(a) detained in prison or in youth detention accommodation, or

(b) residing in approved premises, or

(c) residing in any other premises because a requirement to do so has been placed on C as a condition of the grant of bail in criminal proceedings, and immediately before such detention or requirement to reside was imposed C was in the care of the responsible authority.

(3) In these Regulations any reference to any document or other record includes any such document or record that is kept or provided in a readily accessible form and includes copies of original documents and electronic methods of recording information.

Amendments—SI 2017/713.

3 These Regulations do not apply in relation to any child who is looked after by a local authority and who has been placed for adoption under the Adoption and Children Act 2002 unless the child falls within regulation 56.

PART 2
ARRANGEMENTS FOR LOOKING AFTER A CHILD

4 Care planning

(1) Where C is not in the care of the responsible authority and a care and support plan for C has not already been prepared, the responsible authority must assess C's needs for services to achieve or maintain a reasonable standard of health or development, and prepare such a plan.

(2) Where C has a care and support plan prepared in accordance with section 54 of the 2014 Act, the responsible authority must take the information recorded in that plan into account in its assessment under paragraph (1).

(3) Except in the case of a child to whom section 31A of the 1989 Act (care orders: care plans) applies, the care and support plan must be prepared before C is first placed by the responsible authority or, if it is not practicable to do so, within 10 working days of the start of the first placement.

(4) When assessing C's needs under paragraph (1), the responsible authority must consider whether the accommodation provided for C meets the requirements of Part 6 of the 2014 Act.

(5) Unless paragraph (6) applies, the care and support plan should, so far as is reasonably practicable, be agreed by the responsible authority with –

(a) any parent of C's and any person who is not C's parent but who has parental responsibility for C, or

(b) if there is no such person, the person who was caring for C immediately before the responsible authority arranged a placement for C.

(6) Where C is aged 16 or over and agrees to be provided with accommodation under section 76 of the 2014 Act, the care and support plan must be agreed with C by the responsible authority.

(7) Where a care and support plan prepared in accordance with this Part satisfies the requirements for a care plan required by section 31A of the 1989 Act, it may be treated as a 'section 31A plan'.

(8) Where C was first placed by the responsible authority before 6 April 2016 the care and support plan must be prepared as soon as reasonably practicable.

5 Preparation and content of the care and support plan

(1) The care and support plan must include a record of the following information –

    (a)   the long term plan for C's upbringing ('the plan for permanence');

    (b)   the arrangements made by the responsible authority to meet C's needs in relation to –

        (i)   health, including the information set out in paragraph 1 of Schedule 2 ('the health plan'),

        (ii)   education and training, including the information set out in paragraph 2 of Schedule 2 ('the personal education plan'),

        (iii)   emotional and behavioural development,

        (iv)   identity, with particular regard to C's religious persuasion, racial origin, sexual orientation, and cultural and linguistic background,

        (v)   family and social relationships and in particular the information set out in paragraph 3 of Schedule 2,

        (vi)   social presentation, and

        (vii)   self-care skills;

    (c)   except in a case where C is in the care of the responsible authority but is not provided with accommodation by it by any of the means referred to in section 81 of the 2014 Act, details of the arrangements made and accommodation provided for C ('the placement plan');

    (d)   the name of the IRO;

    (e)   details of the views, wishes and feelings of those persons ascertained and considered by the responsible authority in accordance with sections 6(2) and (4), 7(2) and 78(3) of the 2014 Act about the arrangements referred to in sub-paragraph (b), the placement plan and any change, or proposed change in the care and support plan;

    (f)   where C is –

        (i)   a victim, or there is reason to believe C may be a victim, of trafficking in human beings within the meaning of the Council of Europe Convention on Action against Trafficking in Human Beings,

        (ii)   an unaccompanied asylum seeking child within the meaning of the Immigration Rules and has applied, or has indicated to the responsible authority an intention to apply, for asylum and has not been granted indefinite leave to remain,

        that fact.

(2) In this regulation, 'Immigration Rules' ('*Rheolau Mewnfudo*') means the rules for the time being laid down by the Secretary of State as mentioned in section 3(2) of the Immigration Act 1971.

6 (1) The responsible authority must keep C's care and support plan under review in accordance with Part 6 and, if it is of the opinion some change is required, it must revise the plan or make a new plan accordingly.

(2) Unless otherwise provided in these Regulations, the responsible authority must not make any significant change to the care and support plan unless the proposed change has first been considered at a review of C's case, undertaken in accordance with Part 6.

(3) Subject to paragraph (4), the responsible authority must give a copy of the care and support plan –

    (a)   to C, unless, in the opinion of the responsible authority, it would not be appropriate to do so having regard to C's age and understanding,

    (b)   to P,

    (c)   to the IRO,

PART VII

(d)   where C is to be placed, or is placed, with F, to the fostering service provider that approved F, in accordance with the Fostering Regulations or the Fostering Services (England) Regulations 2011,

(e)   where C is to be placed, or is placed, in a children's home, to the person who is registered under Part 2 of the Care Standards Act 2000 in respect of that home, and

(f)   where C is to be placed, or is placed, in accordance with other arrangements under section 81(6)(d) of the 2014 Act, to the person who will be responsible for C at the accommodation.

(4) The responsible authority may decide not to give a copy of the care and support plan, or a full copy of the care and support plan, to P if it considers to do so would put C at risk of harm.

7 Health care

(1) Before C is first placed by it or, if that is not reasonably practicable, before the first review of C's case, the responsible authority must make arrangements for a registered medical practitioner or a registered nurse to –

(a)   carry out an assessment of C's state of health, which may include a physical examination, and

(b)   provide a written report of the assessment, addressing the matters specified in paragraph 1 of Schedule 2 with particular reference to C's state of mental health, as soon as reasonably practicable.

(2) Paragraph (1) does not apply if, within a period of 3 months immediately preceding the placement, an assessment of C's state of health has been carried out and the responsible authority has obtained a written report that meets the requirements of that paragraph and it is satisfied that no significant changes have occurred within the period since the assessment was made.

(3) The responsible authority must make arrangements for a registered medical practitioner or a registered nurse or a registered midwife acting under the supervision of a registered medical practitioner to review C's state of health and provide a written report of each review, addressing the matters specified in paragraph 1 of Schedule 2 with particular reference to C's state of mental health –

(a)   at least once, and more frequently if C's wellbeing requires it, in every period of 6 months before C's fifth birthday, and

(b)   at least once, and more frequently if C's wellbeing requires it, in every period of twelve months after C's fifth birthday.

(4) Paragraphs (1) and (3) do not apply if C refuses consent to the assessment, being of sufficient age and understanding to do so.

(5) The responsible authority must take all reasonable steps to ensure that C is provided with appropriate health care services, in accordance with the health plan, including –

(a)   medical and dental care and treatment, and

(b)   advice and guidance on health, personal care and health promotion issues.

(6) The responsible authority must ensure that C is –

(a)   registered with a general practitioner as soon as practicable and in any event not later than 10 working days after the placement is made; and

(b)   under the care of a registered dental practitioner as soon as practicable and in any event not later than 20 working days after the placement is made.

(7) The responsible authority must ensure as far as practicable, that C continues to be registered with a general practitioner and under the care of a registered dental practitioner, throughout the duration of the placement.

(8) Where C was first placed by the responsible authority before 6 April 2016 and paragraph (2) does not apply, and no assessment of C's health has taken place or C has not been registered with a general practitioner or placed under the care of a registered dental practitioner, this regulation applies as if that placement had been made on 6 April 2016.

8 Contact with a child in care

When considering whether contact between C and any of the persons mentioned in paragraphs (a) to (d) of section 34(1) of the 1989 Act is consistent with safeguarding and promoting C's well-being, the responsible authority must have regard to C's care and support plan.

9 (1) This regulation applies if C is in the care of the responsible authority and the responsible authority has decided under section 34(6) of the 1989 Act (refusal of contact as a matter of urgency) to refuse to allow contact that would otherwise be required by virtue of section 34(1) of the 1989 Act or an order under section 34 of that Act (parental contact etc with children in care).

(2) The responsible authority must immediately give written notification to the following persons of the information specified in paragraph (3) ('the specified information') –

    (a)   C, unless it would not be appropriate to do so having regard to C's age and understanding,

    (b)   P,

    (c)   where immediately before the care order was made a person had care of C by virtue of an order made in exercise of the High Court's inherent jurisdiction with respect to children, that person,

    (d)   any other person whose views, wishes and feelings the responsible authority consider to be relevant, and

    (e)   the IRO.

(3) The specified information is –

    (a)   the responsible authority's decision;

    (b)   the date of the decision;

    (c)   the reasons for the decision;

    (d)   the duration of the decision (if applicable); and

    (e)   remedies available in case of dissatisfaction.

(4) The responsible authority may depart from the terms of any order made under section 34 of the 1989 Act by agreement with the person in relation to whom the order is made, provided that –

    (a)   C, being of sufficient age and understanding, also agrees, and

    (b)   written notification of the specified information is sent within 5 working days to the persons listed in paragraph (2).

(5) Where the responsible authority has decided to vary or suspend any arrangements made (otherwise than under an order under section 34 of the 1989 Act) with a view to affording any person contact with C, the responsible authority must immediately give written notification containing the specified information to the persons listed in paragraph (2).

PART VII

(6) The responsible authority must record any decision made under this regulation in C's care and support plan.

PART 3
PLACEMENTS – GENERAL PROVISIONS

10 Placement plan

(1) Subject to paragraphs (2) and (4), before making arrangements in accordance with section 81 of the 2014 Act for C's placement, the responsible authority must –

    (a) incorporate within C's care and support plan details of the plan for C's placement ('the placement plan') which –
        (i) sets out how the placement will contribute to meeting C's needs, and
        (ii) includes all the matters specified in Schedule as are applicable, having regard to the type of the placement, and
    (b) ensure that –
        (i) C's views, wishes and feelings have been ascertained and given due consideration, and
        (ii) the IRO has been informed.

(2) If it is not reasonably practicable to prepare the placement plan before making the placement, the placement plan must be prepared within 5 working days of the start of the placement.

(3) The placement plan must be agreed with, and signed by, the appropriate person.

(4) Where the arrangements for C's placement were made before 6 April 2016, the responsible authority must prepare the placement plan as soon as reasonably practicable.

11 Avoidance of disruption in education

(1) Subject to paragraphs (2) and (3), if C is a registered pupil at a school in the fourth key stage, a decision to make any change to C's placement that would have the effect of disrupting the arrangements made for C's education must not be put into effect until it has been approved by the nominated officer.

(2) Before approving a decision under paragraph (1), the nominated officer must be satisfied that –

    (a) the requirements of regulation 10(1)(b)(i) have been complied with,
    (b) the educational provision made for C at the placement will promote C's educational achievement and is consistent with C's personal education plan,
    (c) the designated person at the school has been consulted,
    (d) the LAC Education Co-ordinator has been consulted,
    (e) the IRO has been consulted, and
    (f) where C is placed in a children's home, C's link worker has been consulted.

(3) Paragraph (1) does not apply in any case where –

    (a) the responsible authority terminates C's placement in accordance with regulation 15(3), or
    (b) it is necessary for any other reason to change C's placement in an emergency, and in such a case the responsible authority must make appropriate arrangements to promote C's educational achievement as soon as reasonably practicable.

(4) In any case not falling within paragraph (1), but where the responsible authority proposes making any change to C's placement that would have the effect of disrupting the arrangements made for C's education or training, the responsible authority must

ensure that other arrangements are made for C's education or training that meets C's needs and are consistent with C's personal education plan.

(5) In this regulation –

(a) 'registered pupil' ('*disgybl cofrestredig*') has the meaning given in section 20(7) of the Children and Young Persons Act 2008, and

(b) 'school' ('*ysgol*') has the meaning given in section 4 of the Education Act 1996.

Placements out of area

12 Placement decision

(1) A responsible authority may only decide to place C outside its area if it is satisfied that there is no placement available within its area capable of meeting C's needs ('an out of area placement').

(2) Where paragraph (1) applies, the responsible authority must seek an out of area placement for C, in accordance with the following order of preference, –

(a) within a local authority whose area borders that of the responsible authority;

(b) within a local authority in England whose area borders that of the responsible authority;

(c) within any other local authority;

(d) within a local authority in England, or

(e) subject to the requirements of section 124 of the 2014 Act, outside England and Wales.

(3) Subject to paragraph (5), where a responsible authority is satisfied that an out of area placement is necessary in C's case, the decision to place C in an out of area placement must not be put into effect until –

(a) the decision has been referred to and approved by a panel,

(b) the panel's approval of that decision is recorded in writing giving reasons for its approval, and

(c) that record of approval is endorsed in writing by the nominated officer to confirm his or her approval.

(4) Before approving a decision under paragraph (1), the panel and the nominated officer must each be satisfied that –

(a) the requirements of regulation 10(1)(b)(i) have been complied with,

(b) the placement is the most appropriate placement available for C and is consistent with C's care and support plan,

(c) C's relatives have been consulted, where appropriate,

(d) the IRO has been consulted,

(e) where C has special education needs met in a special educational plan, the local authority or local authority in England in whose area is it proposed to place C has been notified of the placement and agreement has been reached with that authority in respect of the meeting of C's special educational needs during C's placement in its area, and

(f) if C has health needs which require attention, the health care provider for the area of the local authority or local authority in England has been notified and, in appropriate cases, agreement has been reached with the health care provider in respect of the meeting of C's health needs.

(5) In the case of a placement made in an emergency –

(a) paragraph (3) does not apply;

(b) paragraph (4) applies subject to the modifications in sub-paragraph (c);

PART VII

    (c)   the responsible authority must ensure that –

        (i)   a record of the decision is made in writing, giving reasons for the decision,

        (ii) the record is endorsed by the nominated officer to confirm his or her agreement with the decision,

        (iii) paragraph (4)(a) and (b) are complied with before the placement is made,

        (iv) paragraph (4)(c) and (d) are complied with within 5 working days of the placement being made, and

        (v) paragraph (4)(e) and (f) are complied with as soon as possible after the placement has been made.

(6) Where a placement is made is accordance with paragraph (5) –

    (a)   the responsible authority must refer the placement to a panel as soon as practicable after the placement is made and in any event not later than 25 working days after the placement is made, and

    (b)   the placement must be notified to the local authority or the local authority in England in whose area C has been placed not later than 5 working days after the placement is made.

(7) The record of any decision made in accordance with this regulation must be made available to the lead member for children's services for the responsible authority.

(8) In this regulation –

    'notified' ('*hysbysu*') in paragraph (6)(b) means that the responsible authority must provide –

        (a)   details of its assessment of C's needs and the reasons why the placement chosen is the most appropriate way of meeting C's needs, and

        (b)   a copy of C's care and support plan if it has not already been provided;

    'panel' ('*panel*') means a panel of representatives from such agencies as may assist a responsible authority in planning the placement for a C and in meeting C's needs during the placement and must include a representative from the local authority or local authority in England in whose area C is to be placed and, in appropriate cases, any relevant health care or education provider.

13 Placement outside England and Wales

(1) This regulation applies if –

    (a)   C is in the care of the responsible authority, and

    (b)   the responsible authority makes arrangements to place C outside England and Wales in accordance with the provisions of section 124 of the 2014 Act (arrangements to assist a child to live outside England and Wales).

(2) The responsible authority must take steps to ensure that, so far as is reasonably practicable, requirements corresponding with the requirements which would have applied under these Regulations had C been placed in Wales, are complied with.

(3) The responsible authority must include in the care and support plan details of the arrangements made by the responsible authority to supervise C's placement.

14 Notification of placement

(1) Subject to paragraph (3), the responsible authority must give written notice to the persons listed in paragraph (2) of the arrangements for C's placement before the placement is made or, if an emergency placement is necessary, within 5 working days of the start of the placement, unless it is not reasonably practicable to do so.

(2) The persons referred to in paragraph (1) are –

(a) C, unless it would not be appropriate to do so having regard to C's age and understanding,

(b) P,

(c) if C is in the care of the responsible authority, any person who is allowed contact with C under section 34(1) of the 1989 Act and any person who has contact with C by virtue of an order under section 34 of that Act (parental contact etc with children in care),

(d) if C is looked after but is not in the care of the responsible authority, any person who has contact with C pursuant to an order made under section 8 of the 1989 Act (child arrangements orders and other orders with respect to children),

(e) any person who was caring for C immediately before the arrangements were made,

(f) the local health board (or, in the case of a child living or to be placed in a local authority area in England, the National Health Service Commissioning Board and the clinical commissioning group) for the area in which C is living and, if different, for the area in which C is to be placed,

(g) C's registered medical practitioner and, where applicable, the registered medical practitioner with whom C is to be registered during the placement,

(h) any educational establishment attended by, or person providing education or training for, C,

(i) the LAC Education Co-ordinator for the area in which C is living, and if different, for the area in which C is to be placed,

(j) the IRO, and

(k) where C is placed in a children's home, C's link worker.

(3) The responsible authority may decide not to give notification to any or all of the persons listed in paragraphs (2)(b) to (e), if to do so would place C at risk of harm.

15 Termination of placement by the responsible authority

(1) Subject to paragraphs (3) and (5), the responsible authority may only terminate C's placement following a review of C's case in accordance with Part 6.

(2) Subject to paragraphs (3) and (4), before terminating C's placement, the responsible authority must –

(a) make other arrangements for C's accommodation, in accordance with section 81 of the 2014 Act,

(b) inform the IRO,

(c) so far as is reasonably practicable, give written notification of its intention to terminate the placement to –

(i) all the persons to whom notification of the placement was given under regulation 14,

(ii) the person with whom C is placed,

(iii) where C is placed in the area of another local authority or local authority in England, that authority.

(3) Where there is an immediate risk of harm to C, or to protect others from serious injury the responsible authority must terminate C's placement, and in those circumstances –

(a) paragraph (1) does not apply, and

(b) the responsible authority must comply with paragraph (2)(a) and (b) as soon as reasonably practicable.

(4) If it is not reasonably practicable to notify any person in accordance with paragraph (2)(c), then the responsible authority must give written notification to that

person, within 5 working days of the date on which the placement is terminated, of the fact that the placement has been terminated.

(5) This regulation does not apply where C's placement is terminated –

    (a)   under regulation 20(c)(ii) (circumstances in which a child may be placed with P before assessment completed),

    (b)   under regulation 24(2) (termination of an emergency placement),

    (c)   under regulation 27(6), or

    (d)   where section 82 of the 2014 Act (review of child's case before making alternative arrangements for accommodation) applies.

PART 4
PROVISION FOR DIFFERENT TYPES OF PLACEMENT

Chapter 1
Placement of a child in care with P

16 Application

(1) This Chapter applies if C is in the care of the responsible authority and the responsible authority, acting in accordance with section 81(2) of the 2014 Act, proposes to place C with P.

(2) Nothing in this Chapter requires the responsible authority to remove C from P's care if C is living with P before a placement decision is made about C.

17 Effect of contact order

The responsible authority must not place C with P if to do so would be incompatible with any order made by the court under section 34 of the 1989 Act (parental contact etc with children in care).

18 Assessment of P's suitability to care for a child

Before deciding to place C with P, the responsible authority must –

    (a)   assess the suitability of P to care for C, including the suitability of –
        (i)   the proposed accommodation, and
        (ii)   all other persons aged 18 and over who are members of the household in which it is proposed that C will live,

    (b)   take into account all the matters specified in Schedule 4 in making its assessment,

    (c)   consider whether, in all the circumstances and taking into account the services to be provided by the responsible authority, the placement will safeguard and promote C's well-being and meet C's needs set out in the care and support plan, and

    (d)   review C's case in accordance with Part 6.

19 Decision to place a child with P

(1) The decision to place C with P must not be put into effect until it has been approved by the nominated officer, and the responsible authority has prepared a placement plan for C.

(2) Before approving a decision under paragraph (1), the nominated officer must be satisfied that –

(a) the requirements of regulation 10(1)(b)(i) have been complied with,

(b) the requirements of regulation 18 have been complied with,

(c) the placement will safeguard and promote C's well-being,

(d) the IRO has been consulted, and

(e) the views, wishes and feelings of any other person, whom the responsible authority considers to be relevant, have been considered.

20 Circumstances in which a child may be placed with P before assessment completed

Where the nominated officer considers it to be necessary and consistent with C's well-being, the responsible authority may place C with P before its assessment under regulation 18 ('the assessment') is completed, provided that it –

(a) arranges for P to be interviewed in order to obtain as much of the information specified in Schedule 4 about P and the other persons living in P's household who are aged over 18 years as can be readily ascertained at that interview,

(b) ensures that the assessment and review of C's case are completed in accordance with the requirements in regulation 18 within 10 working days of C being placed with P, and

(c) ensures that a decision in accordance with regulation 19 is made and approved within 10 working days after the assessment is completed, and –

    (i) if the decision is to confirm the placement, review the placement plan and, if appropriate amend it, and

    (ii) if the decision is not to confirm the placement, terminate the placement.

21 Support for P

Where C is placed, or is to be placed, with P, the responsible authority must provide such services and support to P as appear to the responsible authority to be necessary to safeguard and promote C's well-being and it must record details of such services and support in C's care and support plan.

Chapter 2
Placement with local authority foster parents

22 Interpretation

(1) In this Chapter –

    'approved' ('*cymeradwy*') means a person has been approved as a local authority foster parent either –

        (a) in accordance with the Fostering Regulations; or

        (b) in accordance with the Fostering Services (England) Regulations 2011; or

        (c) in the case of a placement of C with a particular prospective adopter ('A'), in accordance with regulation 28; or

        (d) in a case of a placement of C with a connected person on a temporary basis, in accordance with regulation 26; and

    'registered person' ('*person cofrestredig*') has the same meaning as in the Fostering Regulations.

(2) Where C is placed jointly with two persons each of whom is approved as a local authority foster parent, any reference in these Regulations to a local authority foster parent is to be interpreted as referring equally to both such persons and any requirement to be satisfied by or relating to a particular local authority foster parent must be satisfied by, or treated as relating to, both of them.

23 Conditions to be complied with before placing a child with a local authority foster parent

(1) This regulation applies where the responsible authority proposes to place C with F.

(2) The responsible authority may only place C with F if –

    (a) F is approved by –
        (i) the responsible authority, or
        (ii) provided that the conditions specified in paragraph (3) are also satisfied, another fostering service provider,

    (b) the terms of F's approval are consistent with the proposed placement, and

    (c) F has entered into a foster care agreement either with the responsible authority or with another fostering service provider in accordance with regulation 28(5)(b) of the Fostering Regulations or in accordance with regulation 27(5)(b) of the Fostering Services (England) Regulations 2011.

(3) The conditions referred to in paragraph (2)(a)(ii) are that –

    (a) the fostering service provider by whom F is approved consents to the placement, and

    (b) where any other local authority or local authority in England currently have a child placed with F, that authority consents to the proposed placement.

24 Emergency placement with a local authority foster parent

(1) Where it is necessary to place C in an emergency, the responsible authority may place C with any local authority foster parent who has been approved in accordance with the Fostering Regulations or the Fostering Services (England) Regulations 2011, even if the terms of that person's approval are not consistent with the placement, provided that the placement is for no longer than 6 working days.

(2) When the period of 6 working days referred to in paragraph (1) expires, the responsible authority must terminate the placement unless the terms of that person's approval have been amended to be consistent with the placement.

25 Placement following consideration in accordance with section 81(11) of the 2014 Act

(1) This regulation applies where the responsible authority decides to place C with a particular prospective adopter ('A') in accordance with section 81(11) of the 2014 Act.

(2) The decision to place C must not be put into effect until it has been approved by the nominated officer and the responsible authority has prepared a placement plan for C.

(3) Before approving a decision under paragraph (2) the nominated officer must –

    (a) be satisfied that the placement is the most appropriate placement available for C and it is in C's best interests to be placed with A,

    (b) be satisfied that the requirements of regulation 10(1)(b) have been complied with, and

    (c) if their whereabouts are known to the responsible authority, notify the parent or guardian of C of the proposed placement.

26 Temporary approval of a relative, friend or other person connected with C

(1) Where the responsible authority is satisfied that –

(a)   the most appropriate placement for C is with a connected person, notwithstanding that the connected person is not approved as a local authority foster parent, and

(b)   it is necessary for C to be placed with the connected person before the connected person's suitability to be a local authority foster parent has been assessed in accordance with the Fostering Regulations or the Fostering Services (England) Regulations 2011, it may approve that person as a local authority foster parent for a temporary period not exceeding 16 weeks ('temporary approval') provided that it first complies with the requirements of paragraph (2).

(2)   Before making a placement under paragraph (1), the responsible authority must –

(a)   assess the suitability of the connected person to care for C, including the suitability of –

(i)   the proposed accommodation, and

(ii)   all other persons aged 18 and over who are members of the household in which it is proposed that C will live, taking account all the matters set out in Schedule 5,

(b)   provide such services to support the connected person as appear to the responsible authority to be necessary to safeguard and promote C's well-being and it must record details of such services and support in C's care and support plan,

(c)   consider whether, in all the circumstances and taking into account the services to be provided by the responsible authority, the proposed arrangements will safeguard and promote C's well-being and meet C's needs set out in the care and support plan,

(d)   unless sub-paragraph (e) applies, make immediate arrangements for the suitability of the connected person to be a local authority foster parent to be assessed in accordance with the Fostering Regulations ('the full assessment process') before the temporary approval expires,

(e)   where the connected person is or will be seeking to be assessed as suitable to be a local authority foster parent under the Fostering Services (England) Regulations 2011, the responsible authority may request the cooperation of the fostering service provider which is undertaking the assessment to complete the process before the temporary approval expires, and

(f)   make a written agreement with the connected person to the effect that the connected person agrees to –

(i)   care for C as if C were a member of the connected person's family,

(ii)   permit any person authorised by the responsible authority to visit C,

(iii)   permit the removal of C from the placement at any time,

(iv)   ensure that all information relating to C and to C's family is kept confidential, and

(v)   honour contact arrangements made in accordance with any order of the court or made by the responsible authority.

27 Expiry of temporary approval

(1)   Subject to paragraph (4), the responsible authority may extend the temporary approval of a connected person if –

(a)   it is likely to expire before the full assessment process is completed, or

(b)   the connected person, having undergone the full assessment process, is not approved and seeks a review of the decision in accordance with regulations made under section 87 of the 2014 Act or under paragraph 12F(1)(b) of Schedule 2 to the 1989 Act.

(2) In a case falling within paragraph (1)(a), the responsible authority may extend the period of temporary approval once for a further period of up to 8 weeks.

(3) In a case falling within paragraph (1)(b), the responsible authority may extend the period of temporary approval until the outcome of the review is known.

(4) Before deciding whether to extend the temporary approval in the circumstances set out in paragraph (1), the responsible authority must first –

    (a)   consider whether placement with the connected person is still the most appropriate placement available,

    (b)   seek the views of the fostering panel established by the fostering service provider in accordance with the Fostering Regulations or in accordance with the Fostering Services (England) Regulations 2011, and

    (c)   inform the IRO.

(5) A decision to extend temporary approval must be made by the nominated officer.

(6) If the period of temporary approval and of any extension to that period expires and the connected person has not been approved as a local authority foster parent in accordance with the Fostering Regulations or the Fostering Services (England) Regulations 2011, the responsible authority must terminate the placement after first making other arrangements for C's accommodation.

28 Temporary approval of a particular prospective adopter as a foster parent

(1) Where the responsible authority is satisfied that –

    (a)   the most appropriate placement for C is with a person who is not approved as a local authority foster parent, but that person is the prospective adopter with whom it proposes to place C for adoption ('A'), and

    (b)   it is in C's best interests to be placed with A, the responsible authority may approve A as a local authority foster parent for a temporary period ('temporary approval period') provided that the responsible authority first complies with the requirements of paragraph (2).

(2) Before approving A as local authority foster parent under paragraph (1), the responsible authority must –

    (a)   assess A's suitability to care for C as a foster parent, and

    (b)   consider whether, in all the circumstances and taking into account the services to be provided by the responsible authority, the proposed arrangements will safeguard and promote C's well-being and meet C's needs as set out in the care and support plan.

(3) The temporary approval period expires –

    (a)   on C's placement with A being terminated by the responsible authority;

    (b)   on A's approval as a prospective adopter being terminated;

    (c)   on A being approved as a foster parent in accordance with the Fostering Regulations or the Fostering Services (England) Regulations 2011;

    (d)   if A gives written notice to the responsible authority that they no longer wish to be temporarily approved as a foster parent in relation to C, with effect from 28 days from the date on which the notice is received by the responsible authority; or

    (e)   on C being placed for adoption with A in accordance with the Adoption and Children Act 2002.

29 Independent fostering agencies – discharge of authority functions

(1) A responsible authority may make arrangements in accordance with this regulation for the duties imposed on it by regulation 15(3) and regulation 23 to be discharged on its behalf by a registered person.

(2) No arrangements may be made under this regulation unless the responsible authority has entered into a written agreement with the registered person which includes the information set out in paragraph 1 of Schedule 6, and where the responsible authority proposes to make an arrangement under this regulation in relation to a particular child, the written agreement must also include the matters set out in paragraph 2 of Schedule 6.

(3) The responsible authority must report to the Chief Inspector of the Care and Social Services Inspectorate Wales any concerns it may have about the services provided by a registered person.

Chapter 3
Other arrangements

30 General duties of the responsible authority when placing a child in other arrangements

Before placing C in accommodation in an unregulated setting under section 81(6)(d) ('other arrangements') of the 2014 Act, the responsible authority must –

  (a) be satisfied that the accommodation is suitable for C having regard to the matters set out in Schedule 7,
  (b) unless it is not reasonably practicable, arrange for C to visit the accommodation, and
  (c) inform the IRO.

PART 5
VISITS BY THE RESPONSIBLE AUTHORITY'S REPRESENTATIVE ETC

31 Frequency of visits

(1) As part of its arrangements for supervising C's well-being, the responsible authority must ensure that its representative ('R') visits C in accordance with this regulation, wherever C is living.

(2) Subject to paragraphs (3) to (6), the responsible authority must ensure that R visits C –

  (a) within one week of the start of any placement,
  (b) at intervals of not more than 6 weeks for the first year of any placement, and
  (c) thereafter –
    (i) where the placement is intended to last until C is 18, at intervals of not more than 3 months, and
    (ii) in any other case, at intervals of not more than 6 weeks.

(3) Where regulation 20 applies, the responsible authority must ensure that R visits C –

  (a) at least once a week until the first review carried out in accordance with Part 6, and
  (b) thereafter at intervals of not more than 6 weeks.

(4) Where regulation 26 applies, or where an interim care order has been made in relation to C under section 38 of the 1989 Act (interim orders) and C is living with P, the responsible authority must ensure that R visits C –

(a) at least once a week until the first review carried out in accordance with Part 6, and

(b) thereafter at intervals of not more than 4 weeks.

(5) Where a care order has been made in relation to C under section 31 of the 1989 Act (care and supervision orders) and C is living with P, the responsible authority must ensure that R visits C –

(a) within one week of the making of the care order, and

(b) thereafter at intervals of not more than 6 weeks.

(6) Where C is in the care of the responsible authority but another person is responsible for the arrangements under which C is living for the time being ('C's living arrangements'), the responsible authority must ensure that R visits C –

(a) within one week of the start of C's living arrangements and within one week of any change to C's living arrangements,

(b) at intervals of not more than 6 weeks for the first year thereafter, and

(c) at intervals of not more than 3 months in any subsequent year.

(7) In addition to visits in accordance with paragraphs (2) to (6), the responsible authority must ensure that R visits C –

(a) whenever reasonably requested to do so by –
     (i)   C,
     (ii) where paragraphs (2), (3) or (4) apply, the appropriate person, or
     (iii) where paragraph (5) applies, the person responsible for C's living arrangements,

(b) within one week of first receiving notification under section 30A of the Care Standards Act 2000 (notification of matters relating to persons carrying on or managing certain establishments or agencies), where the children's home in which C is placed for the time being is referred to in the notification.

32 Conduct of visits

(1) On each visit, R must speak to C in private unless –

(a) C, being of sufficient understanding to do so, refuses,

(b) R considers it inappropriate to do so, having regard to C's age and understanding, or

(c) R is unable to do so.

(2) When visiting C in accordance with this Part, R must –

(a) ensure that C's views, wishes and feelings are ascertained and given due consideration,

(b) consider whether C's well-being is being adequately safeguarded and promoted within the placement,

(c) monitor the achievement of actions and outcomes identified in the care and support plan and contribute (if required) to the review of the care and support plan,

(d) monitor any contact arrangements in place and, where necessary, consider whether support, or additional support, is required to promote contact arrangements,

(e) identify whether additional support or services are required to support the placement.

33 Consequences of visits

Where as a result of a visit carried out in accordance with this Part, R's assessment is that C's well-being is not adequately safeguarded and promoted by the placement, the responsible authority must review C's case in accordance with Part 6.

34 Advice and other support for the child

When making arrangements in accordance with section 97(3)(b) of the 2014 Act for advice and other support to be available to C between R's visits, the responsible authority must ensure that –

(a) the arrangements –
  (i) are appropriate having regard to C's age and understanding, and
  (ii) give due consideration to C's religious persuasion, racial origin, sexual orientation, cultural and linguistic background, and to any disability C may have,
(b) C's views, wishes and feelings about the arrangements are ascertained and taken into consideration, and
(c) as far as is reasonably practicable having regard to C's age and understanding, C knows how to seek appropriate advice and other support from it.

35 Records of visits undertaken by R

R must ensure that a written record is made of any visit undertaken in accordance with this Part which must include –

(a) R's written assessment, having regard to C's views, wishes and feelings, as to whether C's well-being is being adequately safeguarded and promoted whilst in the placement,
(b) details of advice or support R considers are required by C.

36 Appointment of an independent visitor

(1) As part of its arrangements for supervising C's well-being, the responsible authority must consider whether it is appropriate to appoint an independent visitor to visit C wherever C is living in any case where –

(a) C has not lived with a parent or a person with parental responsibility during the previous 12 months,
(b) contact between C and a parent or a person with parental responsibility has not occurred or has been infrequent, or
(c) it would be in C's best interests to do so.

(2) When making a decision under paragraph (1), the responsible authority must consider –

(a) whether the appointment of an independent visitor would make a positive contribution to C's well-being;
(b) where C is placed at a distance from home, or where C is placed in the area of another local authority or a local authority in England, whether the placement makes it difficult to maintain contact arrangements;
(c) whether C is able to go out independently or whether C experiences difficulties in communicating or with building positive relationships;
(d) whether C is likely to engage in behaviour which may put C at risk of forming inappropriate relationships;

(e)   where C is placed in a children's home, whether C's well-being would be promoted by the opportunity to establish a relationship with an independent visitor.

37 Where the responsible authority determines in accordance with regulation 36 that it is appropriate to appoint an independent visitor for C, it must explain to C (according to C's age and understanding) the role of an independent visitor.

PART 6
REVIEWS OF THE CHILD'S CASE

38 General duty of the responsible authority to review the child's case

(1) The responsible authority must review C's case in accordance with this Part.

(2) The responsible authority must not make any significant change to C's care and support plan unless the proposed change has first been considered at a review of C's case, unless this is not reasonably practicable.

(3) Nothing in this Part prevents any review of C's case being carried out at the same time as any other review, assessment or consideration of C's case under any other provision.

39 Timing of reviews

(1) The responsible authority must first review C's case within 20 working days of the date on which C becomes looked after.

(2) The second review must be carried after an interval of not more than three months after the first, and subsequent reviews must be carried out at intervals of no more than 6 months.

(3) Nothing in this regulation prevents the responsible authority from carrying out a review before the time specified in paragraph (1) or (2) and it must do so if –

(a)   the responsible authority considers that C is, or has been, persistently absent from a placement,

(b)   the responsible authority is notified by the appropriate person, P or the area authority is concerned that C is at risk of harm,

(c)   subject to paragraph (4), if C so requests,

(d)   the IRO so requests,

(e)   regulation 33 applies,

(f)   where C is provided with accommodation under section 77(2)(b) or (c) of the 2014 Act and a review would not otherwise occur before C ceases to be so provided with accommodation,

(g)   where C is in the care of the authority and is detained and a review would not otherwise occur before C ceases to be so detained, or

(h)   where C is looked after but is not in the care of the responsible authority and –

(i)   the responsible authority proposes to cease to provide accommodation for C, and

(ii)   accommodation will not subsequently be provided for C by C's parents (or one of them) or any person who is not C's parent but who has parental responsibility for C,

(i)   C is part of a family whose case has been referred to an IFS team and the family has been notified their case will be supported by such a team.

(4) The responsible authority is not required to carry out a review pursuant to paragraph (3)(c) if the IRO considers that a review before the time specified in paragraph (1) or (2) is not justified.

Conduct of reviews

40 Responsible authority policy on reviews

(1) The responsible authority must prepare and implement a written policy regarding the manner in which it will review cases in accordance with this Part.

(2) The responsible authority must provide a copy of its policy to –

(a) C, unless it would not be appropriate to do so having regard to C's age and understanding,

(b) C's parents, or any person who is not C's parent but who has parental responsibility for C, and

(c) any other person whose views the responsible authority considers to be relevant.

41 Considerations to which the responsible authority must have regard

(1) The considerations to which the responsible authority must have regard in reviewing every case are set out in paragraphs 1 to 17 of Schedule 8.

(2) The additional considerations to which the responsible authority must have regard in reviewing C's case where C is part of a family which is being supported by an IFS team are set out in paragraphs 18 to 26 of Schedule 8.

(3) In paragraph (2) and in Schedule 8 –

'family' ('*teulu*') has the meaning given in regulation 18(3) of the Partnership Regulations.

Amendments—SI 2017/713.

42 Role of the IRO

(1) The IRO must –

(a) as far as reasonably practicable, attend any meeting held as part of the review ('the review meeting') and, if attending the review meeting, chair it,

(b) speak to C in private about the matters to be considered at the review unless C, being of sufficient understanding to do so, refuses or the IRO considers it inappropriate having regard to C's age and understanding,

(c) ensure that, so far as reasonably practicable, the views, wishes and feelings of C's parents, or any person who is not C's parent but who has parental responsibility for C, have been ascertained and taken into account, and

(d) ensure the review is conducted in accordance with this Part and in particular –

(i) that the persons responsible for implementing any decision taken in consequence of the review are identified, and

(ii) that any failure to review the case in accordance with this Part or to take proper steps to implement decisions taken in consequence of the review are brought to the attention of an officer at an appropriate level of seniority within the responsible authority.

(2) The IRO may, if not satisfied that sufficient information has been provided by the responsible authority to enable proper consideration of any of the matters in Schedule 8,

PART VII

adjourn the review meeting once for not more than 20 working days, and no proposal considered in the course of the review may be implemented until the review has been completed.

43 Arrangements for implementing decisions arising out of reviews

The responsible authority must –

(a) make arrangements to implement decisions made in the course, or as a result, of the review, and

(b) inform the IRO of any significant failure to make such arrangements or any significant change of circumstances occurring after the review that affects those arrangements.

44 Records of reviews

The responsible authority must ensure that a written record of the review is prepared, and that the information obtained in the course of the review, details of proceedings at the review meeting, and any decisions made in the course of or as a result of the review are included in C's case record.

PART 7
ARRANGEMENTS MADE BY THE LOCAL AUTHORITY FOR CEASING TO LOOK AFTER A CHILD

45 Decision to cease looking after C

(1) In any case where C is aged 16 or 17 and is not in the care of the responsible authority, the decision to cease looking after C must not be put into effect until it has been approved by the responsible authority's director of social services.

(2) Before approving a decision under paragraph (1), the director of social services must be satisfied –

(a) regulation 10(1)(b)(i) has been complied with,
(b) C's IRO has been consulted,
(c) C's relatives have been consulted, where appropriate, and
(d) regulation 46, or regulations 47–51 (as appropriate) have been complied with.

46 Arrangements for ceasing to look after a child who is not a category 1 young person

In any case where C is not in the care of the responsible authority and is not likely to be a category 1 young person when the local authority cease to look after him or her, the care and support plan (or where regulation 58 applies, the detention placement plan) must include details of the advice and other support that the responsible authority intends to provide for C when C ceases to be looked after by it.

Category 1 young persons

47 Meaning of category 1 young person

(1) For the purposes of section 104(2) of the 2014 Act the prescribed period is 13 weeks and the prescribed age is 14.

(2) For the purposes of section 104(6)(b) of the 2014 Act, if C is a child to whom regulation 62 applies, C is not a category 1 young person despite falling within section 104(2) of that Act.

48 General duties

If C is a category 1 young person, the responsible authority must –

    (a)   assess C's needs in accordance with regulation 49, and
    (b)   prepare C's pathway plan in accordance with regulation 51.

49 Assessment of needs

(1) The responsible authority must complete the assessment of C's needs in accordance with section 107(1) of the 2014 Act not more than 3 months after the date on which C reaches the age of 16 or becomes a category 1 young person after that age.

(2) In carrying out its assessment of C's likely needs when C ceases to be looked after, the responsible authority must take account of the following considerations –

    (a)   C's state of health (including physical, emotional and mental health) and development;
    (b)   C's continuing need for education, training or employment;
    (c)   where C falls within regulation 5(1)(f), any needs C has as a result of that status;
    (d)   the support that will be available to C from C's parents and other connected persons;
    (e)   where C is a category 1 young person who has been placed with a local authority foster parent –
        (i)   whether C and F have decided that they wish to make a post-18 living arrangement, or
        (ii)   what information the responsible authority must provide C and F to assist them in making such a decision;
    (f)   C's actual and anticipated financial resources and capacity to manage personal finances independently;
    (g)   the extent to which C possesses the practical and other skills necessary for independent living;
    (h)   C's need for continuing care, support and accommodation;
    (i)   the views, wishes and feelings of –
        (i)   C,
        (ii)   any parent of C's and any person who is not C's parent but who has parental responsibility for C,
        (iii)   the appropriate person;
    (j)   the views of –
        (i)   any person or educational institution that provides C with education or training, and if C has a statement of special educational needs, the responsible authority that maintains the statement,
        (ii)   the IRO,
        (iii)   any person providing health (whether physical, mental or emotional health) or dental care or treatment to C,
        (iv)   the personal adviser appointed for C, and
        (v)   any other person whose views the responsible authority or C consider may be relevant.

PART VII

50 Pathway assessments and plans: post-18 living arrangements

(1) In order to discharge its duty under section 108(2) of the 2014 Act, a responsible authority must provide the information referred to in paragraph (2) about post-18 living arrangements to the following persons –

    (a)   C, where C is placed with F or in a children's home, when preparing or reviewing C's pathway plan;

    (b)   C, where C is a category 1 young person who has been placed with F, when preparing or reviewing C's pathway plan;

    (c)   any F with whom the responsible authority has placed C, when preparing or reviewing C's pathway plan;

    (d)   any former foster parent of C;

    (e)   a parent or other person who had parental responsibility for C before C was placed with F (unless to do so would place C at risk of harm);

    (f)   where C is placed in a children's home, C's link worker;

    (g)   the IRO;

    (h)   R;

    (i)   where one has been appointed for C, an independent visitor;

    (j)   a category 3 young person who is participating in a post-18 living arrangement;

    (k)   a former foster parent who is participating in a post-18 living arrangement;

    (l)   any other person whom the responsible authority considers requires such information.

(2) The information referred to in paragraph (1) –

    (a)   includes –

        (i)   details of the responsible authority's duties under section 108 of the 2014 Act,

        (ii)   a copy of the responsible authority's policy on post-18 living arrangements,

        (iii)   information about the financial implications attendant upon the making of a post-18 living arrangement as they apply to both C and to F,

        (iv)   information about the eligibility for and alternatives to a post-18 living arrangement that are available for C,

        (v)   details of other sources of information, advice and support available to help C and F make a decision about seeking to make a post-18 living arrangement,

        (vi)   information about the support available to category 3 young persons and their former foster parents who make a post-18 living arrangement during the course of such an arrangement,

        (vii)   updates on any changes to the responsible authority's policy or practice relating to the making and support afforded during a post-18 living arrangement, and

    (b)   must be provided in a format that is appropriate for the age and understanding of the recipient.

51 The pathway plan

(1) The pathway plan must be prepared as soon as possible after the assessment of C's needs and must include, in particular –

    (a)   C's care and support plan, and

    (b)   the information referred to in Schedule 9.

(2) The pathway plan must, in relation to each of the matters referred to in paragraphs 2 to 11 of Schedule 9, set out –

    (a)   the manner in which the responsible authority proposes to meet C's needs, and

(b) the date by which, and by whom, any action required to implement any aspect of the plan will be carried out.

52 Functions of the personal adviser

The personal adviser's functions in relation to C are to –

(a) provide advice (including practical advice) and support,
(b) participate in reviews of C's case carried out under Part 6,
(c) liaise with the responsible authority in the implementation of the pathway plan,
(d) co-ordinate the provision of services and take reasonable steps to ensure C makes use of such services,
(e) remain informed about C's progress and wellbeing, and
(f) maintain a written record of their contacts with C.

PART 8
INDEPENDENT REVIEWING OFFICERS AND INDEPENDENT ADVISERS

53 Additional functions of independent reviewing officers

(1) The IRO must ensure that, having regard to C's age and understanding, C has been informed by the responsible authority of the steps C may take under the 1989 Act and the 2014 Act and in particular, where appropriate –

(a) C's right to apply, with leave, for an order under section 8 of the 1989 Act (child arrangements orders and other orders with respect to children) and, where C is in the care of the responsible authority, to apply for the discharge of the care order, and
(b) the availability of the procedure established by it under section 174 of the 2014 Act for considering any representations (including complaints) C may wish to make about the discharge by the responsible authority of its functions, including the availability of assistance to make such representations under section 178 of the 2014 Act.

(2) If C wishes to take legal proceedings under the 1989 Act, the IRO must –

(a) establish whether an appropriate adult is able and willing to assist C to obtain legal advice or bring proceedings on C's behalf, and
(b) if there is no such person, assist C to obtain such advice.

(3) In the following circumstances the IRO must consider whether it would be appropriate to refer C's case to a Welsh family proceedings officer –

(a) in the opinion of the IRO, the responsible authority has failed in any significant respect –
  (i) to prepare C's care and support plan in accordance with these Regulations,
  (ii) to review C's case in accordance with these Regulations, or to implement effectively any decision taken in consequence of a review, or
  (iii) is otherwise in breach of its duties to C in any material respect, and
(b) having drawn the failure to the attention of persons at an appropriate level of seniority within the responsible authority, it has not been addressed to the satisfaction of the IRO within a reasonable period of time.

(4) When consulted by the responsible authority about any matter concerning C, or when informed of any matter relating to C in accordance with these Regulations, the IRO must –

PART VII

(a) ensure that the responsible authority has ascertained, and, subject to C's age and understanding, given due consideration to, C's views, wishes and feelings concerning the matter in question, and

(b) consider whether to request a review of C's case.

54 Qualifications and experience of independent reviewing officers

(1) The IRO must be registered as a social worker in a register maintained by Social Care Wales or in Part 16 of the register maintained by the Health and Care Professions Council under article 5 of the Health and Social Work Professions Order 2001 or in a corresponding register maintained under the law of Scotland or Northern Ireland.

(2) The IRO must have sufficient relevant social work experience with children and families to perform the functions of an independent reviewing officer set out in section 100 of the 2014 Act and under these Regulations in an independent manner and having regard to C's best interests.

(3) The responsible authority must not appoint any of the following as the IRO –

(a) a person involved in preparing C's care and support plan or the management of C's case,

(b) R,

(c) C's personal adviser,

(d) a person with management responsibilities in relation to a person mentioned in subparagraphs (a) to (c), or

(e) a person with control over the resources allocated to the case.

Amendments—SI 2017/52.

55 Independent visitors

A person appointed by the responsible authority as an independent visitor under section 98 of the 2014 Act is to be regarded as independent of that authority where the person appointed is not connected with the responsible authority by virtue of being –

(a) a member of the responsible authority or any of its committees or sub-committees, whether elected or co-opted,

(b) an officer of the responsible authority employed in the exercise of any of the following functions –

(i) the functions conferred on or exercisable by the responsible authority in its capacity as local education authority,

(ii) the functions conferred on or exercisable by the responsible authority which are social services functions (within the meaning of Schedule 2 to the 2014 Act so far as those functions relate to children),

(iii) the functions conferred on the responsible authority under sections 61 to 63 and 103 to 118 of the 2014 Act (so far as not falling within sub-paragraph (ii)),

(iv) the functions conferred on the responsible authority by sections 25, 26, 28 and 29 of the Children Act 2004,

(v) the functions conferred on the responsible authority in accordance with section 33 of the National Health Service (Wales) Act 2006 or section 75 of the National Health Service Act 2006, or

(c) a spouse, civil partner or other person (whether of different sex or the same sex) living in the same household as the partner of, a person falling within paragraphs (a) or (b).

PART 9
APPLICATION OF THESE REGULATIONS WITH MODIFICATIONS TO CHILDREN ON REMAND OR TO CHILDREN WHO ARE DETAINED

56 Application of these Regulations with modifications to children on remand and to children who are detained

(1) These Regulations apply with the modifications set out in this Part while C is –

    (a)   remanded to local authority accommodation,

    (b)   remanded to youth detention accommodation ('YDA'), or

    (c)   detained.

(2) In these Regulations –

    (a)   where C is remanded to local authority accommodation or to YDA, references to the 'responsible authority' are to be read as if they were references to the local authority designated by the court under section 92(2) or section 102(6), as the case may be, of the 2012 Act,

    (b)   where C is remanded to YDA or is detained, references to being 'placed' are to be read as if they were references to C being so remanded or detained,

    (c)   where C is remanded to YDA or is detained –

        (i)   references to the 'placement plan' are to be read as if they were references to the 'detention placement plan', and

        (ii)   where C is a looked after child only by reason of being so remanded, references to the 'care and support plan' are also to be read as references to the 'detention placement plan'.

57 Modifications to Part 2

(1) Part 2 (arrangements for looking after a child) applies with the following modifications.

(2) Where C is a looked after child only by reason of being remanded to local authority accommodation –

    (a)   in regulation 4(3), the care and support plan must be prepared within 5 working days of C being so remanded, and

    (b)   regulation 5(1)(a) does not apply.

(3) Where C is remanded to YDA and was a looked after child immediately before being so remanded, or where C is detained –

    (a)   regulation 5(1)(c) does not apply, and instead the care and support plan must include a detention placement plan,

    (b)   in regulation 6(3), the responsible authority must also give a copy of the care and support plan to the director, governor or registered manager (as the case may be) of the prison or YDA, and

    (c)   regulation 7(1) to (4) does not apply.

(4) Where C is a looked after child only by reason of being remanded to YDA –

    (a)   regulation 5 does not apply, and instead the responsible authority must prepare a detention placement plan, which also includes details of the views, wishes and feelings of the persons that are ascertained and considered by the responsible authority in accordance with sections 6(2) and (4), 7(2) and 78(3) of the 2014 Act about the detention placement plan, and the views, wishes and feelings of those persons in relation to any change, or proposed change, to the detention placement plan,

PART VII

(b) regulation 7(1) to (4) does not apply, and regulation 7(5) applies with the modification that for 'health plan' there is substituted 'detention placement plan'.

Amendments—SI 2017/713.

58 Modifications to Part 3

(1) Part 3 applies with the following modifications.

(2) Where C a looked after child only by reason of being remanded to YDA, regulations 10, 11, 12 and 15 do not apply, and instead –

(a) the responsible authority must prepare a plan for the remand ('the detention placement plan') within 10 working days of C's remand to YDA which –
   (i)   sets out how the prison, YDA or premises in which C is required to reside will meet C's needs, and
   (ii) includes the name and address of the YDA and the matters specified in Schedule 10.

(3) Where C is remanded to YDA and was a looked after child immediately before being so remanded or, where C is detained –

(a) regulations 10, 11, 12 and 15 do not apply, and instead the responsible authority must prepare a detention placement plan in accordance with sub-paragraph (b);
(b) the responsible authority must prepare a detention placement plan for the remand or detention (which will be included within C's care and support plan) within 10 working days of C's remand to YDA or detention, which –
   (i)   sets out how the prison, YDA or premises in which C is required to reside will meet C's needs, and
   (ii) includes, as appropriate, the name and address of the prison, YDA, or premises in which C is required to reside and the matters specified in Schedule 10;
(c) the IRO must be informed of the remand or detention.

(4) Where C falls within paragraph (2) or (3) –

(a) the responsible authority must ensure that C's views, wishes and feelings have been ascertained and given due consideration;
(b) the detention placement plan must be agreed with and signed by the director, governor, or registered manager (as the case may be) of the prison or YDA. or the premises in which C is required to reside.

(5) Where C is remanded to local authority accommodation, regulation 10(1) applies with the modification that the placement plan must be prepared within 5 working days of C being so remanded.

59 Disapplication of Part 4

Part 4 (provision for different types of placement) does not apply where C is remanded to YDA or where C is detained.

60 Modification of Part 5

Part 5 (visits by the responsible authority's representative etc) applies with the modification that in regulation 31(7)(a), the responsible authority must ensure that R visits C, where C is remanded to YDA or C is detained, whenever reasonably requested to do so by the director, governor or registered manager (as the case may be) of the prison, YDA or the premises in which C is required to reside.

61 Modification of Part 6

Part 6 (reviews) applies with the modification that in regulation 41, the considerations to which the responsible authority must have regard in reviewing C's case where C is remanded to YDA or where C is detained are set out in paragraphs 1, 4, and 6 to 13 of Schedule 8 (considerations to which the responsible authority must have regard when reviewing C's case).

PART 10
MISCELLANEOUS

62 Application of these Regulations with modifications to short breaks

(1) In the circumstances set out in paragraph (2), these Regulations apply with the modifications set out in paragraph (3).

(2) The circumstances are that –

(a) C is not in the care of the responsible authority,

(b) the responsible authority has arranged to place C in a series of short-term placements with the same person or in the same accommodation ('short breaks'), and

(c) the arrangement is such that –

(i) no single placement is intended to last for more than 4 weeks,

(ii) at the end of each such placement C returns to the care of C's parent or a person who is not C's parent but who has parental responsibility for C, and

(iii) the short breaks do not exceed 120 days in total in any period of 12 months.

(3) The modifications are that –

(a) regulations 5 and 10 do not apply, but instead the care and support plan must set out the arrangements that have been made to meet C's needs, with particular regard to –

(i) C's health and emotional and behavioural development, in particular in relation to any disability C may have,

(ii) promoting contact between C and C's parents and any other person who is not C's parent but who has parental responsibility for C, during any period when C is placed,

(iii) C's leisure interests, and

(iv) promoting C's educational achievement, and must include the name and address of C's registered medical practitioner, and the information set out in paragraph 3 of Schedule 3, where appropriate,

(b) regulations 7, 14 and 63(2)(b) do not apply,

(c) regulation 31(2) does not apply, but instead the responsible authority must ensure that R visits C on days when C is in fact placed, at regular intervals to be agreed with the IRO and C's parents (or any person who is not C's parent but who has parental responsibility for C) and recorded in the care and support plan before the start of the first placement and in any event –

(i) the first visit must take place within the first 7 placement days of the start of the first placement, or as soon as practicable thereafter, and

(ii) subsequent visits at intervals of not more than 6 months, for as long as the short breaks continue,

(d) regulation 39 does not apply, but instead –

(i) the responsible authority must first review C's case within 3 months of the start of the first placement, and

(ii)   the second and subsequent reviews must be carried out at intervals of not
more than 6 months.

63   Records – establishment of records

(1) The responsible authority must establish and maintain a written case record for C
('C's case record'), if one is not already in existence.

(2) The case record must include –

(a)   C's care and support plan, including any changes made to the care and support
plan and any subsequent plans,
(b)   reports obtained under regulation 7,
(c)   any other document created or considered as part of any assessment of C's
needs, or of any review of C's case,
(d)   any court order relating to C,
(e)   details of any arrangements that have been made by the responsible authority
with any other local authority or with an independent fostering agency under
regulation 29 and Schedule 6, or with a provider of social work services, under
which any of the responsible authority's functions in relation to C are
discharged by that local authority or independent fostering agency or provider
of social work services.

64   Records – retention and confidentiality

(1) The responsible authority must retain C's case record either –

(a)   until the seventy-fifth anniversary of C's birth, or
(b)   if C dies before attaining the age of 18, for fifteen years beginning with the date
of C's death.

(2) The responsible authority must secure the safe keeping of C's case record and take
any necessary steps to ensure that information contained in it is treated as confidential
subject only to –

(a)   any provision of, or made under or by virtue of, a statute under which access to
such a record or information may be obtained or given,
(b)   any court order under which access to such a record or information may be
obtained or given.

65   Revocations

The Regulations set out in Schedule 11 to these Regulations are revoked to the extent
specified in that Schedule.

SCHEDULE 1

PROVISIONS CONFERRING POWER ON THE WELSH MINISTERS WHICH
ARE EXERCISED IN THE MAKING OF THESE REGULATIONS

Enactment conferring power

The 2014 Act	Sections 81(6)(d), 83(5) 84, 87, 97(4)(a), 97(5), 98(1)(a), 100(1)(b), 100(2)(a), 102(1), 102(2), 104(2)(c), 104(6), 106(4), 107(7)(c), 107(8), 107(9), 108(6), and 196(2)
The Children Act 1989	Sections 31A and 34(8).

SCHEDULE 2

CARE AND SUPPORT PLANS

1 Information to be included in the health plan

(1) C's state of health including C's physical, oral, emotional and mental health.

(2) C's health history including, as far as practicable, C's family's health history.

(3) The effect of C's health and health history on C's development.

(4) Existing arrangements for C's medical and dental care, appropriate to C's needs, including –

    (a)   routine checks of C's general state of health, including dental health;

    (b)   treatment and monitoring for identified health (including physical, emotional and in particular mental health) or dental care needs;

    (c)   preventive measures such as vaccination and immunisation;

    (d)   screening for defects of vision or hearing; and

    (e)   advice and guidance on promoting health and effective personal care (including mental health and oral care).

(5) Any planned changes to existing arrangements.

(6) The role of the appropriate person, and of any other person who cares for C, in promoting C's health.

2 Information to be included in the personal education plan

(1) C's educational and training history including information about educational institutions attended and C's attendance and conduct record, C's academic and other achievements; and C's special educational needs, if any.

(2) Existing arrangements for C's education and training including details of any special educational provision and any other provision made to meet C's particular educational or training needs and to promote C's educational achievement.

(3) C's leisure interests.

(4) Where any change to the arrangements for C's education or training is necessary, provision made to minimise disruption to that education or training.

(5) The role of the appropriate person and of any other person who cares for C in promoting C's educational achievements and leisure interests.

3 Family and social relationships

(1) If C has a sibling for whom the responsible authority or another authority is providing accommodation, and the children have not been placed together, the arrangements made to promote contact between them, so far as is consistent with C's wellbeing.

(2) If C is looked after by, but is not in the care of, the responsible authority, details of any order relating to C made under section 8 of the 1989 Act.

(3) If C is a child in the care of the responsible authority, details of any order relating to C made under section 34 of the 1989 Act (parental contact etc with children in care).

(4) Any other arrangements made to promote and maintain contact in accordance with section 95 of the 2014 Act, so far as is reasonably practicable and consistent with C's well-being, between C and –

PART VII

    (a) any parent of C's and any person who is not C's parent but who has parental responsibility for C; and

    (b) any other connected person.

(5) Where section 98(1) of the 2014 Act (independent visitors for looked after children) applies, the arrangements made to appoint an independent visitor for C or, if section 98(6) of that Act applies (appointment of independent visitor not made where child objects), that fact.

SCHEDULE 3
MATTERS TO BE DEALT WITH IN THE PLACEMENT PLAN

1 Information to be included in C's placement plan

(1) How on a day to day basis C will be cared for and C's well-being will be safeguarded and promoted by the appropriate person.

(2) Any arrangements made for contact between C and any parent of C's and any person who is not C's parent but who has parental responsibility for C, and between C and other connected persons including, if appropriate –

    (a) the reasons why contact with any such person would not be reasonably practicable or would not be consistent with C's well-being,

    (b) if C is not in the care of the responsible authority, details of any order made under section 8 of the 1989 Act,

    (c) if C is in the care of the responsible authority, details of any order relating to C made under section 34 of the 1989 Act,

    (d) the arrangements made for notifying any changes in the arrangements for contact.

(3) The arrangements made for C's health (including physical, emotional and mental health) and dental care including –

    (a) the name and address of C's general practitioner and registered dental practitioner and, where applicable, any general practitioner or registered dental practitioner with whom C is to be registered following the placement,

    (b) any arrangements for the giving or withholding of consent to medical or dental examination or treatment for C.

(4) The arrangements made for C's education and training including –

    (a) the name and address of any school at which C is a registered pupil,

    (b) the name of the designated person for looked after pupils at that school (if applicable), the name and address of any other education institution that C attends, or of any other person who provides C with education or training,

    (c) where C has a statement of special educational needs, details of the local education authority that maintains the statement.

(5) The arrangements made for R to visit C in accordance with Part 5, the frequency of visits and the arrangements made for advice and other support to be available to C between visits in accordance with regulation 34.

(6) If an independent visitor is appointed, the arrangements made for that person to visit C.

(7) The circumstances in which the placement may be terminated and C removed from the appropriate person's care in accordance with regulation 15.

(8) The name and contact details of –

    (a) the IRO;

(b) C's independent visitor (if one is appointed);

(c) R; and

(d) if C is a category 1 young person, the personal adviser appointed for C.

2 Additional information to be included where C is placed with P

(1) A record of –

(a) the assessment of P's suitability to care for C, including consideration of the matters set out in Schedule 4,

(b) C's views, wishes and feelings and those of any other person whose views are sought by the responsible authority,

(c) the decision of the responsible authority to place C with P.

(2) Details of support and services to be provided to P during the placement.

(3) The obligation on P to notify the responsible authority of any relevant change in circumstances, including any intention to change address, any changes in the household in which C lives, and any serious incident involving C.

(4) The obligation on P to ensure that any information relating to C or C's family or any other person given in confidence to P in connection with the placement is kept confidential, and that such information is not disclosed to any person without the consent of the responsible authority.

(5) The circumstances in which it is necessary to obtain prior approval of the responsible authority for C to live in a household other than P's household.

(6) The arrangements for requesting a change to the placement plan.

(7) The circumstances in which the placement will be terminated in accordance with regulation 20(c)(ii).

3 Additional information to be included where C is placed with F, in a children's home or in other arrangements

(1) A record of the responsible authority's determination under regulation 23(2).

(2) The type of accommodation to be provided, the address and, where C is placed in other arrangements under section 81(6)(d) of the 2014 Act, the name of the person who will be responsible for C at that accommodation on behalf of the responsible authority (if any).

(3) Where –

(a) the responsible authority has, or is notified of, child protection concerns relating to C, or

(b) C has gone missing from the placement or from any previous placement, the day to day arrangements put in place by the appropriate person to keep C safe.

(4) C's personal history, religious persuasion, cultural and linguistic background, sexual orientation, and racial origin.

(5) Where C is looked after but is not in the care of the responsible authority –

(a) the expected duration of the arrangements and the steps which should be taken to bring the arrangements to an end, including arrangements for C to return to live with C's parents, or any person who is not C's parent but who has parental responsibility for C; and

(b) where C is aged 16 or over and agrees to being provided with accommodation under section 76 of the 2014 Act, that fact.

(6) The respective responsibilities of the responsible authority, C's parents, and any person who is not C's parent but who has parental responsibility for C.

(7) Any delegation of authority to make decisions about C's care and upbringing by the persons mentioned in sub-paragraph (6) (as appropriate) to –

    (a)   the responsible authority,

    (b)   F, and

    (c)   where C is placed in a children's home, the appropriate person,

in relation to the matters set out in sub-paragraph (8), and identifying any matters about which the persons mentioned in sub-paragraph (6) consider that C may make a decision.

(8) The matters referred to in sub-paragraph (7) are –

    (a)   medical and dental treatment,

    (b)   education,

    (c)   leisure and home life,

    (d)   faith and religious observance,

    (e)   use of social media,

    (f)   any other matters which the persons mentioned in sub-paragraph (6) consider appropriate.

(9) The responsible authority's arrangements for the financial support of C during the placement.

(10) Where C is placed with F, the obligation on F to comply with the terms of the foster care agreement made under regulation 28(5)(b) of the Fostering Regulations or regulation 27(5)(b) of the Fostering Services (England) Regulations 2011.

SCHEDULE 4

MATTERS TO BE TAKEN INTO ACCOUNT WHEN ASSESSING THE SUITABILITY OF P TO CARE FOR C

1 In respect of P –

    (a)   P's capacity to care for children and in particular in relation to C to –

        (i)   provide for C's physical needs and appropriate medical and dental care,

        (ii)   protect C adequately from harm or danger, including from any person who presents a risk of harm to C,

        (iii)   ensure that the home environment is safe for C,

        (iv)   ensure that C's emotional needs are met and C is provided with a positive sense of self, including any particular needs arising from C's religious persuasion, racial origin, sexual orientation, cultural and linguistic background, and any disability C may have,

        (v)   promote C's learning and intellectual development through encouragement, cognitive stimulation and the promotion of educational success and social opportunities,

        (vi)   enable C to regulate C's emotions and behaviour, including by modelling appropriate behaviour and interactions with others, and

        (vii)   provide a stable family environment to enable C to develop and maintain secure attachments to P and other persons who provide care for C;

    (b)   P's state of health including –

        (i)   P's physical health,

        (ii)   P's emotional health,

        (iii)   P's mental health,

        (iv)   P's medical history,

        (v)   any current or past issues of domestic violence,

        (vi)   any current or past issues regarding substance misuse, and the relevance or otherwise of any of these factors upon P's capacity to care for children and in particular C;

    (c)   P's family relationships and composition of P's household, including particulars of –

        (i)   the identity of all other members of the household, including their age and the nature of their relationship with P and with each other, including any sexual relationship,

        (ii)   any relationship with any person who is a parent of C (whether or not resident in the same household as P),

        (iii)   other adults not being members of the household who are likely to have regular contact with C, and

        (iv)   any current or previous domestic violence between members of the household, including P;

    (d)   P's family history, including –

        (i)   particulars of P's childhood and upbringing including the strengths and difficulties of P's parents or other persons who cared for P,

        (ii)   P's relationships with P's parents and siblings, and their relationships with each other,

        (iii)   P's educational achievement and of any specific learning difficulty or disability,

        (iv)   a chronology of significant life events, and

        (v)   particulars of other relatives and their relationships with C and P;

    (e)   particulars of any criminal offences of which P has been convicted or in respect of which P has been cautioned;

    (f)   P's past and present employment and other sources of income; and

    (g)   the nature of the neighbourhood in which P's home is situated and resources available in the community to support C and P.

2 In respect of members of the household aged 18 and over, so far as is practicable, all the particulars specified in paragraph 1 except sub-paragraphs (d), (f) and (g).

SCHEDULE 5
MATTERS TO BE TAKEN INTO ACCOUNT WHEN ASSESSING THE SUITABILITY OF A CONNECTED PERSON TO CARE FOR C

1 In respect of the connected person –

    (a)   the nature and quality of any existing relationship with C;

    (b)   their capacity to care for children and in particular in relation to C to –

        (i)   provide for C's physical and emotional needs and ensure that C will have appropriate medical and dental care,

        (ii)   protect C adequately from harm or danger including from any person who presents a risk of harm to C,

        (iii)   ensure that the accommodation and home environment is suitable with regard to the age and developmental stage of C,

        (iv)   promote C's learning and development, and

        (v)   provide a stable family environment which will promote secure attachments for C, including the promotion of positive contact with P and other connected persons, unless to do so is not consistent with the duty to safeguard and promote C's well-being;

    (c)   their state of health, including current state of physical, emotional and mental health and medical history including any current or past issues of domestic violence, substance misuse or mental health problems;

PART VII

(d)   their family relationships and the composition of their household, including particulars of –

   (i)   the identity of all other members of the household, including their age and the nature of their relationship with the connected person and with each other, including any sexual relationship,

   (ii)   any relationship with any person who is a parent of C,

   (iii)   any relationship between C and other members of the household,

   (iv)   other adults not being members of the household who are likely to have regular contact with C, and

   (v)   any current or previous domestic violence between members of the household, including the connected person;

(e)   their family history, including –

   (i)   particulars of their childhood and upbringing, including the strengths and difficulties of their parents and other persons who cared for them,

   (ii)   their relationships with their parents and siblings, and their relationships with each other,

   (iii)   their educational achievement and any specific learning difficulty or disability,

   (iv)   a chronology of significant life events, and

   (v)   particulars of other relatives and their relationships with C and the connected person;

(f)   particulars of any criminal offences of which they have been convicted or in respect of which they have been cautioned;

(g)   their past and present employment and other sources of income; and

(h)   the nature of the neighbourhood in which their home is situated and resources available in the community to support C and the connected person.

2   In respect of members of the household aged 18 and over, so far as is practicable, all the particulars specified in paragraph 1 except sub-paragraphs (e), (f) and (g).

SCHEDULE 6

AGREEMENT WITH AN INDEPENDENT FOSTERING AGENCY RELATING TO THE DISCHARGE OF THE RESPONSIBLE AUTHORITY'S FUNCTIONS

1   The agreement must contain the following information –

(a)   the services to be provided to the responsible authority by the registered person,

(b)   the arrangements for the selection by the responsible authority of F from those approved by the registered person,

(c)   a requirement for the registered person to submit reports to the responsible authority on any placements as may be required by the responsible authority, and

(d)   the arrangements for the termination of the agreement.

2   Where the agreement relates to a particular child, it must also contain the following information –

(a)   F's details,

(b)   details of any services that C is to receive and whether the services are to be provided by the responsible authority or by the registered person,

(c)   the terms (including as to payment) of the proposed placement agreement,

(d)   the arrangements for record keeping about C and for the return of records at the end of the placement,

   (e)   a requirement for the registered person to notify the responsible authority immediately in the event of concerns about the placement, and

   (f)   whether and on what basis other children may be placed with F.

SCHEDULE 7

MATTERS TO BE CONSIDERED BEFORE PLACING C IN ACCOMMODATION IN AN UNREGULATED SETTING UNDER SECTION 81(6)(D) OF THE 2014 ACT

1 In respect of the accommodation, the –

   (a)   facilities and services provided,

   (b)   state of repair,

   (c)   safety,

   (d)   location,

   (e)   support,

   (f)   tenancy status, and

   (g)   the financial commitments involved for C and their affordability.

2 In respect of C, C's –

   (a)   views about the accommodation,

   (b)   understanding of their rights and responsibilities in relation to the accommodation, and

   (c)   understanding of the funding arrangements.

SCHEDULE 8

CONSIDERATIONS TO WHICH THE RESPONSIBLE AUTHORITY MUST HAVE REGARD WHEN REVIEWING C'S CASE

1 The effect of any change in C's circumstances since the last review, in particular of any change made by the responsible authority to the C's care and support plan, whether decisions taken at the last review have been successfully implemented, and if not, the reasons for that.

2 Whether the responsible authority should seek any change in C's legal status.

3 Whether there is a plan for permanence for C.

4 The arrangements for contact and whether there is any need for changes to the arrangements in order to promote contact between C and P, or between C and other connected persons.

5 Whether C's placement continues to be the most appropriate available, and whether any change to the placement plan or any other aspects of the arrangements made to provide C with accommodation is, or is likely to become, necessary or desirable before the next review of C's case.

6 Whether C's placement safeguards and promotes C's well-being, and whether any safeguarding concerns have been raised.

PART VII

7 C's educational needs, progress and development and whether any change to the arrangements for C's education and training is, or is likely to become, necessary or desirable to meet C's particular needs and to promote C's educational achievement before the next review of C's case, having regard to the advice of any person who provides C with education or training, in particular the designated person of any school at which C is a registered pupil.

8 C's leisure interests.

9 The report of the most recent assessment of C's state of health obtained in accordance with regulation 7 and whether any change to the arrangements for C's health care is, or is likely to become, necessary or desirable before the next review of C's case, having regard to the advice of any health care professional received since the date of that report, in particular C's general practitioner.

10 Whether C's needs related to C's identity are being met and whether any particular change is required, having regard to C's religious persuasion, racial origin, sexual orientation, and cultural and linguistic background.

11 Whether the arrangements made in accordance with regulation 34 continue to be appropriate and understood by C.

12 Whether any arrangements need to be made for the time when C will no longer be looked after by the responsible authority.

13 C's wishes and feelings, and the views of the IRO, about any aspect of the case and in particular about any changes the responsible authority has made since the last review or proposes to make to C's care and support plan.

14 Where regulation 31(3) applies, the frequency of R's visits.

15 Where C is a category 1 young person who has been placed with a local authority foster parent, ascertain whether C and F intend to make a post-18 living arrangement.

16 If paragraph 15 applies and if C wishes to make such an arrangement but F does not, consider whether C should be placed with a different local authority foster parent in order to facilitate the making of such an arrangement when C ceases to be looked after.

17 Where C falls within regulation 5(1)(f), whether C's needs as a result of that status are being met.

18 Details of any care plan or health treatment plan for P.

19 Details of any support or services provided for P by any person.

20 Any changes in P's capacity to care for children, and in particular in relation to C, as a result of the health or social care services provided by any person, or as a result of any other factors.

21 Any changes in the family circumstances since the last review.

22 Any significant events outside the family which are relevant.

23 Any difficulties which the family may have had in engaging with the IFS team.

24 Whether there is any conflict between the needs of C and the needs of P, or any other member of P's household, and how this can be resolved.

25 The need to prepare for the ending of the involvement of the IFS team.

26 In paragraphs 18 to 25 –
'P' is to be construed as though it were a reference to 'parent' within the meaning given in regulation 18(5) of the Partnership Regulations.

Amendments—SI 2017/713.

SCHEDULE 9
MATTERS TO BE DEALT WITH IN THE PATHWAY PLAN

1 The name of C's personal adviser.

2 The nature and level of contact and personal support to be provided to C, and by whom.

3 Details of the accommodation C is to occupy when C ceases to be looked after.

4 Where C wishes to make a post-18 living arrangement, details of the advice and support the responsible authority will provide to facilitate and support C in the making of such an arrangement.

5 The plan for C's continuing education or training when C ceases to be looked after.

6 How the responsible authority will assist C in obtaining employment or other purposeful activity or occupation.

7 The support to be provided to enable C to develop and sustain appropriate family and social relationships.

8 A programme to develop the practical and other skills C needs to live independently.

9 The financial support to be provided to enable C to meet accommodation and maintenance costs.

10 C's health care needs, including any physical, emotional or mental health needs and how they are to be met when C ceases to be looked after.

11 The responsible authority's contingency plans for action to be taken in the event that the pathway plan ceases to be effective for any reason.

PART VII

SCHEDULE 10
MATTERS TO BE DEALT WITH IN THE DETENTION PLACEMENT PLAN

1 How on a day to day basis C will be cared for and how C's well-being will be safeguarded and promoted by the staff of the prison, YDA or premises in which C is required to reside.

2 Any arrangements for contact between C and any parent of C's or any person who is not C's parent but who has parental responsibility for C, and between C and any other connected person including, if appropriate –

    (a)   the reasons why contact with any such person would not be reasonably practicable or would not be consistent with C's well-being,

    (b)   if C is not in the care of the responsible authority, details of any order made under section 8 of the 1989 Act,

    (c)   the arrangements for notifying any changes in the arrangements for contact.

3 The arrangements made for R to visit C in accordance with Part 5, the frequency of such visits and the arrangements made for advice and other support to be available to C between visits in accordance with regulation 34.

4 If an independent visitor is appointed, the arrangements made for them to visit C.

5 The arrangements made by the staff of the prison, YDA or premises in which C is required to reside for C's health (including physical, emotional and mental health) and dental care.

6 The arrangements made by the staff of the prison, YDA or premises in which C is required to reside for C's education and training including –

    (a)   the name and address of any educational or training institution C was attending, or any other person providing C with education or training, immediately before C's remand o detention,

    (b)   where C has a statement of special educational needs, details of the local authority (or local authority in England) that maintains the statement.

7 C's personal history, religious persuasion, cultural and linguistic background, sexual orientation, and racial origin, and the arrangement put in place by the staff of the prison, YDA or premises in which C is required to reside for meeting the needs relating to C's identity.

8 The arrangements put in place by the staff of the prison, YDA or premises in which C is required to reside for supporting C to develop self-care skills.

9 The name and contact details of –

    (a)   the IRO,

    (b)   C's independent visitor (if one is appointed),

    (c)   R,

    (d)   if C is a category 1 young person, the personal advisor appointed for C.

10 Details of how C's well-being should be adequately safeguarded and promoted when C ceases to be remanded to YDA or detained, in particular –

(a) whether C will be provided with accommodation by the responsible authority or another local authority or a local authority in England, and

(b) whether any other services should be provided by the responsible authority or by another local authority under the 2014 Act, or a local authority in England in exercise of its duties under the 1989 Act.

SCHEDULE 11

REVOCATIONS

The Regulations set out in the Table are revoked to the extent specified –

Regulations revoked	Series number	Extent of revocation
Contact with Children Regulations 1991	SI 1991/891	The whole Regulations
Definition of Independent Visitor (Children) Regulations 1991	SI 1991/892	The whole Regulations
Placement of Children with Parents etc Regulations 1991	SI 1991/893	The whole Regulations
Children (Shortterm Placements) (Miscellaneous Amendments) Regulations 1995	SI 1995/2015	The whole Regulations* (*regulation 2 has already been revoked in relation to Wales)

Children (Secure Accommodation) (Wales) Regulations 2015, SI 2015/1988

1 Title, commencement, interpretation and application

(1) The title of these Regulations is the Children (Secure Accommodation) (Wales) Regulations 2015.

(2) These Regulations come into force on 6 April 2016.

(3) These Regulations apply in relation to Wales.

(4) In these Regulations –

'the Act' ('*y Ddeddf*') means the Social Services and Well-being (Wales) Act 2014;

'independent visitor' ('*ymwelydd annibynnol*') means a person appointed by a local authority under section 98 of the Act;

'local authority' ('*awdurdod lleol*') means a Welsh local authority unless the contrary is indicated;

'secure accommodation' ('*llety diogel*') means accommodation –

(a) which is provided for the purpose of restricting the liberty of children to whom the criteria in paragraphs (a) and (b) of section 119(1) apply, and

(b) which is situated in either Wales or England unless the contrary is indicated.

(5) In these Regulations a reference to a children's home being registered, or to a person registered in respect of a children's home, is a reference to registration under Part 2 of the Care Standards Act 2000.

Amendments—SI 2016/312.

Maximum Period Without Court Authorisation

2 Maximum period in secure accommodation without court authorisation

(1) Subject to paragraph (2) and (3), the maximum period beyond which a local authority or a local authority in England may not keep a child in secure accommodation in Wales without the authority of the court is an aggregate of 72 hours (whether or not consecutive) in any period of 28 days.

(2) Where –

    (a)   a child is kept in secure accommodation at any time between 12 midday on the day before and 12 midday on the day after a public holiday or a Sunday,

    (b)   during that time the maximum period of 72 hours would otherwise expire, and

    (c)   the child has in the 27 days before the day on which the latest period in secure accommodation began, already been kept in secure accommodation for an aggregate of more than 48 hours, the maximum period is extended until 12 midday on the first day which is not a public holiday or a Sunday.

(3) Where a court gives authority for a child to be held in secure accommodation, any period during which the child was kept in secure accommodation prior to that period of authorisation shall be disregarded in calculating the maximum period in relation to any subsequent periods in secure accommodation after the court-authorised period has expired.

Amendments—SI 2016/312.

3 Requirement where child detained without court authority

(1) Before a local authority places a child in secure accommodation without court authority it must first create a written record setting out –

    (a)   the reasons why it believes the grounds under section 119(1) of the Act are met;

    (b)   the purpose of the placement; and

    (c)   the reasons why it considers that the placement is necessary.

(2) The local authority must provide a copy of that record to –

    (a)   the child and any person providing legal representation to the child;

    (b)   the child's parents;

    (c)   any person who is not a parent but has parental responsibility for the child;

    (d)   the child's independent visitor, if one has been appointed; and

    (e)   any other person who that local authority considers should be informed.

Court Authorisation

4 Applications to court

(1) Applications to court under section 119 of the Act may only be made by the local authority (including an English local authority) which is looking after the child (subject to the power of a local authority to arrange for its functions to be carried out by another person under section 101 of the Local Government Act 1972 or sections 14 to 20 of the Local Government Act 2000).

(2) But where regulation 16 of these Regulations applies to modify section 119 of the Act so that it applies in relation to children other than those being looked after by a local authority, then applications to court can be made by the Local Health Board, NHS Trust or local authority in the exercise of education functions which is providing accommodation for a child and to whom section 119 of the Act applies.

5 Duty to inform parents and others of intention to place child in secure accommodation

Where a local authority intends to apply to a court to place a child whom it is looking after in secure accommodation, it must, as far as is reasonably practicable, notify, as soon as possible –

  (a)   the child's parents;
  (b)   any person who is not a parent but has parental responsibility for the child;
  (c)   the child's independent visitor, if one has been appointed; and
  (d)   any other person who that local authority considers should be informed.

6 Maximum periods of authorisation by the court

(1) Subject to paragraph (2), where a child has been made the subject of an application under section 119 of the Act, the maximum initial period for which a court may authorise the child to be kept in secure accommodation is three months.

(2) Where a child is subject to an application to extend the period in secure accommodation under section 119 of the Act the maximum further period which a court may authorise at any one time is 6 months.

7 Maximum period of authorisation for remanded children

(1) The maximum period for which a court may from time to time authorise a child who has been remanded to local authority accommodation under section 91(3) of the Legal Aid, Sentencing and Punishment of Offenders Act 2012 to be kept in secure accommodation (whether the period is the initial period or a further period) is the period of the remand.

(2) The reference to 'local authority' in paragraph (1) includes an English local authority.

(3) Any authorisation in respect of such a child must not exceed 28 days on any one occasion without further authorisation.

Amendments—SI 2016/312.

Requirements in relation to placements in secure accommodation

8 Placement in a children's home which is registered

A local authority may only place a child in secure accommodation in a home which is registered as a children's home providing accommodation for the purpose of restricting liberty.

9 Duty to give information of placement in secure accommodation

(1) Where a child is placed in secure accommodation in a children's home in Wales which is provided by a person other than the local authority which is looking after the child, the person registered in respect of the children's home must inform the local authority which is looking after the child that the child has been placed there within 12 hours of the placement beginning.

(2) The local authority looking after the child must then confirm to the registered person –

  (a)   its authorisation for the child to be held in secure accommodation;
  (b)   the period of authorisation; and

PART VII

(c)   details of any order made by a court authorising the placement.

Amendments—SI 2016/312.

10 Appointment of persons to review placements

A local authority which decides to place a child in secure accommodation must appoint at least 3 persons to review the decision within 15 working days of the start of the placement and then at intervals not exceeding three months where the placement in secure accommodation continues.

11 Reviews of placement in secure accommodation

(1) The persons appointed under regulation 10 must consider, having regard to the welfare of the child in question –

- (a)   whether the criteria for keeping the child in secure accommodation continue to apply;
- (b)   whether the placement in secure accommodation continues to be necessary or whether any other description of accommodation would better meet the child's needs.

(2) In undertaking a review of the placement, the persons appointed must, so far as is reasonably practicable, ascertain and take into account the wishes and feelings of –

- (a)   the child;
- (b)   the child's parents;
- (c)   any person not being a parent but who has parental responsibility for the child;
- (d)   any other person who has had care of the child whose views the persons appointed consider should be taken into account;
- (e)   the child's independent visitor if one has been appointed;
- (f)   the person managing the secure accommodation in which the child is placed.

(3) The persons appointed must make a recommendation to the local authority about whether the placement of that child in secure accommodation should continue.

(4) The local authority must, as far as is reasonably practicable, inform all those whose views are required to be taken into account under paragraph (2) of the recommendation made by the review and of what action, if any, it proposes to take in the light of the recommendation.

12 Records to be kept in respect of a child in secure accommodation in a children's home

When a child is placed in secure accommodation in a children's home in Wales the persons who are registered in respect of the children's home must maintain a record for that child which includes –

- (a)   the name, date of birth and sex of that child;
- (b)   details of the care order or other statutory provision by virtue of which the child is placed in the children's home;
- (c)   details of the local authority or local authority in England placing the child and the name of the authorising officer;
- (d)   the date and time of the start of the placement in secure accommodation;
- (e)   the reason for the placement;
- (f)   the address of the place where the child was living before the placement;
- (g)   the names and relevant details of the persons informed by virtue of regulation 5 of the child's placement;
- (h)   details of any court orders made in respect of the child under section 119;

(i)   details of reviews undertaken under regulation 11;

(j)   the date and time of any periods when the child is locked on his own in any room other than his bedroom during usual bedtime hours, the name of the person authorising this action, the reason for it and the date on which and time at which the child ceases to be locked in that room; and

(k)   the date and time of the child's discharge and the child's address following discharge from secure accommodation.

Amendments—SI 2016/312.

Application of section 119 to particular categories of children

13   Placement of a child aged under 13 in secure accommodation

(1) A local authority may not place a child under the age of 13 years in secure accommodation without the prior approval of the Welsh Ministers in relation to the placement of that child.

(2) The Welsh Ministers may make the approval subject to such terms and conditions as they see fit.

14   Children to whom section 119 does not apply

Section 119 does not apply to a child –

(a)   who is detained under any provision of the Mental Health Act 1983 or in respect of whom an order has been made under section 90 or 91 of the Powers of the Criminal Courts (Sentencing) Act 2000 (detention at Her Majesty's Pleasure or for specified period);

(b)   who is the subject of a child assessment order made under section 43 of the Children Act 1989 and who is kept away from home pursuant to that order;

(c)   *(revoked)*

(d)   who is remanded to youth detention accommodation and is treated as looked after by virtue of section 104(1) of the Legal Aid, Sentencing and Punishment of Offenders Act 2012.

Amendments—SI 2016/312.

15   Detained children to whom section 119 applies subject to modifications: children detained under the Police and Criminal Evidence Act 1984

(1) Section 119 of the Act has effect subject to the modification specified in paragraph (2) in relation to children who are being looked after by a local authority and are aged between 12 and 17 and are detained under section 38(6) of the Police and Criminal Evidence Act 1984 (detained children).

(2) The modification in paragraph (1) is that, for the words 'unless it appears' to the end of subsection (1), there shall be substituted the following words –

'unless it appears that any accommodation other than that provided for the purpose of restricting liberty is inappropriate because –

(a)   the child is likely to abscond from such other accommodation, or

(b)   the child is likely to injure himself or herself or other people if he or she is kept in any such other accommodation.'

Amendments—SI 2016/312.

16 Children to whom section 119 has effect subject to modifications

(1) Subject to regulation 14 and paragraphs (2) and (3) of this regulation section 119 of the Act applies, in addition to children looked after by local authorities (including English local authorities) –

    (a)   to children, other than those looked after by a local authority (including an English local authority), who are accommodated by –

        (i)   Local Health Boards;

        (ii) National Health Service Trusts ('NHS Trusts');

        (iii) local authorities in the exercise of education functions;

    (b)   to children, other than those looked after by a local authority, who are accommodated in care homes or independent hospitals.

(2) In relation to children specified in paragraph (1)(a), section 119 has effect subject to the following modifications –

    (a)   in subsection (1) replace the phrase 'who is being looked after by a local authority or a local authority in England' with 'who is being provided with accommodation by a Local Health Board, an NHS Trust or a local authority in the exercise of education functions';

    (b)   in subsection (2)(c) replace the phrase 'by a local authority' with 'by a Local Health Board, an NHS Trust or a local authority in the exercise of education functions'.

(3) In relation to the children specified in paragraph (1)(b), section 119 of the Act has effect subject to the following modifications –

    (a)   in subsection (1) replace the words 'who is being looked after by a local authority or a local authority in England' with the words 'who is being provided with accommodation in a care home or an independent hospital'; and

    (b)   in subsection (2)(c) replace the phrase 'by a local authority' with the words 'by a person carrying on a care home or an independent hospital'.

Amendments—SI 2016/312.

17 Disapplication of the Children (Secure Accommodation) Regulations 1991 to Wales

Insert into the Children (Secure Accommodation) Regulations 1991 the following regulation after regulation 1 –

'1A Disapplication to Wales

(1) These Regulations do not apply –

    (a)   in relation to the placement of a looked after child by a Welsh local authority;

    (b)   in relation to the provider of a children's home in Wales;

    (c)   in relation to an application to a court for authority to place a child in secure accommodation in Wales.

(2) In relation to cases to which paragraph (1) applies refer to section 119 of the Social Services and Wellbeing (Wales) Act 2014 and the Children (Secure Accommodation) (Wales) Regulations 2015.'

18 Revocations

The following Regulations are revoked –

(a) the Children (Secure Accommodation) (Amendment) (Wales) Regulations 2006;

(b) the Children (Secure Accommodation) (Amendment) (Wales) Regulations 2013.

19 (*revoked*)